British Factory – Japanese Factory

The Origins of National Diversity in Industrial Relations

by the same author

City Life in Japan
Land Reform in Japan
Education in Tokugawa Japan

British Factory
Japanese Factory

The Origins of National Diversity
in Industrial Relations

by
RONALD DORE

London   George Allen & Unwin Ltd
Ruskin House   Museum Street

First published in 1973

ISBN 0 04 658169 3 hardback
     0 04 658170 7 paperback

Printed in Great Britain
in 10pt Times Roman type
by Alden & Mowbray Ltd
at the Alden Press, Oxford

For Nancy

Preface

It may be a relief to some to find a book about Japanese industry which is not intended as a homily. Voltaire's trick of praising Chinese civilization as a means of obliquely castigating his contemporaries was not the intended model for this essay in comparative sociology. It does not purport to tell British managers how they, too, by taking thought can double their turnover every three and a half years. Rather, the primary purpose is to describe, through a detailed study of one British and one Japanese firm (chiefly of two factories in each of those firms) the various ways in which two methods of organizing industry differ from each other and to *explain* the differences.

Sometimes, it is true, the effect also is to judge. Even the most objective of comparisons are from some points of view invidious, and it may frequently be obvious to the discerning reader *which* side seems to me to come better out of any particular comparison. The only thing to be said in mitigation is that my unconscious biases, when I manage to catch them in the act of expressing themselves, do not appear wholly to favour either one side or the other. As I make clear in the explicit evaluation attempted at the end of Chapter 10, it seems to me that there is a lot to be said for the reasonableness, the mutual consideration, the co-operativeness and the orderliness with which the Japanese manage their affairs, but they pay a heavy price in the sacrifice of individuality and of independence and of those other enjoyments besides pride in work which can bring happiness to men and women. The British manage to preserve these virtues better, but in preserving them they too pay a heavy price in suspicion and bad-tempered obstinacy, in inertia and in a shifting mixture of complacency and national self-doubt. If I come down harder on the faults of one side rather than the other – as some British friends accuse me of doing – it may be because Britain is, after all, the society in which I grew up. A good deal of what I saw in both societies appealed to my sense of humour; both provided occasions for a slight sense of nausea – though more often, perhaps, Japan where rather more hypocrisy has to be used to oil the wheels of the system. But as far as I can remember it was only in England that I occasionally experienced that much more dangerous emotion, indignation.

But, to reiterate, the main purpose of this book is not to judge, but to explain. And why explain? One reason is because some people might well look at these comparisons for practical ideas, for features of the Japanese system which might be imported into England or vice versa. One purpose, then, of 'explaining' is to show how the various parts of a national industrial system fit together and fit with other characteristics of society at large, and thus to show the possible pitfalls of *piecemeal* borrowing. Before one decides that the Japanese system of, say, seniority wage increments is a good thing, one needs to understand how it relates on the one hand to the general security of employment in Japan, and on the other to the general cultural assumptions about the importance of age common in other spheres of Japanese society.

There is another sense of 'explain' – to give a causal account of the genesis of. In that sense, the answer to the question 'why explain' is simply: because it is there; because it is a challenge to one's intellectual curiosity to explain how there should be built around two all but identical physical processes of building all but identical electric generators, two such very different ways of ordering the social relations (including the economic relations) between the people involved. It is all the more challenging in view of the assumptions commonly made about the inevitable 'convergence' of all industrial societies on a common pattern.

The most influential of the writers who have subscribed to some theory of convergent social evolution – from Marx in the last century to Galbraith or Clark Kerr among our contemporaries – have all seen the gradual accumulation of ever more sophisticated and productive technology as the driving engine of change. Theories differ about that engine's motive power – whether it be the cupidity of individual men, their drive to maximize their profits or to optimize the return to all factors, or their lust to gain power or prestige, or whether it be collective urges to national aggrandizement or to keep IBM on top – but in their effects these motives are all the same; they transform the *opportunities* of technology into the *imperatives* of technology; they provide a justification for moulding men and the relations between men in such a way that the machines can be as productive as possible. And, by and large, so the convergence thesis assumes, since human nature is basically much the same anywhere,

10

the same technology is likely to produce the same sort of institutions.

It follows from this that the institutions most closely determined by technology and therefore most closely tending to international conformity should be those surrounding the organization of work. Family institutions and political institutions, moulding themselves to the work institutions, might have more scope for variation; other social spheres – art, literature and religion – even more. If one finds, then, that even in the world of work two capitalist societies manage to get along with widely different ways of recruiting, training, supervising, motivating and rewarding people one is entitled to be sceptical about the whole convergence thesis. If the theory does not work for the central core institutions closest of all to material technology and its needs, there is even less reason for expecting it to explain the structure of whole societies.

Having a general suspicion of all grand theories of social evolution it gave me great pleasure in writing this book to highlight the fairly radical differences between British and Japanese patterns of industrial organization and to marshal the evidence against the popular assumption that the Japanese are only suffering from a slightly prolonged form of industrial immaturity – that sooner or later they will shed their aberrations and become just like us. (An assumption, I may say, popular in Japan as well as in the West.) I discovered to my consternation, however, that in the course of trying to demolish the generally accepted versions of the convergence thesis I was, in fact, developing my own alternative version. I could not, though, entirely rid myself of my original suspicion of grand theories; it *is* inherently implausible that the directions of social evolution can be deduced from a few simple tendencies or principles. Hence, the final version of my convergence thesis is, I trust, suitably modest in its pretensions and not overly deterministic. It differs from most other versions of the thesis in three respects.

The first concerns the basic secular trends seen as determining the direction of development. In addition to increasing technological complexity and increasing organizational complexity, I give considerable weight to an increasingly general desire for social equality (which, indeed, a succession of French nineteenth-century writers – Guizot, de Tocqueville, Bouglé – were much concerned with as a major *consequence* of technological change and the division of labour).

My second suggestion is that most versions of the traditional theory are at fault in assuming that the market-oriented forms of work organization which developed in the early-industrializing countries are permanent – part of a state of 'modernity' which, once reached,

11

is never likely to be abandoned. (See, for example, the writings of Moore and Feldman or Hoselitz or Clark Kerr.[1]) I would, on the contrary, argue that they are giving way to what one might call 'organization-oriented' forms – by which I mean that the terms and conditions of employment are less and less influenced by considerations of the price a worker might get for his skill from another employer in the external market, more and more fitted into an internal structure of relative rankings peculiar to the enterprise and predicated on the assumption of relatively stable long-term employment. In this sense my thesis is not contrary to, but rather complements, Galbraith's version of the convergence thesis, suggesting the transformation of labour markets likely to accompany the other transformations with which he is chiefly concerned – of product and capital markets and of management organization.[2]

The third part of the thesis concerns what might be called the 'late development effect'. It is generally recognized that late-starters have some advantages – Germany leapfrogging over Britain in steel technology in the nineteenth century, for instance, or Japan in shipbuilding after the Second World War, starting, with her yards completely destroyed, unencumbered with all the nineteenth-century machinery which clutters the Clydebank. What is not so generally recognized is that there is a late development effect also in (a) social technology – educational systems, methods of personnel management, committee procedures, and (b) ideologies which – in the case of the egalitarian democratic ideologies germane to the present argument – although orginally consequences of an advanced stage of industrialization in the societies in which those ideologies *first appeared*, can have independent life and force of their own when diffused to societies just beginning industrialization. I suggest that by these processes of diffusion late-developing societies can 'get ahead' – can show in a 'more developed' form, patterns of social organization which, in the countries which industrialized earlier are still emerging, still struggling to get out from the chrysalis of nineteenth-century institutions. I suggest further that evidence for this thesis can be seen in certain similarities between institutions in Japan and in the contemporary developing countries of Asia, Africa, and Latin America, and that these factors are a partial

---

[1] W. E. Moore and A. Feldman (eds), *Labor Commitment and Social Change in Developing Areas*, 1960, Introduction; B. F. Hoselitz, 'The Development of a Labor Market in the Process of Economic Growth', *Trans. of the 5th World Congress of Sociology*, vol. 2, International Sociological Association; Clark Kerr et al., *Industrialism and Industrial Man*, 1960.

[2] *The New Industrial State*, 1967.

though not a complete, explanation of the differences between British and Japanese ways of organizing the world of work.

That it is not a complete explanation is important. There remains a good deal of the differences between Japan and Britain which it seems only reasonable to ascribe to their different cultural traditions or to the particularities of their respective histories. Those who (intellectual agreement or disagreement apart) *dislike* the convergence thesis because they dislike the process of world homogenization or can't bear the thought of being indistinguishable from the Americans, can take heart. Even my amended version of the thesis still allows for a good deal of idiosyncratic national variation.

I do not expect the reader to be already convinced by this bald statement of the thesis, but I hope that when he has read the book he might be. To help the busy man to get to the meat of the arguments I have provided summaries of the more tedious descriptive chapters dealing directly with the factories which were the object of the study. These are to be found at the end of Chapters 2, 3, 8 and 9, while Chapter 7 summarizes Chapters 4 to 6. Chapter 10 attempts a 'who gets what' sort of evaluation of the two systems. Chapter 11 is the 'functionalist' chapter suggesting ways in which the industrial systems of the two societies fit together with other social institutions in those societies. Chapter 12 has the dual purpose of 'placing' Hitachi, the firm studied, in the context of Japanese industry as a whole and of assessing trends of change in Japanese society over the last decade, and the following Chapter, which contains the heart of the convergence argument, is concerned with trends of change in Britain. Chapter 14 offers an historical account of the origins of the Japanese system, and the last chapter tries to analyse the reasons why different systems emerged in the two countries and to generalize from that analysis to the thesis of the 'late development effect'.

The research on which this book is based was a co-operative effort with Martin Collick (who also helped considerably with the writing of Chapter 14), Hiroshi Hazama, Hideaki Okamoto and Keith Thurley, supported by Gill Palmer, our research officer. It was financed by a generous grant from the Nuffield Foundation which permitted the English members of the team to visit Japan and the Japanese members to visit England and which covered the cost not only of the general institutional studies in factories in the two countries but also of a factual and attitude survey of samples of 300 workers in each of three industries in each of the two countries. The whole study covered, in addition to the two factories of Hitachi and English Electric (the two electrical engineering firms described in this book), two steel firms and a number of construction sites. After some initial joint work, responsibilities were divided: Thurley and Oka-moto concentrating on construction, Hazama and myself on electrical engineering and Collick, Okamato and Hazama on the steel firms.

The agreed basis of co-operation was that all notes would be pooled, the English members of the team using them to write for an English-speaking audience and the Japanese members for a Japanese audience. The fact that the engineering study has been finished first is due to the generosity of the Institute for Advanced Study, Prince-ton, which provided a year of leisure and tranquillity for the purpose. Studies of the other industries will follow.

The original intention was that the samples for the interviews would be drawn from the factories initially studied, so that the replies could be interpreted in relation to some detailed knowledge of the particular institutions and work practices which the respondents could be expected to have in mind when answering. Unfortunately, by the time we were ready to do the interview study at the English Electric factories the firm had merged with General Electric and the delicate state of industrial relations which resulted from the fear of redundancies prompted managers to refuse us permission to take the addresses of a sample of the workers at the Liverpool and Brad-ford factories. We were forced to turn, as a second best, to other factories. Still trying to get a balance between heavy and light en-gineering, we finally secured the co-operation of the management at Babcock and Wilcox in Glasgow, and of Marconi, in Chelmsford. In the text the 'British engineering sample' means the approximately 150 workers at each of these factories, who were interviewed (at home). In Japan we were able to draw the sample of 300 engineering workers from the two Hitachi factories whose institutions we had studied. The interviews among steel workers are also sometimes used in the text for purposes of comparison. They were conducted among workers at the Yawata works of the Nippon Steel Corporation and at the Appleby Frodingham works of the British Steel Corporation. Further details of the survey are to be found in the appendix.

My debt to all my colleagues, for amiable co-operation and stimu-lating discussion, is great – particularly so to Gill Palmer who held the team together and ran the interview survey almost single-handed and to Hiroshi Hazama who joined me in the electrical engineering study. He and I visited the Hitachi factories together and separately, but his first lengthy visit with a group of students provided the founda-tion for the study. In the British factories his 'stranger's eyes' provided many shrewd observations which I alone would not have made, and his was the responsibility for organizing the interview study in the Hitachi factory.

14

For financial help I am indebted not only to the Nuffield Foundation and the Institute for Advanced Study, but also to the Nomura Cultural Foundation which provided research assistance in Japan, and to the Japan Institute of Labour which supported the initial research of our Japanese colleagues. The Japan Institute also provided me with a splendid base in Japan and access to its library whose admirable staff not only knew where all their books and documents were, but also what was in them.

Acknowledgements are also due to the many people, managers, workers and trade unionists, who not only tolerated our inquisitive visits but responded to them generously – some from an intellectual interest in the problems we are tackling, some from sheer good nature. Those whose special helpfulness deserves particular mention include: Messrs R. Andrews, J. W. Brown, F. Butterfield, N. Goji, B. Goldthorpe, T. Kashiwagi, T. Kominato, H. Kurokawa, Lord Nelson, Messrs R. M. McArthur, T. Shirochi, S. Suzuki, P. Sullivan, T. Tsuru, E. Ward, W. Wolsey, M. Yakushige, E. Young, Hiroshi Hazama.

For research assistance I am indebted to Yoshihiko Hirata, Toshihiko Machida and to Kay Adamson. Chapters 10, 12 and 13 respectively owe a good deal to their help.

Anyone who has my facility for appropriating the ideas of others finds it hard to recall the provenance of any particular one, but I do remember especially helpful discussions at seminars run by Carl Kaysen and Marius Jansen at Princeton, by Messrs Okita, Omura and Ujihara in Tokyo, by Henry Rosovsky at Harvard, by H. A. Turner at the other Cambridge and with my colleagues at the Institute of Development Studies. Mike Burrage, Ernest Gellner, Brian Goldthorpe, Keith Hopkins, Henry Phelps-Brown, Barry Supple and Keith Thurley have all read parts or all of the manuscript and helped enormously to improve it. Perhaps some of these people also share the responsibility for my errors and misconceptions, but I doubt it.

Finally, grateful thanks to those who have helped with the secretarial work, especially Anna-Marie Holt and Ethel Royston.

Contents

Abbreviations

AEU	Amalgamated Engineering Union
ASTMS	Association of Supervisory, Technical and Managerial Staffs
AUEW	Amalgamated Union of Engineering Workers
CBI	Confederation of British Industry
CIR	Commission for Industrial Relations
CSEU	Confederation of Shipbuilding and Engineering Unions
DATA	Draughtmen's and Allied Technicians Association (*now* AUEW)
DEP	Department of Employment and Productivity
EE	English Electric
ETU	Electrical Trades Union
GEC	General Electric Company
GMWU	General and Municipal Workers Union
OECD	Organization for Economic Co-operation and Development
TGWU	Transport and General Workers' Union

PART ONE

The Factories

Chapter 1

Four Factories: A First Look

Factories look very much alike anywhere except in those few countries where the corporation has thoroughly taken over from Church, Prince and Robber Baron the role of patron of the arts, providing architects and landscape gardeners with fat contracts to beautify the temples of the post-industrial age. Both Japan and England are countries where the covert, unacknowledged transition from a production orientation to a consumption orientation which Galbraith holds to be one of the hall-marks of the affluent society, has not gone so far. They are still less affluent societies; industrial life is real and earnest, more philistinely single-minded. There is certainly nothing very much that is graceful about either of the factories of the English Electric Company – the Bradford and the Liverpool factories – with which we shall be concerned in this book. One of English Electric's 'home' factories does indeed have a well-tended piece of lawn, a circular drive, a flag-pole and a quasi-country-house portico gracing the frontage of its main office, but neither the Bradford nor the Liverpool factories show reliance on any but the most utilitarian architectural advice. The Liverpool factory sprawls spaciously over a still not much built-up area; the neatly serried bays making an orderly pattern. Outside the long three-storey front office a few spare trees among the managerial car-parks represent the only piece of indulgence.

The main Bradford factory is one whose size it is hard to get an impression of, since it is hemmed in by rows of 1910-ish houses, as dully greyish-brown in appearance as the high brick wall which surrounds the factory. The same colour, too, is the older office block which fronts directly on to the main road with no forecourt or front garden – a modest huddle of a building whose main architectural feature is the big weighbridge door painted in hard-wearing municipal green. Above it, a little frayed and smoke-dulled, flies the Queen's Award for Industry flag. Opening equally directly on to a side-street is the newer, glassier entrance to a block in light-brown brick which houses the slightly more spacious offices of the two top managers, the wages department, and the drawing and design departments. The only part of the factory with a remotely post-war look, it rises several stories above the jumble of factory bays, ridges odd-angled to each other, the product of improvised *ad hoc* expansion within a confined space.

Nor are things so very different at the two factories of the Hitachi Company – the Furusato and the Taga factories – which were the subject of the Japanese end of our comparative study. (The real name of the Furusato factory is in fact Hitachi factory. I have arbitrarily renamed it to avoid confusion between factory and firm.) As befits the modern successor of the company's original home (it started as the machine repair shop of a nearby mine in 1910) the Furusato factory does have a lawn and an ornamental pond in front of its main administrative block, but the block itself looks even more uncompromisingly utilitarian than either of the English ones. So are the offices inside; managers sit at desks which are a little less solid, less polished, than those of their English counterparts. The wooden window frames do not fit quite as well. The armchairs appear to be stuffed with the most unyielding of synthetic horsehair. The building is a product of the austerity days of the immediate post-war period, the days when Hitachi was picking up the pieces, rebuilding its technical cadres, finding out how to sell things to people other than army procurement officers, above all repairing the physical damage of those days in June and July 1945 when first the bombers, then the battleships and finally, with firebombs, the bombers again, reduced the Furusato works to a blazing shell and half destroyed the Taga works as well. Until rusty disintegration made it a hazard in 1968, the second floor of one of the office blocks was carefully preserved as a jumble of tangled girders.

Its loss is hardly regretted: it was an ambiguous memorial in any case. To many younger managers in the late forties it may well have meant 'Never forget the dangers of developing a military-industrial complex and letting it run the country.' (And Hitachi remains, in 1970, unusual in having no major contracts for Japan's defence forces.) But the consciously anti-nationalistic, past-rejecting attitudes of the late forties have become mellowed since – as is attested by that other symbol, the national flag which one day in the early sixties was run up outside the main office block and has flown there every day since.

More probably the tangled memorial wreckage used to stand as a nostalgic reminder of the exciting days of reconstruction, when nothing was routine, everything was improvision, a reinvention; days when an industrial manager could find almost daily some sense of achievement which half-compensated for the fact that there were holes in his shoes and he was physically hungry. Or perhaps, by the time they were ready to bother with rebuilding that office block they had already pulled far enough out of the disaster to be glad to have something proudly to remind them of how far they had come – in the way that the rags-to-riches tycoon keeps on his study wall the bag from which he sold newspapers as a boy.

English Electric's outward patriotism is subdued and conservative. It does not normally fly a Union Jack outside its factories, but entrance halls do have a picture of the Queen. A photograph in the Bradford dining room has minor royalty visiting the works in the course of a civic visit; at Liverpool, near his constituency, the then Prime Minister walking through the works with the chairman. And, of course, somebody, once, did decide to call the firm *English Electric*.

Nor is there any evidence of more local pieties at the English Electric factories. 'The father of the present Lord Nelson' as he is called by most people or 'Old George Nelson' to those whose memory of him antedates both his baronetcy and his peerage, is still remembered fondly at Bradford, at least by some long-serviced chauffeurs (non-unionists and 'deferential' Conservatives), as someone whose drive and ingenuity and sense of responsibility kept the Bradford works open during the depression days when unemployment was a prospect of real dread. But there are neither plaques nor portraits. Whatever the English Electric cult is, it is not of the personality. At Hitachi, by contrast, the founder Odaira, who died in 1951, is a shadowy and legendary figure who nevertheless plays a well-defined symbolic role in defining the ideology by which, as we shall see later, the identity of the firm is in part established. At what is now a branch of the main factory where the original mine workshop was situated, there is even a Shinto memorial shrine in his honour. And outside the headquarters building at the main site a large memorial stone bears a single four-character Chinese motto, incised in the rock in the founder's own calligraphy. 'Harmony', it says, 'is much to be prized.'

Perhaps it is the fact that you can so easily convey exhortation and admonition in a few crisp Chinese characters, as much as the fact that the Chinese and Japanese have a long tradition of mural moral exhortation, that explains the fact that the Furusato factory is much more liberally festooned with slogans than either of the English ones. Enormous 'Safety First' slogans, notices proclaiming that this is the nth day without an accident in the works, blackboards chalked up with a gruesome account of what happened to a slinger in another Hitachi works who recently did *not* put Safety First, appeals to craft pride and urgings to eliminate faulty workmanship or to 'promote creativity' are displayed in a profusion which – while still perhaps somewhat reticent compared with the screaming didacticism of the walls of a modern Peking factory – is still way beyond the range of what any English Electric factory, with a few modest safety slogans, could possibly match.

Deserted, on a Sunday afternoon, there may not be all that much difference in appearance between an Hitachi and an English Electric factory, but around 7.30 (Bradford) or just before 8 (Liverpool, Taga and Furusato) on a summer's morning, the differences enlarge. Work begins at 8 a.m. at Furusato. But one should be more precise. *Work* begins at 8 a.m. at Furusato. The whistle blows at 7.50 a.m., as the last few stragglers come running in – office workers and operatives indistinguishable in their white short-sleeved shirts, most carrying their lunches in tins wrapped in the standard Japanese furoshiki cloth, foremen carrying theirs – and perhaps some other things as well – in a brief case. Most people are already at the bays where they work, have already changed into working overalls, are sitting, talking, smoking, reading a newspaper. Each one has a little badge on his left breast pocket. At the top of the badge is his department, in the middle is his name, at the bottom a very revealing number, 580003, for instance, means that the wearer was the third new entrant to be registered in 1958. He 'belongs to the 1958 intake', as managers say when discussing whether so-and-so's promotion to, say, section chief rank indicates that he is moving ahead faster than the seniority norm or slower.

For some time before the whistle blows, loud-speakers have been playing Liszt's Hungarian Rhapsody rather loudly but (the heavy electrical end of the firm indicating its contempt for the niceties of electronics?) with cracked infidelity. Suddenly there is a silence. Liszt gives way to the tum-tum-ti-uuum-tum of rhythmic piano – the standard set of physical-jerk music which many workers will be hearing for the second time that day since the national radio and television play it at 6.15 each morning. With lesser or greater enthusiasm everyone gets up and joins in five minutes of swinging, swaying and bending. Those who work in the bay opposite the power house where the noise of the generators makes the music inaudible turn to face a demonstrator pace-setter, positioned far enough from the noise to hear the beat of the piano.

The music stops and the men gather in small groups around their respective foremen. The foreman in the direction of the group, the group in the direction of the foreman, bow to each other – not very deep bows, rather perfunctory in fact, with little more significance than a morning handshake in France. All simultaneously chorus 'good morning!' The erection team foreman clears his throat. 'Now, let me see. . . . Yes, points to note. . . .' And he offers that day's ration of reminders, tips and hints; mottoes for the day, as it were, drawn up by the shop supervisor (a young engineering graduate) and designed to keep people up to the mark, to remind them of places where things can go wrong if they are not careful. When you temporarily fix in the pedestal bearing the rotor, remember to test its insulation before fixing, because you can't do it afterwards. Don't test-turn the rotor in reverse, because it gets the oil holes jammed up. Today there are three such tips, received with signs neither of boredom nor of interest, though it may be that an observing foreigner induces some tenseness and hence a greater-than-usual impassivity of expression. Then comes the work allocation for the day. Most of his team of nine men (seven others are away doing on-site erection jobs) will be continuing to work on a job they have already started. The one among his subordinates who is clearly older than himself the foreman addresses with the somewhat polite suffix – san. The others with the male-comradely – kun. He remarks on the absence of one of the team. A readjustment is made. If there were any overtime to be done, this is when it would be allocated. 'That's all.' The foreman uses a phrase which is almost, but not quite, as formal as a military 'End of message'. As the group dispersed to their jobs one of the younger men who had been too shy to give his message in front of the whole group, comes to explain the absence of the missing member. 'His sister has come from the country, and it appears he's got something on today.' 'You mean he's taking the day off because he's got a visitor?' The foreman is clearly put out. The young man gives a responsibility-discarding shrug: 'Well, anyway, he said to please count it out of his annual holiday allowance.'

At Bradford and at Liverpool, without punctuation by any formal act or ceremony other than the sounding of the hooter, work begins in a more gradual way. As they stream into the factory, the 'hourly-rated men' and the 'staff' are fairly clearly distinguishable. Manual workers generally wear the same clothes – mostly boiler suits – as they work in. The collars and ties belong to the office workers, or to the foremen who will change into white, or once-white, overalls, or to the shop-floor quality control inspectors, testers and viewers who will exchange their jackets for a red coat (at Liverpool) or a duller utility brown at Bradford. But whereas Hitachi workers mostly come

25

on foot – from their nearby homes or from the railway station, or else on a bicycle, a large proportion of Liverpool and Bradford workers come in twos and threes by cars which they park in muddied cinder car parks at some distance from the actual place where they work.

As they come into the factory each goes to punch his time card at a clock conveniently close to the bay where he works. (At Furusato the time clocks are at the main outer gate – many minutes walk from some of the workshops. But whereas in English Electric one is deemed absent unless proved by the clock-punch to be present, in Hitachi one is deemed present and punctual unless proved otherwise. One has to punch the clock only if one enters the gate after 7.50 a.m. or leaves early.) Fifteen minutes before the Liverpool hooter blows a good many people are already at their benches. There is an air of complete relaxation, induced by the silence, slightly hollow under the high roof, in a place where usually one has to shout to make oneself heard. A few men are cleaning their tools; most are reading a newspaper, chatting. A small group of women are brewing the day's first cup of tea. After the hooter the pace of movement gradually increases; the noise level rises as machine after machine is switched on, but it may still be some time before things are fully under way. One Monday morning at the Liverpool plant people were still moving around the floor exchanging morning pleasantries at five minutes past eight when the foreman finally switched on the washing-machine assembly belt and work began. Immediately a worker waved a pump at him from across the line and he hastened to the store to find a supply of pumps, leaving the pool-leader, his second-in-command, to sort out the absences and rearrange positions on the line. A few more stragglers came in. At 8.30 a.m. the foreman finally takes stock. Eleven of his forty-five workers are missing. Someone is recruited from another line to do the leg-and-castor assembly and while the pool-leader is showing him how to do the job, washing-machines go on past him as legless as ever. They will provide a job for the snaggers – the all-purpose defect-correctors at the end of the line.

In this domestic appliance division overall absenteeism had been 13·6% a day for the worst six months of the year, September to March, 12·6% in the washing-machine assembly shop (though falling to a remarkable 5·2% two weeks before Christmas). This particular day on which we had the opportunity to observe the start of work was untypical because it was a Monday, because there was a bus strike (though, being in its third week, one to which people had accommodated themselves) and because it was raining. In all probability, said the foreman, those who had been accustomed to walking to work since the strike looked out of their windows in the wet half-light of that April morning, asked themselves if they really needed a full wage packet the following week, said 'Oh, sod it' and went back to bed. 'The typical Kirkby attitude', he added. (Kirkby is the name of the New Town a large proportion of whose inhabitants had been transferred from Liverpool's dock areas, and which had a reputation for preserving some of the toughened fecklessness of the Liverpool slums.) 25% absence at 8.30 a.m. was unusually bad, but nevertheless, according to the foreman, to lose 50% of production in the first hour was normal, not only because of the rearrangement induced by absences, but also because someone was bound to have slipped up and failed to keep up the supply of components. The large chart at the end of the bay showing numbers of units completed in each hour of the day for the past week – the only visual exhortation in the shop apart from a few 'lower your head' notices – roughly bore out his 50% figure.

At Bradford, with a higher proportion of skilled workers – and, indeed, in some of the other divisions of the Liverpool factory – the morning start to work was said to be more prompt and efficient, and absenteeism was certainly lower. There is, indeed, a considerable difference in the social character of the four factories. Liverpool is not an area with a long manufacturing tradition. Until the war its chief industries were shipbuilding and dock work – industries notorious for ruthless hiring and firing, the insecurity of which bred a tough, militantly self-protective, short-horizoned working-class culture. After the war Merseyside was declared a development area and manufacturing firms were given special inducements to build factories. With many new factories, the area today is different from what it was when the English Electric factory was built at the beginning of the Second World War, then the only sizable manufacturing plant in the neighbourhood. Still, however, attitudes towards and expectations held about work remain somewhat coloured by the casual-labouring, insecure past, and somewhat different from those of Bradford workers whose mills, however dark and satanic, offered relatively more stable employment.

Bradford too has changed considerably. Once a predominantly woollen town, the number of engineering firms has increased in recent years, though the English Electric plant – originally the Phoenix Dynamo Works, started independently during the first world war and absorbed into the company in the 1920s – remains the biggest in the district. But there are many alternative employment opportunities for its workers in other nearby firms.

Hitachi workers, too, have alternative employment opportunities in a sense, but *not* – for they are in the elite half of Japan's 'dual structure' of employment – opportunities offering equally good wages and conditions. The town of Hitachi by now has many factories beside the Hitachi Company's Furusato factory. There are some 200 other firms in the electrical and kindred trades, employing over 15,000 workers – half as much again as the Furusato factory itself. But most of these firms are satellite sub-contractors, or sub-sub-contractors, of the Furusato factory. Their workers, belonging to the ill-favoured half of the dual structure, work longer hours for less money and have lesser security and other benefits. The Furusato factory not only dominates Hitachi City; it is its main *raison d'être*. In 1910, when it was founded, there was no town; only a village. And even today some 45% of the factory's male workers are the sons of farmers.

As it has expanded the company has put up new factories all over the prefecture, and indeed all over Japan. The Taga factory, the other of the two Hitachi factories which we studied, is of medium vintage, dating from 1939. It is about two miles away from the Furusato factory, about half an hour's walk along the coastal road, past a fishing village in a cove where the television aerials reach up from the dense huddle of houses and where few people actually fish any more except for fun. It is somewhat different in atmosphere from the Furusato factory. The latter concentrates on generators and turbines and the other on heavy engineering goods. There is little flow-line work. Most of its products are custom-made one-off jobs. Taga, by contrast, manufactures a variety of domestic appliances, car instruments, meters and other kinds of small-scale electrical equipment. It has, in fact, manufactured a variety of things since it was founded in 1939, but they have nearly all been of the size and type that lend themselves to large batch or mass production. Hence it has a higher proportion of girls, less grease, smoke, noise and dust, more clean windows, light and air, fewer skilled workers and especially fewer older skilled workers, and a shallower, less venerable and less stiff 'tradition' of the factory. Taga workers for instance, also carry a badge. But the badge shows only name and department. The seniority-revealing number is missing.

Much the same difference in product range exists between Liverpool and Bradford. Liverpool's biggest department was the domestic appliances division, though it also manufactured switch-gear and fuse-gear. Bradford had a somewhat narrower product range than the Furusato factory – the biggest generators and turbines were made at Rugby and Stafford, and Bradford's main concentration was on medium-size generators and electrical machines of relatively unstandardized types. There was also, organizationally a part of the factory, but a couple of miles away, a new plant for small fractional horse-power motors produced on a much more standardized flow-line basis.

As far as possible we tried to select for this study matched pairs of factories – Taga corresponding with Liverpool; Bradford with Furusato. Many of the matters to be discussed in the following

Table 1.1   *The four factories*

	Bradford *c*. 1916	Liverpool 1942	Furusato 1910	Taga 1939
Built				
Main products	medium industrial machines, electrical motors, etc.	domestic appliances, switch-gear, fuse-gear, etc.	generators, industrial machines, turbines, etc.	domestic appliances, pumps, small motors, meters, etc.
Employees in 1969				
Total	4120	9030	10440	7850
Proportion of non-manual workers	45%	44%	48%	29%
Proportion of women	20%	29%	10%	26%

Table 1.2   *The two companies*

	English Electric Company Ltd (Dec. 1967 or calendar 1967)	Hitachi Company Ltd (March 1969 or fiscal year April 1968–March 1969)
Founded	1918 (from amalgamation of older engineering firms)	1910 (as offshoot of a mining company)
Employees	126,000	85,000
Share capital	$217m.	$276m.
Fixed assets	$234m.	$303m.
Total funds employed	$754m.	$1,782m.
Turnover	$987m.	$1,501m.
Gross value added[a]	$518m.	$434m.

[a] These figures are not entirely comparable owing to different methods of calculating value added. No doubt the same problem applies to the valuation of fixed assets and the calculation of funds employed.

The big discrepancy between the ratios of turnover to value added in the two firms is largely due to the fact that Hitachi buys a larger proportion of parts and sub-assemblies which English Electric makes in its own factories.

chapters concern policies and practices of the companies as a whole so that the exact matching of the factories does not matter very much. (Though the extent to which there *are* company policies differs between the two countries of course. Hitachi Company is much more uniform in its personnel policies than English Electric where much more is left to local factory managements.) Below the factory level, when dealing with more detailed matters such as modes of supervision or job allocation, we concentrated on the washing-machine assembly line at Taga and Liverpool, and on the shop in which small groups of fitters were engaged in erecting medium-to-large-size generators and motors at Bradford and Furusato.

A few basic facts about the firms which the reader might like to have are given in Tables 1.1 and 1.2.

Chapter 2

The Workers: Who They Are, How They Are Recruited and Trained

In the first systematic study of a Japanese factory to be published in English, James Abegglen coined the phrase 'lifetime commitment' to describe one of the most striking characteristics of the Japanese employment system – the fact that almost the only way to get into a big Japanese firm in the elite half of the dual structure is at the beginning of one's working life, and that having got in one expects to stay until retirement.

Consider, by way of illustration, the differences in the average *age of entry* for men, shown in Table 2.1a. Bradford has a much more stable work force than Liverpool, but the difference between Bradford and Taga (the Furusato factory would not be much different) is still striking. (If figures for manual workers only had been available from Taga the differences would have been greater, since manual workers leave school earlier and enter earlier.) In England people enter and leave employment at all ages, though with lessening frequency as they grow older. When recruiting new workers English Electric managers by and large are more pleased to get people with

Table 2.1a   *Age and length of service: Men*

	Taga	Bradford	Liverpool (Domestic Appliance Division)
	1967 (all grades)	1968 (manual only)	1968 (manual only)
Average age	31·3	40·0	38·1
Average years of service	9·5	9·4	4·1
Average age of entry	21·8	31·6	34·0

Table 2.1b   *Age and length of service: Women*

	Taga 1967 (all grades)	Liverpool Domestic Appliances Division 1968 (Hourly rated workers)
Average age	20·8	33·0
Average years of service	2·5	3·9
Average age of entry	18·3	29·1

experience than people without, and make only a somewhat cursory check to make sure that neither criminal activity nor excessive union militancy were the reason why they left their previous job. In Hitachi, by contrast, once the wartime upheaval had passed and its post-war workforce had been pieced together, then recut down to size in the mass dismissals of 1950 – once this stage was passed, the orthodox way to get into Hitachi has been to be recruited immediately on leaving school or university. A proportion of those recruited decide, usually within a year or two, that a lifetime with Hitachi is not for them. Ideally the company replaces them with new school-leavers the following April.

However, some manpower needs cannot be foreseen a year ahead, and in any case, the acute shortage of labour in the school-leaving market has in recent years made it impossible to get as many recruits as they want at the ability level they require. As a consequence the status of 'temporary worker' has become in recent years a secondary channel of recruitment. (The 'temporary worker' is a necessary complement of the 'permanence' of the regular work force. See *infra* p. 38 and Chapters 12 and 14. A large contingent of easily dismissable temporary workers was once a means of maintaining a flexible buffer force against recession.) Those recruited by this route are mostly under twenty-five and never over thirty-five – so that they are still capable of being socialized into good Hitachi men. It is an indication of the tightness of the labour market that whereas it was possible a few years ago to recruit men through this route with the promise of permanent status after two years, the probationary period cannot now be longer than one year or even six months.

As will be seen from the manpower balance sheet shown in Table 2.2 a small number of workers with experience are also recruited directly from the labour market without a period of temporary worker status. Most of these are girl secretaries in the big towns where there is a more than usually acute shortage of workers. Somewhere between 50 and 100 only were male graduates hired for a particular expertise – computer experts, system engineers, etc. – who were poached from other firms. In principle the personnel department still strongly prefers to get new graduates and train them within the firm, but in some cases expansion has been too fast, with too short a lead time between the planning for a new departure and the beginning of execution for that to be possible.

Table 2.2   *Hitachi Manpower Balance Sheet 1 April 1969–31 March 1970*[a]

Employees at 31 March, 1969	80,829 (plus 7,796 'temporary workers')		
	1st half-year	2nd half-year	Total
Leavers:			
Transfers to related firms	216	112	328
Retirements, death, etc.	199	539	738
Girls leaving for marriage	853	1,038	1,891
Dismissals	8	49	57
Voluntary leavers, less than 3 years' service	2,022		
3–4 years' service	491	2,762	5,793
5–10 years' service	442		
over 10 years' service	76		
Total leavers	4,307	4,500	8,807
Recruits:[a]			
New graduates of universities	622		
New graduates, higher technical schools	113		
New graduates, high schools and middle schools	7,230	1,885	10,405
Experienced workers directly employed	555		
Temporary workers upgraded to permanent status	2,853	2,991	5,844
Total recruits	11,373	4,876	16,249

[a] New graduates are normally recruited in April, at the end of the school and university year.

The differences in average age at entry are just as marked for women as for men, as Table 2.1b shows. Girls working at Hitachi are predominantly youthful. They are also predominantly unmarried and destined to leave the firm at marriage or first pregnancy, never to return. Formerly it was the policy to require girls to retire on marriage – they were thought to be more prone to absenteeism and likely to be an 'upsetting' influence on younger innocents. While this is no longer true – labour shortage put an end to that kind of policy – it is only recently that the Furusato factory has begun to recruit older women – and then only as *pāto-taimas* (Japanglish for part-timers) under somewhat different terms and conditions from other women – i.e. not as 'regular' employees. (They are not included in the above statistics.) At Taga, for example only 8% of the women are over 25, and only a dozen have any children.

The English factories, too, employ many girls at similar ages, who are similarly likely to leave soon after marriage. (Contraception is less often used to postpone first births in Japan than in England, but on the other hand Japanese girls marry later. The average age of mother at first birth is in Japan 25·2 and in Britain 23·5.[1]) But a large number of the English women factory workers are older women, not much different in average age and length of service from the semi-skilled men they work with.

Apart from the figures of Tables 2.1a and b, the only other statistical comparison easily possible between the two companies is the crude separation rate – the number of leavers as a proportion of the labour force at the beginning of the period. The Hitachi rate (see Table 2.2) works out at about 10% for a full year. At Bradford it has been running steadily for several years at around 20–25% for men and 50% for women manual workers, 10% for non-manual men and 25–30% for non-manual women. Liverpool has higher – unusually high – figures approaching 100% a year for both sexes among the mainly unskilled workers in the domestic appliances division. The difference between male manual workers in that division and male manual workers at Bradford (which is apparent also in Table 2.1a) is partly due to the difference between the two factories and the two areas, partly due to the fact that the Bradford labour force contains a higher proportion of skilled workers.

Some idea of the nature of this turnover, may be gained from the leavers' register at the Liverpool factory. Of a sample who left between April 1967 and March 1968, about 15% were dismissed and another 5% died or reached the age of retirement. The others had their own reasons for leaving, though how often the probable imminence of dismissal figures among them it is impossible to tell. (At Hitachi, it will be seen, hardly anyone gets dismissed, though there, too, rather more may be 'taking the hint' and leaving to avoid dismissal.)

Another indicator of the difference may be found in the questionnaire answers. In the sample of Hitachi workers, both for those over 50 and for those between 25 and 34, the average number of previous

[1] Figures for 1967 and 1966 respectively, Central Register Office, *The Registrar General's Statistical Review of England and Wales*, 1966, part II, pp. 148–9. Kōseisho, Tōkeichōsabu, *Shōwa-41-nen jinkō dōtai tōkei*, 1, pp. 269–7.

jobs held was 1·1. In the British engineering workers sample the figures were respectively 4·5 and 2·4.

STABILITY OF EMPLOYMENT

It takes two parties to make an employment contract, and it takes certain attitudes on both sides to make for stability of employment of the Hitachi type. On the worker's side is the expectation that he *will* be able to stay with his chosen firm, and the intention to do so, an intention which is conditioned by the fact that staying is the norm of Japanese occupational life and is bolstered by the knowledge that he has a good deal financially to gain by staying on. (See the next chapter.) On the employer's side is an expectation that (provided he offers 'standard' wages and conditions of employment – of which more in the next chapter) the workers will *wish* to stay. This expectation is combined with a sense of obligation to provide work for them as long as they do so – an obligation conditioned by the fact that it is one normally assumed by Japanese employers, and sanctioned by the employer's knowledge that he stands to meet tough union resistance and to lose a great deal in work motivation if he departs from the norm.

Of course, as with most of the differences between Britain and Japan described in this book, the difference in expectations is only one of degree. Of those Hitachi workers who were under 35, 92% answered a question about their likely whereabouts in five years' time on the assumption that they would still be with the firm. Of their contemporaries in the two British engineering firms, 61% claimed to have the same expectation.

[It would be wrong, indeed, to think of these as all-or-nothing differences. English Electric, like many other English firms did not work on the straightforward 'hire and fire' basis of British shipyards or construction firms, adjusting its work force from week to week in the light of the needs of that week, caring little what happened outside its doors and assuming that somebody would ensure that workers were there, in the market, reasonably well-fed and capable of work, whenever needed. As a trade union representative said at a local conference in Bradford – a conference called to resolve a dispute arising from the Bradford works' decision to declare twenty-one maintenance men redundant:]

'English Electric have had a very good name in the City of Bradford and its environs where they have had and maintained – more than, I would say, any other firm – a policy of full employment. The worry that we have, quite frankly, is that the policy of full employment seems to be going. . . . It seems to be substituted by something that we certainly do not like at all – a policy of "hire and fire" according to requirements at a particular point in time. This has never been the policy before.'

What, in British terms, a 'policy of full employment' meant was roughly this. First, if an older man suffers an incapacitating illness he is not just fired. If he cannot do the job he was formerly doing then he is found another job. If he is a manual worker or a routine clerical worker, he may have to take a loss of money – perhaps moving down from a skilled man's to a labourer's rates. If he is a member of the staff in the managerial grades he is likely to stay, even in a lesser position, at the salary he was formerly receiving.

Secondly it means that, in order to hold a labour force together, managers will sometimes keep on more workers than they need when the market is slack. At the conference mentioned above, an English Electric manager explained that of the three separately-accounted profit centres one had,

'. . . lost money substantially last year and has lost even more this year. Because we have a policy of stable employment, we act maybe rather more slowly than some people would do in similar circum-stances. We have not wished to make very large reductions in the labour force, based on one year's operating results. . . .'

Managers will explain that in the post-war full-employment period skilled men – and even more, skilled men who are also good workers – have been hard to find. Hence it is worth the expense of paying a retainer through the slack times so as to be able to meet orders when they come in. Perhaps, indeed, in the thirties, when there was a buyer's market for skilled labour, the management was not quite so reluctant to let people go. But it is also true that in addition to having these reasons why it might be rationally profit-maximizing to keep unnecessary labour on for a period, managers *do* value English Electric's reputation as a 'good employer' and would like to keep it.

In the case of white-collar workers there is also a conscious ap-preciation of the connection between the company's reputation and the loyalty and work motivation of the staff. When one Bradford department proposed to reduce the period of warning for redundant technical staff and give money instead of notice, one manager wrote objecting to such a scheme. Many of those involved, he pointed out, were older men. 'Many have long service and a considerable number are either unqualified or not highly qualified. In the current labour market they will not easily find new places. From a humanitarian ethical approach, the minimization of warning will have repercussions on the company's "image" both internally and externally.'

When the crunch comes, however, and there is a forced choice between this reputation and profitability, there is no doubt which has to go. In the same conference, upholding the decision to declare twenty-one men redundant, a management representative said to the trade unionists:

'The decision of the company to declare a redundancy is made on the need to cut costs in order to maintain a viable operation for the future. And, whilst you say that the company must have consideration for the individual – this is so – surely it must also have consideration for the security of employment of the whole labour force. . . . It has to provide the conditions for a viable operation and a successful, efficient operation if it is going to survive.'

The point does not need to be laboured. A 'shake-out' of hoarded under-utilized labour appears on most British lists of the prerequisities for industrial advance. The closing of a Woolwich, the near-closing of an Upper Clyde, may be deplored if it is done in a particularly sudden or inconsiderate way, but even those who condemn such closures usually do so on the grounds that considerateness *ought* to count for as much as profits, rather than on the grounds that considerateness is the 'best' – the ultimately most profit-making – policy. A reporter on *The Times* was only voicing generally received opinions on these matters when he remarked, apropos of English Electric's vulnerability to take-overs, 'one cannot help thinking that the recent profit records might have been somewhat better if all that humanity [i.e. of English Electric] had been tempered by the cold steel of radical decision.'[2]

The Redundancy Payments Act was designed precisely to prevent this inevitable irreconcilability of ends – the profit of the employer and the job security of the employee – from issuing in overt conflict, to facilitate job mobility by sweetening the pill of dismissal. Cutting down the labour force remains, indeed, the most common of prescriptions for cases of falling profit. When mergers take place, the man whom the new management sends in to a 'slack' plant to introduce a note of wholesome fear and inspire a few conversions to the doctrine of efficiency is usually a cost accountant looking for signs of adiposity which he can cut off.

One meets such 'inspector generals' in English Electric dining rooms since the merger. One teases them by explaining that if this

[2] *The Times*, 30 August 1968.

were a Japanese firm they would be playing a very minor second fiddle to a product engineer, that when you start from the premise that the only way your workforce will ever diminish is by death or retirement, then the question with which you begin a clean-up operation is not: 'How can we cut labour costs; whom can we do without?' but 'What new markets or product lines can we open up so that we can fully employ our workers?' The response is at best an incredulous denial that that could possibly be the way it is; at worst a faint condescending smile at the thought of the terrible cropper these poor Japs are eventually going to come, once this American-sponsored flash in the pan has burnt itself out.

Japan is, of course, the country whose economy has grown more rapidly in the last decade than any other, a country where a recession is defined as a year when the growth rate falls to around five per cent. Cutting back production until the outlook improves, and so making men idle, is not a necessity which many firms have often had to face. Nevertheless, in Japan as much as in other countries – or in fact even more so because of the rate of growth – changes in technology and consumer taste do constantly make certain skills obsolete. Men who have acquired an automatic facility in a certain job are liable to find overnight that that job has disappeared. And, even though the over-all growth rate is high, in the capital goods industries like Hitachi's heavy electrical engineering, the accelerator effect can cause swings in the national growth rate, albeit between 5% and 15%, to lead to wide fluctuations in demand.

FLEXIBILITY WITH A PERMANENT WORK FORCE

The ways in which Hitachi deals with this situation *without* sackings and *ad hoc* hirings may be summarized as follows:

1. One way formerly employed to obtain an element of flexibility was to hire a sizeable number of 'temporary workers', clearly distinguished by mode of recruitment and training and by their payment system and other marks of status from the 'permanent workers', and hired on a short-term contract. Now, however, as already discussed, this status has become a kind of probationary limbo, given almost exclusively to those whom, on the prima facie evidence, the Company considers fit to be hired as permanent workers after six months' or a year's probation. The Furusato factory has about 200 of these youngish 'mid-career recruits' of temporary status.

In addition there are some 200 'temporary workers' of the old type – distinguished as a separate category. These are older men and women engaged entirely – and out of a departmental, not from the central budget – as labourers for the menial fetching and carrying jobs. They are employed on a three-month contract, but some have been with the firm for well over ten years, and they too receive annual increments in wages – though, since they are not union members, not on the same scales as the permanent workers.

Yet a third category of non-permanent members are the part-timers. The Taga factory in particular has started using farm housewives on production work during the agricultural slack seasons, but still in relatively small numbers and chiefly for holiday relief. They certainly represent an element of flexibility similar to that of the old-style temporary workers, and so, to a more limited extent, do the probationers, 'temporaries' who have only a conditional promise of permanent status. But the shorter the probationary period becomes with the tightening of the labour market, the less room for such manoeuvre. And as for the other category of sweepers and cleaners, the company may skimp on such things at a pinch, but it would be hard to get rid of these people and transfer permanent workers from production work to such low status jobs.

2. Both Hitachi factories do less of their own machining and fabricating and founding than their British counterparts. The Taga factory, for example, buys a sizeable proportion of finished or semi-finished parts for its washing-machines – an amount almost equivalent in value to the total value of raw materials purchased. Another rougher indicator of Hitachi's dependence on sub-contractors is found in the fact that, in 1966, for the whole company gross value added amounted to only 30% of turnover, compared with a figure of 52% for General Electric of America, and the same figure for English Electric in both 1960 and 1967, the only two years for which figures are available.[3] At Liverpool, for example, bought-in parts amount to a negligible proportion of the material costs of the Domestic Appliance Division. The Hitachi factories, consequently, have the advantage that they can cut back production and still keep their own workers occupied by making within the factory parts which they were formerly buying. However, the reorganization required, together with the fact that they cannot afford to kill off their dependent suppliers in too cavalier a fashion for a variety of reasons (among them the 'extra-economic' one that many retired Hitachi employees are found jobs with these suppliers) mean that they must use this

---

[3] The General Electric figures are drawn from material prepared by the Hitachi union to support its wage claims. On the difficulties of international comparisons of value added see later, p. 266.

adjustment mechanism sparingly. At the Taga factory, the proportion of the total cost of parts and raw materials accounted for by these semi-manufactured parts was said to have varied only by 1 or 2% over a period of six years which included the recession period of 1964–5.

3. As we shall see when discussing wages and skill grades, there is greater job interchangeability in a Hitachi than in an English Electric factory. At Bradford too, where fitters, say, are employed in several departments, a reduction in the work for fitters in one department may be dealt with by moving them to other departments, to fill gaps caused by natural wastage or even to increase the labour force where there is work to be done. In Hitachi this happens on a bigger scale because (a) there is no separate costing of small departments' performance; consequently, not automatically having to bear the cost of workers transferred to them, departments are not as likely to make nice calculations of the marginal productivity of an extra worker or two, and (b) there are few divisions between trades and a man can be transferred to any job which he is capable of doing or of learning to do. *And* if his new job requires less skill than his old one, he does not suffer a loss in wages. (See next chapter.)

4. The same process of readjustment takes place on a larger scale than the individual factory. The Hitachi Company has 90,000 workers in a score of factories. Its product range is very wide. If one factory's order book is light, the odds are that another is short of labour. Workers can be 'posted' within the firm from one factory to another for months or years at a time, much as soldiers are posted to a new station. (English Electric tries to offer jobs to redundant workers in other company plants – at least since the Redundancy Payments Act – but rarely outside the immediate district except to higher grade *staff* workers. The offer may well not be accepted. There is no question of 'posting'.)

5. The adjustment process within Hitachi can be even more far-reaching. If necessary, workers can be 'seconded' for a period to other firms which are in a semi-dependent sub-contracting relation to Hitachi. This device, however, is as often resorted to in order to help these sub-contractors to fulfil their orders as to take up surplus men.

6. If a man is redundant because technological progress has swallowed up his job, then he is simply retrained for another, perhaps totally different type of job.

Inability to declare redundancies hardly inhibits Hitachi's technological flexibility, therefore (whereas English Electric often *was* so inhibited because union strength made managers scared to resort to the redundancy dismissal solution they were accustomed to – and retraining, if it *were* considered as an alternative, would be severely hampered by union craft rules). Structural adjustment apart, however, Hitachi is less well placed than it was to make *overall* adjustments in the total size of its labour force. It operates on the assumption that recessions calling for more than a mere cessation of recruitment[4] are unlikely – an assumption which the experience of the last twenty years has reinforced.

RECRUITMENT AND TRAINING: BRITISH MANAGERS

Clearly, when you recruit a man for life you take rather more deliberate care in his selection than you do when both parties to the contract have reservations about its permanence. You are also likely to lavish more resources on preparing him for his working life.

The difference between English Electric and Hitachi in this respect is a little less in the case of managers than in the case of manual workers. The principle that one appoints to a vacancy the best man available in the market, irrespective of whether or not he is already employed, was applied more vigorously in the early sixties when a number of outsiders were brought in. Central policy changed somewhat later when it was realized how difficult it was to judge how well a man would 'fit in'. In practice English Electric was not a firm in which top managerial positions were easily given to outsiders.

How, in English Electric, age and long-service loyalty are balanced out in practice against competence demonstrated on the job may best be illustrated by describing how one particular vacancy was filled at Bradford. There were three candidates. The oldest was over 40, had been at Bradford since the age of 15, had considerable experience in the works, but had no formal technical qualifications and was judged in the interview to be, as our informant put it, 'already at the limit of his potential, both intellectual and emotional'. The second oldest was 35 and highly qualified. He had responded to a newspaper advertisement and was clearly ahead of the other two in technical excellence and practical experience. The third was younger; had been at Bradford for one year, but for 15 years in other English Electric plants. He 'did not have the technical know-how, but he was a loyal company man, youthful, but acceptable to the organization and capable of the job if we gave him a planned programme of training over the course of a year'. They chose, eventually, the last, though tempted to appoint the second. The deciding factor was that the department had

[4] An embargo on recruitment for 1972 was announced by Hitachi after the 'Nixon shock' surcharge of August 1971.

Table 2.3 *Age and length of service of men at Bradford (various grades) and English Electric key executives*

	Manual workers	Weekly paid staff	Monthly paid staff		
			No qualification beyond elementary or grammar school	University graduates	29 key English Electric executives immediately below executive director level[a]
Average age	40·0	41·3	46·2	35·9	47
Average years of service	9·4	11·9	21·6	10·7	18
Average age of entry	31·6	29·4	24·6	25·2	29

[a] Figures from a *Times* profile of the firm which quoted these figures as showing a most unusual pattern of long service which was partly responsible for the strength and uniqueness of the top management team (30 August 1968).

recently had too many changes in organization and the appointment of another outsider might have been too bad for morale.

Table 2.3 shows clearly that English Electric managers approach closer to the youthful-entry-internal-promotion model than other workers. But still the average entry age of 25 – of the Bradford sample both of university graduates and of the other managers who had worked themselves up from the ranks over a long period of service – was two or more years higher than for their Hitachi counterparts. It is the exceptional man at English Electric who has not worked for another firm, at Hitachi it is the exceptional man who has.

In marked contrast, as we shall see, to the Hitachi situation, a university degree is by no means a normal qualification of English Electric managers. In Bradford and the Domestic Appliances Division of Liverpool, there were altogether some 879 men receiving monthly salaries. Of these 167 might be considered as managers or senior technologists – they were either over 30 and earning over £2,000 a year (in 1967) or were over 25 and earning £1,500 a year. The university graduates in this group amounted to 24%; those with a full-time technical college education, 10%. The rest had either a part-time further education (50%) or none at all. Many of the latter group had gained Institution membership, and thereby a status equivalent to that of a university graduate, through evening courses and a protracted series of examinations. Accountants may have started by being articled to a practising accountant. The Institutions and other professional bodies have long performed an important role in prescribing curricula for technical institutes, organizing examinations and providing certificates of competence.

In contrast with Japan, where nearly all managers are university graduates, this multiplicity of routes to managerial status means that a man's schooling is not a definitive determinant of his status in the firm, nor is it an important element in his self-definition or the way he is viewed by others. Thus for a chief shop steward who had dealt with a succession of general managers, the natural way to categorize them was in terms of class status rather than of education.

Witness this interview record.

'— Mr A was a more soft-spoken type of person than Mr B, more of a thinker. Mr B was a man who would jump over a wall and then explore what he'd jumped into. Mr A would look over first, and we admired him for the cool manner in which he used to approach things.'

'— What kind of a training did he have?'

'— Mr A? I wouldn't know. Not the same kind as Mr B. I should say Mr B was basically practical whereas Mr A was theoretical.'

'— Had he been to a university?'

'— I think so. If I'd hazard a guess, I'd say "Yes", A, "No", B.

'— There was another manager before A, a Mr C. He was a right aristocrat *but* humane; he'd stop in the main aisle to the man who was sweeping the floor and ask, "How is your Missis?", Now you wouldn't get that with either Mr A nor Mr B. . . .'

'— How do you mean that he was an aristocrat?'

'— Well, I may have used the wrong word when I said aristocrat. He gave one the impression of being of the upper crust. Do you follow what I mean? His speech, his demeanor, his mannerisms, his stature, everything – everything about him. And yet, he had a light humorous touch with it. He was well respected.'

Until relatively recently English Electric did not treat new graduates very differently from others, graduate or non-graduate, who were qualified for managerial jobs. They would be recruited by individual plants to specific junior positions, though it would be appreciated that they would need rather more time to work into a job than others. English Electric was one of the earliest British firms to begin the systematic central recruitment of university graduates, but it was not until the early fifties that it did so. At that time it became common for plants to take graduates, not for specific posts, but as trainees for a range of posts in a specific department – or even in a range of departments, but it was not until 1959 that the firm began a formalized graduate apprenticeship involving centrally organized systematic training.

Even at the time of the firm's demise, however, the centralized recruitment of graduates was more a matter of providing common services than of central control. The head office collated the stated requirements of the various factories, provided the recruiting literature, contacted the university appointments boards and made up teams from the personnel departments of various factories to interview aspiring graduates-to-be. These teams did the initial sifting and then passed on the applications of which they approved to the factory or factories which the applicant opted for or was guided into opting for. A small number of the most promising of those interviewed were invited to apply for one of six two-year Industrial Fellowships available annually. Those (sometimes only two or three) who were eventually deemed qualified – after a civil service-type country-house selection process – remained under the direction of head office and moved round to several factories in the course of their two years. They received £1,400 a year (in 1968) or £300 more than an ordinary graduate entrant with first or second class degree.

The final selection of the other graduates was left to individual factories. At Liverpool in 1967, 12 new graduates were recruited. Their salaries depended on the class of their degree – £1,100 for a second or better, £1,050 for a third, though with some decrease if training was to be of some specialized kind involving out-of-factory study and lasting longer than a year. Most of the graduate entrants, however, had a standard programme for the first six months. They began with a production engineering course for three months at English Electric's country-house training centre. The emphasis, according to those who designed it, was on making them cost-conscious, time-conscious, profit-conscious, on the assumption that their university had already made them sufficiently craft-conscious and that English Electric's traditional 'highest engineering standards' pride had been indulged at the expense of profits for long enough. Bradford, however ('We are not one of the well-to-do works. We are cost-conscious.') had sent its graduate entrants to a similar three-month course at Colchester College. There the fee was £13 for the twelve weeks, compared with the £120 which English Electric charged its own factories and in the view of the personnel manager the course was better. (Training was not treated as a Group overhead; its services were separately costed.)

Then the new graduates returned to their factory and were given three months, mixed group as they were, to conceive and carry out some project of their own devising; perhaps a new tool for a specialized tricky operation, or a machine to perform some quality control operation. As they planned, designed and made a trial product they were expected to learn how to work with men of different specialities, how to operate the firm's purchasing and costing procedures, how to get co-operation from the design departments and the tool room and so on.

Thereafter, for six months, or as much as eighteen months, they were posted around the factory in various jobs most relevant to their future branch of activity – all of them managerial jobs. Formally they had a training programme worked out by their 'guardian' senior manager or the chief training officer, but in effect they were given a very free choice as to where they might spend their time, unless someone who needed reinforcement insisted on pre-empting their services. Sometimes they were given tasks designed with the partial aim of giving them a broad view of what the factory was doing, in part they learned just by being around and seeing what happened – the time-honoured method of 'standing by Nelly'.

This route of entry, however, accounted for only about half of English Electric's initial recruitment of graduates and quasi-graduates. There was also the contemporary equivalent of the part-time night school courses through which many of the present generation of middle managers (and some senior managers) got their qualifications. These are sandwich courses at universities and institutes of technology. They were of several types – the thin sandwich course alternating six months in the factory and six months at a (usually nearby) university or technical institute; the thick ones – with one year at the factory, three years of study and then one year of factory training – and the new slightly thinner variation on this which puts the first factory year in between the second and third academic years. The student apprentices, as these were called, received a regular local authority student grant while they were at the college, and a standard (and modest) wage while they were at the factory. They got from their study a full university degree or the equivalent offered at colleges of technology by the Council for National Academic Awards, or (from a shorter course) a higher diploma which may or may not later be topped up to a level equivalent to a degree.

Some 18-year-olds actually prefer this route into the firm to the graduate one – those who want some early assurance that their career is settled or those who like to be assured of paid working vacations. But most whose abilities give them no cause for anxiety about their future and who have every prospect of getting a university place prefer to keep their options open. Consequently the majority of student apprentices (commonly referred to just as 'students') are of lower academic attainments – men who have barely acquired the minimum two passes at A-level. Nevertheless, the dominant ethos at Bradford and Liverpool was such that many managers preferred the products of student apprenticeships to ordinary graduates. 'When they come up for their regular panel interview around 23 or so', said one manager, 'it's the students who show the greater confidence. They're the ones who'll bang the table and tell us what we ought to be doing.' University graduates often seemed rather lost by comparison; they found the discipline of factory life hard after the freedom of the university, whereas the student apprentices had been schooled in regular hours and regular work habits from an earlier age. Many university graduates, it was said, left quite soon under the impression that they had chosen a bad factory, whereas it was really factory life itself they found hard to adjust to. Another explanation was that the graduate recruits were just of poor quality – a reflection of the difficulty not only English Electric but British industry in general finds in attracting good graduates.

Not, however, that these factories were good at keeping their student apprentices either, even if the reasons for their leaving were different. Bradford, for instance, lost a good many young managers, although it tried to minimize its losses by taking no one from south of the Midlands at the graduate level (so as not to compound the problem with southerners' revulsion to the misty smoky north). In the years 1962 to mid-1967, it recruited 35 new graduates, and in the same period lost 16. It fared no better with students – 23 newly recruited and 12 leaving.

RECRUITMENT AND TRAINING: MANAGERS IN JAPAN
If the recruitment of new graduates is only one aspect – albeit one which is receiving increasing attention – of the recruitment of technologists and managers at English Electric, it is the whole story of their recruitment at Hitachi. What is more it has been the whole story for twenty years, and it has been the dominant mode of recruitment since the 1920s. Of the 305 men who in 1967 occupied departmental chief positions and head office section chief positions, only 9 had not been either to a university or to one of the pre-war technical high schools of quasi-university status. All but 26 of them had spent their

whole working lives in the firm or in other firms which Hitachi later absorbed.

The obverse side of this contrast is that the alternative route to managerial status – job performance plus the mid-career qualifications provided by institutions and professional associations – does not exist in Japan. Japan does, to be sure, have flourishing professional associations which function to disseminate information and ideas. They differ from their British counterparts, however, in two respects. First, the Japanese bodies are dominated by university professors and are centred in university departments, whereas the British institutions are dominated by professional practising engineers. Second, none of the Japanese bodies is concerned with what has always been a major function of the British Institutions – maintaining professional standards by testing and certifying the competence of individuals.

These differences clearly reflect the histories of the two countries. In Britain, professional engineers came together to form their societies and to protect the status of engineers by testing the competence of those who aspired to enter the profession *before* the first university courses in engineering were created. But late-developing Japan did not repeat the history of the pioneer of industrialization (any more than did other late-developing countries like Germany). Modern engineering in Japan was not gradually created by practising engineers; it was brought (by Scottish teachers imported to found the Tokyo University of Technology) as an already systematized body of knowledge to be transmitted in educational institutions. The apprenticeship/mid-career qualification route to professional status – which is only now being superseded in Britain – was never established in Japan. Japan jumped straight into the phase of pre-career university qualification which Britain is only now reluctantly (and there are very good reasons for reluctance[5]) reaching.

Moreover, given the lifetime employment system, an Hitachi engineer is not very interested in a specifically *professional* qualification. Such qualifications exist. There is, in Japan, a fully developed system of national certification for technological skills which is operated by the various relevant ministries – the prototype being the certification of doctors by the Ministry of Health. The Ministry of Trade and Industry ran a state examination for engineers on these

[5] On the irrelevance of much of the ritualistic pre-career qualifications by which employment opportunities are obtained in advanced societies see I. Berg, *Education and Jobs: The Great Training Robbery*, 1969. The consequences are even more deplorable in late-developing countries which adopt pre-career qualification patterns rather than apprenticeship from the beginning of industrialization.

lines, but few Hitachi engineers – or engineers of any other firm, for that matter – bothered to gain this qualification. Given that an Hitachi engineer is unlikely to envisage that he might one day be in the market *needing* an objective certification of his competence, given that he is likely to define himself as an Hitachi man first and as an engineer second, the difference is not surprising.

The degree, then, is the ticket-of-entry into managerial ranks. And in Japan, unlike Britain, since the post-war elevation of the technical high school to university status, there has been only one level of tertiary institution (if one excludes the two-year colleges of very little significance for professional training except for teachers) and only one tertiary qualification of any significance – a degree taken after 4 years (beginning at 18 or later) at an institution called a university. Part-time, correspondence and evening students (who make up about 15% of the student population and probably, therefore, something over 5% of graduates) take these same degrees.

Just as, within each of the British levels, there is a prestige gradation, Japanese universities are also very steeply graded in reputation. In fact the prestige gap between the top and the bottom is rather greater than that between Oxbridge and a rather unhappy polytechnic. In both countries this gradation is to be accounted for partly by the supposed quality of the teaching at these different establishments, partly by the system-reinforcing effect of prestige on student recruitment and of student recruitment on prestige. (The 'best' universities can pick the 'best' students. The superior quality of their graduates – due to their native brightness rather than their education – enhances their reputation for being 'best'.)

The resulting prestige gradient is that much steeper in Japan precisely because this sorting out process is more deliberate and – using more nationally homogeneous standards of what constitutes 'better' and 'best' in a student – more efficient; selection by the universities at the top of the prestige scale is more rigidly meritocratic. Entrance to all universities is by competitive examination, which at the 'top' universities is very stiff indeed. You do not get into Tokyo University because your father went there, or because you went to the right school, or because you have poise and sophistication in interviews. You get there because, helped by x amount of brains and y hours of anxious sweat, you are among the 3,000 of your Japanese contemporaries who scored more marks than anybody else in written papers in calculus, English translation, history and several other subjects.

It is the general opinion of personnel managers that this composite test for brains and capacity for anxious sweat provides the best predictor of useful lifetime employability. They are prepared to believe, and nothing much in their experience has served to persuade them otherwise, that those who have entered the most competitive faculties of Tokyo University are (from their point of view) among the 1% most desirable recruits their age group could produce. Those from other state universities and some of the 'better' faculties of other universities can be relied on, they consider, to be within the top 5%. And so on.

Since these evaluations are generally shared by all employers, the prestige level of university from which one can recruit one's graduates is a function of the prestige rating of the firm itself. Hitachi, in the past, has done rather well. Of the 305 middle managers mentioned, just one quarter had been at the 'top' university – Tokyo University; a little over a sixth had been to one of the other state universities which occupy the second rank, and most of the rest had been to prewar technical high schools of good reputation. In recent years, as the number of industrial giants of Hitachi size and repute competing for university manpower has increased, it has probably had to dip a little further down the prestige scale. Exactly which universities the 623 [sic] graduates recruited in 1969 (485 of them engineers and scientists) actually came from was one piece of information the firm was not prepared to disclose. It was not clear whether, as seemed to be suggested, they did not wish unnecessarily to become an object of envy of their rivals, or accused of hogging the market from the top universities, or whether, on the contrary, their score was not particularly good that year. It might also have been because they did not wish to discourage too much the appointments officers of the 180 or so lesser universities the firm also contacted (partly in the hope of finding men of good calibre 'misplaced' in the prestige hierarchy, partly to show how democratic they were). They might well have been discouraged if it were revealed how slim the actual chances of the graduates of these universities were.

Hitachi recruits centrally and has done so since the Second World War. Selection is entirely in the hands of the head office's personnel section though quotas for graduates of different specialisms are set in consultation with the various departments. The universities' appointments bureaux are contacted and invited to recommend up to a given quota of suitable students to take Hitachi's entrance examinations – tests in the candidate's special subject, a personality test and, for non-technologists, translation from English. Those who pass this written examination are further screened by interview.[6] The competi-

[6] For a detailed description of this process see K. Azumi, *Higher Education and Business Recruitment in Japan*, 1970.

tion for graduates of Tokyo and one or two other first-rank universities is nowadays such, however, that one does not prejudice one's chance of attracting them by submitting them to the indignity of an examination. They are simply interviewed.

The final step in selection is a personal check, a rather more elaborate investigation than the letters of recommendation required for English Electric recruits, into the personal circumstances and family background of otherwise suitable applicants. This is usually farmed out to an agency which specializes in such matters and which makes discreet enquiries of teachers and possibly neighbours – just to make sure that there are no indications of hereditary disease, mental instability or dissolute tendencies in the family which might suggest that a young man is a bad risk. Since the interview is a major part of the selection process relatives of members of the firm or the sons of important customers may be given a slight preference – but only if all other considerations are all but equal; if, that is to say, they seem to be of adequate ability. With the labour shortage of recent years Hitachi does not fulfil its graduate recruitment target. In 1969 when they recruited 623 graduates they were hoping to find some 1,100.

Those who are selected spend two years as management trainees. During April and May, the first two months of their employment, all collectively attend an induction course which includes visits to some of the firm's factories, lectures on the structure and history of the company, together with a few broad lectures on management science and engineering technology. The English Electric production engineering course devoted the first three or four days to lectures on the structure and history of the firm. The Bradford graduate trainees missed this by being sent for the alternative course at Colchester, though the Bradford personnel manager did give them lectures on the structure of the firm on their return. That induction of this kind should be treated in such an offhand fashion would be unthinkable in Hitachi for it is considered the most important part of the two-month course. Nor is the course concerned merely with the cognitive process of getting to know one's way around the firm, but more particularly with the related process of being socialized into the Hitachi community. As the official description of the course puts it, it is designed 'to enable new graduates to grasp the history of the company and of its separate establishments; further it seeks to develop within them the spirit and attitudes appropriate to Hitachi men, and, while imparting certain basic knowledge and skills relevant to their professional status as technologists and managers, to promote the development of character and of their general education'.

Since they represent important instruments in this process of character building and attitude formation, one might as well quote here as anywhere else, the 'Guiding Spirit of Hitachi' (a document promulgated for educational purposes in 1959) and secondly the Hitachi firm song, written many years ago.

The Guiding Spirit of Hitachi

1. The first principle of our firm is 'sincerity'. This above all is the basis of our company's reputation. Our company owes its present position entirely to the unflagging efforts which have been devoted to every aspect of technology and management – with sincerity of heart. That solid core which enables us, however rapid the progress of technology, to produce high quality goods and thus promote the welfare of society is none other than sincerity. To deceive neither others nor oneself, to act always in sincerity of heart, sincerity of mind – these are the fundamental moral principles for all employees to observe.

2. The second principle is the spirit of forward-looking positivism – the most prominent characteristic of our firm. Our former chairman, Odaira, was noted for his deep love of the Japanese people and his high opinion of their capacities. It was precisely through his spirit of forward-looking positivism that he was able, without any reliance on foreign capital, exclusively by the technical skill of Japanese born and bred, to lay the foundations from which our company has grown to its present powerful size. It is precisely this spirit which should prompt each of us to develop the limitless potential which lies within us, to sharpen our wits and redouble our energies. It is this spirit which should make even a moment's slackness a matter of grave self-reproach, as we seek to attain a level of technical skill and managerial efficiency which, not just in Japan, but also in the world at large, will be recognized as in the highest class.

3. Third comes harmony. The spirit of harmony is one which has always been most highly valued in our firm. That we have been able first to accomplish our mission to produce all-Japanese electrical machines, that we have been able to go further, develop our skills further to the point at which they outstrip world levels, diversify widely under integrated leadership and create one of the biggest firms in our country, is to be attributed precisely to the fact that each individual opinion is listened to, each individual is given the opportunity to expound his views and principles, but, the decision once taken, all co-operate in a common endeavour to move triumphantly forward to the common goal. Henceforth this spirit of

51

harmony will be even more essential as we strive for greater integration of our widely ramifying divisions, and seek ever greater success in our operations as a manufacturing complex with a wide variety of products in every sphere.

The Hitachi Song
Over hill, over valley, each calls and each responds.
We are united and we have dreams,
We are Hitachi men, aroused and ready
To promote the happiness of others.
Great is our pride in our home-produced products.
Polished and refined our skills.

With a sincerity that pierces steel,
Unflaggingly we strive.
Difficulties we overcome, treading the thorny path.
The spirit of Hitachi carries us forward,
Conscious of the honour of our race.
Already we are world-famed Hitachi.

Filled with the hopes of dawn,
We make ready for the morrow.
Stretch the shining rainbow,
Over the seven great seas.
Forward to new fields with burning zeal,
The youthful blood of Hitachi courses in our veins.

Some of them who get to be in charge of production departments will be singing the song frequently thereafter on drunken social occasions with some of their older and more maudlin foremen. Perhaps, too, half mockingly and half seriously the song will be sung at their own reunion parties. (Each year's intake gathers from their respective factories for a weekend celebration, usually at a hot spring hotel with a golf course. At first this happens once a year, later every five years or so, after they reach marrying age and when status differences between the high-flyers and those promoted slowly get to be more embarrassing.) At the Furusato factory the enterprise song is almost unknown, but there is a *factory* song which is often sung on social occasions. Taga, too, an upstart plant by Furusato standards, decided recently that it also ought to have a factory song, offered prizes for the words, commissioned a composer to write the tune, had it recorded by Japan's equivalent of the Red Army choir and distributed a copy to every employee. There are other factories, though, where, once his induction course is over a graduate is never likely again to have to take these songs seriously except when, perhaps, eminence eventually requires him to distribute sports day prizes and stand on a rostrum as the factory band cymbal-clashes its way through the verses, noiselessly but semi-respectfully moving his lips in the manner of a Labour cabinet minister submitting to the Red Flag. Generally speaking, one head office personnel manager claimed that in these matters Hitachi was a pretty *dorai* (dry) firm. The *uetto* ones have induction courses and periodic ritual observances designed to achieve such a complete conditioning of the subject that ever thereafter tears well automatically at the mere mention of some of the more illustrious moments in their firm's history.

After the first general course is completed the new graduates disperse to the factories to which they are initially posted. The first induction month at Hitachi has included, since 1968, 140 hours of computer training. Then follows a couple of months moving round the factory doing manual work on the shop floor.[7] For the rest of their first two years they are still, though posted to operational jobs, officially designated as trainees. Only after they have presented to a managers' study group at the factory a formal 'graduating' paper (later printed in the study group's mimeographed journal) do they move in to the lower management work proper as 'planners'.

During those two years it used to be the practice to put all non-technical graduates into a relatively humble supervisory position in the *production* shops, but policy has recently changed. Paralleling the attempt to balance cost-consciousness against pride in engineering craftsmanship at English Electric, henceforth all non-technical managers at Hitachi will spend most of their formative probationary years in *accounting* departments. Their jobs in these years are likely to be humble. A technical graduate may well spend most of his time working as a draughtsman. On the administrative side, though more frequently charged with draft planning exercises a man may find himself given jobs which could well be done by far less qualified people.

The senior managers who designed this policy doubtless had in mind the thought that they had come up the hard way and it did them good. It does ensure, however, that later in their careers managers have a reasonably intimate knowledge of the actual work of those whom they supervise.[8] Two conversations in English Electric

[7] In 1970, because of the pressure of work and the shortage of staff the original four months' induction was reduced to less than three. The manual training bore the brunt of this reduction.

[8] A sample study of members of the British Institute of Mechanical Engineers found that of the graduates in the sample, only a half had ever worked in a drawing office. J. E. Gerstl and S. P. Hutton, *Engineers: the Anatomy of a Profession*, 1966, p. 87.

come to mind. One was with an unusually thoughtful personnel manager who had long experience in the firm and was responsible for many reforming innovations. Reflecting on the embittered relations between most English Electric managements and their draughtsman's union representatives, he remarked that a major source of trouble lay in the fact that hardly any of the men who negotiated with DATA – works managers, design engineers, personnel managers – had a very clear idea of what draughtsmen actually *do*, or could make any real assessment of how much contribution a new type of drawing board, say, might make to their welfare, their productivity or their morale. The other was with a gay, slavishly hard-working rough-talking deputy works manager who had left school at 14 and worked his way up. He called himself one of the last representatives of a dying breed and spoke of those who had come to the department from student apprenticeships with envy. 'I'd have given my right eye to know at the age of 21 what they know. With their book knowledge and their ideas, if only they'd put in a couple of years there on the shop floor and get a real feel of what a factory's like, they'd be superb managers. But they won't do it, you know. They'll always be half-baked.'

ENGLISH ELECTRIC: TECHNICIANS, CRAFTSMEN AND OPERATORS

Below the graduate level, in both countries, recruitment and training are a matter for individual plants. English Electric recruits at five levels: technicians, skilled men, clerical workers, semi-skilled operators and labourers. As with managers, most of those recruited are men and women with experience. Neither factory, in fact, either seeks or admits school-leavers for the last two categories since they take no one (except a few girls) below the age of 18 and nearly all workers in these categories leave school at 15.

Technicians, men of relatively narrowly specialized skills, draughtsmen, laboratory technicians, computer programmers, some quality control inspectors, have only recently been recognized as forming a general category. Various training programmes for those leaving between 15 and 17 years of age with some O-level qualifications (for draughtsmen, for instance) have existed for some time, but only recently has a general pattern of engineering technicians' training been formulated, and only in 1967 was a special certificate devised for them, distinct from the 'papers' received by craft apprentices. The complaint at both factories was that this was a difficult category to recruit for. Most boys who got the requisite four passes at O-level preferred to stay at school for a further two years and aim for the student category. Supposedly a bridge between the two nations in the factory – the technologists and the manual workers – technicians were seen as uncomfortably neither fish nor fowl.

Within the factory their training is little different from that of craftsmen for the first year, except that, starting from a higher level of basic education they take technical courses of a higher level and are given longer periods of block release to take them. Later they serve their on-the-job apprenticeship in laboratories and drawing offices rather than in production shops.

Craft apprentice training, by contrast, is the epitome of British industrial traditions, as is symbolized in the formalities of acceptance. Graduate students, and now technicians, receive a letter of agreement 'to confirm that we are prepared to offer you an engagement as a graduate apprentice for training at our works . . . subject to your acceptance of the terms of this letter': they are signed up by the simple act of endorsing a copy of the offer and conditions. Apprentices, on the other hand, together with their guardians, 'set their hands and seals' to an imposing green document which begins in large Gothic characters 'This Agreement Witnesseth' and goes on to talk of the employer 'receiving the Apprentice into his Service'.

Apprenticeship is no simple instrumental matter of acquiring necessary skills. It is surrounded by ritual; its conventions still have something of the flavour they had when apprenticeship was a very personal relation between a man and a boy. These elements serve, in older craftsmen, to enhance the normal nostalgia for their youth. The resistance of trade unions to any shortening or rationalization of apprenticeships is not simply a monopolistic reaction designed to prevent dilution and a cheapening of wages; it also expresses a conservatism which is as much soft-hearted as bone-headed. It is something of the reaction of the old Wapshottian who hears with horror of the things they are doing nowadays to the old school. The reminiscences of a shop steward who served his apprenticeship at Bradford in the thirties give something of the flavour.

'There was a far better atmosphere here before and during the war. I suppose you could say that people weren't so interested in money. You didn't get up on Monday morning and think, 'Oh, my God! Another week of it.' There was plenty going off in the shop; there was always one or two characters who were the life and soul of the party. Somebody told me the other day that I'm the last character left. It's a shame that all that's changed. After all, you spend more of your life at work. You're better off having a better atmosphere than getting a fabulous wage and having a miserable time.

Take these apprentices, for instance. The lads today are dead. If some of today's foremen had to cope with us, we'd all have been sacked. We used to get up to typical boys' tricks, teasing the gaffers. In 1938 we thought we'd revive the traditional half-holiday for apprentices on Shrove Tuesday. The supervisor said we couldn't do that. So we used the old method. We threw a cap up in the air and we said, "now, if it comes down we work; if it doesn't we take the day off." And do you know, it stuck up there on a girder. Seven or eight of us took the day off. 'Course, next morning we were in the office. . . .

Of course we had night-school too – a one-year course to start with. At the end there was an exam which was one big bloody fiddle. There wasn't any relation at all between the course and the exam. The teacher said, "There's been a right botch-up here", and there was; it was a bloody carve-up. I thought "Bugger it. I'm not wasting any money next year."

If you didn't enrol for night-school you likely got a black mark counted against you. We used to have an interview every year. There was the deputy manager, an under-manager, a superintendent and the principal of the technical college. It was the usual do – a right Spanish Inquisition; kids coming out with tears streaming down their faces. When it came to my turn I wasn't afraid of them. The under-manager was a sarcastic sort of bloke who thought he was God's gift to everybody. When they got to asking about the technical college I said that I didn't mind being robbed and not knowing, but I don't like being bloody robbed and knowing it. The principal nearly fainted. So they went on at me. "What do you want to be. You'll end up pushing a broom." That kind of thing. Then this under-manager asked me, "What does your father do?" "Is that relevant?", I said. "I've asked you a question." "He drives a bus." "Well, and why does he drive a bus?" "Because he earns a bloody sight more driving a bus than he would as a skilled man." "Does he have a trade?" this bloke went on. So I told him he was a fully qualified engineer with his 1-2-3-4-5 ticket as a ship's engineer. "And", I said, "he's been a bloody sight farther than Saltaire Park." The deputy manager who didn't go much for this under-manager bloke nearly threw a fit when I said that, and whenever he was walking round the floor and saw me he'd always say, "Ah, and you're the lad whose father's been farther than Saltaire Park." But they didn't go on at me about the night-school. We were never press-ganged into it; never dictated to.'

It is still possible to complete an apprenticeship without gaining a certificate at technical college. Ideally the Liverpool factory would like to take no one who was not capable of completing a City and Guilds Craft Practice Certificate – and no one ('horses for courses' is the principle) who was capable of much more, lest they get dissatisfied with their lot, and seek to 'escalate into the technician's grade' thus, presumably, involving the factory in additional expense and upsetting manpower plans, in so far as they exist. They aim for the 'bottom of the A stream or the top of the B stream in a secondary modern' – and they use intelligence tests as well as teachers' reports to help in the diagnosis. They are setting their sights lower than they used to. The shop steward's impression of a decline in the average brightness and vivacity of apprentices is a general one. The kind of bright child whose parents in the thirties could just about afford an apprenticeship but not much more, nowadays is much more likely to get to a grammar school and aim for something better.

Today apprentices are given greater opportunities for systematic study than they were in the pre-war days when they attended night-school classes only in the evenings. Now they do not move into the factory proper until their second year. Liverpool, which accepts some sixty or more apprentices each year, provides a systematic course in a special training school within the works – three weeks at desks, then three weeks at one type of machine, three weeks block release to study for a City and Guilds certificate at a local technical college, alternating in twelve-week cycles through the rest of the year. In their second year they move into the works and learn the traditional way – by doing and watching other people doing – but nowadays receiving instruction also from special instructors dotted about the works or from foremen who have taken a Ministry of Labour course in instruction techniques. In each of the second and third years they are given three-month periods of block release to attend the technical college.

In the later years of their training apprentices do ordinary production work, being distinguished by the green overalls they wear (issued by the company; one of the compensations for lower wages), by the somewhat paternal attitude which older workers take towards them, by their right to have things explained or demonstrated to them when others are not too busy, by the occasional concern of foremen to give them – in shops where the opportunities arise – interesting jobs which will provide useful learning experience, and by their eligibility for certain privileged outings and training opportunities. Their wages depend on the merit-rating their foreman gives them in his quarterly report – a rating by the six criteria of practical ability, conduct ('his demeanour, i.e. the way he accepts discipline'), reliability, progress, keenness and co-operation. They may also be on piecework. The average apprentice wage increases gradually from around 35% of a skilled worker's wages at the age of 16 (apprenticeships begin at 16, or at 17 if the additional year is spent at school) to around 80% at the age of 20.

Vestigially – as exemplified in some of the headings of the merit-rating form – the factory accepts some responsibility, *in loco parentis*, for developing the characters as well as the skills of its apprentices, particularly at Liverpool where a dozen apprentices are sent each year to develop healthy minds in healthy bodies at the Outward Bound training school. Apprentices are also eligible for a partially subsidized continental holiday, and the firm provides free use of the training shop for the model club and a minibus for the apprentices' football team and other outings. An institutionalized remnant of the master-craftsman's pride in the progress of his apprentices remains in the foreman's shield, for which a dozen or so of the best apprentices are invited to compete in a test of skill devised each year by the foremen (*not* the managers) and rewarded by them with £20 or £30 contributed out of their own pockets. The factory sends the prize-winners in a group with prize-winners from other Merseyside factories to spend a continental holiday in the company of Swiss and German apprentices. There is also a foremen's silver medal awarded – to demonstrate the worthiness, if slightly lesser worthiness, of work with hand as well as with brain – to the most skilled among those who are 'not very good at book-work' and fail to complete their technical college training.

Apprentices, in fact, are at the centre of most of such community life as exists at the factories, much as the social life of many families centres around its children. An annual parents' Saturday provides the opportunity for relatives and friends to inspect the training school, see an exhibition of apprentices' projects, partake of a cup of tea and a cake and assist at the award of the foremen's shield and medals by a prominent trade unionist or politician or industrialist. The final granting of indentures to the 21-year-olds is marked by another social occasion – in the managers' mess this time. There are tea and cakes – a 'tilly and a wad' – and the general manager presents the 'papers' and makes a speech.

The burden of his remarks usually is: you have completed your training now; we are proud of you. Now you can go out into the world holding your heads high as skilled men if you wish to – though of course we hope you will stay. Not many do however. The Liverpool factory estimated that it had trained 2,400 craftsmen since 1945, and lost 1500 of them. At Bradford 301 apprentices completed their training between 1962 and mid-1967; 228 ex-apprentices left the factory in the same period. The wide world has considerable attractions, partly, as was clear from questionnaires completed by ex-apprentices who left the Bradford factory, for the same reason as children leave home, because it is hard for foremen and older workers to drop their former avuncularity and accept former apprentices as skilled adults.

To train 300 for a net gain of 73 is not an attractive proposition and explains the lukewarmness of many managers towards their training programmes. There is direct compensation, of course, in the fact that in their final years of apprenticeship many apprentices do a full man's work for 70–80% of a man's wage. (One reason why managers are not too upset by union resistance to new Training Board schemes for shorter apprenticeships.) The other consolation is the swings-and-roundabouts one. Each factory also recruits skilled men whose training has been at the expense of other firms. But this, of course, is not necessarily a stimulus to effort, provided that one's own neglect of training is not imitated by other firms.

Operator Training

It is primarily to stimulate social conscience and to prompt each firm to play its part in contributing to the pool of skilled workers available to the industry as a whole that the Training Boards were set up under the Industrial Training Boards Act of 1964. Until the recent changes, the Board exacted a levy from each firm according to its size, and redistributed the money as subsidies to in-factory training schemes. The Board for the engineering industry paid the capital cost of buildings for off-the-job training facilities, 75% of the cost of new, and 50% of the cost of second-hand machinery for training, plus a grant for running costs and overheads depending on the number of instructors and students.

English Electric's levy was £250,000 per annum and its subsidy receipts £210,000 in 1967. The gap between these figures was responsible for a noticeably enhanced interest on the part of managers in plans for new training schemes. This interest was reputedly responsible for the fact that Liverpool started in 1967 to provide formal one-week training courses for semi-skilled operators. (The manager in charge of the course not unnaturally denied that anything other than its intrinsic virtues was responsible for the introduction, but he did so with an abundance of enthusiasm which suggested that he had a lot of surrounding scepticism to deal with.) Formerly, semi-skilled operators had been taught informally on the job by a foreman or pool-leader. Now, after the first half-day's induction – short talks about the firm, explanations of factory rules, wage systems, etc. – which had always taken place each Monday for newly hired workers, operators spend the rest of the week on a series of exercises to familiarize them with tools, to teach them to use both hands together, to screw in screws with the left hand, to position themselves correctly, to take the odd few seconds rest in the most effective way, and so on. Opinions differed as to the efficacy of such training. 'They sent me a man who was supposed to be capable of any job on the line', said one foreman, 'I had to put him on packing so that he couldn't do any harm.' That there might well be some grounds for scepticism was suggested by the fact that three of the scheme's defenders offered the same single concrete example of the benefits of the training – that women who would remain frightened of a power screw driver for a couple of weeks if they used it only once every eight minutes on a job, overcome that fear immediately now that the training course gives them two or three hours' continuous practise.

In-service Training: English Electric
The inducement offered by Training Board grants has also stimulated the creation of a management and supervisory training department at Liverpool. Foremen are given two-week courses on human relations, work study techniques and the nature of the supervisor's job. The same department was also developing short single-purpose courses for middle managers, though for the most part the training of technicians and technologists in some particular technique is accomplished by sending them away to a special course run by a university or by a private 'knowledge firm', occasionally by English Electric's own central training establishment.

HITACHI: TECHNICIANS, CRAFTSMEN AND OPERATIVES
'Technician' and 'craftsman' are not easily translatable into Japanese. The terms most likely to be used to make a similar distinction between general categories are 'middle-school-graduate employee' and 'high-school-graduate employee' (both terms capable of abbreviation to less ponderous four-character phrases). Formerly the distinction used to indicate a probable difference of ability as well as length of schooling. Only fifteen years ago some 60% of Japanese boys left school at the end of the compulsory middle school, and only 40% (including most of the brighter children) went on for the further three years of high school. High school education had become a good deal less indicative of ability in 1968 when the proportion staying at school had risen from 40% to 70%. For girls the proportion staying at school in the prefecture in which Hitachi is situated was still

something like 55%, so that Taga still finds it possible to select from among the 45% of 15-year-olds who are available, most of the semi-skilled girls it needs to work its domestic appliance assembly lines, though it has also started taking high-school-leavers, and paying them more than office workers of the same educational level, in order to fill the gaps in its ranks.

Not only schooling but the school itself also plays an important part in the recruitment process. Among the younger third of the Hitachi sample 32% said in answer to a question asking how they came to find their job, that they had been recommended by the school or by a particular teacher (compared with less than 1% of the British engineering sample). Mostly the rest were introduced by relatives and friends; only 6% came (like 50% of the British sample) in response to an advertisement or by direct application unmediated by any personal connection.

Personal connections are important. Although nowadays not many firms, apart from the banks, require their workers to have a personal guarantor (who accepts responsibility for any malfeasance of which the employee might be guilty[9]) – individualism has at least got that far – firms do like to know whom they are employing. Hitachi still has means – and uses them – of checking to make sure that the family of prospective employees has no criminal record.

To anticipate what will be said later about the importance of group cohesion in Japanese society and Japanese factories, just as a marriage in Japan used to be not a mere matter for two individuals, but a 'handing over' of a woman by her parental family to that of her husband's, so recruitment can be seen as the 'handing over' by school and by family, of one of its members to the firm. The individual nature of the contract is clearer at English Electric. Parents may come to enquire about apprenticeship opportunities, but the Liverpool factory insists on the boys making *personal* applications. They used formerly to send parents reports on apprentices' progress – until some of them had wives who objected that they, now, were next of kin!

To train its workers, Hitachi has created its own schools. The variety of training institutions is shown in chart form on the next page.

Craftsmen

The youngsters who go straight into the firm at the age of 15 and enter the Furusato Technical Training Centre are Hitachi's closest

[9] A special law was passed in 1933 to regulate the terms of such personal guarantees (Mimoto hoshō ni kansuru hōritsu).

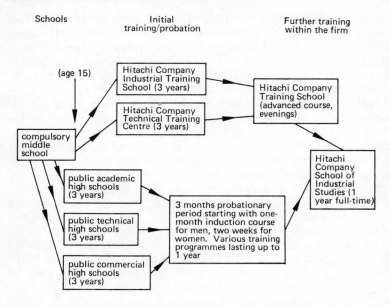

analogue of English Electric's apprentices. Their number is diminishing as most bright 15-year-olds go on to further education. In 1967, 93 out of 235 applicants were selected; several years earlier much larger numbers had been admitted, despite a much higher proportion of rejects.

After a year spent entirely within the centre's training shops and classrooms, the apprentices move into the factory and come to the training centre for only two days a week in their second year, and for only one in their third. At the end of the course there is a final test of skill. These tests are devised by the firm, and the certificates of competence which are gained through them are Hitachi certificates. The standards do, however, conform to standards laid down by national statute. Trade unions – unlike the situation at English Electric – are not involved in the setting of these standards.

Japan does have a universally recognized system of skill certification, however, though only since 1959. The state examinations instituted in that year, are of a relatively exacting standard (failure rate 1959–69, 58%)[10] and the number of candidates, particularly from

[10] Rōdōshō Shokugyō-kunrenkyoku, *Ginō-kentei oyobi ginō gorin yosen* 1969. It is striking that of the first-class craft certificates awarded in the first ten years 45% were in the (relatively mobile) building trades; only 22% in engineering – thus underlining the connection between the existence of a real labour market and

big firms, has not been large. After some initial hesitation Hitachi began mildly to encourage its workers to take these examinations – to the extent of letting them use the firm's machines to practice on, but not to the extent of paying entrance fees or giving holidays for the examinations (which are held, anyway, on Sundays). They decided that to *seem* to be afraid of possibly losing skilled men who got a nationally valid qualification would be bad for morale. In the event such fears have proved to be groundless; the tests have proved to be yet another outlet for the expression of the need for achievement, and have not stimulated desertions.

Particularly gifted young workers are encouraged to aim higher than an imposing craft certificate bearing the signature of the Minister of Labour: they are coached for the national qualifying rounds of the International Apprenticeship Competition. This competition, of which only the training officers at English Electric seem to be aware, is known to the Japanese as the skill Olympics and is a focus of great interest as an occasion for the Japanese to win the world's applause. Hitachi workers always manage to get into the Japanese team, and in 1969 at Brussels they got five of Japan's nine gold medals.

Skill levels, of course, are not the only concern of the teachers at the Technical Training Centre. They are also explicitly concerned with the formation of *character* and of the *attitudes* appropriate to Hitachi men. They are generally of the opinion that they have a duty to retrieve some of the damage done by lax post-war standards of parental upbringing by enforcing strict discipline. In addition to the formal notebook trainees receive a little booklet entitled *Standards of Conduct* which prescribes such things as the clothes they should wear (giving an example of the form to be filled in if for some good reason they should seek permission, say, to wear wooden clogs instead of the regulation shoes) and the manner in which they should address superiors. In order to induce a proper seriousness of mind they are required to produce weekly, on a prescribed pro-forma, a daily record of what they have learned in the class-room or the work-shop, together with their 'reflections on the week' (self-critical, not self-congratulatory reflections). There is also an (optional) space for 'dissatisfactions, worries, wishes and queries'. Teachers and foremen then reflect on their reflections, answer their queries, offer consolation for their worries, and correct their grammar, in spaces provided for these purposes on the form, stamp it with their personal seals and

the interest shown in the universally valid certificates. Government stipulations that, e.g. welding work on government contracts should only be done by certified welders, have added extra incentives in recent years.

– after the document has passed to the superintendent and the department chief to collect *their* signature seals – return it to the trainee. Reflections and dissatisfactions have been taking a somewhat worrying turn lately however. The centre's director recently received a petition, signed by every member of the third year, requesting an end to the rule that hair should be worn not more than twenty millimetres long.

Of one recent intake some 17% failed to complete the course. One or two were dismissed for violent behaviour or other misdemeanours, but most just could not keep up or decided that they had chosen the wrong vocation. The loss is higher than at Liverpool where it was said that, apart from a loss in the first year of 1 or 2% who decide that they have made a mistake, hardly anyone fails to complete an apprenticeship. The British factories have no final qualifying tests of the kind that Hitachi has. Provided one sticks it out until the age of 21, one is a skilled man; there is no question of failing.

Technicians

The Technical Training Centre was not established until 1958. Until then the factory relied exclusively on its other school, the Hitachi Industrial Training School, founded in 1910 and as old as the factory itself.

There is now a difference of level between the two institutions, a difference which corresponds roughly to the British distinction between craftsmen and technicians. The Industrial School gives a broader and more theoretical training, and its students do not go into the factory until the last quarter of their second year.

The Industrial School, consequently, seeks students of a higher level of ability and recruits them more widely. (Some 200 are selected each year by an elaborate written examination, half of them from Hitachi and its environs, most of the rest from other parts of the same prefecture, and about 10% from even further afield.) However, the school does not offer quite as desirable a training in the eyes of those from whom it recruits, as do the ordinary technical high schools (most of which are public, though some, with equally open recruitment, are private fee-paying foundations). Although the course lasts for the same three years it is recognized by the Ministry of Education – because of its heavy vocational bias – only as a 'training school' and not as a 'high school'. The firm itself, in fact, requires graduates of the school to take a further year's course of evening classes before they can be admitted, on a par with technical high school graduates, into the Hitachi School of Industrial Studies. Although the school does offer the sizeable inducement of a steady scholarship income from the age of 15, whereas nearly all high school education involves some considerable cost, it nevertheless draws its recruits by and large from a level somewhat lower in the ability range than technical high school entrants. The increasing capacity of these high schools and their tendency to absorb more and more of each age group is causing concern in the firm at the declining quality of Industrial School apprentices. The number of applicants fell from 1,300 in 1964 (of whom they took one in six) to 800 (of whom they took nearly a quarter) in 1969. Soon, in the words of Liverpool's training officer, they fear that there will be no horses for their courses.

Moving up the scale of technical sophistication we next come to the graduates of technical and commercial high schools, who in fact account for the bulk of Hitachi's intake below graduate level. There is a certain amount of centralization of recruitment here, the Furusato factory acting on behalf of all four of the company's factories in the prefecture. As in the case of graduates, recruitment is on a national scale and applications can be initiated only from selected schools. Hitachi has connections with some 140 schools throughout Japan – many of these connections being personal ones between members of the firm and their former teachers. In fact, an earnest recommendation from a former teacher on behalf of a favourite pupil is the decisive factor in the selection of a good many of those eventually accepted into the firm. Even the best of recommendations is not enough, however, if the candidate's academic qualifications are below the required level – in most schools roughly within the top 15% in academic standing. Exceptions are made, however, for a leavening of 'sportsmen'. Hitachi doesn't like its teams to lose and sportsmen may well have leadership qualities which in certain selected positions may substitute for brains.

In-service Training: Hitachi
The most distinctive features of Hitachi's in-service training are, first, the fact that it provides its own courses, and secondly that they are of an elaborate kind; a whole year of further technical training for those of technical high school graduate standard, in one of two special schools which the firm owns. The one which serves the Furusato factory has dormitories for all its students and can take over 300 pupils at a time. Entrance to this school is by competitive examination taken by technical high school graduates usually three or four years after entering the firm. Of recent intakes about a quarter have been managing to secure entrance to this school – and thereby to ensure themselves higher positions, eventually, within the firm. Some of them stay on for a further period in the school's re-

search section. Some graduates of this school might be eligible, along with university graduates, for a period of university post-graduate research. In 1969 Hitachi had ten such students abroad, and another eight in Japanese universities, most of the latter engaged, with university teachers, in a piece of contract research for Hitachi.

In addition, the factories organize a large number of special *ad hoc* training courses. The preparation for the manufacture of gas turbines in conjunction with General Electric was an example. It began with the selection from within the firm of half-a-dozen bright young men who had been employed on related work. (Not, be it noted, with a search in the labour market for already experienced engineers.) They formed the nucleus of the new department. They were given the best part of a year to prepare themselves, partly by self-organized study, partly by taking courses available in Japan, partly through a stay of four weeks at General Electric. They then held special classes for two hours a week for foremen who would be supervising the machine shops making parts. Simultaneously a different set of classes were held for a skilled group of erection fitters, formerly employed on marine reduction gear. These classes were held after hours, and paid for at overtime rates.

Apart from formal training there are also professional 'clubs' as they might best be called. At the Furusato factory there is the Engineering Study Group whose main function is to have read to them the papers which graduate trainees write at the end of their training period.

The similar club at the Taga factory includes both administrative and technical graduates and publishes a quarterly mimeographed journal with the Smilesian title of *Self Admonition*. A recent issue contains, for example, a recorded discussion on the effects of the five-day week, a comparative analysis showing why Matsushita's profit record is better than Hitachi's, a study of the problems of operating girls' hostels, an application of computer simulation techniques to a baseball game, and a discussion of the possibilities of automating the production of stators. At a different level, there is a Craft Club to which those who have been involved in the skill Olympics, hobby model builders and so on belong. Another, perhaps more important, device for developing pride in craft and intrinsic interest in the work itself is the competition. In the course of 1966, 436 men and women took part in slide-rule contests, 52 girls in card-punching contests, 21 teams of crane-drivers and slingers in a crane contest, 679 men in a welding contest, 683 men and 396 girls in different kinds of clerical speed contests, and an unspecified number in abacus calculation races!

Many Furusato workers were teaching themselves English in an amateurish kind of way and the firm was contemplating conversion to English terms for all parts and specifications – many of which are already in Japanglish, anyway. This was intended to aid export efforts. English Electric was at least, albeit reluctantly, going metric.

PROMOTION

The comparison of promotion systems is complicated by one difference. English Electric does not have a distinction between ranks (e.g. 'captain') and functions (e.g. 'company commander'). All titles refer to functions. Hitachi does make such a distinction. It is possible, therefore, for promotion systems to provide for a regular progression through ranks without necessarily involving a succession of functions. This, essentially, is what Hitachi provides for its manual and routine clerical workers, as is best described in more detail in the next chapter when we come to discuss wages.

As for promotion proper – to functionally higher positions such as foremen, superintendent foremen, chief clerk, etc. – the prospects for shop-floor and clerical workers are much the same in both the British and the Japanese firm and the criteria for promotion – skills and personal qualities – are similar. Having been a shop steward may be an advantage in both cases, though given the state of labour relations in Hitachi there is less suggestion of 'buying a man over'. The methods of selection differ only in that Hitachi's personnel department has extensive dossiers and records of earlier merit ratings for each of the possible candidates for a foremanship. The recommendations of the immediate shop superintendents and department managers can be, therefore, and in fact are, checked and possibly questioned at a higher management level before appointments are made, whereas in English Electric this check is largely a formality.

It is hard to say what are the effects on work morale of these differences in promotion methods. We asked in the interview survey whether those chosen for promotion to foreman were the right persons, and whether they were accepted by their men in general. There was little difference in the balance of opinion between Hitachi on the one hand and the British engineering sample on the other. (Except that the British engineering workers were more likely to give a decided 'yes'/'no' opinion rather than 'half are, half aren't' kind of answers.) But when asked about their own personal chances of promotion, only 13% of the Japanese sample, compared with 46% of the British samples said that they had no chance at all. And of those who said that they had little or no chance at all, 28% in Britain, compared with 16% in Hitachi, gave as their reason the injustice of the firm's methods of selection rather than their own lack of qualifications or personal deficiencies. (In passing: in answer to the question about promotion chances, while there was no doubt that the British sample was generally more pessimistic, at the extreme end of the scale only 7% of the Japanese were prepared so far to throw modesty to the winds as to say that they had a 'very good chance' (42% said 'some chance') compared with 11% in England ('some chance': 23%).)

At the managerial level the distinction between rank and function still applies, but there is a slightly closer correspondence between the two as can be seen in Table 2.4.

Table 2.4

Rank[a]	Positions held by most men of that rank
Assistant principal (fuku-sanji)	Section chief
Under principal (sanji-ho)	Department chief, plus some older section chiefs
Principal (sanji)	General managers (factory and branch managers), department chiefs in key head office departments, some other older department chiefs

[a] In 1970 a fourth upper rank, between director and principal (*sanyo –* counsellor) was created to relieve frustration at the top as the whole pyramid expanded without expansion of the board of directors.

The advantage of this flexible system is that it allows faithful service by men of mediocre ability to be rewarded by an increase in rank without the disadvantage of dysfunctionally promoting them to positions of greater authority. (Salary scales are tied to ranks rather than to positions.) The system also offers a fair security of prospects. A Hitachi graduate, joining the firm at the age of 22 knows that if he is very bright indeed he will reach an assistant principal/section chief position by the age of 32. He has an 80% chance of getting there by the age of 36, and he will have to have distinguished himself in some way for gross inefficiency or unco-operativeness not to get there by the age of 40. (At the same time some high school graduates will reach this rank at any time between the age of, say, 34 and 50.) The spread of appointment ages for graduates to the under principal rank is of course greater. The system, in fact, bears a close resemblance to that in the British civil service (Table 2.5).

Speed of promotion is not the only criterion for judging future prospects. It also matters which section one is made chief of. There

Table 2.5

British Civil Service 1960–mid-1966

Rank	Youngest age at promotion	Median age at promotion	Oldest age at promotion
Assistant secretary	33	42	60
Under secretary	39	48	65
Deputy secretary	44	50	60
Permanent secretary	46	52	59

Hitachi 'in recent memory'

Rank	Youngest age at promotion	Median age at promotion	Oldest age at promotion
Assistant principal	32	38–9?	
Under principal	39	45–6?	
Principal	44	50–1?	
Director	50	52	57

Sources: Great Britain, Civil Service Commission, *The Civil Service* (Fulton Commission Report), vol. 4, p. 562. For Hitachi the median figure is a rough guess; the minimum ages indicate the youngest actual cases managers could remember over the last three or four years. For Hitachi directors the figures refer to the 25 members of the board in 1970. Age of retirement, of course, is 55 in Japan (except for directors) and 65 in England.

are no clearly marked-out key departments in which experience is necessary for later promotion, but the high flyers who are possible candidates for directorships will be moved around and will be likely to spend a fair proportion of their time at the Tokyo head office. The 'sportsmen' are likely to find themselves allotted the housing and welfare sections.

No comparable degree of career planning is provided for in English Electric, though tentative moves in this direction are apparent. As long, however, as mobility between firms is as common as it is at present, and as long as a man's chances of reaching the dizzier heights are considered to be enhanced if he spends the first ten or fifteen years of his career moving from firm to firm, broadening his experience and raising his salary with each move, it is unlikely that any tightly formalized promotion system will develop. The personnel manager at Liverpool, however, had a particular interest in management development techniques. One of his devices was a salary progression chart (see next chapter) as a guide for merit increases. Another was a management succession chart. For each department an organizational chart was drawn. Against each position was a space for the name of a possible replacement should the present incumbent leave. The details of this chart were known only to the department chief. It was his duty to ensure that possible replacements were given experience and training to fit them for the tasks to which they were contingently assigned.

SUMMARY OF THE DIFFERENCES

1. Employment with Hitachi is in principle for life. Entering English Electric involves a less permanent commitment in the understanding of both employers and employed.

2. The distinction between permanent employees – presumptively life-time employees – of the firm and temporary employees is an important one at Hitachi, novel and of relatively little importance at English Electric.

3. English Electric provides jobs for, and accepts into employment, men and women from the whole ability range – from just above the educationally sub-normal level up – and it accepts without question its duty to employ its legal quota of physically handicapped. Hitachi seeks to ensure that its permanent employees constitute a quasi-elite force, recruited only from the upper ranges of the intelligence distribution. The menial jobs which can be done by those of lesser ability – packing, cleaning, fetching and carrying – are carried out by temporary workers, or by the workers of on-site contractors.

4. Most of those recruited to English Electric are recruited for quite specific work roles; recruitment into Hitachi is for a more general range of work roles, and for all permanent employees there is a reasonably clear career progression.

5. In English Electric there is a considerable difference between managers, skilled men, and operators in the degree to which they are given cause to consider themselves 'members of the firm' rather than mere employees. This difference is much less marked at Hitachi; the official ideology, in fact, holds there to be no difference.

6. The importance attached to educational qualifications in re-cruitment has for a long time been greater at Hitachi than at English Electric. Initial educational qualifications have also been a more important determinant of subsequent appointments – i.e. it has been more difficult to work one's way up from the shop floor to a mana-gerial position. English Electric is becoming more like Hitachi in this respect. The change in Britain is due not only to the greater com-plexity of engineering and managerial technology, but also and more importantly, because there is now thought to be – thanks to the rising level of living and of parents' educational aspirations for their children – a much tighter correlation between level of schooling and innate potential; the level of terminal education is seen (the 'horses for courses' philosophy of the Liverpool education officer) as a much more certain indicator of ability than it was before the war when many bright working class children had no chance of a grammar school education and many bright public school boys couldn't be bothered going to a university because they didn't need to.

7. In both countries the importance attached to educational qualifications lies chiefly in the indication that they give of 'general ability'. There is, however, a slightly greater importance attached in Japan to the substantive content of the education itself – a reflection, as is the different nature of their professional associations, of the fact that engineering science came to Japan initially as a systematized 'bookish' body of knowledge to be taught in schools and colleges. Though to this factor – an element of the universal 'late industrializa-tion effect' – should be added the particular circumstance of Japan's Confucian tradition and the high importance it gives to education.

8. Reflecting (presumably) this greater belief in education as a good thing, as well as its better chance of getting its money back from those it trains, Hitachi provides a good deal more continuous in-service training than English Electric.

9. Because, presumably, of the greater seriousness of the commitment involved, more systematic care is given to the recruitment of employees at Hitachi than at English Electric.

10. Recruitment in English Electric is seen as exclusively a matter between the individual and the firm – even in the case of apprentices the role of parent or guardian is of diminishing importance, and university appointments boards act only as mediators. In Hitachi the process of recruitment may be seen with only slight exaggeration – *vide* the practice of taking applicants recommended by schools, for instance, the personal check into family background, the requirement of a guarantor – as the handing over by a group (school, family) to another group (the firm) of one of its members – much as a traditional marriage involves the transfer of a girl from one family to another.

11. Training at English Electric is very largely a matter of providing opportunities for an individual to 'better himself'. Men are trained for specific tasks, but except in the case of a very specific training for a highly specialized post of which there might be only one or two in the factory, their subsequent loss is not seriously deplored. The underlying principle is that in so far as vocational training is a cost to the firm, it represents the firm's contribution towards creating a pool of skill available to the industry as a whole. The Industrial Training Board's operations are based on this principle and are designed to ensure that each firm's contribution to and benefits from that pool are evenly matched. At Hitachi the assumption underlying the training programme is that the firm trains men who afterwards use their skills in the firm. The return on investment is direct. Becker's distinction between specific training which the firm may have to invest in and general training which can be charged to the individual, has no relevance.

12. Skills belong, at English Electric, to individuals. A man's craft 'papers', his Institution membership, are guarantees of his level of competence, a certified indication to possible buyers of what he has to sell in the market. At Hitachi whether the skill of a man 'belongs to' him or to the firm is a question which would be likely, one suspects, to receive a different answer, though in practice it is one which hardly arises. (Though smaller firms which cannot and do not expect to retain workers the way Hitachi does have been known to bind trainees over to a minimum period of post-training service, and even to sue them – unsuccessfully – when they have defaulted.)

13. For English Electric workers the function of validating competence by the issue of certificates is performed by public educational

institutions; in the case of professional level workers by associations of professionals themselves, and at the apprentice level by the employers, though the power of unions to claim monopoly rights to skilled jobs means that they have to be consulted about the standards of skill to be certified as acceptable. In Japan this function is performed only by public authorities and almost exclusively for lower-level skills. Moreover, these certificates are of limited importance for Hitachi workers. Neither professional associations nor trade unions of manual workers are involved in setting standards of competence.

14. Public authorities contribute less, the individual being trained contributes less, and the firm contributes more, to the costs of in-service vocational training of Hitachi workers than to the costs of training English Electric workers. And Hitachi has, whereas English Electric has not, long since sponsored and subsidized its own vocational training school. The rationale for the involvement of public authorities and public-authority supported schools and colleges in this matter is, in both countries, an amalgam of three elements:

a. The State is concerned to replenish and expand the pool of skill available to the nation as one of several nations in a competitive international system.

b. The State, as an association of its citizens, provides facilities, open to all citizens, which give them a chance to 'better themselves'.

c. The State, as an 'executive committee of the bourgeoisie' helps employers to get their employees trained.

Among these three justifications (b) is less often met with and is less often automatically used by those concerned with planning public vocational training in Japan than in England.

15. Training at Hitachi is more 'bookish' than training at English Electric; it places more reliance on the written word, on paper tests of competence and on articulate cognition as opposed to inarticulate skill. (The graduates' essays, the apprentices' diaries, have no counterpart at English Electric; the foreman's medal to be competed for only by those who fail written examinations no counterpart in Hitachi.)

16. Training at English Electric is concerned with a man's working competence; only apprentices have attention given to their general education or their soul – and then only marginally. Soul is a prime concern of Hitachi induction training at all levels. The courses aim to impart attitudes and moral principles appropriate to Hitachi men. English Electric managers hold only the most tenuous conception of how English Electric men might differ from other varieties of men.

Chapter 3

Wages

One thing the wage systems of Japanese and British factories have in common is complexity. But whereas the remuneration system of a British factory has the lush complexity of a jungle, full of dark unsavoury corners which no one dares touch for fear of finding a viper's nest, that of a Japanese factory has the aseptic complexity of an over-planned maze.

Apart from complexity, the two systems have almost nothing in common. Just as the lifelong contract implicit in the employment relation involves looking at that relation as a good deal more than a temporary arrangement for the purchase of a particular type of skill, so the wages paid in Japanese factories take account of many factors – a man's age, seniority, education, demonstrated 'co-operativeness' and so on – which have little to do with the notion of a 'market price' for skills determined by a balance between supply and demand. In Britain, on the other hand, although some other factors may be taken into account in practice, the notion that there *is* a market which operates to standardize the price of various skills is the starting point for all discussions of wage determination.

The two systems are so different that there seems no way to compare them except by describing the English Electric wage structure as a whole, then that of Hitachi, and finally pointing out some of the underlying differences between them.

STAFF IN BRITAIN

On the British side, to begin with, employees can first be divided into three broad categories. The first, those in the higher management categories (who also get *more*) are paid an annual salary in monthly instalments in arrears. The amount paid does not vary with the number of hours worked,[1] and payments continue during absence

---

[1] A survey by the personnel manager at Bradford in 1967 found that senior managers worked an average 57-hour week and took 10 days' holiday a year.

through sickness, for thirty-nine weeks in the case of the highest grade, for between six and thirty-nine weeks, depending on length of service, for the next grade. The amount of one's annual salary is a matter for individual negotiation at any time with one's immediate superiors.

Annual reviews are also carried out to award, selectively, merit increases. 'Salaries . . .', says an English Electric recruiting handbook, 'do not follow set minima and maxima within a known sequence of grades, but reflect individual ability and responsibility.' This still accurately describes the Bradford situation. At Liverpool, however, the personnel staff were attempting in some small degree to rationalize the pattern of managerial careers. On the one hand, they were evaluating and grading managerial jobs on a much finer scale than the existing three managerial categories and setting maxima and minima for the grades (divulging only the minima, and keeping the maxima a closely guarded secret). Then, starting from the other side, they were assessing individuals according to their ultimate potential (from the alpha pluses deemed possible future general managers, to the gammas likely to end up with little more than a rather unexciting department to run). For each of these ability categories, a standard salary-age curve was drawn on the basis of general information about the managerial job market. Merit increases were decided in light of these curves – that is, they tried to ensure that no one whom they did not wish to encourage to leave, was too far below the curve for his ability level.

The second category comprises those in the lower reaches of the staff hierarchy – some foremen and inspectors, clerks up to clerical section leaders, draughtsmen, technicians, typists, etc. They are known as 'weekly paid staff' because they are paid by the week – though many of them directly into a bank account. Unlike the managers, they receive additional payment – at premium rates – for overtime. Depending on their length of service they may receive two to twenty-two weeks' sick pay. They also have the same possibility of merit increases, though for certain categories regular annual increments are guaranteed as a result of negotiation. Draughtsmen for example, negotiated in 1965 a scale rising from £15.85 at age 21 to £26.15 at age 25, and have since sought to extend the system of automatic increases up to the age of 30. The clerical workers union is also seeking a similar automatically rising scale.

It is possible to give some statistical indications of the distribution of salary differentials at the Bradford factory and it would be useful to do so since they throw light on the question: how sharp is the contrast between the Japanese system based explicitly on payment according to age and length of service, and the British system overtly based on payment according to function – the purchase of skills at their market value?

Table 3.1 *Liverpool and Bradford: Salary, Age and Service: Correlation Coefficients*

	Salary and age	Salary and length of service	Number
University graduates	0·68	0·47	68
Technical college and correspondence course graduates	0·32	0·22	409
Weekly paid staff	0·11	0·26	946

The correlation between age and salary is quite high for university graduates, lower for graduates of technical and correspondence courses, and lower still (though still significant) for weekly paid staff. This result conforms reasonably well with functional market principles since it is in the more responsible occupations likely to be filled by university graduates that the accumulation of experience has the greatest functional importance.

Another calculation confirms the impression that function is more important than age – a comparison of the spread between the highest and lowest salaries, first among managerial staff occupying the same managerial position but of different ages, and secondly (limiting the sample to technical college and correspondence course graduates only) among managers of the same age but occupying different positions. The average spread within age groups (-24% of the mean to $+40\%$) is a good deal greater than the average spread within job classifications (-17% of the mean to $+19\%$).[2]

Nevertheless, the fact that *some* considerations over and beyond the market value of work performed to enter into the determination of salaries is clear from the fact that for weekly staff (foremen, etc.) the correlation between salary and *length of service* is higher than that between salary and *age*. There must, therefore, be some premium paid for 'loyalty', not simply for accumulated experience.

BRITISH MANUAL WORKERS

A third category of workers – the 'hourly-rated' – are paid according to a variety of methods of calculation. They are collectively dis-

[2] The figures represent the average for 37 managerial occupations (409 individuals) and 40 ages (477 individuals). This is a straight unweighted average – i.e. the highest salary and the lowest salary and the average salary for each age (and for each job classification) were summed and the percentage variation worked out from these totals.

tinguished from the others by a variety of differences in fringe benefits (see a later chapter), secondly, by the fact that their wages are
paid in cash and not into a bank, and thirdly, by the fact that their
wage rates are still in many cases conventionally described in terms
of shillings and decimal points of a shilling per hour. Until 1966 they
were paid only for days on which they worked; in that year the
company introduced a system of sick payments which – while not
providing full earnings as for the staff – might provide as much as
85% of normal earnings for up to twenty-six weeks for skilled workers
and up to thirteen weeks for others, depending on length of service.

The means of calculating the actual weekly sums due to a man or
woman within this category are infinitely varied, but basic to them
all is a concept of a worker's 'rate', differentials between which
represent the basic presumed differences of worth between different
skills. This *rate* depends on:

1. One and only one ascribed characteristic – his or her sex. At
every skill level, women receive less than two-thirds of the male
wage, even when doing exactly the same job.
2. The worker's qualifications by virtue of which he is categorized
and identified, and
3. The nature of the job he is actually doing.

Thus a skilled fitter might have a rate of 49p per hour. In theory, if he
were to do a job which did not require his fitting skills, he should
receive a lesser rate, but then, by convention backed by unions sanctions, he could refuse to do that lesser job on the grounds that the
company had an obligation to provide him, as long as they are employing him *as* a fitter, with a job appropriate to his talents. Consequently,
in practice, he retains his fitter's rate whatever the job he does. This
does not work the other way around, however. If a semi-skilled
man is 'upgraded' – put on to work which by workshop convention is
one which can only be done by someone with higher qualifications
than himself – he will, if the union concerned agrees to his doing the
job in the first place, receive the skilled man's rate for the job.

These differential rates – x p per hour for this skill; y p for that –
are based on minima laid down in national agreements. Local bargains can raise all or some of these *rates* above these minima, though
not much alter the relative rank order of different skills (even though,
under piecework schemes *earnings* of semi-skilled workers can sometimes exceed those of skilled men). Generally speaking, however,
with the exception of the tool room 'merit pay' to be mentioned later,
an *individual* man's *rate* is not open to bargaining. Changes are made
only as the result of a bargain between the company and a whole

77

BRITISH FACTORY—JAPANESE FACTORY

group of workers doing the same job. Naturally, some scope exists for redefining the functional category for a particular job (many man-hours of negotiating time were spent at Bradford, for example, negotiating a claim that 'markers off' were as skilled as fitters and should have the same rate) but that scope is limited.

Note that the principle is pretty generally accepted that a man is paid for what he *does* (actually or fictionally) not for what he *can* do. (Or rather for that amount multiplied by the masculinity factor. A woman is also paid for what *she* actually does, multiplied by the femininity factor). One of the union arguments in favour of the markers off in the negotiations just mentioned was to the effect that most markers off were formerly fitters (few people ever 'served their time to marking off') and that consequently they were 'dual trades-men'. The argument was sharply rejected by the management negotia-tor. 'I just want to remove any idea that the company uses them as dual people. They are markers off and they are not used alternatively in other trades.' The union did not press the argument. In the context of English bargaining, it is a weak one.

Ways of translating a man's rate into his weekly wage, however, are multifarious. We shall list most of them below.

The simplest is a method by which most indirect workers are paid – the straight *time rate* of the labourers, the fetchers and carriers, crane drivers and slingers, cleaners, and so on. The Liverpool factory in the autumn of 1967 achieved a very substantial rationalization of these rates. Twenty-four formerly different rates were collapsed into four grades; the lowest – sweepers, toilet attendants, and trainee drivers of the internal trucks, received £13 per week. Window cleaners, car washers, labourers who deliver supplies of parts to the shop floor, an extra £1. The next grade were storekeepers and checkers, some un-skilled inspectors and the slingers who attach loads to crane hooks. They received yet an additional pound to make £15 a week. The last grade, at £15.15 a week, included eight jobs such as that of crane driver, internal truck driver, etc. The four grades were intended to act in part as a promotion ladder.

At the other extreme from the time rate is the system of *individual piecework*. The basic principle is simple. The pieceworker has two hourly rates, one called the piecework supplement and one called the base rate, both of which vary according to skill and sex status. Sample rates at Liverpool in 1968, expressed in new pence per hour, were:

	Base rate	Piecework supplement
Skilled fitter	19·0	7·5
Semi-skilled man	17·9	6·4
Semi-skilled woman	14·7	3·9

Contrary to what one might suppose, the piecework supplement is a straightforward time rate: it is multiplied by the number of hours worked to provide a more or less invariate (i.e. apart from variations due to overtime) contribution to the weekly wage. The base rate, on the other hand, is the one which is used to pay a man not for the hours he works, but for his production during those hours. A machinist given, say, a batch of 100 gaskets to shape used to receive with the job a specification of the amount of time deemed necessary to prepare his machine for the task, and to shape each of the 100 gaskets. If the total was four hours he received four times his notional 'base rate' even if he did it in less than four hours.

If he actually did it in two hours, his hourly earnings on this piecework would obviously be twice what they would be if he took the standard four hours. To confuse the uninitiated, this is referred to variously as having a '200% bonus', or as having, in addition to his base rate of (say) £5 a week, a 'piecework bonus' of £5 making his total 'piecework earnings' £10. (To add to the confusion the invariate piecework supplement is also sometimes called – even on some of the Liverpool factory's official forms – a 'piecework bonus'.) In the subsequent discussion 'bonus percentage' will be used to indicate a percentage multiplier applied to a base rate to make total 'piecework earnings'.

Clearly the difficult and ambiguous factor in such a payment system is the notion of a 'normal' or 'standard' time. Someone has to fix these times. That unfortunate man is the rate-fixer. And it is hardly a novel observation to say that in engineering for the last thirty years, the rate-fixer has slowly been losing the battle of wills and wits with the workers whose rates he fixes. This battle takes place directly with the workers concerned and for many years, the actual terms of the bargaining process have been straight cash, rather than time. The following, for example, are typical examples of the kind of reports of these negotiations one hears:

'So I told him, I said: "But you can't expect us to do this job for 21s a hundred. That lot's 20s and they are only to be finished to six thou' [6 thousands of an inch tolerance] not three thou' like this lot." '

Or, perhaps, from a rueful rate-fixer:

' "Nine bob?!" he said, "You must be bloody crazy", and he gets out his little black book. " 'Ere you are. I got it down in black and white. Last time I turned out a job like this it was 10s 6d. And that was in 1966. It'll be 11s 3d now." So what do you do? Your job is

79

to get the production out. So you settle for 10s 9d and he goes off happy.'

Despite the straightforward cash terms of the bargain, time generally being used only relatively ('this takes longer than that, therefore it should pay more') the results of these bargains were until recently always translated into 'standard time' terms on the piecework tickets which accompanied jobs onto the shop floor. Consequently, upward drift of piecework prices meant a gradual lengthening of nominal standard times. A useful fiction resorted to in the early stages was to increase the actual job time by a percentage known as 'contingency time'. However, as the contingency allowance crept up from 10%, 20%, towards 100%, even this subterfuge began to wear an air of slightly ridiculous complicity. The Liverpool factory eventually dealt with the situation by a reform of their piecework ticketing system in January 1968 – they omitted all reference to times on piecework tickets, which then specified (in addition to information necessary for cost accountants) only the type of job, the base rate payable for the skill required to do the job, and the cash amount to be paid for doing it. The standard time could still be deduced from the last two figures, but at least attention was not drawn to it.

The individual piecework system clearly has many complications. What happens when a fitter assembling a machine discovers that the driller in another department has drilled a hole in the wrong place? This is a contingency not allowed for in the original pricing of his assembly operation. If he were just to get a drill and redrill it, he would be making a gratuitous contribution to the welfare of his employers, unrequited in his wages. So he goes off to find the foreman, who phones for a rate fixer to come and write him out a 'rectification ticket' giving details of the extra uncovenanted job the worker has to do, and authorizing that he be paid an appropriate sum for it.

What happens when a machine breaks down? The worker finds his foreman, who writes him out a pink 'waiting time ticket', showing that he is unable to work at his piece work job for X hours for reasons beyond his control. The bonus percentage paid for those hours varied from shop to shop in the factories between 180% and 280% depending on the general level of piecework earnings. But it was always such that workers received for doing nothing a good deal less than for working.

What happens when a worker leaves his job for other reasons – to attend a works committee of which he is a member, for example, or if he is senior shop steward, to go out to another work shop to help sort out a dispute? He gets his foreman to write him out a maroon 'factory expense ticket' indicating that he should be paid for so many hours at an agreed rate, also a multiple of his base rate, but a slightly larger one than for waiting time.

What happens if a worker discovers that certain necessary operations of a job seem not to have been taken into account in the specifications on the piecework ticket – if, for example, he discovers that three holes have to be drilled in a bracket whereas the job was priced on the assumption that there were two? He goes to his foreman to complain and, if he puts his point forcefully enough or if his foreman is indulgent enough, he gets an 'additional piecework ticket' allowing him extra payment.

What happens if the job is new so that the rate fixers are unable to estimate the amount of time a job will take by adding together standard times for various parts of the job or by analogy with other jobs? The worker gets an 'unpriced ticket' or 'open ticket' – an ordinary piecework ticket with all the normal specifications of the job, but lacking the usual job price. Again, the basis for payment is the actual length of time taken on the job, which should, in theory, be accurately measured by the man 'clocking on' to the job in the time clerk's office, and 'clocking off' when he has finished. (Recent regulations in the Bradford factory specify for one department tightened procedures for such cases. Foremen will see to it that clocking on and off is properly done. They will then sign the bill with a recommendation for payment. This then goes to the rate-fixing department 'who will approve payment and calculate the appropriate base time equivalent to the payment recommended' – a curious illumination of the now ritual nature of the standard time concept.) The regulations do not specify the basis of the payment recommendation. The unwritten convention is that the payment should yield per hour 90% of the average yield of piecework. Foremen deviate from this convention at their peril – except upwards, though hardly even then, for favouritism is not generally liked, and instances of overpayment are likely to become known and hence to raise the subsequent expectation of all workers.

'Open tickets' are also used for other exceptional work. It is not unusual to find, for example, a ticket on which the foreman has simply written '8·7 hours: urgent work to instructions Mr X [the departmental superintendent]. Pay 47½p [per hour].' The ticket bears his signature and the counter signature of the superintendent.

In fact, the discretionary power of supervisors (with their immediate superior's approval) to award extra money to individual workers is considerable. The wage summations in one Liverpool department had a special column for 'supervisors' allowance'. These include payments to raise to a normal level the earnings of the blind and handicapped (the proportion of which, in their work force, is prescribed by law) together with a number of payments made for various reasons, to bring a man's wages up to a 'reasonable' level.

The latter requires some explanation. The bargaining balance is now such in these factories that managers find it very hard to introduce any changes in work organization except under guarantees that no one will lose financially. Hence, if the work flow in a high-earning shop falls off temporarily, they can only make a temporary reduction in manning, sending some people elsewhere – perhaps even to low-paid labourer's jobs – if they can guarantee that 'we'll see you don't lose by it'. The transaction is effected by paying the transferees the lower rate appropriate to the job they actually do, but writing them in addition an 'open ticket' to raise their wages to the level of those who are not transferred. In one Liverpool department the amount paid on these various kinds of discretionary 'open tickets' amounted in some weeks to as much as 11% of the total wage bill.

The Pitfalls of Piecework

The feeling that the payment systems just described represent an unsatisfactory way of organizing work and its payment is widespread in British industry and well reflected in the excellent report *Payment by Result Systems*, by the Prices and Incomes Board. One cannot spend long in either the Bradford or the Liverpool factories without hearing the system attacked – most often by managers, but frequently by shop stewards or by workers, too. The grounds of criticism are multiple.

1. First, there is the direct cost of operating the system – the cost in salaries for rate-fixers, time clerks, and extra wage clerks. Well over 40 people were so employed for the 4,000 manual workers at Liverpool. However, the work of about half of them serves the dual function of fixing wages and of cost accounting each job which goes through their factory. Hence, if it were in any case desired to make the same detailed analysis of labour costs on each product for accounting purposes, the saving of abandoning the piecework system for wages might not be so great.

2. There is a further indirect cost in the time spent arguing/ bargaining about piecework prices. One manager, persuading workers to go off individual piecework onto a new scheme (to be described later) used the argument that, since they now spent 15% of their time arguing about rates, they could expect a good increase in wages

if they were to eliminate the source of argument and share the proceeds from using that time productively. Doubtless he exaggerated.

3. There is a further, intangible, cost in disaffection and suspicion. Because the whole system is geared to keep their earnings level constantly salient in the workers' consciousness, they carefully calculate what their earnings *ought* to be. Frequently, there is a discrepancy between what they get and what they expect. Sometimes they have miscalculated; sometimes the wage clerks have miscalculated; sometimes there are just two principles to apply to the case – as in matters of appropriate bonuses in lieu of piecework when people move jobs, and so on. Whichever the case, they complain. In one week, at the Liverpool wage office, 300 of the 4,000-odd workers came to register complaints: the average weekly score is over 100. Even if a rectifiable error is found, the worker does not necessarily go away happier – the admission of error may be grudging; he may reflect on all the other possible occasions when he might have been cheated without knowing it. And if it *is* a matter of interpretation, and all he gets are the persuasive arguments of the chief clerk explaining why the principle of payment adopted by the office was the right one, he is likely to go away distinctly *un*happy.

4. There is a further morale cost. The very wide discretion given to supervisors to make payments on 'open tickets' to make up a worker's wages leads to a certain amount of favouritism, and to much *more* suspicion of favouritism. Equal occasion for favouritism and the suspicion of favouritism is provided by the allocation of jobs. Some jobs have 'tight' times, others 'loose' times. The foreman has to decide who gets which.

Dissension within the work group can occur even more directly as workers compete for the loosely-timed jobs not just by arguing with the foreman that it is 'my turn', but by deliberately slowing down one job so as not to be available for the next, particularly nasty, job coming up.

5. Objective measurement of the length of time a job should take for an 'average worker' is extremely difficult and always – however careful the 'observations' taken – subject to elements of intuitive and arbitrary decision by the rate fixer. (Whatever the claims to the contrary invariably put forward by the exponents of whatever happens to be the latest school of job measurement. The missionary passion with which they usually argue the case for the superiority of their methods and their total difference from all other methods is generally a good indication of the weakness of those claims.) Consequently, as one

83

superintendent put it, 'the result of an argument about piece rates depends on the strength of character of the individual rate fixer'.

Actually this needs elaborating: any battle of wills between two individuals of different and, in some senses, opposed groups, cannot but be affected by the relative power balance existing between the groups to which they respectively belong. In a feudal society, for instance, as de Tocqueville shrewdly pointed out, a master who was by temperamental disposition shifty-eyed and feeble, could, nevertheless, command with unassailable authority because, in a feudal society, 'the servant is weighed down by the weight of the whole class of masters'. In post-war Britain, full employment – and the experience of full employment for long enough for it to enter into general expectations and assumptions about the immediate future, has made workers less fearful of dismissal and employers more anxious not to lose skilled men. The translation of this change in the economic position into effective organizational power through the growth of the shop steward system has affected the relative 'starting weights' of individual workers and rate fixers. Winning an argument now requires a greater natural endowment of 'strength of character' on the part of a rate fixer than it used to. Their power to prevent an upward creep of prices has diminished.

6. Piecework drift results also from other characteristics of the system and from the power of workers to manipulate it. In a shop where much of the work involves one-off jobs which are new and cannot easily be pre-priced, a worker may work for 20 hours on a normally priced job and for another 20 hours of 'open ticket' work on a job that cannot easily be pre-priced. Supposing that in his 20 hours of regular piecework he did jobs equivalent, according to the entirely notional standard times, to 50 hours of work – say £10 worth at a base rate of 20p per hour. For the other 20 hours of 'open ticket' work he would be paid at 90% of whatever is the average piecework earnings in his shop during the previous week. Let us assume that the average was 250% bonus, which would give him 90% of 250% of 20p (or 45p) for each of the 20 hours.

In practice, however, it is not easy to enforce rules that a worker should clock on and off his separate jobs at the time office so that the actual 20/20 division of his hours of work would be ineluctably recorded. He can find ways of presenting a bunch of tickets together and telling the time clerk, retrospectively, how much time was spent on each. Thus it becomes possible, in our hypothetical example, for the worker to make it appear that he in fact spent 18 hours on his pre-priced jobs and 22 hours on his unpriced jobs. This has three consequences. First, while still getting the same amount for his pre-

Table 3.2

	Hours worked on pre-priced jobs	'Hours-worth' of work done on pre-priced jobs	Bonus %	Bonus rate	Piecework earnings
Actual	20	50	250	20p	20p × 250% × 20 = £10
Reported	18	50	278	20p	20p × 278% × 18 = £10

	Hours of open ticket work	Hourly pay for open ticket work (90% of average bonus)	Piecework earnings
Actual	20	20p × (say) 250% × 90% = 45p	20 × 45p = £9
Reported	22	ditto	22 × 45p = £9.90

Total entitlement: fixed piecework supplement (+ overtime premia) + £10 + £9.
Actual receipts: fixed piecework supplement (+ overtime premia) + £10 + £9.90, or 90p extra.

priced jobs, he gets more for his open ticket work. Secondly, he chalks up a bonus percentage for his pre-priced work that week of 278% instead of 250%. Provided that three or four people in a shop can manage to pull off such a feat every week, the 'piecework average' for the whole shop can gradually creep up from 250% to 253% to 256% and so on. In subsequent weeks the *rate* for unpriced, open ticket, jobs also rises as a consequence: at 256% it would be 46p, not 45p, per hour. A third, long-term consequence is that a job which, worked at a reasonable pace, yielded 240% bonus percentage and which when the average was 250% would be looked on as a job with 'tight times' that paid badly but was still not something to make an issue of, becomes, when the average rises to 280%, a cause for rebellion. There is a demand that it be repriced, which eventually succeeds. When new jobs have to be priced, it becomes impossible to put on them a price that would yield much less than a 280% bonus percentage.

'Manipulating the average' thus has undeniable pecuniary advantages and some workers develop considerable skills, both arithmetic and social, in the service of this end. The essential thing is that the upward creep should go slowly so as not to arouse suspicions of higher echelons of management. This may require that jobs performed in one week are transferred to the next week. If, as in the above example, a worker had the chance to inflate his unpriced job time from 20 to 25 hours, he would be ill-advised to present all his piecework tickets with the claim that he had done all that work in 15 hours – thus suspiciously raising his piecework average from 250% bonus percentage to 330% all in one jump. He would keep some of his tickets 'at the back of his book' so as to boost his average gradually, or use some of them in order to take things easy occasionally when he is feeling off colour without lowering his average. Equally, when the work-flow temporarily falls off, it is possible, with the co-operation of the time clerk to keep up the average by mortgaging the future – presenting for payment as already completed tickets for jobs not yet done. In one factory (not an English Electric factory), recently a walk-out occurred when the foreman discovered, and made an issue of the fact that, one of his workers had presented for payment a job which was still three weeks away from arriving on the shop floor!

Most foremen who would prefer to keep a 'happy shop' are careful not to make such discoveries. Or, more accurately, they are discriminating in the discoveries they make. A glaring instance such as the one just mentioned would be unlikely to get past a British foreman. On the other hand, the rigid insistence on clocking on and off jobs which would prevent these manipulations is clearly ridiculously wasteful of time – in searching for the foreman for his counter-signature, in trips to and from the time office, as well as in preventing a worker from having two jobs under way at the same time, so that while for example, waiting for the crane or for the supply of a part for one job, he can fill in the time by working on the other. Consequently, an understanding soon develops as to how far one can go in 'beating the book'. The odd fifteen minutes here, ten minutes there, and the foreman will sign with a telescope to his blind eye. But a whole hour and the foreman, cornered, will feel obliged to raise questions. This leads not only to hard words and diminished future opportunities to stretch the truth by the odd few minutes, but also to the embarrassments which are always caused when one party can no longer use covert warning signals to deter the other from breaching the unacknowledged, illicit conventions established between them, and has to resort to the gaucherie of overt remonstrance.

Clearly, this characteristic of the piecework system is most pronounced in heavier engineering shops, with a large number of one-off jobs to be done and a high percentage of new work which it is hard to pre-price. It is less pronounced in mass-production departments. Nevertheless, few factories are wholly one or the other, and it is just impossible to have bonus percentages of 400% in one department and of only 200% in another over a long period of time. The leaders pull up the rest.

The total effect of these various devices is clear enough in the official statistics. From October 1964 to April 1967 average hourly earnings (excluding overtime premiums) rose by 17·9%. During that time hourly *rates* rose by only 7·5%. The remaining 12·4% can be attributed to wage drift.

For managers these characteristics of the piecework system constitute its greatest drawback. They see the wage bill as essentially outside their control. A few of the more thoughtful ones see it also as a system of condoned illegality which has a pervasive effect on morale and on the general tenor of management–worker relations. From some points of view, of course, it could be argued that this is its virtue. Workers can derive from the game of 'beating the book' a good deal more fun and opportunity to display arithmetical virtuosity than from football pools. The fact that they *do*, as managers complain, have partial control over their own wages gives them a sense of their own personal worth, redresses the status balance of inequality between management and men in a society where equality is held to be a not insignificant value. And this, it is reasonable to suggest, reduces alienation and raises morale. But the topic of the sources of satisfaction and self esteem available respectively to Japanese and British workers is one to which we shall return more systematically later.

7. It is further often argued that the piecework system does not even act as an incentive – *because* it is not fully under management's control. 'It's my opinion', said one bright young manager, 'that the man on the shop floor under the present system can determine how much he is going to earn. If he is determined to make £25, he damn well makes it – unless we refuse to give him work.' Every man has, it is argued, a pace at which he normally works and feels comfortable at working. Secondly, he has a fairly clear standard in mind for the amount of money he expects to take home each week – not yet, for most Liverpool or Bradford workers, an amount as high as £25 a week, but one which imperceptibly rises both with inflation and with rising living standards. These are the independent variables. The dependent variables are his effort-output and the piecework price system. If his normative wage can be secured for less than his normative effort, then effort slacks off. But, on the other hand, as soon as the effort required to produce his normative wage rises above his normative effort level, instead of responding with greater effort, he restores equilibrium by means of his partial control of the piecework prices – through manipulation of averages and by rebellious protest against 'tight prices'. The efficacy of the piecework system in serving the purposes for which its later nineteenth century inventors devised it – the maximizing of effort-output for a given wage – depends entirely on the piecework price system being, for the worker, an independent not a dependent variable – which it clearly is not.

8. Piecework systems impose on supervisors the very considerable burden of monitoring the quality of work. Prices can be made to vary only according to quantity, not quality. True, minimum quality standards can be imposed; both factories have well-developed testing systems. Rectification tickets work back to the shop responsible for the faulty part, and the worker responsible is not paid for his botched job. But four, five, even fourteen or fifteen brackets out of one hundred with the hole drilled in the wrong place? Do you go through the complicated business of sending the tickets through that will ensure that the machine shop, not your assembly shop is charged for the loss? If you are a harassed foreman, fully occupied trying to keep your workers' supplies running smoothly to their point on the assembly line, you do not bother. 'Scrap! That's another thing', said a Bradford shop steward in the course of a general denunciation of the inefficiency of his management. 'I've never seen such scrap! It's

WAGES

chronic. Every week tons of the stuff goes out through the door!' He was exaggerating, but managers will admit that their losses are not inconsiderable. And where it is a matter of the odd thousandth of an inch in a milling tolerance, the tightness of a screw, the soundness of a wire soldering, when prices *do* mean that the worker has to put the heat on to reach his normative pay packet, sloppiness can be the result.

9. Even when the system is working properly, it contains ambiguities. What constitutes a laudable increase in productivity, what a 'fiddle'? This ambiguity was well illustrated by a Bradford dispute over the piecework rates to be paid to plastic press operators. Since the piecework prices had been fixed output from the presses had improved considerably. There was some dispute as to whether this was due to the management's modification of the machines or to the increasing skill of the workers, but managers wished to retime and reprice these tasks to take into account the 'realistic' processing times – thus, in effect, cutting back the operators' earnings. The argument of the union representative was that 'basically, when piecework is operated in engineering, particularly under the older arrangements, it was anticipated that the operator would, in the course of time, cut a few corners and improve on the times which the management had anticipated would be taken'. That, he said, was perfectly in order; the management got higher production, the workers higher bonuses and everybody was happy.

The resolution in this case, was to reduce the standard times by 50% of the saving, thus splitting the gains.

The proponents of the new work study unit at the Liverpool factory (adherents of the MTM System who had some prominence in the British 'movement' and whom their colleagues delighted in teasing into near apoplexy by calling them 'just glorified rate-fixers') married a fundamentalist, revivalistic puritanism about piecerates to new notions about productivity bargaining and incremental-income division. They insisted on a clear distinction between increase in effort and improvement in technique. Someone who improves technique may be personally rewarded with a prize for his suggestion, but the job must be retimed to take account of his innovation. The higher proceeds would be redistributed in the form of an increase in the *rates* paid for 100% performance (doing 6 hours' work in 6 hours) rather than by making it possible, without any increase in effort, to do the 6 hours' work in 5½ hours and so earn more money at the same rates.

'Yes, and how long does it take to get the rates changed?' is a natural worker reaction. The ambiguity surrounding this matter, and

89

BRITISH FACTORY—JAPANESE FACTORY

the different conceptions of justice held by managers and workers concerning it are not unrelated to the 'condoned illegality' of the subterfuges described earlier. Thus, a shop steward explained with some sense of outrage, the MTM doctrine which he had just heard expounded at a lecture on work study given for shop stewards at the Liverpool factory.

'Take a skilled man whose job it is to mark off work. He's been at it twenty years and he finds a new way of doing it. Instead of using a ruler or a tape, he makes himself a jig. Then work study comes along and they use his technique. Now, how's he getting paid for the benefits of his experience? *They* say it isn't experience. He's just fiddling the times. . . .

When management say this kind of thing, how can you take too much notice of what they say is right and wrong? After all, in private enterprise if you do this kind of sharp practice against your competitors, you're supposed to be doing well!'

In other words, the principled objection to what is seen as an immorally grasping attitude of management on this issue, becomes a justification for the subterfuges of manipulating the average which are *not* principled and which *do* count as a misdemeanour according to the norms of both management and most workers (except in those areas where the superior morality of the class war has penetrated rather deeply). The beam in management's eye justifies the mote in the eyes of the workers.

Reform of Piecework?
For all these reasons, disillusionment with the piecework system is widespread. *But*, say most of the people who express such disillusionment, what can you do? Thus, a manager who spoke of a change in the payment system as (along with new systems of industrial relations and apprenticeship) one of the three major pre-requisites for better productivity:

'But piecework will have to stay until people can be educated to give of their best as long as there is work to be done. If you take it away now, there will be a tremendous loss in output, because people just aren't geared to be self-motivating and none of the exhortations of our political leaders are going to make them so.'

Or an older, experienced chief shop steward who spoke of tentative informal discussions he had had with managers who were seriously

90

considering abolishing the piecework system and putting everybody on a time rate:

'There will have to be tighter control if they do that. It's quite obvious that you'll get a certain class who will sit back and do nothing all day. There needs to be stronger discipline. Supervisors will have to supervise. We haven't reached Utopia yet. I recognize we've got problems on our side too.'

The solution generally favoured among reform-minded managers is the measured day work system whereby a standard time rate is linked to performance norms based on careful work study. The question of the sanctions to be employed if the performance consistently falls below the norms remains a source of doubt and misgiving. Given that, 'You can't go back to the old whip-cracking mill-master days', can you get supervisors with the moral authority to induce good work? If you try to build in bonus incentives, do you not find yourself back where you started?

Alternatives to Piecework

So far, experimental moves in this direction have been made at both the Bradford and Liverpool factories. Two forms are described below.

The first, at Bradford, is the *step bonus system*, a modification of the piecework system designed – for individually working machinists and millwrights – to lengthen and to make more tenuous the connection between work done this week and wages received next week. The essentials of the piecework system – standard times for each job, arrangements for waiting time and open ticket work, etc. – are retained but the relationship between performance and payment is blurred: (a) by paying an unvarying wage for each 8-week period based on that worker's performance in the previous 8 weeks, and (b) by 'stepping' the connection between performance and wage according to a scale such as the following:

Hours' worth of work produced in 42 hours	Gross wages
29·1 – 35	£14
35·1 – 40	£15.25
40·1 – 45	£16.25
45·1 – 50	£17.25
and so on	

Moreover, a worker who has for two consecutive two-monthly periods been in, say, the £16.25 bracket and whose performance falls only just below the corresponding performance level is allowed to go on receiving the same wage for the fourth period. Only after a further period of lower performance is his wage stepped down.

The agreement with the unions lists the purposes of the change. It will level out fluctuations in wages and enable operators to achieve and maintain a higher and more consistent working tempo. 'Some of the day-to-day pressures of the piecework systems will be removed and operators will need to spend less time disputing and negotiating piecework times.' More stable pay conditions should reduce turn-over. New starters (who are given a guaranteed minimum for an initial period) would be able more easily to settle in. There is a general view that the scheme was working well, though no hard before-and-after figures were available to show how far some of these objectives were achieved.

A second type of scheme, introduced at both Bradford and Liverpool, was the *group bonus scheme*. The assembly of washing-machines at Liverpool, for example, was subjected to exhaustive work study. Improvements were made in layout, tooling, and job divisions. Each operation was devised, in theory, to take exactly the same amount of time as every other. The standard number of washing machines which a 40-hour week would produce was then calculated. For producing exactly that number of machines each man in the group (apart from the 'pool leader' who received an extra bonus) was paid 46½p per hour; each woman, 32p. For producing 10% more they would receive an extra 4½p and 3½p per hour respectively; 4½p and 3½p less for producing 10% less. The earnings appropriate for 80% production – 38p and 26½p respectively – were guaranteed minima even though production fell below that level. To iron out fluctuations and produce a steadier wage level, each week's pay was determined by the average production over the previous four weeks.

There were the usual arrangements to compensate for additional work caused by resetting of tools for different models or rectification of deficient parts – additions to the top half of the fraction:

$$\frac{\text{hours' worth produced}}{\text{hours worked}}$$

and for waiting time (subtraction from the divisor in the above fraction and separate – lesser – payment for the idle hours).

Given that one week's activity of some 40-odd people was involved, the complications which these latter adjustments implied for the weekly accounting were very considerable. The shop steward for that department, a quiet and somewhat self-effacing young man, claimed that he had been elected to the task solely because he had something of a head for figures. He was quite shrewd about devices for using waiting time to pre-assemble parts that could be pre-assembled (instead of sitting quietly with hands in lap as the regulations prescribed), but he was not altogether clear about the precise mechanisms by which he had achieved the considerable feat of keeping the earnings of his fellows pretty constant around the 90–95% of parity mark, despite rather wild fluctuations in output.

The answer seems to be roughly as follows. It is expected with any new scheme such as this that the first few weeks will be difficult. In order not to lower morale, therefore, earnings are boosted by what appears in the calculations as a 'policy allowance'. When that tapered off according to the prescribed rules, and the prospect of a real drop in wages loomed up, the foreman and shop steward jointly and severally made representations to the factory manager and to the work study team in charge of operations, claiming that the times were too tight. This charge was hotly denied by the team. Their times were the synthesized product of the highest ergonomic science, and if only the foreman and workers would set their minds to it, they would soon be proving that even the impossible was possible. The usual weekly resolution of these arguments was for the work study man to go to the deputy divisional manager and ask him: 'Okay. So how much do you want to pay them this week?' It would then be his job to modify the additions to the top variable of the fraction (to be made in respect of the 'objectively ascertained' work involved in rectifications, re-toolings, etc.), thus inflating that figure sufficiently to produce the desired earnings level – a concession to the weakness of the flesh which was justified on the grounds that these were, after all, teething troubles.

After several months, however, the pretext began to wear uncomfortably thin. Most teeth do not take that long to break through. Meanwhile, the youthful foreman was replaced by an older, more experienced, and tougher man. He, too, was of the opinion that the times were tight, but he used rather different tactics of persuasion. He drove his workers hard and got them actually working according to the prescribed times. He 'belted the line'. One consequence of this was that, after three or four hours, the people on the later operations found themselves having to move gradually on towards the end of the line in pursuit of the washing machines they were working on. As soon as he had five or six people jammed elbow to elbow, working furiously on the very threshold of the test-beds, he called in the work study team to witness the reduction of their science to absurdity. Thus, finally, cycle times were lengthened. The original plan whereby

28 average sensual human beings given the advantages of modern scientific organization could produce 156 machines in a day was substantially modified to allow thirty-three people to produce 141. Earnings improved slightly, but not much. The biggest improvement was in tempers, and now the desired normative level of earnings was produced by playing the scheme straight – without stretching anyone's conscience by the issue of inflated additional work tickets.

There is a final category of payments methods linked to the piecework system and also of long standing. It is that of workers with a *variable lieu bonus.* (Bonus 'in lieu of' piecework payments. Those workers on a fixed day-rate are also, in formal terms, receiving a lieu bonus but theirs, once negotiated, is fixed until renegotiated.) The period within which the variable bonuses vary may be as short as a week – a crane driver's wages, for instance, are calculated weekly to give him a bonus percentage equal to the average bonus percentage of all those in the shop he serves. The period may be as long as eight weeks, as in the case of the highly skilled tool-room fitters (most of whose work involves the preparation of new jigs and tools, etc., which it would be impossible to pre-price). Their bonus percentage is fixed for eight weeks at a time and is calculated from the average bonus percentage of all skilled workers on piecework in the whole factory.

Having mentioned *time rates* (including the fixed z pence per hour $- z \times 133\%$ or 150% pence per hour of overtime – of the pieceworker's piecework supplement) and having described how the pieceworker's base rate is used to calculate a production bonus by various *payment by results* schemes, one has fairly exhaustively covered the two principles which determine the pay of manual workers in the Liverpool and Bradford factories – with one small exception: the merit pay in the Bradford tool room. This consisted, in 1969, of an addition of 1 to 4 old pence per hour to the wage. It was said that seniority played an important part in determining whether one was a penny man or a fourpenny man. Since a fourpenny man got only 2% more than a penny man in his wage packet, however (the toolroom elite averaged £23 per week in May 1968), it cannot be said that merit pay was of overwhelming importance.

JAPANESE PAYMENT SYSTEMS

Japanese payment systems are somewhat different. To begin with, one cannot divide employees into three broad groups of monthly salaried, weekly salaried, and hourly rated, as in an English factory. Everyone is paid monthly. Everyone's payment is officially called *Kyūyo* – i.e. 'remuneration', though thanks to trade union tradition *chingin* ('wages') are what union bargaining is officially about, and white collar workers will colloquially call what they receive *kyūryō* ('salary'). (*Chingin* and *kyūryō* – as opposed to *kyūyo* – are hangovers from a pre-war staff/worker division similar to the contemporary British one, and they have much the same connotations as the English 'wage' and 'salary'.)

There *are* divisions of status and methods of payment, however. The clearest, and the nearest approximation to the staff/hourly rated line in Britain, is that which divides all those who are union members, or (see p. 120) would be union members but for the fact that they occupy posts of special responsibility, from the more senior managerial and technical employees. The former are paid according to a public scale negotiated with the union (all manual and routine clerical workers together with junior managers and graduate technologists in their twenties and early thirties), while the salaries of senior managerial and technical employees, like those of their British counterparts, are fixed at the discretion of their superiors.

The way salaries are fixed for the latter group differs, though, from the practice in English Electric, in three respects. First, a Hitachi manager does *not* bargain. 'Asking for a rise' is against the whole ethos of the firm and it is out of the question to back such a request with the threat to go elsewhere. Either that threat is not taken seriously, or it *is* taken seriously as an indication that the loyalty of the querulous manager is now so attenuated that if he feels unwanted and leaves, the firm will suffer no great loss.

Secondly, Hitachi salaries for senior managers have long since been governed by pre-determined scales – of the kind Liverpool (p. 75) is beginning to adopt. The scales are extrapolations of the scales for junior managers which (since they are union members) are publicly negotiated with the union. The senior managers' upper reaches of these scales are not publicly known, but your superior will let you know (and you can only *hope* honestly) whether you are getting par for your grade and seniority, or whether your merit rating is above or below average.

Thirdly, although there is no individual bargaining pressure to raise salaries there *is* what might be called dispersed collective pressure. A section chief in the personnel department – who has the records – will compute the average salary for section chiefs at various levels of seniority, and swap the information informally with his opposite numbers in the three other big electrical firms. If it turns out that Hitachi comes badly out of the comparison, the word will be spread around and individual section chiefs will send the message up through their immediate superiors that there are certain obvious remedial measures which would visibly enhance their sense of dedication to Hitachi.

The same dividing line between senior managers and the rest separates those who are believed to be inner-directed, and the others who are thought to require some extra money incentive to make them stay on after hours. In the matter of sick pay everyone is treated alike from general manager to the newest manual recruit – there is no deduction for the first month. But in the case of overtime, senior managers get no extra pay however hard they work, whereas others do, and at premium rates, though junior managers, although they normally clock on for overtime in the office, make no claim for work taken home. The more one behaves like a senior manager, the quicker one might get to be one.

(In Hitachi one does, incidentally, clock *on* for overtime. Unlike English Electric where one is deemed to be absent unless proved by the evidence of a clock card to be present, in Hitachi one is deemed to be present during normal working hours and punches a card only for deviations – late arrival, early leaving, hours off in the middle of the day, overtime, etc. Supervisors report absences.)

Before going more deeply into Hitachi wages, it might be useful to summarize at this point some of the differences in hours, holidays and overtime premia between the two firms (Table 3.3). The most striking difference is the differential between senior staff and manual workers at English Electric, contrasting with the absence of such differentials in Hitachi. The intermediate category at English Electric – the weekly-paid staff and some junior monthly-paid staff – is omitted from the table in order not to overburden it.

Table 3.3   *Hours, overtime premia, holidays, etc. in the two firms*

	Hitachi 1969		English Electric 1968	
Overtime	Senior managers	All others	Senior staff	Hourly rated
Premium for first 2 hrs overtime		25%*		33%
Premium for further hrs overtime		25%*		50%
Premium for overtime hrs at night[a]		30%*		50%
Premium for regular shifts at night		30%*		33%
Premium for Saturday[b] work		30%*		50%
Premium for Sunday and bank holiday work		30%*		100%

Hours of work

Regular weekly hrs; spring and autumn	44 (av.)[b]	44 (av.)	37½	40
Regular weekly hrs; summer and winter	40	40	37½	40

Holidays

Annual paid holidays for first 5 yrs of service (days)	10*	10*	18–20	10(10–11)[c]
5–9 yrs service	15*	15*	19–20	10(11–12)
10·or more yrs service	20*	20*	20	10(13)
Other days of paid holiday[d]	16	16	6	6

Sickness and pension

Number of wks of sickness during which state insurance benefits supplemented by *ex gratia* payments, after 10 years' service:				
When the illness is tuberculosis	60	60	39	6–10[e]
For high blood pressure, cancer	52	52	39	6–10
For other illnesses	48	48	39	6–10
Non contributory pension[f] received after 25 yrs service (% final salary)			25%	0
Non-contributory lump-sum pension after 25 yrs service (multiple of final monthly salary)	25	23		

[a] Japanese night: 10 p.m. to 5 a.m.; British night, 12 a.m. to 6 a.m.

[b] In Hitachi alternate Saturdays in spring and autumn remain regular working Saturdays. This makes the 44 hour average.

[c] Figures in brackets represent the result of a new agreement, at the Bradford factory only, in 1969. Hourly-rated workers will receive an extra day after 3 yrs, another after 5 yrs, and a third after 7 yrs.

[d] In Britain the 6 bank holidays; in Japan the 12 legal holidays, plus 2 extra days at New Year, May Day and Hitachi Foundation Day.

[e] Skilled workers receive 10 and others 6 weeks continuation of payments.

[f] This indicates only the company's contribution to the pension. Actual pensions were larger by virtue of the employee's own contributions. Normal retirement age is 56 in Hitachi, 65 in English Electric. A lump sum of 30–5 months' pay would be required in Britain to produce an annuity equal to 25% of final salary. Japanese retiring at 56 normally, of course, have more than 25 years' service. In 1971 average retirement bonuses were reported to be running at around £4,000 for manual workers and double that for managers. In Japan as a whole they were reported to average £7,000 for manual workers with 41 years' service and £11,500 for college graduates with 32 years' service (*Japan Labor Bulletin*, 12, i, Jan. 1973 p. 5).

* Items asterisked are statutory minima imposed by the Labour standards Law of 1947.

How a Japanese wage is made up

A man's wage at Hitachi is a total of four component elements. Table 3.4 shows the proportion of the total monthly wage paid out under each of these four heads. The figures refer to payments in cash to all those below the dividing line just mentioned – i.e. union members. Although these figures are for the enterprise as a whole, individual factories do not deviate much from the average.

Table 3.4 *Hitachi Manufacturing Company Wage Composition: 1967–70*

	1967	1968	1969	1970
Basic salary	42·4	39·1	35·0	41·8
Merit Supplement	33·4	31·7	31·2	23·3
Job-level supplements	20·7	25·3	29·3	31·0
Various allowances	3·5	3·9	4·5	3·9

First, the *basic salary* is a function of seniority plus merit. To begin with there is an agreement with the union concerning the minimum amount of basic salary to be received by those joining the firm directly from schools of different levels. Secondly, there is an agreement concerning the *minimum* basic salary to be received by men and women of different ages – up to 30 for women and to 40 for men. (To be more precise, for men too the *guarantee* extends only up to the age of 30. The contract has a note to the effect 'for men over 30 the payments are "standard" not "guaranteed" amounts'. The union has sought annually to extend the guarantee but without success so far.) The age minima and the minimum starting salaries can be conviently reproduced together here (Table 3.5) in an abbreviated form which shows how small is the initial advantage of lengthening one's education beyond the school-leaving age of 15. The figures show the 1969 agreements. They represent, of course, only the basic salary element in the monthly wage. About 8,500 yen equalled £10 in 1970.

Thirdly, a very complex set of agreements limits the amount to which a man's basic salary may be raised above the minimum. Every employee receives annually in April a rise in salary. In the limiting case the minimum rise would, of course, be fixed by the age minima of the above scale, but there is a further *agreed minimum increase* for each grade of workers. (Which has the effect of ensuring that those who are some way off the floor for their age are not reduced to the floor level at the next age.) No *maximum* increase is set for each grade, but the *average* rise is – and in practice most workers get something reasonably close to the average.

Fourthly, the final institutionalized element limiting managerial discretion in wage increases is an agreement concerning the speed of

Table 3.5 *Minimum monthly starting salaries and age-linked salaries (Basic element only)*

Age	Minimum Women	Salary Men	Starting salaries for graduates of:				
			Hitachi apprentice schools	Technical high school	Ordinary high school	Higher technical institute	University
15	7,700	8,100					
18	8,690	9,200	9,300/9,400	9,600	9,200		
20	9,350	9,900				10,900	
22	10,010	10,700					12,700
25	11,000	11,900					
30	11,750	13,400					
35		14,800					
40		15,800					

promotion from grade to grade. The average and minimum salary increases, and the maximum and minimum promotion speeds are set out in Table 3.6.

Note that, with the exception of those in the foreman category, these grades have *no functional connotation whatever*. Promotion from grade to grade simply means more status and a higher level of annual salary increases. It is not, in other words, a seniority promotion system of the kind found in British railways or blast furnaces; promotion does not depend on someone retiring, leaving his shoes to be stepped into. It is a scale of 'person-related payments' – as opposed to 'job-related payments' – to use the everyday language of Japanese wage lore. (A lore which has developed to such arcane dimensions that a trade union publisher recently put on the market all one could wish to know about wages in a 900-page, six guinea *Encyclopaedia of Wages*.) It is an intricate set of rules, based on the exponential principle that the higher you go the faster you rise, designed to give recognition to both seniority and assessed merit. The seniority principle requires that everybody goes up a notch every year of some minimal proportions. The merit assessment is two-fold – first in determining how quickly a man shall be promoted to the next highest grade, secondly in determining whether his annual rise shall be higher, lower, or the same as, the average for workers in his grade.

Of course, the system does not work with quite the rigorous regularity prescribed, but only a small number of the 48,000 Hitachi men and women in the ordinary manual and clerical grades who responded to the union's 1968 questionnaire reported themselves as being in a grade which fell outside the proper limits for their age. The vast

Table 3.6 *Salary increases (basic element only) by grade and standard ages for reaching grades (Hitachi, 1969 agreement)*

Grade	Salary increases (yen)		Age on reaching that grade		
	Average	Minimum	The high flyer	The median[a] worker	The plodder
Managerial workers	7%	600			
Specially titled workers					
Master craftsmen/master clerks	1,500	900			
Craftsmen/clerks-in-chief,					
first class	1,200	720			
second class	1,000	600			
Supervision and guidance workers					
First class foreman	1,000	600			
Second class foreman	900	540			
Third class foreman					
Basic salary over 17,000	800	480			
Basic salary under 17,000	700	420			
Skilled workers and administration workers: various grades					
Grade 1	800	480	36	46	54
Grade 2	750	450	32	39	46
Grade 3	700	420	28	33	38
Grade 4	650	390	25	28	31
Grade 5	600	360	22	24	25
Grade 6	550	330	20	21	21
Grade 7	500	300	18	18	18
Grade 8	450	280	15	15	15

[a] i.e. the middle worker if all those in any one age group are lined up in the order in which they get promoted.

majority of these were technical workers between the ages of 21 and 26 appointed two or three years ahead of the high-flyer schedule into grades 6 and 5. The reason for their accelerated promotion is interesting. It reflects the marginal influence of market forces. These were technicians in short supply for whom rather high wages were being bid – particularly by smaller firms with more flexible wage structures. The Hitachi personnel managers said that they were not greatly worried that they might leave to go elsewhere (though this is the most footloose period of life when some people *do* decide to move – not just out of their firm because there still is no route into comparable big firms – but out of the big-firm sector as a whole to try their luck in one of the smaller specialized or consulting firms).

Rather, they said, they were worried about the general effect on the morale of these workers if they saw themselves as seriously under-appreciated in comparison with others of their age and skills.

The 'higher the faster' principle means that over the years considerable disparities can develop between the basic salaries of men and women of identical ages. But everybody goes up to some degree. The picture revealed by a union survey is shown in Table 3.7. Two things should be remembered when interpreting the figures. First that the very tight grading and promotion system was not negotiated until the early sixties. Until then the company had greater discretion in raising basic salaries, consequently the wage spread for 45-year-olds is now greater than it is likely to be in future. Second, that the figures refer only to those who had spent all their working lives in Hitachi. Mid-career entrants are not included. They are, in fact, a mixed bunch. A large number of those who were very glad to get into Hitachi are receiving wages lower than the minimum listed here. Likewise, a number of skilled men whom Hitachi was glad to get are higher than the maxima for the home-bred.

Since final wage packets are fairly closely related to basic salary (in ways to be discussed later) the figures of Table 3.7 are not too misleading if taken as an indication of total wages as well as of the basic salary element in wages. It will be seen that even the least favoured worker is getting more than two-and-a-half times his 18-year-old salary at the age of 45. Moreover, thanks to the grading system, everybody goes through formal changes in status which give

Table 3.7 *Salaries (basic element only) of Hitachi male life-time employees*[a]

(Minimum for 18-year-old middle school graduate = 100)

Age	Middle school graduate (i.e. compulsory education only) Minimum	Maximum	High school graduate Minimum	Maximum	University graduate Minimum	Maximum
18	100	121	117	117		
22					157	157
23	133	160	134	176		
30	155	209	195	257	198	324[b]
45	267	317/356[c]	359	476		

[a] Based on a union survey of Hitachi employees. 70% responded.

[b] A very small number of 30-year-old graduates may already have been promoted beyond the union-scale range – i.e. to a higher figure than this.

[c] The higher figure is the maximum for those who have already been promoted to foreman grades: the lower for those still in the basic manual or clerical grades.

him or her a *sense* of getting on. Even the least meritorious worker reaches grade 1 eventually – albeit only a year before his retirement. For those who have got to the same place already at the early age of 36 – having received a formal promotion nearly every other year – there are still four foremen grades to go to, and beyond them the upper 'specially titled' grades of master-craftsman etc. (These special titles are also means for 'kicking upstairs' foremen who have out-lived their usefulness, and means for rewarding good experienced craftsmen who lack the power of personality to become foremen.) Beyond that again is the possibility of promotion to the managerial grades. That possibility – particularly promotion to managerial posi-tions in production departments – is now extremely remote for manual workers and diminishing with time. For the clerical (so-called 'administrative workers') the chances of moving into mana-gerial jobs are considerably better, especially for those – the majority – who have had a high-school education. Such promotion is more likely to take place fairly early, when they are in grades 4 to 3, rather than later, and similarly workers in the same manual grades (so-called 'skill workers') are more likely to move into foremen grades – beginning with a vice-foremanship – at around the same stage in their career.

So much for the basic salary.

The second element in the wage, the *merit supplement*, is exactly what it says, an additional payment of a percentage of the basic wage, the percentage being determined – like promotion though this time on a monthly basis – by one's superiors' assessment of one's merit. This element of the wage does, however, operate in practice to accelerate the effect of the seniority element of the wage since the *average* percentage merit rating which individuals shall receive, and also the *minimum* rating, are subject to annual contract with the union and are set to rise from grade to grade. Thus, by agreement, workers in the lowest and youngest grade will on average receive a 59% rating and never less than 48%. For top grade I workers, however, the average is 78% and the minimum 62%.

The senior workers with the special titles all, predictably, have a high rating. Master clerks and master craftsmen get 117% – i.e. their basic salary is more than doubled. For the others, there is a range, not a fixed rate – between 76% and 94% for the second-class crafts-man or clerk-in-chief, for example. Thus, even for these honoured veterans, there is still over and above their long-term hopes of eleva-tion from second to first class, the short-term hope of a higher rating and a higher salary next month, to make it worthwhile keeping their willing smiles brightly polished.

For senior managers, monthly adjustment of the merit supplement had become entirely notional (managers were assessed only in the annual round of basic salary increases) and recently this was acknowledged in the formal redesignation of managerial salaries as an all-inclusive fixed monthly amount. A certain proportion of that salary however – now an invariate proportion – still has to be considered as the notional merit supplement element for the purposes of sick pay. (For all workers full salary is paid during the first month of prolonged sickness, full salary *less* the merit supplement for several weeks or months thereafter depending on the nature of the illness. See Table 3.3.)

The third component of the wage, the *miscellaneous allowances*, is also a person-related component, but one related to characteristics of the person less obviously of moment to the company's profits than are his diligence and skill. An example is the payment of the total cost of rail and bus season tickets beyond the first two kilometres. One could argue, possibly, that there is an instrumental rationale. One might say that the company does not get its best out of a man who has walked to work, or even that workers should be encouraged to live at a distance because the company gains from having them kept in a state of rude health by the country/suburban air, and the exercise they get in helping out on their father's/brother's/wife's farm in their spare time. But the reasoning would be somewhat specious. Family allowances are also paid: 3,700 yen (about £4.40) per month for the first dependent, if she is a wife; 3,100 yen if he/she is somebody else; and 300 yen each for the next four. Presumably this also could be given a directly instrumental rationale: the worker is not going to give of his best if he is half starved from having to feed a large family. It is curious, however, that British employers have not generally seen this as a likely or as a consequential contingency. Family allowances are paid in Britain, in fact, only to members of the middle class such as university professors who are not particularly noted for starving themselves to feed a family.

In point of fact, apart from fitting into a management ideology and a theory of motivation which will be discussed later, the family allowances are largely a product of the particular exigencies of the immediate post-war period. Then, after so much destruction, in the chaos caused by the need to adjust the world's most totally war-mobilized economy to peace, GNP fell back to less than 40% of 1940 levels. Simply staying alive meant spending a high proportion of wages on food. Family size seemed a reasonably sensible criterion to adopt for distributing a large part of the wage bill and the practice became common, sometimes under union pressure, sometimes at the initiative of managers. Since then, however, this element has been gradually whittled back, largely under union pressure, but not against any great resistance by managers, though with occasional upward revisions as in 1968.[3]

The fourth part of the wage, *the job-level supplement*, which now accounts for nearly one third of the wage bill, is a recent innovation – brought in for manual workers in 1964 and for clerical workers in 1966. It is the only part of the wage which is 'function-related' rather than 'person-related'. All jobs are graded, supposedly by a rather elaborate job evaluation technique. To each grade is attached a job payment; payments for the highest and lowest grades being as follows.

Table 3.8 *Dimensions of job-related payment ladders, 1969*

Ladder	Number of grades	Payment for highest	Payment for lowest	Difference
Foreman	3	20,000	16,400	3,600
Manual	11	17,640	9,240	8,400
Non-manual	6	16,400	8,900	7,500

The introduction of 'western-style' job-related wages has been hailed as a great advance, the final breakthrough out of a transitional adolescent stage of repressive feudalism into a state of full maturity in which workers are paid 'properly' – as economists would say, according to market principles, or as sociologists would say, according to achievement rather than ascriptive norms.

To say the least this is an exaggeration – for three reasons. First, although the relative weight of the job-related element has been gradually increased, and although there is agreement between management and union to increase it further until it accounts for as much as 50% of the wage bill, no one is proposing to take it *beyond* 50%. 'Given our Japanese traditions and present circumstances', they say, a balance between the seniority scale and the function scale is obviously needed – though why that balance should be 50:50, rather than 25:75 or 75:25 (as it is in some other firms) no one seems to know.

Secondly, despite rapid increases in the *total amount* of the wage being paid on this scale, the floor remains high, and the differentials

---

[3] According to the explanation of managers, this was a device to raise the wages of men over 40 without too much upsetting the general pattern of salary scale. Some such adjustment was considered necessary to restore age differentials. Younger workers' wages had been raised considerably in order to improve the firm's competitive position in the virgin labour market.

relatively small. It will be seen that the difference between the job-related payment for the highest supervisory grade and that for the humblest manual grade is only 11,000 yen, which in itself would give rise (if the other elements in earnings were equal) to a spread of only $\pm 12\%$ of the average total monthly wage. If one takes the spread for manual workers only – as between the least skilled workers in the bottom grade and the most skilled workers in the top grade – it is $\pm 8\%$ of the average wage. By contrast, according to the Department of Employment and Productivity's figures for June 1968, the spread of earnings, not between the extremes but between the *average* British skilled worker and the *average* unskilled worker was $\pm 17\%$ of average hourly earnings.[4]

Thirdly, the assertion that this scale is 'function-related rather than person-related' is itself open to question. How does one define a 'function'? In Britain manual job descriptions are broad and simple. A man is a centre-lathe turner, or he is a generator erection fitter. To be sure, if a team of three men are put on to erecting a generator, one may be able to do, and naturally assume the task of doing, jobs that the other two cannot do. But this does not change his formal designation or his rate. Not so in Hitachi where a man is a first-class lathe mechanic, or a second-, third-, or fourth-class lathe mechanic; a first-class, or a second- or third-class generator erection fitter. Lathe mechanics, therefore, spread themselves from the third step on the job-related scale to the eighth – from 10,920 yen to 15,120 yen, depending on their skill and experience. In fact the only jobs which are not so classed are those such as temperature tester in a foundry which are part of a normal promotion ladder *of jobs* within a work team.

Hence the so-called job-evaluation exercise turned out to be not an evaluation of jobs, but an evaluation of chaps. By the workers this was explicitly understood to be its intention. Some said, for example, that they thought the introduction of the new scale was an improvement because the evaluators really took the trouble to find out what a man *could* do, and had looked at a man's skills more objectively than the foreman did for his periodic merit ratings.

One consequence of the fact that *everyone* has some prospect of advancement up the job-scale is that there is a high correlation between this scale and the seniority scale (which comes out very clearly in the union's survey of wages). The odds are that when a man is upgraded from a third-class assembly fitter to a second-class

[4] *D.E.P. Gazette*, Dec. 1968, p. 1057, to be precise, not of actual average earnings but of an unweighted average of the average skilled and the average unskilled wage.

assembly fitter, and thus from grade 4 to grade 6 on the job scale, he will also move from grade 6 to grade 5 on the basic salary scale. (And if he is intelligent and spends long enough on the wage scales at the back of his free copy of his Hitachi Workers Trade Union Diary, he might even be able to work out what all that *means* in terms of wages. It is not made easier for him that all the words translated here 'class' or 'grade' are all *kyū* in Japanese. The quickest way to lead a conversation with an Hitachi worker into total confusion is to ask him what '*kyū*' he is.)

Finally, the rigours of this scale are further modified in practice. The 1970 wage contract contains the following two clauses:

'1. If a man is moved from one job to another of lower grade, he shall continue to receive the same job-related payment applicable to his previous job for six months or until job-grade rates are raised by wage negotiations, whichever is the sooner.

2. Any man over 40 whose job falls in grades 1–4 shall, notwithstanding his actual grade, receive grade 5 payment.'

If, it might then be asked, the introduction of this complex system of job-related payments produced very little change in individual pay packets, why was it embarked on? One part of the answer probably lies in something to be discussed later – the scientism, intellectuality and fashion-proneness of Japanese managers, their exaggerated respect for American management consultants, and their willingness to believe that their wage system left workers 'without incentives'. The other part of the answer is that it did produce *some* change in the distribution of wages. First, it flattened the age/wage gradient somewhat. On the 'basic salary plus merit' scale, the average 50-year-old received (before and after the change) something like 300% of what an 18-year-old received. On the new functional scale, those in the top grade (for manual workers), received 190% of those on the bottom. By taking increasing amounts of the wage bill off the first very steep scale, and using it for the new, more gently graded, scale the gradient of total wages is being somewhat flattened (when the proportions paid are 50:50 the gradient would become 100 to 236 rather than 100 to 300).

In effect, this means a redistribution from older to younger workers, though in practice, the transfer is being done in stages in the form of differential *increases*, so that those at the upper ages never suffer any actual reduction in wages. This was an end earnestly desired by Japanese managers. Since the early 1960's the shortage of labour in the virgin school-leavers' market had led to competitive bidding for the brightest workers. Able youths would still come to

Hitachi for 85% of the starting wage at small firms with less prestige and less attractive prospects, but still the differential could not be allowed to become too great. The job-level scale offered a device for raising starting wages much more rapidly than average wages.

A second, more particular, intended effect was to raise the salary of young, particularly competent, high school graduates, relative to that of older, less well-trained workers. This was thought desirable to assuage what was considered to be a growing resentment on the part of the well-trained bright young technicians at the disparity between contribution and reward. Although the 'older = more experienced = better worker' argument is not by any means the major justification for the seniority wage system, it is *one* justification, and too great a disparity between contribution and wage certainly was seen by some as an injustice.

There is one further refinement on the job-level scale. Not content with inventing the complexities of the system just described, Hitachi managers have been unable to forbear from borrowing all the complexities of the British piecework system too. Briefly, it is operated as follows. There is all the paraphernalia of job tickets and standard times. Total time actually taken is set against the standard times for the work done and a 'performance percentage' is worked out – for a month at a time. The payment due to a man on the job-related scale is then multiplied by this percentage.

The system works differently at Hitachi from the way it works at English Electric in several respects. First, few people are on *individual* piecework – only 13% of all the piecework workers at the Hitachi factory. (As at English Electric most indirect workers simply get their flat job-grade payment on a straight time basis, though some, like setters, tool-room workers and crane drivers are, as at English Electric, paid a factory average or a shop average.) Of the other 87% of pieceworkers some are in groups of two – the two workers who operate the same machine on each of two shifts – but most are in much larger groups. At Taga whole departments of several hundred people are collectively rated. The connection between an individual's effort and his wage is thus tenuous.

Secondly, since it alters only the job-related payment, performance has a lesser effect on wages than in Britain where the invariate part of the wage is smaller.

Thirdly, the fiddling of tickets by the foreman with the willing connivance of his superiors is sufficiently standard practice for the rating of large groups of workers never to deviate from the average performance percentage of 103% by more than four or five points. At Hitachi, where whole groups under a single foreman will often have a group rating, foremen not only hold back tickets from one month to the next; they also borrow from and offer loans of tickets to, each other. Occasionally something will go wrong and an individual worker will come out with a percentage as low as 60% or as high as 135%, but these are exceptional cases, soon 'corrected'.

Fourthly, quite apart from these under-the-counter modifications, there is formal official readjustment. The 1970 wage contract states 'if the average piecework performance rate of any factory varies by more than 7% from the standard norm, adjustments shall be made to bring it back within the 93%–107% range'.

Fifthly, as a consequence of these features, the piecework system is seen by most workers to be of little consequence to their welfare. There is little bargaining over rates – not just because bargaining is 'not done', but because few people see much danger of serious loss or hope of substantial gain. Thus the system can be operated very loosely without it becoming a major bone of contention. For example, waiting time is not normally counted out of operational time on the grounds that the standard times are very generous anyway – a principle of operation which would have any British trade unionist sharpening his knife and his righteous indignation, filled with gleeful anticipation of the large killings to be made.

If no one cares very much about the system, it is hard to see how it operates as an incentive. The union is in favour of abolishing it (largely because a lot of the union department representatives are foremen who bear the brunt of the very tedious administrative work involved and have the responsibility for fiddling the averages). The managers, however, are reluctant to abandon any incentive to diligence, of however theoretical a kind.

This completes the discussion of the monthly wage.

An explanation of how the *monthly* wage is calculated does not, however, conclude the analysis of the cash wage bill. It accounts, in fact, for less than two-thirds of it. The rest is paid in two bonuses; one at mid-summer and one at year's end, each amounting to the equivalent of (in 1969) almost three months' salary. The total size of the bonus is negotiated separately on each occasion. The formula for its distribution to individuals is also determined by negotiation with the union and may be altered from time to time. It always involves a large element of pro-rating according to the basic salary, plus a merit premium. The latter accounts for as large a proportion of the total as the company can make it and as small a proportion as the union can make it. Merit rating for this purpose is separate from the regular monthly rating and is supposed to measure a man's performance and development over the previous six months.

Table 3.9   *Average earnings by age, and spread within each group*

Age group	Hitachi 1968-9 Primary school leavers (inc. some foremen)				Bradford 1967-8 manual workers			Liverpool and Bradford managers and technologists 1966	
	Top of bottom decile	Average	Bottom of top decile	University grads, average	Top of bottom decile	Average	Bottom of top decile	University grads average	Tech. Coll. grads, average
15-19	69	71	74		49	25(a)	120	85	94
20-24	78	85	92	71	79	80	125	100	100
25-29	88	100	111	100	87	100	125	130	108
30-34	102	115	132	130	78	103	125	146	123
35-39	113	132	153	177	87	101	105	179	121
40-44	123	158	188	237	73	102	129	180	128
45-49	141	173	205	287	73	100	134	182	131
50-54	152	179	215	–	73	97	115	–	
55-59					73	93	111	–	130
60-64						86			128

ª The low figure for the under-twenties at Bradford (similar also at Liverpool) is because both factories employ no under-18s and few under-20s in semi-skilled and unskilled jobs. Hence almost all in this group are apprentices.

Sources: Hitachi figures from respondents (70% of total members) to a union questionnaire. Bradford manual figures from a random sample of 292 PAYE tax records. Bradford and Liverpool managers from staff cards for total of 82 university graduates and 484 technical college graduates or diploma holders.

Owing to the small numbers in each age group, particularly for Bradford manual workers and Bradford and Liverpool university graduates, no great importance should be attached to small differences. (Also, the figures for the top of the bottom decile and the bottom of the top decile have an extra element of uncertainty in that they were calculated from a summation of earnings in fifty steps.) The general pattern of these figures, however, seems to be clear, and for manual workers is reproduced in a similar calculation for manual workers' earnings at Liverpool.

Finally, to sum up the most important consequence of the structure of earnings, Table 3.9 shows the difference between the lifetime earnings pattern of Hitachi and English Electric workers. Its purport is easily summarized. British manual workers reach their peak earnings in their twenties. Thereafter there is little change in their earnings level until (for those who are not made foremen) they decline somewhat in their fifties and rather more in their sixties. Japanese workers' earnings rise throughout their working life at a rate which does not vary very greatly, though the gradient steepens somewhat in the late thirties and levels off after 45. At the end of their working life they are likely to earn two and a half times their beginning wage. The pattern for British university graduates is similar to that of Japanese manual workers. British technical college graduates' wages show a pattern intermediate between that of university graduates and that of manual workers. As to what these indexes mean in cash terms, some indication is given in Table 10.2 (p. 268).

SUMMARY OF THE DIFFERENCES

1. At English Electric one assumption underlying the approach of both employers and employees to wage negotiation is that they are dominated by a market situation; that the market does more or less determine a going price for a particular skill, and that employers ought to pay that price, not merely because it is 'just' but for the self-interested reason that workers will drift away elsewhere if they do not. In Hitachi such considerations enter into managers' calculations only with regard to temporary workers, and to new school- and university-leaving workers. (Though in the latter case the consideration is not the fear of losing workers so much as the fear of not attracting them.) Managers must, to be sure, keep their eyes on other firms when fixing wages – but not so much other engineering firms in the same district (at English Electric much more telling for negotiating purposes than, say, evidence of wage rates at other, distant, English Electric factories) as the other comparable electrical engineering firms in Japan. These are the firms whose wage levels are quoted in wage negotiations by the Hitachi Union. These are the firms with which they need to maintain parity if they are to keep their workers satisfied.

2. Apart from the very big difference that negotiations take place exclusively within the firm at Hitachi, but partly on an industry-wide basis in England, the size of the total wage/salary bill is determined by a similar bargaining process in both firms (though much more formally and systematically at Hitachi as we shall see later), and the

110

principles invoked by the two sides in the course of bargaining are the same.

3. The principles governing the *distribution* of that wage/salary bill are quite different, however. Since an English Electric wage or salary is considered as the market price of a particular skill, the distribution of the wage/salary bill becomes a matter of determining appropriate skill differentials. Argument about these differentials involves the same factors as marketplace arguments over the proper relative prices for different types of cooking pots; that is to say:

a. Relative levels of demand – as indicated by the relative wages paid by other firms.

b. The relative scarcity of the necessary raw material – i.e. the level of genetic capacity required by different jobs; that is to say which is the job any fool could be taught to do and which only the particular intelligent or dexterous; or, in other words, the relative intrinsic complexities of different jobs, and

c. The production cost – the relative cost in time and money of training for different jobs.

These are, indeed, the staple arguments invoked by unions and employers in wage bargaining about differentials; i.e. about the distribution of the wage bill.

Hitachi by contrast, does not buy skills. Instead, it admits men to the enterprise, as it were, to serve the enterprise to the best of their abilities. When a firm goes into the virgin labour market, it considers itself to be buying, not a skill but a lifetime's work. The relevant categorization of the people available to be bought, therefore, is in terms of their development potential, their capacity to acquire skills. The best indicator of this is said to be their educational level which reflects both their 'native ability' (in so far as achievement selection affects access to higher education), and the level of basic training already received. These judgments about relative desirability, together with relative scarcities, determine the relative starting salaries for people from different educational levels. And these differences in educational levels and in expected lifetime total contribution to the firm, justify each category being launched on a different career track and a different pay scale track. This is the only one of the factors governing the distribution of the wage/salary bill between individuals (i.e., pay differentials) which is market determined. The others are:

a. length of service;

111

b. age (which, of course, correlates highly with length of service but *is* separately recognized);[5]

c. sex;

d. merit as rated by supervisors – predominantly co-operativeness, diligence, etc.;

e. family responsibilities.

To these have recently been added a sixth factor:

f. function currently performed in the firm, a factor ostensibly designed to allow, on just price principles, for what *would* be the result in differentials *if* a market in labour existed.

4. English Electric provides two different types of monetary incentives for different types of worker (non-monetary incentives we shall consider later). The salaried manager has the prospect of his extra effort being rewarded by promotion to a different job at a higher salary, or by a merit increase in salary while in the same job. The wage worker on piecework has a pay packet which varies directly with his own output. The latter may be called a direct incentive; the former a contingent incentive because the relationship between performance and reward is mediated by *some superior's* subjective assessment of that performance. The manager's incentive is also clearly a more long-term one (longer time elapse between performance and reward) than the wage worker's. In English Electric, long-term and contingent incentives are offered to wage workers only very marginally indeed; first, there is the hardly significant, residual fourpence for merit in the Bradford tool-room and the merit pay for apprentices. Secondly, there is the prospect of gaining a foremanship, though only a small proportion of workers at any one time are likely to consider their chances sufficiently good for the incentive to be a strong one.

At Hitachi, by contrast, apart from the piecework system which is of small importance, monetary incentives are:

a. identical for every type of employee, manual or managerial;

b. almost exclusively contingent rather than direct;

c. of longer rather than shorter term;

d. quite consequential (by the age of 35, for example, the high flyer who races up the manual ladder can be getting more than half as much again as the slowest plodder with whom he started out);

[5] Until 1970 mid-career recruits were slotted into the seniority scale on the principle that ten years' experience elsewhere equalled nine years in Hitachi. In the 1970 union contract, however, this 10% discount was abolished (to make mid-career recruitment easier) so that the scales became, in effect, age scales though still spoken of as service scales.

e. multiform, with the assessments involved in the different forms recurring at different intervals. There is annual assessment in April for promotion, monthly assessment for the merit premium, and twice yearly assessment for the bonus payments in June and December.

Direct piecework incentives are also found at Hitachi, but they are of minor importance compared with contingent incentives, and they are for the most part group not individual incentives, designed in such a way as to promote co-operativeness between workers and to blur the connection between an individual's efforts and that individual's wage. Such group incentives are found also at English Electric, though they are generally operated only in shops where there are obvious difficulties in measuring an individual's separate contribution to the shop's output. A whole factory direct group bonus is not found or contemplated, though sometimes, under such formulae as the Scanlon Plan, in a desultory way discussed.

Chapter 4

Unions: Membership and Organization

The last two chapters have dealt with two of the major points of difference between our two firms: a relatively high rate of mobility *versus* a stable, almost permanent, commitment, and a pay system based on function *versus* a pay system based substantially on seniority. The third major difference is between Britain's structure of craft and industrial unions, and Japan's structure of enterprise unions. English Electric workers belong to a variety of national unions like the Electrical Trades Union, the Transport and General, etc. Hitachi workers all belong to the Furusato Plant Workers' Union, the Taga Plant Workers' Union, etc., which are integral parts of the Federation of Hitachi Company Unions.

The intimate interrelation of these three differences is obvious. The British electrician is assumed to need a strong local and national organization to ensure that the skills of electricians are given their proper price, and that work which should go to electricians is not given to others – and that requires defining both what is electrician's work *and* who should be entitled to call himself an electrician. He shares his concern for these things equally with other electricians in other firms. An electrician working for Hitachi, on the other hand, probably did not become an electrician until he passed out of the labour market into Hitachi. Once in the firm he is never likely to go into the market again to sell his electrician skills and so he has no particular interest in keeping up their price. Within the firm, given the wage system, his interests coincide rather more with those of non-electricians of the same age as himself than with those of older or younger fellow electricians. And on matters which affect, not the distribution of rewards as between different types of workers, but their distribution as between the workers on the one hand, and the shareholders, the firm, the consumers or the state on the other, his interests are the same as those of other Hitachi workers. And, if not totally different from, they are at least not closely identical to, those of workers in other firms.

One can put the effects of different degrees of permanency of employment in another way. If you meet a Bradford English Electric foundryman on a train and ask him what he does, the first thing he will probably say is that he is a foundryman, the second thing that he comes from Bradford, and the third that he works for English Electric. His Japanese counterpart would most naturally define himself first as a member of the Hitachi Company, secondly as working at such and such a factory, and thirdly as being a foundryman.

Most of the differences in trade union structure follow naturally from this difference – heightened by two particular historical factors which deserve mention at the outset.

BACKGROUND FACTORS

The first is the fact that British trade union institutions developed, and acquired a mature rigidity, at a time when plants were smaller, employment was less stable and local labour markets would have been very close to a state of perfect competition except for the unions' and employers' associations' attempts regulate them. By contrast, Japanese unions were still weak and plastic in structure until the big corporation stage was reached – and it *was* in the big companies rather than in the smaller enterprises that the strongest, pace-setting unions developed.

The second circumstance is that Japanese industry has had, whereas British industry has not, its social democratic revolution. In Britain such rights as the unions possess have been gained by continuous inch-by-inch pressure against dogged managerial resistance. Sometimes the circumstances of the times have strengthened the power of managers; sometimes they have strengthened the power of the unions. But such shifts in the power balance have led only to small incremental gains and losses in union rights. There has been no breakthrough, no sudden revolution or even comprehensive reform.

In Japan, on the other hand, such a breakthrough did occur – in the period when Japan was occupied by American troops. For the space of two or three years, all who held formal authority in all spheres of Japanese life, including industry, were demoralized and no longer confident of their power to command. The shattering effect of the defeat reverberated throughout Japanese society. Japan at war had been all but totally mobilized, ideologically as well as economically. Managers and workers believed, and constantly thought in terms of, the 'home front' rhetoric they so frequently used; their organic unity was part of the cohesion of the Japanese nation accomplishing its glorious mission in Asia.

But when the defeat came, those who had been on the receiving end of commands 'in the name of Japan and the Emperor' were the ones who felt they had been deceived; those who had been giving the commands saw themselves as implicated in the deceiving. The organs of public opinion became, in a space of a couple of months, filled with vituperative rejection of Japan's vainglorious 'mission' and of her wartime leadership. Exhortations to loyalty and service gave way to the propaganda of democracy, equality, liberty and individual dignity. The atmosphere was ideally propitious for the formation of trade unions and there were plenty of people ready to take the initiative – men who had had experience of trying to organize trade unions in Japan in the 'democratic twenties', even in the repressive thirties, and just as importantly junior managers who had absorbed a not inconsiderable dose of Marxism in their high schools and universities and knew something about the trade unions in Weimar Germany, Britain and America. They set about transforming the wartime 'unions' – the factory branches of the Society for Service to the Nation through Industry – into militant instruments for the erosion of management's authority.

In their efforts they were given every encouragement by the Labour Section of the American Occupation Administration which contained a fair sprinkling of New Dealers anxious to bring to Japan some of the democratic reforms which American society resisted back home. Three laws passed in the occupation's first fifteen months added immensely to the power of the unions. The Trade Union Law of December 1945 gave organized unions not only immunity from conspiracy charges, but also rights of access to organizational facilities – office space, use of the check-off for union dues, etc. – to which no British government has ever contemplated giving statutory support. A Labour Conciliation Law set up a system of tripartite conciliation committees (representatives of unions and of employers and independents). The Labour Standards Law laid down maximum hours, minimum holidays, overtime provisions, etc., which were more generous than in any other capitalist country. (Only at the end of the sixties did Japanese society reach a level of affluence sufficient for the unions to begin to use some of their bargaining power to improve on these minimum legal standards rather than concentrating exclusively on wages – first pressing for a reduction in hours below the regulation forty-eight hour week, then beginning, tentatively, with overtime premium rates, see Table 3.3).

The sheer bargaining power of the unions grew as successful wage negotiations strengthened their members' loyalties: so did the cohesion of their national organizations (so that successes in one part of Japan provided forceful examples for other firms) and so did the influence of the Communist party within the major national federation and within individual unions. At the Furusato factory – and the story was not very different at Taga – the power of the unions became firmly entrenched. The manual workers' union and the white collar union, formed within two weeks of each other at the beginning of 1946, and merged by May – as much through the leadership of radical junior managers as from any other influence – had achieved equality in almost everything except wages for workers of all grades. The union continued to use rooms it had 'occupied' in early 1946 on the second floor of the company's administrative building. It very rapidly established a closed shop *de facto*, and enshrined it *de jure* in its first constitution-making contract signed with the management in June 1946. Gradually it extended its interpretation of the principle to the point at which it held a virtual veto power over all personnel movements. In October 1946 the final surrender of management prerogatives was signalled by the union's successful insistence that the new edition of the Works Rules should bear a simple preface explaining that they were decided by agreement between company and union.

The union's militancy was not accompanied by a total lack of productivity consciousness, or lack of concern for the fortunes of the firm. Within limits, the union remained mindful (as it was perhaps hard not to be in the devastated Japan of 1946) of the need to reconstruct Japan's productive capacity. Hence its development of a sophisticated range of graduated deterrents – for example the 'silent strike' in which work went on as usual but all managers were sent to Coventry, and what might be called the 'service strike' in which only those categories of workers traditionally expected in England to be loyally unlikely to strike – the security guards, the chauffeurs, and the secretaries – came out on strike, leaving the production departments at work.

The discipline and solidarity which made this sort of strike possible were needed for continuous pressure on the company over the one thing the union could not directly control – the level of wages. And it *was* continuous pressure that was needed because the rapid inflation – which left the 1949 yen at less than 1% of its 1945 value – was continuously in progress throughout the first three years of the occupation. In late 1947, all the constituent unions of the Hitachi Workers Federation maintained a strike which lasted forty-seven days.

This was perhaps the high tide of union power in Hitachi, but it

117

was not until 1949 that a second, cold-war generation of American Occupation Labour Officials, together with the Japanese government and Japanese industrialists, concerted their efforts to begin the roll-back. By now the initial American concern with democratizing Japan had given way to the objective of making her a prosperous bulwark against communism. The first really stable post-war government elected in January 1949 – a conservative one – was now able to tackle the inflation and use deflationary measures to get the economy on a firmer base. The politicians' financial patrons, the industrialists, had long since recovered from the demoralization of the defeat, and could find a ready hearing for their request for labour-curbing legislation.

In May 1949 a restrictive revision of the 1945 Trade Union Law passed the Diet. Already, before it had become law, the Furasato Plant Workers Union received the management's declaration of war. First, under the provisions of the new law the company would no longer allow the seven or eight full-time union officials to draw a salary for their nominal post in the company; secondly, union meetings were no longer to be held in paid-for working time; thirdly the company no longer considered itself bound by the 1946 constitutional contract.

It was September before the company won even that battle and the war continued for a further nine months of increasingly bitter conflict throughout the company. The climactic period began on 9 May 1950 when the company announced its intention, in view of the company's critical financial position and the need to rationalize, of dismissing an average of 17% of its employees throughout its factories. At the Furusato Works it ended on 19 July when, after a two-day strike followed by a two-week lock-out, the union finally acknowledged defeat and accepted the dismissal of over 650 of the 5,700 employees – dismissals which included many men who were without doubt selected for their troublesome militancy.

There was never very much doubt about the outcome. The Government and the occupation forces were strongly behind the company, and the police were quick to prefer charges against disturbances of the peace. And since they were with increasing frequency called into the factory to rescue section chiefs made the focus of 'collective workshop struggles'– i.e. exposed for several hours in the broiling sun to vociferous and often abusive attempts to persuade them to refuse to co-operate in making up lists of those to be dismissed – the number of arrests increased. The union was weakened by the internal struggle between the socialists and the communists, and the communists fatally weakened by MacArthur's quasi-suppression of the party just before and after the beginning of the Korean war.[1]

Communist power in the union was practically destroyed by the defeat and the subsequent dismissals, and it was a socialist leadership which finally picked up the pieces after the defeat and accepted a new balance of power finally formalized in a new contract of March 1951. The constitutional structure then established has hardly changed to the present day. The management was able to reassert its authority on the shop floor and in matters of job allocation – more completely than any modern British manager could hope for. But the counterattack could go only so far and no further. Two great changes of the post-war years were accepted as irreversible – the two changes which justify by their completeness and their suddenness the assertion that Japanese industry has had its social democratic revolution whereas British industry has not. The first is the unquestioning acceptance of the union as a legitimate bargaining agent in matters of wages and the protection of persons with rights to full facilities within the factory to do its legitimate job. The second is the abolition of all but monetary distinctions between the formerly separate 'statuses' of staff and manual workers.

THE STRUCTURE OF UNIONS: MEMBERSHIP

It is impossible to say how many of those employed at the Bradford and Liverpool factories are union members; they belong to a wide variety of unions, and even the chief representatives of the main unions in the factory do not know how many fellow-members they have, since they are members not of any union organization in the factory, but of various local branches scattered about the cities. Nevertheless, it is a fairly safe bet that some 90% of all below staff status belong to one of a dozen or more unions. At Bradford the list is: the Amalgamated Engineering and Foundry Workers, the Electrical Trades Union, the Plumbers Union (the last two recently amalgamated), the Transport and General, the Municipal and General, the Patternmakers, the Metal Dressers, the Woodworkers, the Draughtsmen and Allied Technicians, the Clerical and Administrative Officers, the Association of Scientific, Technical, Supervisory and Managerial Staff, and (one solitary member who took several months after his

---

[1] Graphic details of this strike are to be found in Hitachi Seisakusho Hitachi Kōba Rōdō Kumiai, *Hitachi rōdō undō shi*, 1964. This splendid history of the Furusato Plant Union – in 700 quarto pages – was written with the assistance of two professors from Ibaragi University. It is the source of all the historical details here described. The strike is also briefly described in Nihon Jimbun-Gakkai, *Kindai kō-kōgyō to chiiki shakai no tenkai*, 1955.

119

arrival at the factory to find the location of his closest union organizer) the Woodcutters.

At the Furusato works everyone who belongs to a union belongs to the same union – the Furusato Plant Workers Union. Belonging or not belonging is not a matter of individual choice. The first article of the contract between the Federation and the company lays down who shall not be a union member; the second accepts the closed shop and means in effect that everyone else must belong. The general categories excluded from union membership are:

1. Senior managers of section chief level and above.

2. Sub-section chiefs in personnel, education and welfare divisions.

3. Sub-section chiefs, and those in charge of planning in departments concerned with management information and research.

4. Sub-section chiefs concerned with estimating for orders and enquiry into production processes.

5. Sub-section chiefs in accounting, and general manager's secretariat section.

6. The private secretary of directors and general managers, and one chauffeur each.

7. Sub-section chiefs and squad chiefs of the security guards.

8. Those in charge of planning in the personnel and education divisions.

9. Others as shall be from time to time decided by agreement between individual unions and managements.

In the Furusato plant contract, these general categories are spelled out in lists of particular functions. Points 2 to 9 exclude in total some 200 people. In addition there are about 740 managers above section chief level. This leaves approximately 500 to 600 junior managers and technologists who are members of the union.

The number excluded under point 9 can vary from factory to factory. Whereas at some factories the senior superintendent in each department remains a non-unionist, at Furusato and one or two other plants with a more militant union tradition all superintendents join the union, and when strikes take place in production departments the section manager is left in splendid loneliness in a deserted workshop.

ORGANIZATION: JAPAN

The internal structure and relation to other bodies of unions in the two factories are contrasted in the accompanying charts.

To begin with the simpler task of explaining the Hitachi situation using the example of the Furusato factory. The basic unit is the

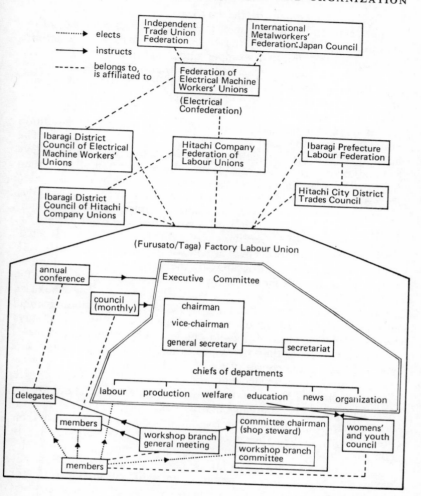

han – the section, shop or department which may have as many as 500 or as few as 50 workers. The *han* elects a committee with a chairman. It also elects, annually, someone else not a committee member – or two others if it has more than 130 workers – as representatives on the council. Thirdly, it elects delegates to the annual conference – one for every twenty to thirty members.

The officers and executive committee members are elected, every other year, by secret ballot of all members. Nine of the twelve executive committee members are elected to specific full-time union posts – the chairman and vice-chairman, the secretary, and the heads of the organizational department, the education department, the welfare department, the union newspaper and magazine department, the production problems department and the wages and conditions department. They are supported by a clerical staff of three men – one accountant, one editor and one chief clerk – nine girls and one living-in caretaker.

This large staff inhabits quite spacious offices in the new union building, across the road from one of the main factory gates. The building, which was completed in the early sixties with a special levy of about 6,000 yen (£7) per head, spread over a period of more than three years, contains committee rooms and lecture rooms and a large auditorium. In 1969, again with a special levy, more committee rooms were being added and the whole building including the auditorium, was being air-conditioned. One room – the front parlour, as it were – is designed for receiving visitors. It is rather nicely carpeted. The arm-chairs are soft. There are one or two pleasant pieces of folk pottery and a piece of calligraphy by the Socialist leader Asanuma – the victim of Japan's most recent political assassination in 1960. It is a simple bold rendering of the word 'Liberation'. The bookcase contains a few casual coffee-table books, including a photographic memorial of the destruction of Hiroshima. If he is lucky and stays long enough, the visitor is likely to be served by attractive girl secretaries with no fewer than two kinds of tea, two kinds of fruit, and a piece of cake in the course of a couple of hours.

All these nine officers have nominal positions in the firm to which they can return if they are defeated, or choose not to stand, at the next elections. The company marks them up for notional pay increases, according to their seniority and job, during the period of their union office, though they receive no salary. Five of them live in company houses. Until recently the union simply paid the salary which its officers were foregoing by taking the union job, but they have recently introduced a separate partially job-related scale for union officers. A vice-chairman would now have to be nine or ten years older than a chairman to be receiving a higher salary than he does.

Four other Furusato works employees are also 'on-leave' as full-time staff members, elected by the Furusato Plant Workers Union, of other organizations to which the union is affiliated. One is chairman of the Hitachi Company Union Federation. The others are chairman of a workers' housing society; chairman of the Prefectural Labour Federation, and chief of the secretariat of the Hitachi City District Trades Council.

Delegates to these various bodies are nominated by the executive and approved by the council. The key body, of course, is the Hitachi Federation, and the Furusato plant's representatives on its committees are all members of the Furusato plant's executive committee. The function of the other bodies is largely political – to co-ordinate support for the Socialist Party in elections.

To be sure they are supposed to have other functions – particularly the Prefectural Labour Federation, and its local constituent, the Hitachi City District Trades Council which are supposed to promote working-class organization wherever possible. Here, though, there is a clear conflict of interest. Hitachi workers form a local elite. Workers in the smaller firms of Hitachi city which sub-contract from the Furusato plant frequently work longer hours for less pay – and are unorganized. So, even, are the workers in local firms within the Hitachi family – firms in which the company has money invested. If these sub-contracting firms were unionized and got themselves better wages, the Furusato plant would have to pay more for the parts it buys from them. There might be a squeeze on Furusato wages. Is there not, then, some awkwardness in the fact that the full-time secretary of the Trades Council is seconded from the Furusato Plant Union, that the president belongs to another Hitachi union, and that most of its funds come from the Furusato Plant Union?

Not at all, said the Furusato union chairman; it might be argued that they had something to gain by the low wages in the sub-contracting firms, but this did not mean that they were inconsiderate, that they could stand by and see their fellows suffering. He mentioned two local firms, both with about 400 employees, where they were at present preparing a foundation committee for a union. Their aim, he explained, was to make a union which could co-exist with the management. They did not use the Communist Party tactics of mass leafleting, creating a minority oppositional union which though a minority was still strong enough to produce deadlocks and sometimes the complete collapse of firms and loss of jobs.

Nevertheless, it is clear from the union's official history[2] that the Furusato Plant Union was only prodded into *some* activity in this direction by pressure on it in the Prefectural Labour Federation, and by a plan (successfully headed off) to send a national organizer from a national federation to Hitachi city. This happened in 1959, and it was in that year that the District Trades Council secretary's post was made a full-time job, and a resolution was passed at the Furusato Plant Union meeting supporting a drive to unionize local workers. The number of unions created since then, however, is not large.

[2] Hitachi Kōba Rōdō Kumiai, op. cit., p. 685–8.

The division of functions between the Furusato Plant Union and the Hitachi Company Federation gives most of the important functions to the Federation. The annual bargaining over wage rates is done exclusively at the central enterprise level, and wage structures and levels are standard throughout the firm – the only differentials being in family allowances which are used to introduce variations according to the local cost of living. The master contract which contains all the works rules and defines the rights of the union and the prerogatives of management, grievance procedures, strike procedures, etc., is a central contract. The local works contract (which is just as thick) is concerned with the application of general rules to the local situation – precisely who shall not belong to the union and what union members shall stay at work during a strike, details of shift times, when the sirens shall be blown, what jobs come in what category of the job classification scheme, how newcomers shall be phased into a group bonus scheme, and so on. Both central and local contracts are looked at every two years and revised as necessary.

The function of the Federation of Electrical Machine Workers' Unions (referred to subsequently as the Electrical Confederation) is of lesser importance. It is not a bargaining body. Its major function is the exchange of information and the co-ordination of bargaining strategy between the major unions which belong to it. It is the place for plotting the 'spring offensive'.

Since the school year ends in late March and hiring takes place in April, this date is the natural date, being also the start of the financial year, for promotions and salary increases. Wage contracts run from April to March. Renegotiation begins with union proposals – 'demands'– made in December or early January. The function of the Confederation is first to ensure that the biggest unions, those in comparable companies, make demands of approximately the same magnitude and synchronize their pressure. One of their number might be picked out to make the running, preferably the union of a firm which has a reasonably good profit margin, but is, say, struggling to keep or expand its market share and so can ill afford to lose production through strikes. If this union forces the pace of bargaining with a series of one-day strikes, the standards they set in their final bargain will usually make it easy for the others to gain comparable increases.

Strategy co-ordination takes place also on an even broader scale. Ever since 1955 a broadly-based national committee has organized a nation-wide strategy in which the Electrical Confederation still takes part.

The second function of the industry-wide Electrical Confederation is political. It channels union funds to the Socialist Party and it is a possible avenue along which union officials can become members of the Diet. It is not so much that the Confederation exists *in order to* exercise political influence on behalf of workers in the electrical industry. Rather, having come into existence and been maintained in existence for other reasons, it represents a considerable reservoir of money and influence in the hands of men who, being political animals, naturally seek to use it for causes dear to their own hearts. Whether the weight of the organization should be thrown behind the Communist Party, the Socialist Party, the Democratic Socialist Party, or none of these, or any of these, has consequently been the single most important divisive issue at Confederation level. A clear declaration in favour of one of these parties is made by explicit affiliation with one of the national labour federations, the tiny Shinsanbetsu (CP), Sōhyō (JSP – the largest with four and a half million members, but now containing more government employees than private-industry unions), and Dōmei (JDSP – with two million members nearly all in private industry). The Electrical Confederation has for many years belonged instead to a fourth national federation, the Independent (or Neutral) Federation which exercises little control over its members and exists largely to press their claims to seats on tripartite government committees and foreign delegations. The leaders of its constituent unions by and large divide their loyalties between the JSP and the JDSP. Since the mid-sixties the Electrical Confederation has also joined the Japan Council of the International Metalworkers Federation, a body known in Japan for its apolitical business-unionist stance.

The Ibaragi Regional Council of the Electrical Confederation in which the Furusato Plant Union is joined together with other electrical industry unions in the prefecture is a body of rather little importance. It consists, with one exception, entirely of Hitachi firms, and exists largely to allocate requests for funds, and invitations to join foreign study missions, or to send union members to camps and oratorical contests which the Confederation organizes.

ORGANIZATION: BRITAIN

The British system is not susceptible of such neat characterization, since every union has a different organization. Perhaps the clearest procedure is to discuss the organization of the AEF, the biggest and oldest engineering union (now even bigger as the AUEW or Amalgamated Union of Engineering Workers, having since incorporated the draughtsmen's union DATA). In 1969 it had over 40% of the membership represented by the engineering industry's thirty-union federation (the CSEU – shown in the upper centre part of the chart).

125

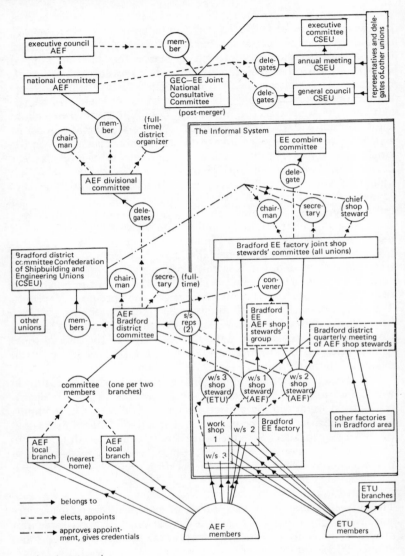

belongs to

elects, appoints

approves appoint-
ment, gives credentials

s/s: shop steward
w/s: work shop

For a Bradford engineer or foundryman the basic status of membership in the AEF is obtained through membership of the *local*
branch closest to one's home, not through any organization centred

on the work-place. The exceptions are a number of managers who have worked their way up from the ranks, who took out a union mortgage on their houses when they were still on the shop floor and have to keep up their membership to retain it. They join special branches for supervisory workers, directly affiliated at the divisional or national level. Some do so for other reasons – in order to get the union literature and keep in touch, or in order, like the former Lord Nelson, first chairman of English Electric, to be able to flash a green AEU card (this is a very status-conscious union: only skilled men have green cards) and say at crucial moments in discussions: 'Don't forget, I'm a skilled man, too, you know.'

Branches are moribund. Worse, according to one AEF district organizer, they are dead. One chief shop steward told a story of,

'. . . one of these national organizer blokes. He came down to give us a talk about organization – all as how the branch was the basis of the union, the source of vitality and all that. And there we were, a branch with 600 members, sitting in a little back room that at most would have held 20 people! I got up, and I told him. "Where've you been these last 20 years", I said.'

Undoubtedly one reason for the decline of the branch is the non-coincidence between branch membership and workplace. The AEF members at both the Bradford and Liverpool factories are scattered, depending on where they live, over fifteen to twenty branches. In their branches, fellow English Electric workers may well be in a minority. There are few problems they have in common with their branch fellows, except the periodic national pay claims put forward by the Confederation, or more peripherally, problems such as pay freezes, the Industrial Relations Act, or the government's policy towards the Common Market. On these matters, the five or six faithful gathered together might occasionally pass a resolution to be sent on to the district committee. Otherwise, branches have no business to conduct except the collection of dues, and the payment of sick benefits.

It is not surprising that whereas at Hitachi, where workshop branch meetings are held in the lunch hour, 62% of the sample said that they had been to the last meeting, the proportions of union members who had attended the last branch meeting in the British sample were 2% at Marconi and 10% at Babcocks. A large proportion – 71% and 39% respectively – said that they did not even know when the last branch meeting was held.

The death of the branches poses a financial problem. How to collect dues if people do not come to meetings? The solution adopted in most unions is to appoint collectors who are given a 5% to 7% commission on dues collected. The AEF firmly held out against this system until recently. It was the view of the executive that the branches were the very root and source of sustenance of the union. Members must be given every incentive to attend. But in 1968 the AEF, too, appointed commissioned collectors.

The effective local body is the district committee. At Bradford this meets in a quite comfortably appointed committee room below the two small austere offices and the two additional committee rooms which make up the total physical presence of this union which has several thousand local members in the town. The offices are for the district secretary (an elected full-time salaried official) and for his secretary-typist. The committee consists of fifteen members besides the secretary: the president, elected for a three-year term, the twelve representatives from twenty-four branches, and the two shop steward representatives elected annually. The committee's activities hinge on the secretary, whose main job, as district organizer, is to go to any factory when called, and sort out disputes affecting his members. A good part of the weekly meetings consists of his reports on the actions he has taken in the past week. Depending on the chance of who is elected from the branches or by the shop stewards, some factories in the district will be completely unrepresented on the committee, and the secretary will be the only real link between factory and committee except for representations that are passed up from individual workers by their branch representatives.

Some district committees play an actively vigilant role in monitoring factory agreements reached in their areas, sometimes actually blocking agreements thought to set dangerous precedents, but the Bradford committee largely left these matters to the judgement of its secretary. Apart from his reports of current disputes and negotiations, other items of business which occupy the two or three hours of each weekly meeting include such as the following, drawn from the Bradford minutes:

'Relaxation agreements. Committee ratifies all agreements reached in individual factories allowing unskilled men (dilutees) to do skilled work in the absence of available skilled men.

Decision to send two members of the committee to William Temple College, Rugby, for course on Responsibility in Industry.

Endorsement and transmission to the National Executive of resolutions from branches [almost never] or from shop steward meetings of particular factories [e.g. from Bradford English Electric asking Union Executive to enforce overtime ban throughout GEEEC until guarantees were given about post-merger redundancies].

Donation of £20 each to five Labour Party candidates in local government elections.

Donation of £10 prize for local technical college speech day.

Payment of legal defence fees for members engaged in compensation, etc. suits.

Organization of a trip for retired members to Blackpool.

Decision, in view of shortage of skilled men, to list local job vacancies in the committee minutes.

Organization of shop stewards' day-release course at local technical college, curriculum suggested by the union. Approval of the guidelines for negotiation with Employers Association on the terms for the day release.

Reports from the committee's delegate to the Regional Council of the Labour Party, from the secretary about his attendance at meeting of the Junior Workers Committee [a forlorn and apparently unsuccessful attempt to recruit a few union activists from among the younger generation], the Industry and Commerce Committee of the local Development Association, etc. [This last he attended *ex officio*. As local organizer of one of the largest trade unions, he is also involved in many other civic functions – as JP, as member of the local race relations board, governor of the local technical college, etc.]

Transmission of requests from Federation of Old Age Pensioners for help with signatures on a petition to extend free bus passes for the evenings, and from the Council for Commonwealth Citizens to publicize English classes for immigrants.

Report of circulars from the executive of such things as coverage of legal expenses of house purchase, officers' train meal allowances, the need to reactivate political sub-committees to co-operate with the local Labour Party, etc.

Consideration of attempts by the Association of Supervisory etc. Staffs (ASTMS) to poach members promoted to foreman status, and decision not to agree to their transfer. [Amicable transfers allow the transferee to take sick benefits rights, etc. Uncondoned transfers do not.]

There are two other trade union bodies at the same local level. The first is the Trades Council which is a local microcosm of the TUC but of little importance except on the rare occasions when there are matters of purely local significance to be urged in the TUC annual conference. In Bradford its full-time secretary is mainly employed as secretary of a trade union social club. The second is the district committee of the Confederation of Shipbuilding and Engineering Unions. This is composed of representatives of the district committees of all engineering unions. One of the full-time organizers – usually from the biggest union, the AEF – is its secretary. It exists largely to exchange information, though it did take up problems like mergers and large scale redundancies which affect several of its constituent unions. Its meetings also get a little more lively when the Confederation is engaged in the only function for which it exists – negotiations with the Federation of Engineering Employers Associations over wages and conditions.

Little explanation is required of the rest of the top half of the chart, except to say that there is also a full-time organizer at the divisional level who comes into the picture for higher level dispute negotiations.

Nor is there much to be said concerning differences between the AEF and other unions. The ETU and the TGWU have bigger branches covering a wider district: about 80% of the Liverpool English Electric members of ETU belong to a single branch with nearly 2,000 members, and some bigger branches have a full-time secretary. Even though branch membership more or less coincides with factory membership, however, attendance at branch meetings is not proportionately greater nor the meetings any livelier. (This should not be taken as proof that a system of factory branches with meetings in the lunchhour or after work at the factory would not bring an increase in members' involvement in the union, however. The ETU branch meetings take place after supper in prime television time and are held off the factory premises.)

The British Dual Organization
The complexities lie rather within that part of the chart labelled 'informal workshop system'. The organs so far described make up the formal, official, traditional structure of the unions. It is the structure through which were negotiated agreements which (until recently) had an immediate effect on every member's wage rates or holidays or hours of work. These have always been important – whole factory strikes, in fact, have only been held in connection with such negotiations. But, thanks to the wage system described in the last chapter, these national negotiations have never by any means been the only determinant of any individual worker's wealth and welfare. Some firms can be induced to pay over the rates (as well as to give additional holidays or, more rarely, a shorter working week). Again, even if the rates paid are formally the national minima, where piecework is involved, the way those rates are translated into earnings is a

matter for endless local negotiation. And changes in these variables are nearly as important as changes in rates. Over certain periods they can be more important. (See the figures quoted on p. 87.)

In response to this situation – itself largely a product of full employment as we saw when discussing wages – there has developed over the last thirty years, a whole new pattern of organization – the shop steward system. This system is so little formalized that although some unions have recognized the existence of shop stewards in a few crisp amendments to their rules, and even, in the last decade, begun to issue shop steward handbooks, no one quite knows how shop stewards ought to be elected. The only rule in practice is that it should be by some means that gives them legitimacy in the eyes of the fellow workers in their shop or department. According to the convener of ETU stewards at Liverpool, if a shop contains, say, 40% AEF men and 60% ETU men, the ETU men alone would vote to elect one of their members steward of that shop. The AEF men could seek his help on matters affecting the work of the department, but might prefer to go to the AEF steward of the neighbouring department for more personal matters such as a threat of dismissal.

In some departments consisting predominantly of skilled men something like this may happen, but there were many other shops in which *all* the workers participated in the election of a shop steward, and where, particularly if few of them were skilled workers, little heed was paid to the identity of the union a man belongs to. The whole washing-machine assembly line, for example, consisting of many ETU and TGWU members as well as members of the National Society of Metal Mechanics, 'went outside the gates' one lunchtime, and after a show of hands, with the metal mechanics factory convener acting as master of ceremonies, came back with a metal mechanic as a steward. There was reported to be a very solid turnout. (Unlike a branch meeting this is a gathering of fellow-workmates. One doesn't want to come back at half-past one and have someone say: 'How come I didn't see you at the meeting.') Once a shop steward is elected, the district committee of his union will ratify his election, and the (full-time) district secretary will write to the factory announcing his appointment and issue him with a card by way of credentials.

In Liverpool on average there is one shop steward for every forty-two manual workers, and the proportion is about the same at Bradford. In both factories the shop stewards have some organization of their own. At Liverpool each of the four unions which are sufficiently strongly represented in the factory to have shop stewards has been allowed for the last ten years or so, to hold a meeting of all its stewards (ranging from the TGWU's twenty-five to the Metal Mechanics thirty-six) and to elect a senior steward whose position is recognized by the company. The conference room is put at their disposal for the last thirty minutes of the working day (for which thirty minutes they are paid at the agreed – somewhat below average – bonus rate) and they may carry on as long as they like. The four senior stewards may also meet to discuss matters of common concern. In the last four years they have been able to do so comfortably by booking a management conference room. Until then, they had to huddle together in a corner of the factory.

At Bradford, on the other hand, a smaller factory with half the total number of stewards, the important body is the Joint Shop Stewards' Committee – a committee of *all* shop stewards irrespective of union. (The stewards of each of the main unions also separately appoint their own convenor, but his functions are limited to liaison with the full-time official of his union.) The joint committee elects a chief shop steward (confirmed in his appointment by the multi-union district committee of the Confederation of Shipbuilding and Engineering Unions.) The chief shop steward is, in effect, a quasi-full-time multi-purpose union negotiator (paid by the company), the most important single influence on the tenor of industrial relations in the firm.

A similar Joint Shop Stewards' Committee became active at the time of the study in Liverpool. It had existed earlier, but since it had been given no facilities or encouragement by management and was forced to meet off the factory in the evenings, it had led a shadowy kind of existence and hardly met. It was reactivated in 1968, largely at the initiative of the AEF senior steward. The increasing pace of company proposals for work study programmes and productivity deals meant an increasing need for a common attitude by the unions agreed to and generally understood by the stewards. The prospect of a takeover and large-scale redundancies made the need for a common strategy acute.

The Liverpool committee made one major innovation: it included the white-collar unions. The 150 stewards who met the week after Plessey's takeover bid at a local labour club elected an executive committee consisting of one representative from each of the four main manual and three staff unions and five others elected at large among the stewards. It was this body which led the militant protests against the management of the new combine after the GEC takeover, and which proposed, in 1969 a protest 'occupation' of the Liverpool factory.

One other body deserves mention. Some years ago, the stewards at the various English Electric factories formed a joint 'combine committee' to discuss problems common to them all by virtue of the fact that they faced a common management. Each factory sent one or two representatives to Rugby, the factory of the combine committee's first secretary, a shrewd, unbending and forceful old unionist, a former National Executive member of the AEF. The company too had found it necessary to respond by strengthening its central personnel services. While individual factories retained autonomy in personnel matters to a degree undreamt of in Hitachi, and while managers of individual factories could, and sometimes did, make concessions locally which broke agreements reached in the firm's central policy committee (and received no more in the way of sanctions than angry letters from fellow managers who had been doggedly resisting similar demands) it became increasingly necessary for the central management at least to try to co-ordinate the strategy.

The combine committee was, of course, not a negotiating body; it never met a representative of management, and received no formal recognition. It provided an opportunity for stewards to exchange information about what various different managements had conceded. Still, however, although the argument that such-and-such an English Electric factory on the other side of England had agreed to pay 90% average bonus for waiting time might *help* in strengthening a case during negotiation, it would help much less than the argument that a similar concession had been granted at Messrs XYZ's factory *in the same town*.

Consequently, the utility of the combine committee was rather limited. A typical example of the way it operated is provided by the concession of service holidays at Bradford. The idea of pressing for an increase in holidays with increased years of service originated with the Bradford shop stewards whose representative had it put on the agenda for a combine meeting in the summer of 1968. A general policy was agreed and a leaflet was printed for the use of member factories, drafted in firm, forceful but convoluted prose. Headed 'Eight major reasons why the Company should grant service holidays to hourly-rated personnel, Now!' it ended, after listing the reasons, with the exhortation to make it 'known to your Management at every available opportunity, that you not only desire; but are entitled and expect; Service Holidays to be granted to you in the very near future; as patience is now becoming exhausted on a very valid entitlement being continually evaded'. Bradford followed through the campaign and won these extra holidays several months later as part of a package deal. The Liverpool stewards, on the other hand, decided that this was not for them the priority issue. They decided to

133

press first for an increase in wages for the lower-paid labourers – a decision related, in part, to the Liverpool joint committee chairman's need, as a skilled AEF man, to retain the support of the other unions whose members were predominantly in the lower paid ranks.

The growth of shop steward organization has produced a double structure, the articulation between the two parts of which is, to say the least, imperfect. The shop steward structure, for instance, receives no support from the dues collected through the branch structure. At Bradford, before the company offered the use of its conference room and half an hour of the firm's time for the purpose, the Joint Shop Stewards' Committee used to meet in a local pub in the evening. The secretary laid his hat on a table near the door and those attending threw in the odd shilling to cover the hire of the hall and perhaps a pint or two to recompense the secretary's labours. When someone was to be sent as a delegate to the combine meeting in Rugby there would be a 'whip-round' among the stewards, the going rate being 12½p a head. Later the Committee organized a regular raffle which raised enough money to cover these expenses, to give the chief shop steward £3 a week for postage and telephone expenses, and to run a small welfare fund.

Even communication between the two parts of the system can be difficult.

To give one example, when the merger took place and wholesale redundancies seemed likely, the Bradford Factory Committee decided to send some of its members to lobby Bradford MPs. One MP caught unawares and unable to give them the attention he would have liked to give, wrote in bitter complaint to the district secretary at the lack of warning. The secretary replied, perfectly reasonably, that he did not know of their plans, and that since it was a shop steward's affair, there was no particular reason why he should have done.

A second example led to greater bitterness. The protocol of levels is an important one. The personnel officer deals daily with a chief shop steward; the general manager of a factory may deal with district and divisional organizers. London head offices and the Employers Federation deal with the National officers. When, therefore, the newly merged GEEC sought to allay widespread fears of redundancy by establishing a consultative committee with unions, the director in charge of personnel matters, Sir Jack Scamp, naturally invited representatives from the national executives of the major unions. But the only channel of communication between the national trade union officers on that consultative committee, and the trade unionists elected through the shop steward organization to the GEEC combine committee – the direct representatives of union members in GEEC factories – was through the district and branch organization to individual shop stewards. The only way from the tip of the stalactite to the tip of the stalagmite was up and across the ceiling, down the wall of the cavern and across the floor. On one occasion the combine committee, impatient at the imprecision of the promises they were receiving, decided to lobby a meeting of the consultative committee at Rugby. They arrived to find that the meeting had been shifted to London. It was said that there *were* reasons for the change other than the top trade unionists' desire to foil the rank and file lobbiers. The fact remains that no message arrived to save the would-be lobbyists a fruitless journey.

The White Collar Unions

The three white collar unions do not differ very much in their pattern of organization from the manual unions, except in the following respects. First, their membership coverage is smaller. At Bradford, only 44% of non-manual workers are in a union, whereas the manual figure was probably in the region of 90%. (At Furusato 80% of the non-manual workers belonged to the union.) The proportion was approximately the same at Liverpool. About half the Bradford foremen and most of the assistant foremen belonged to ASTMS (the Association of Supervisory, Technical and Managerial Staffs), but hardly anyone of any higher supervisory rank, despite some full-page advertisements in *The Daily Telegraph* during 1969 telling managers that nowadays they too needed protection and ASTMS could afford it. The membership of DATA, the draughtsmen's union, too, is largely rank and file. Until recently section leaders in one drawing office had remained members (despite a certain feeling that they no longer really belonged to the underdog category) but a one-hour stoppage in sympathy with another factory and the stern insistence that they stay at work on the part of the chief draughtsman (another ex-member) precipitated their withdrawal.

Secondly, the factory is more explicitly recognized as a unit of organization by the white collar unions. DATA has local branches, but the factory is recognized as a sub-unit within them, the clerical workers have only factory branches.

Thirdly, they do not call their shop stewards 'shop stewards'; they have 'staff representatives', 'corresponding members', or 'chairmen of office committees'.

Fourthly, they tend to have a less rigidly hierarchical organization. A factory convenor of AEF stewards might conceivably, in emergencies when he disagrees with his district secretary, go to the divisional officer. A DATA office committee chairman can telephone national officials as a matter of course, if the matter can more easily be dealt with at the central than at the district level. There is also greater freedom of lateral communication. DATA's co-ordination of strategy between English Electric factory committees was probably more important in forcing the company into a more centralized personnel policy than the manual workers' combine committee.

Fifthly, the white collar unions do not negotiate through the Confederation. They each negotiate separately with the Engineering Employers Federation.

FINANCE

Union dues in Hitachi are pro-rated according to earnings. Each member pays monthly the equivalent of 2·52 hours' regular pay as a basic contribution to cover the union's operating costs. In addition, he pays 50 yen (6p) into a basic fund, 40 yen into a sick fund and 400 yen into an individual strike-fund account. (As soon as his account reaches the sum of 25,000 yen – a month's salary when the amount was fixed – he may withdraw any surplus when he needs it. It *is* a matter of withdrawal rather than of stopping payment since the contributions are paid by automatic check-off from wages.) The annual general meeting frequently decides on supplementary levies for a fixed term and a fixed purpose – such as for building offices or an auditorium for the union or for one of the federations to which it is affiliated, or to support socialist candidates in local and national elections.

British union dues are a fixed weekly sum (not, therefore, automatically rising with increasing wages). The amount depends not on earnings but on skill status. The range in 1969 was from 15–16p weekly for a skilled man to 5–8p for a woman. There may be small additions for a sick fund and one ½p of the subscription was an optional contribution to Labour Party funds. When these two items are excluded, the Donovan Committee found[3] that the average union contribution amounted to 0·39% of weekly earnings in 1966. Allowing a very generous element of overtime in the composition of those earnings, this might be the equivalent of 0·8 hours' wages a month – or about one third of the proportion a Hitachi worker surrenders from his wage.

The correlates of this difference are easily discerned. In 1966 there were 4,027 members for each full-time ETU official, 6,807 for each AEU official.[4] The Furusato Plant Union had one full-time local official for

[3] Royal Commission on Trade Unions and Employers' Associations, *Report* ('The Donovan Report'), 1968, para. 714.

[4] Ibid., para. 702.

every 1,272 members, and the ratio would be even better if the Hitachi Federation officials were included. The cramped, dingy, lonely silence of an English union's mid-town district office, some miles from the factories at which most of its members work, or the even more dingy back room of a local pub or parish hall where branch meetings are held, contrast sharply with the Furusato Union auditorium, its smart offices and modern office equipment, the constant lunch-hour traffic in and out of the union building directly across from the factory gates – the flocks of young girls and men going into the building after work for a five-thirty stereo concert (with two music critics to introduce each item); the not-so-young coming for a lecture on health in middle age; smaller groups of girls practising the tea ceremony or flower arrangement in one of the building's three traditional, matted, Japanese-style rooms; or the older men of the fishing club or the Noh-play chanting circle. *The Struggle*, the Hitachi Plant Union's 2- or 4-page weekly newspaper, with a good proportion of local factory news, contrasts with a British union's national monthly journal, of interest to those few union activists who know who's who or how the factions go in the Union's National Council, and destined to be left in piles at branch meetings for anyone interested to take. (Or perhaps the closer British analogy would be the single mimeographed sheets which senior stewards get printed at district offices and distribute throughout the factory on special emergency occasions – usually only when support for a strike is being sought.) The union card (invidiously different in colour depending on a man's skill status), the only thing an English Electric worker carries around with him to remind him of his union membership, contrasts with the pocket diary issued to every Hitachi member. With a soft imitation leather cover and large 4½- by 3-inch pages of good quality thin paper, it contains 27 pages for engagements, etc., 44 pages for notes, and 71 pages of useful information – 27 devoted to union rules, 22 pages with all (or nearly all) anyone could need to know about wages, then overtime regulations, allowances and loan schemes, charts showing the union's structure and its relation to other bodies, the words of the union song, and a lengthy table showing where to go for what – for everything from getting a house loan or a burial allowance for a wife to lodging a complaint against your union section chairman or acquiring the services of a lawyer.

Efficiency and Tradition

The much larger resources at the disposal of the Furusato Union also explains in part why it seems such a generally more efficient, formally well-thought-out, and more literate organization than its British counterpart. Compare, for instance, the slap-happy method of electing British shop stewards by a show of hands with the secret-ballot elections of their Furusato counterparts, or the trim, functional organization of Hitachi unions with the archaic complexities of a British union structure. The Confederation of Shipbuilding and Engineering Unions managed, with the research resources of member unions representing over a million workers, to produce in the three years between the 1964 and 1967 pay claims a creditable array of a dozen statistical tables and six graphs to bolster its new 1967 claims. But it was left to the Employers' Federation to publish this material (in the shorthand report of the negotiations). It was not made generally available to union members except in brief summaries in some union magazines. The Hitachi Federation, by contrast, with 77,000 members, manages to produce every year a seventy- to eighty-page printed booklet of statistical analyses for internal union consumption – chiefly for use in offices. The 1969 edition of these *Materials for the Spring Offensive*, for instance, has 63 tables and 23 graphs. Many of them show the results of a computer analysis of members' responses to a questionnaire enquiry on wages (material which was drawn on in Chapter 3). The rest are detailed comparisons of wages by age and grade in Hitachi as compared with the other big electrical firms, and in the electrical as compared to other industries, an analysis of the company's announced five-year expansion plan, and a detailed comparison of the financial structure, ratios of labour costs, depreciation and profits to value added and turnover as between Hitachi, General Electric (US), Westinghouse and Siemens. The CSEU's pay claim, by contrast, confined itself almost entirely to British data culled from the Board of Trade Journal, the DEP's monthly bulletin of statistics and the Financial Times' analyses of company reports.

These differences are only partly due to the differences in resources available. Organizations tend to preserve features characteristic of society at large at the time of their foundation.[5] British unions acquired their main structural outlines at a time when British social institutions were much less formally structured than were Japanese social institutions in the late forties which saw the birth of Japanese unions. British factories, for example, relied much more on informal, unrecorded, oral communication than on the written word preserved for the record, much more on the diffuse authority of superiors rather than on the 'legal–rational' authority of objective rules.

[5] For a very able elaboration of this thesis, see the article by A. L. Stinchcombe in J. G. March, *Handbook of Organization*, 1965, largely reprinted in T. Burns (ed.), *Industrial Man*, 1969.

Japanese unions, by contrast, first took shape in enterprises with highly formal, rule-governed forms of bureaucratic organization which rely extensively on paper and ink. The founders of Japanese modern unions included a number of university graduates. Even those who had not been to universities were products of a modern system of primary and secondary education articulated with the university centres of research. It is natural that they should have shown a more lively appreciation of the usefulness of explicit constitutional rules, and of the need for research–the need to beat the bosses with *knowledge* – than products of a more traditional kind of education in British elementary schools who relied primarily on the weapon of worker *solidarity*.

Another source of the difference is that Japanese unions had less *need* of solidarity and self-sacrificing loyalty in their early stages, formed as they were, at a time when the world at large accepted unions with enthusiasm as wholly legitimate organizations. The rhetoric of Japanese union speeches and publications preserves much of the language of post-war, left-wing politics, but internal communications have nothing equivalent to the embattled sectarian 'Dear Sir and Brother/Yours fraternally' style of British union business; there are no rituals like never closing the door at a branch meeting when strangers are present. Nor (although men are not supposed actually to profit from union activities) is there much of the feeling traditional to the British 'movement' that the true union man should give his energies to the cause at some financial cost to himself. Elected officials at Hitachi lose nothing and may gain slightly by their union job. Their non-elected professional research workers are paid salaries comparable with those in industry.

Chapter 5

Industrial Relations: Mainly England

The Japanese system of industrial relations, it was said in the last chapter, has passed through its social democratic revolution in a way that the British system has not. One justification for that statement can be found in the different notions of legitimacy and the different degrees of consensus in the two countries. One way of putting it would be to say that in Britain many among both unionists and managers, while accepting the inevitability of the other's existence, refuse fully to accept its legitimacy – or at least to accept the legitimacy of the power which the other enjoys. Both sides are apt to consider an ideal society as one in which the other does not exist, and to believe, or at least sometimes to act as if they believed, that such a society is possible. In Japan on the other hand, although the union songs may hail the breaking of a socialist dawn, and although a few old-time managers reminisce sometimes about the pre-war days when unions did not have to be reckoned with, both sides look forward to an indefinite future in which their relations will not be very different from what they are now. Britain's is an Arab-Israeli situation with shifting frontiers which only constant vigilance can defend. Japan's is a Franco-German situation; there are memories of monumental disputes over Alsace and the Saar, but now the border is not an issue. These are exaggerations, but they indicate the nature of the difference in question.

The reason for this difference lies partly in the nature of the Japanese post-war breakthrough and roll-back, described in the last chapter, partly in the fact that industrial relations in Britain are less institutionalized than in Japan. The 'constitutional' contract renewed at Hitachi with some adjustments every two years, provides for practically every eventuality – who should be a member of the union, who should stay on duty during strikes, where and when meetings may be held and at whose cost, grievance procedures, etc.

In the English Electric factories, by contrast, there was no such document.

The only formal agreements of a constitutional kind are as follows:

1. The general national procedure agreement between the union Confederation and the Engineering Employers' Federation, an agreement renounced by the unions since this study was completed. This provided what was essentially mediation of disputes between workers and their employers by other employers. The unions agreed not to take strike action until this mediation had been through a series of stages – a Works Conference, a more formal Local Conference, and finally a national Central Conference. Between 1898 and 1922 the agreement could be interpreted to give unions the right to demand that, where the dispute was started by some innovative act of the managers, that act should not take effect until the procedure was exhausted. By the 1922 amendment, carried through at a time when the market situation put employers in the ascendant, the situation was changed. Employees were required to obey first and protest afterwards.[1] In the negotiations for revision of the agreement started in 1969 the unions have tried to restore the pre-1922 *status quo* provisions, but so far without success. It is a perfect illustration of the ding-dong Arab-Israeli nature of British industrial relations that the dispute should essentially be about pushing the frontier back to where it was in 1921.

2. Certain domestic elaborations of this procedure may be formalized unilaterally by the factory management. At Bradford, for example, the management reorganized the system of works committees in 1965 and took the opportunity fully to spell out how appeals and grievances from groups and individuals should be processed. (An individual complains to his foreman and if unsatisfied may go to two higher levels within the department – superintendent or departmental manager – either alone or accompanied by his shop steward. At the next stage, the chief personnel officer or the general manager and the chief shop steward take up the matter, and if they disagree, the Works-Local-Central Conference procedure involving full-time union officials from outside is activated.) Although there had been consultation with union representatives on this pronouncement, it is not a negotiated agreement like the national or procedural agreement, and the unions were in no sense committed to support it. Nevertheless,

[1] See A. I. Marsh and W. E. J. McCarthy, *Dispute Procedures in Britain*, Royal Commission on Trade Union and Employers' Associations, Research Papers 2, part 2.

since the procedures outlined followed those which had been established by convention – they 'conformed to custom and practice' – they
were generally followed.

For the rest, the definition of the relative rights and duties of
union and management were entirely a matter of unwritten convention or oral agreement.[2] Conveners of stewards at Liverpool had
the right to a meeting with their union's stewards for half an hour
a month in the firm's committee room and in the firm's time, but
there was no document in anyone's possession which validated that
right. Since no one challenged it, no problems arose, but they do
arise on other matters where convention is far from unambiguous
about rights. Did the chief shop steward at Bradford have the *right*
to be present when any man was given a final warning of impending
dismissal for bad work, bad conduct, or bad time keeping? Some divisional managers thought he did, some thought it very useful to im-
plicate him. Some saw his presence as a derogation of their authority.
And since autonomy in these matters rested with divisional managers
– and was even delegated to foremen in some divisions – the absence
of any agreed rules in the matter meant that every other case of dismissal was a cause of dispute.

The same applies to other doubtful questions. Does the shop
steward have the right to be in attendance when the rate-fixer is
observing a new job in order to fix the price? When can union meetings be held inside the factory? How much time should the senior
steward be allowed to devote to union business? What facilities can a
shop steward claim in order to carry on his work?

The following account by a chief shop steward of his early days in
that office is a good example of the uncertainties of the situation, and
of the general assumption of union officials that the present balance
of rights is inequitable, and that constant pushing is necessary to
redress the balance. He explained that his predecessors had been able
to use during the daytime the night office of the fire officer, fully
equipped with lockers and a telephone, but this building had been
pulled down. Eventually after much protest at the failure of management to provide him with a substitute office, he was given a fenced-off
corner of a warehouse – an enclosure with walls of which the lower
six feet were of steel sheeting and the rest wire mesh up to the ceiling.
But he never succeeded in getting a telephone. He was told that there
were no extra lines. With the co-operation of the chief electrician who

2 As generally in British industry. For the reasons why, see W. E. J. McCarthy,
The Role of Shop Stewards in British Industrial Relations, Royal Commission on
Trade Unions and Employers' Associations, Research Papers 1, pp. 26–9, and
also Research Papers 10, pp. 73–5.

passed him information about comings and goings in the factory, he asked for every spare line as it became available,

'But I always got the same answer; they're required for somewhere else. So I gave up. I thought, "Well, look. It's no skin off my nose to lose all these hours production", and – well, you know the works, how far it is from one end to the other. Well they used to come down from the far end – ten minutes walk it was – and if I wasn't in they'd sit down in my chair and wait for me, and they didn't know where I was. In the meantime, probably there would be a stoppage of work up there, and I wouldn't know anything about it. . . .

It was like – well, victimization. Victimization is the hardest thing in the world to prove, even though *you* know it is taking place and the person who's *involved* knows it is taking place. . . . I knew from the beginning of me taking office, their efforts were to obstruct as much as they can. They went to the extent of sending instructions out: "Mr Hines must not be contacted before ten o'clock in the morning" – although I were chief shop steward. What they did, they put a runway over a bench. There was this runway – they got all the large chucks for met to repair – and they put a bench under, and I had to strip these chucks down, repair them and then put them down to be taken away. They always saw to it that a pile of chucks were there and if ever Albert Hines were called on, me hands were as black as the ace of spades, and I had to start washing up. So I had to do something about it. So suddenly one morning there was a downing tool at work in one of the departments. All it wanted was a little bit of a get together. Well work stopped about quarter to eight and the Tannoy [loudspeaker] went for me – and I wouldn't answer it. I refused to answer management or men before 10 o'clock in the morning. Well, the manager of 26 Department came into my department: "Please will you come down, please will you." I said, "No. Sorry you have had your instructions." "What the hell were the instructions?" he said. "No", I said. "Go and get Mr M. [the deputy general manager]. Put him on the job."

Anyway there was no more working for me after then, because I thought things had got to a pitch where I had to make a stand, so I never turned up in the department to repair a chuck the morning after. And my superintendent, Mr Alfred Hardcastle – bless his soul, he is dead and gone now – he said to me: "Albert, Mr K's been on. He hasn't seen Mr Hines on that bench this morning." [i.e. the department manager has been complaining that you're not at work.] So I looked down into the department and I said, "Damn me, he isn't there yet, is he?" So he said, "No, and it's no laughing matter." "No," I said, "It isn't, Alfred, but tell Mr K. that next time he sees Albert Hines on that bench he's got to go up to him and tell him he hasn't seen him there, because I doubt whether he'll ever see him there again. That's it. Now tell Mr K. he can do what he wants. There's nothing will do. Nothing whatever to do." You've got to take that stand you see. And it's bad when they're forcing you – all the way along the line to take stands of this nature. You've enough to do with worrying about the everyday occurrences in the works, and the trouble created by the stupidity of various people, without management going out of their way to obstruct you. This doesn't lend itself to good relationships.'

The two characteristics on which we have dwelt so far – the absence of written agreements and the permanent state of latent belligerency – clearly reinforce each other. Imprecision multiplies the occasion for misunderstanding, giving rise to disputes which provide further occasions for each side to nurture a negative image of the other. Conversely, the assumption of permanent belligerency makes each side – whenever it sees itself as making a concession in any change of the *status quo* – reluctant to record the fact because there is always hope of some *de facto* retrieval of the concession at a later date. There is also a fear that one may inadvertently give away more than one intends. As one older manager insisted: 'Never give 'em anything in writing. They'll only take advantage. They'll twist your words and get all kinds of meaning out of them that you never intended.' When anxieties were at their height after the merger, the Bradford general manager started to call *ad hoc* meetings of all shop stewards and staff representatives to give them information about the company's reorganization plan as it was released. They arrived back on the shop floor with the hottest news, frequently before their foreman had heard it from their divisional manager. Some were a little embarrassed at thus upstaging their foreman, and others got tired of their responsibility of verbally transmitting these news items to forty or fifty fellow-workers. They asked that there should be a written announcement that could be posted on the bulletin board. The general manager then agreed that there should be a record of the meetings, including his answers to questions, to be printed and posted. The personnel officer who had the task of making the record, and who quietly sabotaged the decision by doing nothing, explained: 'These were, after all, very informal exchanges about possibilities and probabilities. Experience has shown if you put down these rather vague assurances in the form of words they are bound to be misinterpreted.'

144

Another factor contributing to this situation is doubtless the ineffable British faith in the superior virtue of relying on ancestral wisdom and the accumulation of 'custom and practice', rather than on the written constitutions which lesser breeds need as a crutch to help them manage their affairs. The difference between parliament and a factory, however, is that parliament does at least have its Erskine May.

SHIFTING THROUGH THE SPECTRUM TO THE CORPORATIST POSITION

Nevertheless, the situation is changing. There are more younger managers with new attitudes – personnel specialists who have taken courses in industrial relations and know all about constitutional management, for instance, or members of the new quasi-classless technocracy with no ingrained sense of the need to defend a crumbling traditional hierarchy.

Some of them are trying actively to change the approach of their fellow managers in the hope that union leaders will respond, cease to be leaders of a rebelliously protesting 'us' against a tyrannical 'them', and accept a role as partners in the making and upholding of agreed rules – *in certain defined areas*. At the same time, the DEP's promotion of productivity bargaining was a major stimulus to a changed approach.

One can roughly chart the spectrum of union attitudes as follows:

1. 'Defend your members right or wrong.' *All* dismissals are wrongful dismissals and must be fought. If a man draws his money and doesn't work, so what? It reduces the bosses' profits and it's one up to us. (The market free-for-all position.[3])

2. A recognition that certain of the rules made unilaterally by management are just rules, and that sanctions designed to uphold those rules ought for that reason to be accepted. (The passive co-operative position.)

3. A willingness to accept responsibility for sharing in the making of the rules as a condition for the right to a say in how they shall be enforced. (The active, co-operative position.)

4. A positive demand for the right to share in the making of the rules and their enforcement springing from a sense that the workers have just as much of a stake in the company and its success as do the managers. (The corporatist position.)

[3] 'Market' is used here not in the sense of 'perfect market', but to refer to the impersonality of the relation between management and (collectivities of) workers and the assumption that each party is solely concerned to maximize his own returns. See below, p. 156.

The position of most union officials, until recently, can be described as hovering between 1 and 2. There were few men in the Bradford factory, and only a fraction more in Liverpool, who displayed the single-minded militancy of position 1, except in occasional moments of exasperation with arrogant or bloody-minded managers. But, on the other hand, there was still a sufficiently ingrained sense of the adversary nature of the worker-manager relation for shop stewards to be sensitive to the charge of 'letting one's own side down'. The result was sometimes subjective attitudes conforming to position 2, but public behaviour conforming to 1. Thus a chief shop steward who described how at one stage shop stewards were paid only 85% of their average bonus for union work, with the result that some of them, in order to make up the money they thereby lost, resorted to the devices described apropos of 'open ticket' work on p. 84.

'Well, I wasn't one for condoning any of this, and the only honest way out, was to see to it that stewards did not lose any wages by virtue of doing their job right. So I opened up negotiations with Mr M. to obtain average earnings for all time spent on shop stewards' duties. Well when you're negotiating a thing like that you've got to recognize that even management aren't prepared to say I'll give you a thing without question. So we agreed that every steward only recorded, or claimed, shop steward's duties when in the presence of management or a representative of management. Which put a bit of a tightener on some of 'em. There's been cases when I've 'ad to defend stewards who I know have put excess time down for shop stewards' duty, even when they've got average earnings. Simply because they wanted a bit more – the old Adam again. I've 'ad to get 'em to one side and give 'em a right ramping, and then go in front of management and defend them with all my might.'

Position 2, a situation of responsibility without power, is in the long run, given British traditions of equal citizenship and insistence on the reciprocity of contract, not compatible with self-respect for a union leader. Position 3 is compatible, however, and younger managers commented on the willingness of most shop stewards to adopt such an attitude if they were given a certain degree of encouragement. To give such encouragement, however, required a certain sacrifice on the manager's part. He must give up his pretensions to possess inviolable 'managerial prerogatives' if the union's share in the rule-making process is to be a genuine one. The first and easiest steps are taken in the area of training, skill status, and piecework prices where the union's right to bargain has long been recognized and where it is now accepted that unions have *de facto* power. In matters such as the use of semi-skilled workers on what might under some definitions be considered as skilled work, or the method of taking observations in order to time work for rate-fixing purposes, an increasing tendency to discuss before acting has modified the traditional method – simply carrying out an immaculate 'managerial act' and then waiting to see if there are any protests.

Sometimes the consultation actually results in a piece of paper signed, perhaps, by a chief shop steward and a departmental superintendent.

'It has been agreed that until such time as adult labour is fully employed in the Turret Section in 11 Department, the skilled setters X, Y and Z, will be allowed to be observed by rate-fixing department for the purpose of establishing floor-to-floor times of any job which is being operated by an apprentice.'

For more extensive changes in payments systems, a formal paper agreement has now become essential. The payment systems described on pp. 91–94, for example, were only put into practice after lengthy consultation between managers and shop stewards and the formal signing of an agreement – in one case only after a ballot among the men in the shop.

Perhaps a slightly larger departure from tradition is implied by the practice (not universal, as we have seen) of having a shop steward present while a man is given a final warning. While on the one hand this represents, from the manager's point of view, a useful endorsement of the work rules by the steward, it admits the right of the steward to participate in both the making and interpretation of the rules concerning what constitutes grounds for dismissal.

An even greater change has been brought about by the Redundancy Payments Act which, by making dismissal for redundancy a relatively attractive proposition in a full-employment situation, has prompted the abandonment of one traditional union weapon for the enforcement of union solidarity – the last-in-first-out principle. That principle belongs to a whole battery of devices whereby unions have traditionally sought to restrict managers' ability to weaken union solidarity by removing all possibility of favouritism. Universal one-price wage rates based on objective criteria are another such device. (Even where the merit system vestigially remains as in the Bradford tool-room (see p. 94) *shop stewards* demand to be present at the periodic reassessments.) Seniority promotion systems are similar devices for allocating benefits or disbenefits strictly on objective

147

criteria. And so, too, the last-in-first-out principle when workers have to be dismissed owing to shortage of work.

At Bradford, however, in the course of 1969, a thinning-out of the workers was carried out in two sections on other than last-in-first-out lines. In both cases, the management first suggested a list of those to be dismissed on the traditional seniority principle. The shop stewards demanded instead that those to go should be in the first place non-unionists, and secondly, volunteers. As the price for agreeing to discriminate against non-unionists, managers insisted in one case on including on the final list one worker who was generally agreed to be a bad time-keeper and poor worker. According to one of the shop stewards who negotiated the agreement, they were uneasy about permitting this reassertion of managerial prerogative and offered to defend the victimized worker, but they were saved from an awkward issue of principle by the man's own decision that he might as well take his redundancy pay and go 'if they've got their knife into me anyway'.

An innovation perhaps even more far-reaching in its eventual consequences is one temporarily stimulated by, but not dependent on, the Prices and Incomes Policy – the general plant bargain of a more formal kind, affecting more than a single department. One single-purpose example was the agreement, mentioned on p. 78, rationalizing the pay structure of indirect workers in Liverpool in 1967. A wider one is the Bradford package deal negotiated by a joint management-union productivity committee over twelve lengthy meetings in 1968. The origin of the deal was the union's request – pressed to a Local Conference – for additional days holiday depending on length of service. Managers decided to make this concession as the cost of 'buying' from the unions certain concessions on their part – agreement to the computerization of the payroll and payment by bank transfer, to an extensive programme of job evaluation, and to the saving of lost production time by reducing waiting time. The 'purchases' were partly genuine, changes which the managers wanted in their quest for greater efficiency. In part (the reduction of waiting time, for example) they were expressions of pious hope intended to impress on the Department of Employment and Productivity that the agreement conformed to the Prices and Incomes Policy and gave nothing away without a corresponding increase in productivity – the managers having decided that some concession on service holidays was necessary for morale anyway.

The use of the 'purchase' metaphor is instructive. It is a recognition that workers do have a stake in the *status quo*, a capacity for resentment at its disturbance, a willingness to express that resentment in non-co-operation, and, most importantly, a lack of fear of the management's only counter-sanction, dismissal, all of which in effect has given them veto power over any change. An abstention from the use of this veto power can be bought at a price. This disturbs many people, including the former director of the Manpower and Productivity Service of the Department of Employment and Productivity who urged in a 1969 speech the need to draw a distinction between changes which really do bring disamenities to workers, and those which they can and ought to be persuaded out of viewing as disamenities.

'The idea that all future changes have a price tag on them is already too widespread. It must be killed before productivity bargaining assumes the characteristics of a sort of national game of Monopoly and before effective far-sighted management becomes impossible.'[4]

But the most important aspect of these 'transactions' is that they bring managers and trade unionists into frequent contact in something other than an embittered dispute situation. As personal encounters, there is all the difference in the world between a friendly haggle in the marketplace on the one hand, and on the other an altercation between the buyer angrily demanding his full change and the storekeeper who is supposed to have cheated him, or an angry storekeeper and the customer accused of slipping a carrot into his pocket. A glance through the diaries of the chief shop steward in the early sixties shows that nearly all his energies were devoted to pouring either water or petrol on flare-ups of the latter types.

The increase in formal contacts of a relatively amicable kind has led also to a great frequency of informal contacts between managers and union officials – sometimes tête à tête in contravention of the rule in nearly every union rule book that no union official should converse with a manager except when accompanied by a fellow unionist. In Bradford, for example, on the day before it was expected that there would be a one-day strike by some unions in support of a national wage claim, the chief shop steward and his deputy spent some time with a manager discussing, in effect, how they could best keep non-strikers out of the factory. The managers' intention was to avoid 'consequential losses' – to prevent anything happening on the strike day which would cause dispute and loss of production on the subsequent days. (They had learned from the bitter experience of a previous one-day strike in 1962 when 'loyal' workers who came into the factory were allowed to do a certain amount of work. Everything

[4] Mr G. H. B. Cattell, address to an *Observer* seminar, 29 May 1969.

they touched was declared 'black' the next day when the strikers returned, and after a month of costly disputes, managers were humiliated into penalizing the loyal workers.) The shop stewards, too, are generally keen to avoid unnecessary unpleasantness and were willing enough to co-operate.

It is a long way from this kind of informal contact to the relations classified above as position 4 – what might be called the corporatist position, perhaps best described in the words of the DEP's Director of Productivity in the speech quoted earlier. To arrive at such a position requires the manager in effect to recognize that:

> His mandate to manage comes primarily from his subordinates: only if they co-operate or at least acquiesce will he achieve his purpose. . . . Consent . . . has to be sought. It requires the creation of confidence by a frank disclosure of full information concerning the business, a sincere invitation to participate in the determination of future objectives, a continuous joint review of overall performance and the predetermined extent to which all interests will participate in success – the slicing and share-out of the cake.[5]

THE SOURCES OF HESITANCY: MANAGERS

This seems a visionary prescription viewed from where most managers are sitting today in either Bradford or Liverpool. At Liverpool, for example, there was not even the same degree of informality between the leaders and managers as at Bradford, and no preparatory talks took place before the threatened strike. There are, in fact, considerable obstacles at both factories to the permanent adoption by the unions even of the actively co-operative position 3, largely springing from a reluctance of managers to take the corresponding attitude.

First, managers are reluctant to make the necessary formal surrender of their prerogatives as already mentioned. Second, the reference above to 'frank disclosure of full information' touches a crucial point. In any organization secrecy is a means of strengthening authority. The more knowledge a man has the stronger his bargaining position. Said a manager:

> 'The big problem in British industry is that in the majority of cases the management is not honest with the worker; often because they themselves are frightened of their superiors. Anyway they don't lay the problem on the table fairly and squarely before the workers and the proposal stops half way.

[5] G. H. B. Cattell, op. cit.

When it comes to money – what we all come here for is money after all – if you're going to get any kind of change you must give something away. Hence the desire of managers to give as little as possible in order to get the change. They are cagey. This is often penny-wise in the long run because the administrative cost of keeping the controls that hold down wages is great.

I believe in being square with unions on the amount of money I can afford to pay, making it clear to them that any further increase over and above that must be the result of increased output. On the bonus, the X Department bonus scheme, for example, it was not until I came that I told the workers that one production unit was calculated to equal 56·8 minutes of work. The chief rate-fixer who was there, nearly had a duck-fit when I told them. He said we'll be in real trouble now. They'll always be doing their own rough calculations as to what the unit value system of every machine should be. But formerly their ignorance had simply created frustration.'

There are two other justifications for secrecy which managers frequently use. The first is that the workers' nerves are not strong enough to stand the strain. If they were regularly told about the length of order books or the state of the firm's profits, they would be constantly worrying about redundancy or short-time working. 'We'd be able to get more forthright if we ever got to the secure situation where you walk through those doors at age 16 and stay until you're 65.'

The final argument against greater candour is that information given to shop stewards will be leaked to competitors and give them an advantage. 'It is true that we are bad about the way we talk to the unions,' said one manager, 'but on the other hand, they don't encourage us when they send everything you tell them to the local newspapers.'

All together, it is hard to see any trend in the direction of greater frankness in management. One manager claimed that there was and that more information was recently being given to unions about the financial state of the works accounts. But he added, 'To be fair, though, this is because we are in a bad way. If the situation improved and we began to show a good profit balance, there would certainly be a swing-back in the opposite direction.'

Machinery for consultation and communication both at the departmental level and centrally do exist in both factories in the form of works committees (for manual workers) and staff committees of a kind first developed at Britain at the time of the first world war and widely diffused during the second. (It is significant that moves in this co-operative direction take place during wars when patriotism and the war effort define goals sufficiently common to both sides to overcome normal suspicions.) The Bradford factory refurbished its works committees in 1965. There are central committees (manual and staff) and departmental committees directly elected from the shop floor. The purpose of the reorganization was to develop 'a more positive approach to industrial relations than in the past – to create a climate in which changes will be considered on their merits by employees at all levels'. The committees were not, however, to deal with matters which were subject to negotiation or appeal (i.e. grievances). They were to be dealt with by the normal negotiating procedures. The committees were for 'consultation' defined as discussion of matters 'in which the management normally takes the initiative and always takes the decisions and responsibility'. Meetings usually follow a standard pattern, perhaps best indicated by the sample minutes of one department below:

'1. Minutes

2. *Safety and Health* [there follow details of all reportable accidents and what ought to be done to prevent their occurrence.]

3. *Production*

In recent months we have received a very large volume of work in certain groups, particularly Group G and deliveries have had to be lengthened due to our extended order book.

Mr P. explained that the work load is measured in output units – loaded to a level of 360–320 from shop and 40 from subcontractors "Unfortunately many of our subcontractors have not come up to expectation, and this has resulted in a progressive build-up of overdues."

The work is planned through various stages from standard lead times, and there is a due date on every component. If the due dates are met then the components will come together to the sub-assembly and assembly stages at the right time, thus enabling machines to be completed at the correct time.

It is imperative that an all-out effort is made to catch up with overdues in each section. The individual position is:

Machine shop ....1 week behind.

Corebuilding shop......6 weeks behind. etc.

4. *Fire prevention* Nothing to report.

5. *Working conditions*

Leaking Roof – a representative complained that the roof was leaking very badly in his department. The chairman told the committee that many of the roofs were in need of repair due to recent gales, but he promised to take the matter up with the maintenance department.

6. *Transport* The question of the Leeds 72 bus was again discussed.
7. *Social and Sports Activities* Nil.
8. *Canteen Services in the Works* Nil.
9. *General Welfare* Nil.
10. *Choice of Representative on the Central Works Committee*

Some managers are more concerned than others to give the fullest possible information and create a sense of 'involvement', and there had been hopes at Bradford that the Central Works Committee might acquire negotiating functions and become a serious factory 'parliament'. In practice, however, few managers set much store by such meetings except as a means of squashing anxiety-generating rumours about impending changes. Nor did the unions set much store by these bodies known to them variously as the 'tea and cakes' or the 'draughts and farts' committees. The chief shop steward at Bradford was by convention normally elected to the chairmanship of the central committee for manual workers and in fact all its members were shop stewards. Equally, the representatives of the three staff unions were given seats *ex officio* on the staff central committee. The DATA representative, however, refused to take up his place. At Liverpool, where managers made more deliberate attempts to keep the meetings off production matters, manual unions and DATA representatives steered clear of the committees, though some shop stewards were individually elected from their department.

THE SOURCES OF HESITANCY: UNIONS
Union leaders are, in fact, very reluctant to be 'drawn in'. The prospects of the 'corporatist' position 4 are both appealing and fraught with danger. In the course of the meetings of the Bradford working party responsible for the productivity package deal, there was, to judge from the minutes, a good deal of self-congratulation by both managers and trade union representatives about the 'new atmosphere' of co-operation, and there was agreement in principle that there should be a job evaluation panel to revise the whole pay structure of the factory to which the shop stewards should nominate two of their number.

Eleven months later the joint shop stewards committee had still not been able to agree on the managers' more detailed proposals for the job evaluation exercise. Many felt that the unions ought to have a hand in it. On the other hand, there was the danger, as one shop

153

steward put it, 'that the people appointed would be brainwashed and become management-minded'. Since they would no longer be on their own shop floor, they would have to give up their shop-stewardship and so get out of touch with union feelings and perspectives.

A second source of the reluctance on the part of trade unionists to be drawn towards copartnership-type arrangements, is the fear – on past experience a realistic fear – that given the managers' superior access to information, and greater experience and financial competence, the union representatives would be out-manoeuvred. There is evidence to support this fear in the record of negotiations of the Bradford productivity package. Managers produced at the first meeting a set of figures showing the cost of extra holidays. The basis of the calculation was clearly explained, but quite clearly involved a dubious double-counting. It was not until the seventh meeting that they were withdrawn and replaced by another figure based on a more obviously justifiable calculation – and then, apparently, at management's initiative rather than because of the union representatives' protests.

In some unions, the fear of any compromise of their independence extends to the point that, despite the great difficulty they have in collecting subscriptions, they would reject any co-operative offer by employers to collect dues on their behalf by a check-off from wages. One district secretary who was in favour of the check-off and who was sure that several firms in the vicinity would be prepared to co-operate, remarked that his union's national executive combined their real ability and intelligence and honesty with such a stiff-necked conservatism that they would never agree. The tradition persists at root level, too. Almost certainly the Liverpool management would be willing to allow workers to use a convenient area in the workshop for the election of a shop steward, but none of the unions is interested in asking for this privilege. 'Going outside the gates' (the means, too, of bringing a dispute to a head) has more a symbolic than a real purpose. There may occasionally be some point in evading the eyes of spies who will report to managers who said what, but more importantly, it is a ritual shaking-off of the dust of the employer's property.

WHITE-COLLAR WORKERS: A DIGRESSION

It is perhaps curious that in both factories the union which is most puritan in this regard – indeed the union which is closest to position 1, the market free-for-all position – is the draughtsmen's union. Few senior shop stewards of the manual unions would feel very uncomfortable about breaking the union rule of never speaking to a manager without a witness. The DATA office committee, however, will formally request an interview with a manager and appear as a five-man delegation merely to announce their acceptance of the agenda for a meeting the following week. DATA, moreover, is the white-collar union whose representative at Liverpool was the first to join a factory joint shop stewards' committee (traditionally a manual workers' preserve) and the first to be sent as a delegate to an English Electric combine meeting.[6] It has been the most militant union, particularly at Liverpool, in pressing wage claims by one-hour strikes and overtime bans, and has attempted to enforce a closed shop by quite ruthless and tension-creating policies of non-co-operation with non-union men.

There may be many reasons for this, but three immediately suggest themselves. First, many of the local leaders being men with a grammar school education, perhaps continuing until eighteen, have not just a tradition of working-class consciousness, but some reasoned ideological commitment to anti-capitalism to provide a principled basis for their adoption of position 1. There is a clear analogy with the well-educated young white-collar workers who led the amalgamation of the manual and non-manual unions in Japan after the war.

Secondly, relations have become especially embittered because of the reaction of managers. As a Bradford memorandum for managers remarked, 'Many managers and supervisors of staff have not yet adjusted to the fact that their freedom to act is becoming limited in much the same way as that of managers and supervisors of manual workers.' It has taken a century or more for manual workers' unions to become accepted by managers as a fact of life. But although DATA

[6] A departure which shocked older trade unionists who find it impossible to perceive of 'the staff' except as part of the enemy. Thus, the minutes:

Brother A opened the meeting by welcoming delegates and commenting on the good attendance. He went on to stress the importance of the National Strike and suggested that it be fully discussed at this meeting. He then informed Brother S (DATA) that as the constitution of the Combine Committee catered only for manual workers' Unions, he could not be allowed to take an active part in the meeting, although he would be allowed to remain as an observer.

Brother S explained that as he was delegated by Liverpool Shop Stewards' Committee to represent them he should be allowed to stay, and at this point Brother L, who is Convener at Liverpool, defended Brother S and explained that at Liverpool Manual and Staff Unions work together on one Committee, and in his opinion this was a good arrangement, but Brother A said he could not alter the constitution to suit this situation and could not allow Brother S to participate in the meeting. After further heated discussion on this point it was

Moved and seconded: That the Chairman leave the Chair.

The Motion was defeated by 9 votes to 8 with 13 absentions.

Since this study, of course, DATA has merged with the AEF to form the AUEW, though the extent to which there has been a real fusion of organization is still limited.

was accepted as a negotiating body by the Engineering Employers Federation as long ago as 1924, there is still a lingering sense that one ought to be able to expect from staff workers a certain loyal deference. The greater the expectation of loyalty the more shocking the demonstration of non-loyalty seems, the more emotional and uncompromising is the managerial reaction, and the more militant the further response provoked.

Thirdly, by very intelligent tactics and good interplant co-ordination, the union *has* secured its members considerable gains which have made even the blazered Young Conservatives among draughtsmen willing to go along with radical and militant local leaders.

UNION HESITATIONS: A SUMMARY

Underlying the reluctance of union leaders to be involved in anything approaching the copartnership of a corporatist pattern of relations, one may elucidate two principles. The first is hinted at in the earlier designation of position 1 as the 'market free-for-all' position. The union is a co-operative organization for regulating the sale of labour to employers. The firm which sells generators to a shipping company does not undertake to help the shipping company to manage its own affairs. If it did get involved, it might find itself under pressure to cut the price of its generators. Similarly, the sellers of labour have no obligation to get involved in running the affairs of the purchasers of labour, and can best safeguard their own position by not doing so. And, as the comment of the shop steward quoted on p. 90 makes clear, if capitalist market relations are seen as involving all kinds of sharp practice, 'fiddles' on the part of workers can be justified as an extension of the same ethics.

The second, related, consideration is that copartnership involves workers as members of an organic factory community. Loyalties can more easily be focused on the company, at the expense of a sense of loyal solidarity with fellow workers in other companies. The rejection of merit pay increases, the seniority rules for promotion, the last-in-first-out principle for deciding the order of redundancy dismissals, are all devices for preventing personal relations of patronage and gratitude between workers and managers which might strengthen those loyalties.

COMPANY MEMBERSHIP VERSUS UNION MEMBERSHIP

This second is a consideration of which local full-time officials of trade unions are particularly aware. Contrary to the frequent popular impression that it is the shop steward who is the wild, uncompromising militant and the local full-time officials who are sober and responsible, from the district official's point of view it was often the other way around. 'Some of these chief shop stewards', said one district secretary (one, be it said, who was much in favour of accepting the check-off and otherwise rationalizing union structures), 'are like clay in the hands of management. It's easy enough. You give them a bit of prestige and then you give them some confidential information and then you've got them fixed. The result is that I never get to hear of some issues which ought to be taken up at the district level because they can set precedents for elsewhere. The managers will say: "I don't think we need to bring the officials in at this stage" and the shop stewards will agree and possibly give something away that they ought not to give away.'

A union district secretary has only one organizational loyalty – to his union. Shop stewards have a divided loyalty. They are union men, but – after twenty or thirty years' service in many cases – they are English Electric men too. A quite militant senior steward at Liverpool, speaking to an outsider about recent changes, said quite unconsciously, 'We [sic] put in work study in X Department.' It will soon become apparent that one of the main differences between British and Japanese union structure is that the latter does not give rise to this conflict of identities.

UNION LEADERS AND THE RANK AND FILE
The district secretary's mention of confidential information as a means whereby shop stewards are softened up is very pertinent. The willing receipt of information compromises. Confidential information compromises absolutely. The crux of the matter is the relationship between leader and led which is already difficult in the trade union movement and which every approach to corporatism makes more difficult.

The organization of trade unions described so far is essentially an organization of activists – of those who hold some union position. Members are rarely more than passive dues-payers. At any branch meeting, most of those in attendance are likely to be shop stewards and collectors, plus a few members who drop in to collect sick benefit. And not all of those become shop stewards from an eager and zestful interest in the union's affairs. Some do. Some are keen Labour Party men, perhaps the sons of trade unionists, with a sharp sense of the need of the working class to defend itself. But others – like the steward on the washing-machine assembly line (p. 92) – have shop stewardship thrust upon them. They are flattered enough to accept, but have no very principled commitment to trade unionism. The fact is that they are not selected from a large group of eager volunteers

157

with some real commitment to the cause. Although some 20% of union members at both of the factories sampled for the interview survey (the same proportion as at Hitachi) said that they would be willing to consider being elected as shop stewards or collectors, not many actively seek such a job.[7]

And with reason, for the shop steward's lot is not a happy one. There are several reasons for this. The first is related to the earlier discussion of information. The generalized suspicion of managers which pervades the shop floor (and ambiguously coexists, often, with a very common view that, all the same, when you compare them with some others, 'Our's is a pretty good firm, really: they treat you fair.') rubs off also onto those who are in frequent contact with managers. Thus, one perceptive young man who had been elected convener by the stewards of his union:

'When I came to this factory, I really hadn't wanted to get involved in union business again. You see, it's the suspicion that members have of their own stewards. Everything you do is questioned. You see it is part of their suspicion of management. We've got to negotiate with management and we've got to play square with them. We accept that management is on the level until it is proved otherwise. But the ordinary member, when he hears of some management scheme, says that it must be a plot to trick the workers, and that the shop stewards have agreed to it, and that they're getting a back-hander, and so on.'

The absence of any system for formal meetings at which shop stewards regularly report back to the people to whom they are accountable (an absence due to unions' neglect of workshop organization) almost certainly exacerbates this situation – though the suspicion that shop stewards were being given cash bribes by managers really does not seem to be widespread. That form of corruption is rare in British trade unionism. More common is a mixture of envy and suspicion of motives – stewards are seen as 'trying to make a name for themselves' – with the suggestion that the position is being used as a stepping stone to other things. One direction a steward's ambition can take is obvious and condemned by no one – a small number hope to go on to become (by election) full-time union officials. But since there is only one official for several hundred

---

[7] Of shop stewards in a national survey, 40% said that they had been reluctantly persuaded to take the job, W. E. J. McCarthy and S. R. Parker, *Shop Stewards and Workshop Relations*, Royal commission on Trade Unions and Employers' Associations, Research Papers, 10, 1968, p. 15.

stewards,[8] the chances are a good deal better of becoming a foreman, a rate-fixer, an inspector, a safety officer within the firm. This is not just because managers are willing to 'buy over' troublesome stewards – though they sometimes do. But the steward inevitably gets noticed. And the force of character which makes a good steward is likely also to make a good foreman, while clearly, from the manager's point of view, to hold out promotion prospects to shop stewards by the occasional judicious example can encourage the others not to alienate the managers too far and give greater cause to the rank and file to be suspicious of stewards' self-interested ambition. Add to this the fact that an ex-shop steward can bring to a foremanship a special expertise. 'It's hell for the men on the shop floor when you do buy a shop steward over. He knows all the "fiddles".' This last consideration, however, cuts both ways. A foreman's over-zealous ferreting out of 'fiddles' can make matters worse and ruin workshop relations. The impression of a senior shop steward at Liverpool was that fewer stewards were being given promotion than several years ago, partly for this reason, partly because of an increasing tendency to promote younger technicians to foreman posts.

There is a further possible upward route for a union activist. Some who have been promoted from shop stewards to full-time union officials may later in life join the managerial ranks as a personnel officer. Liverpool's industrial relations officer was an example (a former officer of a union which had no formal representation in the Liverpool works) and there were at least four other examples in the neighbourhood. Such men may refuse to accept that they have 'changed sides'. 'I don't see it as the other side', said one. 'I never have. The function of the trade union officer and the function of the industrial relations officer is the same – to secure a reasonable compromise.' Nevertheless, many others do so see it, and an industrial relations officer with a union background may face a certain amount of hostility on that account. At the same time, few people are prepared to maintain that a loyal trade unionist should forever renounce all possibilities of self-advancement. A certain ambiguity remains. Here is a chief shop steward's diary entry, doubtless the basis of a brief speech at the next shop stewards' meeting.

'Today Sister Wilkinson takes on the duty of supervisory instructor of the cutting department (new section) and I feel sure we all wish her every success in this post. Sister Wilkinson has proved

[8] W. E. J. McCarthy and S. R. Parker, op. cit., p. 87. According to their survey the average number of stewards for each full-time officer was 172. In the AEF the figure was as high as 477.

herself a stalwart for the union and I feel certain that she will do credit both for the people she deals with and all concerned as she herself said that she will never change her outlook on life and there-fore approve the policy and aim of all Unions that we educate our people not to lord over other workers but to take their just place in industry and share the responsibility of running it to benefit of the people and the country as a whole.'

Suspicion, envy or dislike of shop stewards was not universal, however. In the sample of engineering workers 60% of respondents (almost the same proportion at both factories) were prepared to say that their shop stewards were doing a good job, and in steel the pro-portion was 43%. The shop steward acting directly as spokesman for a group of workers in a pay dispute, or defending someone who has been 'picked on' by an unfair supervisor can usually count on the support of his fellows. But – precisely because of the disjunction between the shop steward system and the union organization proper – such support for the shop steward does not necessarily spill over into general backing for the union, certainly much less so at a factory like Marconi's than in the more traditional Glasgow firm of Babcock and Wilcox. At Marconi, only 19% of the sample were in favour of a union shop, and only 23% were prepared to pay higher union sub-scriptions. At Babcock's the percentages were 61% (very close to Hitachi's 58%) and 38% respectively. (The Hitachi question about union dues was not properly comparable.)

TRADE UNIONISM AND THE SOLIDARITY OF THE WORKING CLASS

To these last figures one might add two other sets. First, 25% of Marconi workers and 10% of Babcock workers said 'no' when asked: 'Generally speaking would you say there was any danger of unfair treatment from management if there weren't any shop stewards to take up grievances?' The other set of figures concern replies to a ques-tion about how workers' participation might work. Should the workers be represented by union officials, by shop stewards, or by specially elected representatives?

	Marconi	Babcock
Officials	13	16
Stewards	23	41
Special representatives	52	37
Don't know	13	5
	100	100

These figures should be enough to make clear that there can be no simple characterization of the attitudes of 'British workers' towards trade unions, but it is fairly safe to say that attitudes are a mixture (in different proportions in the average Marconi worker from that in the average Glasgow worker) of several strands, identified also in a recent study of Luton workers.[9]

1. An acceptance of, and some support for, the unions as instrumentally useful to the workers in getting higher pay.

2. A tendency to accept the unions and one's obligation to pay union dues as part of the traditional order.

3. More or less positive feelings towards workshop representatives.

4. More or less antipathetic feelings towards union leaders, and to 'the unions' as reified actors in the national political scene.

5. Sometimes, but sometimes only vestigially, a positive feeling of loyalty to 'the union movement' associated with feelings of solidarity with other workers.

Discussion of this last theme is best postponed to a consideration of general differences in class consciousness between Japan and England (Chapter 11), but it might be worth quoting here one incident and some reactions to it, as illustrating the difficulties of any attempt to generalize about the nature of such sentiments of class solidarity.

After the merger between EE and GEC there was widespread anxiety about rationalization and redundancies. It finally emerged that the Bradford factory was likely to survive more or less intact while a similar factory in Manchester would bear the brunt of the rationalization in that branch of production. When cuts at the Manchester factory were announced, there were proposals for a sympathetic strike. It was actually the DATA representatives who were most in favour of striking – see the earlier remarks about DATA's probably being a more educated and principled militancy. The manual unions showed little enthusiasm, however. 'You've got to be a bit parochial about these things', said one senior steward, 'Of course, you don't like to see anybody else suffer, but if somebody is going to suffer you thank God it isn't you.' He added that in any case the Manchester factory was only getting what it deserved. Their shop stewards had failed to mount demonstrations, newspaper campaigns and MP lobbying on the same scale as Bradford, and they had not answered earlier

[9] J. H. Goldthorpe, et al., The Affluent Worker in the Class Structure, 1969, p. 167–70.

letters suggesting a co-ordinated campaign before the choice of cuts was made.

At Liverpool, a shop steward leader who was one of those involved in plans for a protest 'factory occupation' proposed largely in support of a sister factory nearby, spoke of the probable imminent collapse of his plans. First, managers were having great effect with the argument that the protest could not win, and that the notoriety it caused would make *other* manufacturers hesitate about moving into the district and offering employment.

'When support weakens, it is either this or the fear of losing a week's money. In fact, pure selfishness is probably the most important. "Blow you, Jack, I'm all right." You know. It certainly doesn't seem to be the old ideas about unity. This affluent society has got something to do with it. Their main concern is to continue to run their car and the television and this sort of thing.

It's shortsightedness really. But then unions are supposed to be a democracy and in a democracy you give people what they want. But, you know, I'm told by my father [who had been a full-time union official] – I used to get emotionally involved in this sort of subject; I imagined that the working class were all of like mind – you know – they all believed in unity and trade union principles. And I think he told me: "Ay, it's very good all that," he said, "but in the twenties and thirties – there's a lot written about those times – the general strike period and all that – but in fact the people that were working really didn't care a damn about those that weren't." You know? And I admit the same is there today, and recognizing that in a democracy it means that you carry out the wishes of the majority – that's a difficult one, but I can't accept that policies have to be determined by the selfish motives of people. Somebody has to make a stand.

How these attitudes all fit together we shall attempt to summarize in Chapter 7, but first it is necessary to take a closer look at the contrasting pattern of relations between union and management at Hitachi.

Chapter 6

Industrial Relations: Mainly Japan

An enterprise union, such as Hitachi's, is bound in some obvious respects to work differently from British unions. Clearly, the 'market free-for-all' position is untenable. Given the lifetime employment structure, one does not take the line: the price of our labour is such and such; if the company goes bust trying to pay it, too bad; we'll go and work somewhere else. The extreme militant position has to be a more class-conscious and apocalyptic one: if we destroy Hitachi in the process of trying to seize control over it, so much the better: one more nail in the coffin of the capitalist system. And, of course, some such principle was indeed followed by the communist group within the union before the roll-back of 1951. There remains a small number of members of the Communist Party youth league in the Hitachi factory, but they have so far made no attempt to penetrate the union. The union itself now rejects such militancy. The phrase 'monopoly capital' is now largely reserved in union documents for general discussions of the Japanese economy. 'Capital' is used occasionally as a means of referring obliquely to the Hitachi management when criticizing them – a means of avoiding being too personal.

Nor are there the same inhibitions as in England to prevent union leaders from accepting a corporatist position. There is no parallel to the conflict between the identification with the firm (however minimal) of a British shop steward and the identification exclusively with the trade union organization of the full-time official. Hitachi full-time officials *are* Hitachi men. Some of them, going about their work in the union office, wear exactly the same denim suit as is standard issue for office workers in the factory. They wear the same badges, surname on top and employee number on the bottom. The only difference is that the centre band contains not the usual abbreviated name of a department in the firm, but the two characters for 'trade union'. Even in the context of the revolutionary overtones of the union song, it is still 'our Hitachi'.

Union Song

The storm still blows, the mountain pass is long
But we will never give up.
Though still the sun gives no glimpse of light
Dawn approaches for the working man.
Our Hitachi! Hitachi where the muscles tense!
Never slacken. Shoulder to shoulder we move ahead.
Soon you shall see! Soon you shall see!

The path is dark, precipitous. Cold penetrates the bone
But no one walks alone.
Though still the sun gives no glimpse of light
Somewhere, faintly, the first cock crows.
Our Hitachi! Hitachi where the muscles tense!
In amity and unison, with laughter and song we move ahead.
Soon you shall see! Soon you shall see!

Now to be born anew: the history of Japan.
Wave the union flag on high.
The sun thrusts up over the horizon
The century of the working man arrives!
Our Hitachi! Hitachi where the muscles tense!
Grit teeth, tighten belts, just one more short haul
Soon you shall see! Soon you shall see!

Similarly managers at Hitachi are not subject to the same fears about divulging confidential information. In the first place, Japanese company law requires annual publication of the most intimate details of the company's balance sheet and profit and loss account within three months of the end of each half-year. The differences between what one can find out from published accounts about Hitachi and what one can find out about English Electric is about the difference between a short book and a table of contents. Somehow, a high degree of secrecy is not thought essential for the running of Japanese business.

Quite apart from these *public* disclosures of information about past performance, it is, in any case, difficult for managers to keep information from the union. Every department in the firm contains union members. Certain plans for the future may be discussed confidentially among a group of senior managers, but except in departments like the personnel department which has quite junior graduate non-unionists who can be given rather tiresome data-collection chores to do, it would be hard for them to develop substantial plans in secret without subordinates who are union members becoming aware of it. This by no means automatically implies that the information will be transmitted to union leaders. One Hitachi union official had no doubt that union members in the personnel office operated according to a strict code of self-imposed discretion. 'To judge from the attitude of the general council members elected from the Personnel office, there's a good deal they don't tell us. The new shift system, for instance, was sprung on us pretty well by surprise. And it must have been two years in the making.'

Nevertheless, there clearly is some variation in this regard. One factory personnel manager claimed that during a previous regime head office operated on the assumption that anything revealed to factory personnel managers about the company's strategy for dealing with the union was bound to leak to the union. They were, consequently, fed an irritating diet of black intelligence deliberately designed to mislead the enemy. He claimed that his own practice, in contrast, was to discuss strategy for dealing with union leaders with his whole department. Generally one could rely on one's subordinates' discretion not to tell all to the union. But even if they did one gained more from building up a reputation for frankness than one lost in being unable to take the 'enemy' by surprise.

A third factor affecting the disclosure of information is the fact that managers have a less powerful *motive* for keeping financial information from the union, inasmuch as the union, indirectly, represents the managers too. The British manager might feel directly threatened by a large wage claim. A tighter purse in the company could reduce his chances of a merit increase. Japanese managers' salaries, however, are paid according to a scale which, by convention, is automatically jacked up by an amount equivalent to the increases negotiated with the union (expressed as an overall percentage). Managers, therefore, do not see themselves as differentiated from the union in interest, only by their possession of a superior sense of responsibility and a livelier appreciation of the need for occasional self-denial in the interests of the firm.

To be sure, in the final bargaining, the firm's directors play a major role, and directors, as well as owning some shares, receive a bonus which is paid out of profits. (As opposed to their salaries which are linked to the general salary scale.) However, even this does not much alter the situation: (a) because by this stage the room for bargaining has already been very much narrowed by the middle-level managers; and (b) because despite the principle that directors' bonuses should fluctuate with profits, in corporations with 'salary-man directors' like Hitachi (as opposed to those where the real founder is still chairman) bonuses have become a relatively standardized part of their income.

In short, on neither side are there such hesitancies about accepting a corporatist position as in England. And, in effect, the Hitachi unions, both at Federation and at the Plant Union level, do claim the right to participate not only in the making of organizational rules, but also in setting the organization's goals. And that right has been conceded, at least in formal terms, in the establishment of joint management councils, both centrally and at each factory. These are made up of ten managers and ten union representatives and meet approximately every three months. The agenda is divided into items for report, and items for consultation. The first category consists of:

1. Explanation of management policy objectives.
2. Production plans and achievements, budgets and financing plans, and financial reports.
3. Major changes in company managerial structure.
4. Manpower plans.

Items for consultation are:

1. The opening and closing of new factories and any other managerial policies which have an important influence on working conditions.
2. Improvements in production equipment and techniques.
3. Improvements in work efficiency.
4. Improvements in advertising and sales methods.
5. The establishment of workshop discipline.
6. The operation and improvement of safety facilities.
7. The operation and improvement of welfare facilities.
8. Other matters of common concern to both company and union.

The reporting process for the first group of items consists, in fact, of handing over to the union the four main budgeting documents – orders and sales, finance, manpower and profits – and the four *post hoc* accounts for these items. They bear a 'secret' stamp, and managers said they thought it was reasonably well respected, though it is somewhat doubtful whether these budget documents really reveal all the company's secret plans.

About the effectiveness of these councils there is room for doubt. One man who had spent four years on the central Federation Executive could remember no occasion on which the union had forced management to change policy. None of the Federation Executive members has any accounting experience, and they employ no university graduates on their research staff. (Not because they could not afford the salary; more probably because educational qualifications carry such prestige in Japan that it would be awkward for them – none of them university graduates – to have such a subordinate). They seek reinforcement by hiring professors from reputable universities at considerable expense to lecture to them on the Japanese economy and on how to analyse company accounts, and they feel reasonably confident of their grasp of what goes on in Hitachi. But they do not feel sufficiently well informed, nor do they feel that they carry sufficient weight, to challenge managers' plans for the development of the firm. So they content themselves with pointing out possible gaps between production plans on the one hand and manpower plans on the other which seem likely to lead to an intensification of work, or to asking for increased expenditure on welfare. 'After all, it's only a place to talk things over. You have your say and they have theirs and that's that. Nothing with any binding force is decided.'

At the central level, the union sometimes raises broader issues. The Federation chairman gave as instances from a 1970 meeting: pollution problems; rumours that the firm was contemplating a joint venture in Taiwan which the union hoped was not true since it would spoil prospects for building relations with China; and armaments. He said that he expressed the hope that Hitachi would not get involved in the armaments industry, particularly in association with American firms. 'I told him that we hoped Hitachi would remain true to the firm's traditions, not getting entangled with foreign capital and concentrating on raising the level of home-grown Japanese technology.'

Some idea of the nature of a council meeting at the factory level may be gained from the Taga union news-sheet's report of the discussion which followed the general manager's report at a meeting in May 1970.

'*Union*: It looks as if market competition is likely to be tougher in the future and the only way to win out will be to cut costs in order to keep prices down. How are you proposing to go about this?

Company: We hope we can cut out a lot of waste here and there and build a high efficiency, high production system. There is also the problem of our sub-contractors whom we hope to give stricter, though understanding, guidance.

Union: There seems to be a great emphasis on exports. Will American trade restrictions – quotas etc. – affect that?

Company: There's not much problem with our products. It is general trade conditions that will affect us, rather; particularly a revaluation of the yen if that should happen.

167

Union: Every month we seem to get a rush to finish orders in the last five days of the month so as to fulfil monthly production quotas, with a great deal of overtime. A more even flow of work would be a more effective way of raising production.

Company: The trouble comes from bottlenecks in the supply of components. We are hoping to improve our system of ordering from sub-contractors and make sure we don't let them take on more than they can deliver. . . .

Union: In these connections what are your manpower plans?

Company: Our number of indirect workers is rather high for our volume of production, but we're hoping to put our spare resources into the development of new products. As far as manual workers are concerned we are not planning to take on any 'mid-career recruits' this quarter. Altogether about eighty or ninety people will be posted as 'helpers' to sales stations. [A device to give the man on the shop floor a sense of what happens to his work.] As for postings to other [sub-contractor] firms, it should run at about thirty people through the year.

Union: We would like to reserve our observations on welfare and on overtime for the appropriate committees.

Company: Agreed.

UNION LEADERS

Although there is no doubt about the intelligence and general efficiency of union leaders, both at plant and Federation level, and both in contexts such as these and in negotiations proper, it was generally thought that union leaders now were less of a match for managers than in the late forties. Then they included a number of university graduates who were among the most able of their generation of recruits to the firm (and many of whom are now in key executive positions in the firm). Since the roll-back, however, university graduates sometimes take union positions at the departmental level (though even there with diminishing readiness), but they do not seek higher leadership positions in the union. Compared with the exciting, hungry days after the war, union activity has ceased to be an adventurous crusade. The career of union leader can no longer be thought of as a stepping stone to a place of eminence in a post-revolutionary government. In fact, it is no longer seen by anybody as a career at all, but merely as an interlude – which might last for ten years or so if one seeks a chairmanship or a secretaryship, but in most cases lasts for four or five. (Even the chairman of the Federation of Electrical Machine Workers Unions, now rather beyond the Hitachi orbit after twenty-five years of union activity, is expected to return to his home factory at some time before he is due to collect his retirement benefit, though the benefit comes to him whether he does so or not.) For a university graduate a spell in union office is now simply an interruption of his career, liable to diminish his promotion chances.

At the lower levels the motives which draw rank and file workers into union positions include many which operate equally in England. It is flattering to have one's leadership qualities recognized; it is gratifying if one has some facility in self-expression or in combative negotiation, to have a chance to exercise that ability. Committee meetings are a welcome break in the routine, and for manual workers who were good at school, the chance to do paperwork again can seem like a chance to revive disappearing skills. 'I took the job because I felt I was getting more and more like a vegetable mentally, working all day with my hands', said one Furusato council member. There are differences too, however. It is probably rarer in Hitachi than in England to enter a union career from any inherited sense of class-conscious trade union militancy. And one motive which, *per contra*, is important in Hitachi and rare in England is the sense of *noblesse oblige* which prompts a foreman or a vice-foreman to take on a union position as the natural leader of his group. An almost analagous situation is not wholly unknown in England. At Liverpool one or two pool-leaders – vice-foremen who receive only a bonus supplement and do not have staff status, very much the opposite numbers of the *bōshin* referred to above as 'vice-foremen' – are at the same time shop stewards. But this was rare, and although foremen sometimes belong to the AEF – the same union as many of the workers whom they direct – they belong to organizationally different branches and are rarely – if ever – active union members.

At the Furusato works, in contrast, some 60% of departmental (workshop) union committee chairmen were foremen or superintendents, and they made up about 40% of the 250 members of the general council, though it was said that in recent years they were increasingly giving way to younger people, which meant partly an increase in the number of *bōshin*, but also of rank and file workers.

This power of the foremen in the union does not amount to quite the same perversion of trade union principles as one might imagine given British trade union traditions. Both foremen and the next rank of supervisors (usually called superintendents in British factories) are union members paid according to the same scales as the other workers. And the older tradition of the foreman, as a kind of paternal master-craftsman leading a small group of workmen who are personal dependents, is not dead. It is, moreover, the foreman who does the

169

bargaining with the rate-fixers over piecework times, and a foreman who is a union official can be 'got at' by the full-time officials and put under moral pressure to drive a stiffer bargain.

In short, Hitachi workers do not conceive of the workshop situation as a straightforward 'us' and 'them' situation in which the foreman is usually seen as one of 'them'. In Britain there is an important dividing line between those who only take orders and those who, in any capacity, give them – a line symbolized by their membership in different unions. In Japan, to anticipate the discussion in Chapter 9, the pyramid of command is seen as more finely graded, and the line of division between foreman and senior workers is not seen as being so definitively more important than that between older workers and younger workers.

There are however, lines which do represent discontinuities in the status system – those which divided fairly effectively the career lines of those who have not graduated from high school from those who have, and the latter in turn from university graduates. For those bumping up against such barriers union activity can seem an attractive proposition. Six of the nine full-time officers at the Furusato factory were graduates of the firm's Hitachi Industrial Training School. They had all reached positions such as that of superintendent, foreman or rate-fixer, but their likely ceiling was only one or two steps higher – whereas those who had spent the years 15 to 18 in a regular high school (academic or technical) had rather better chances of further promotion. Resentment at this blocking of their career chances was generally thought to be a fairly powerful source of their interest in union activity. Similarly, the age 24 to 25 was said to be a good time to recruit high school graduates into union activity. They are too busy studying until that time, but even those who succeed in getting a year at one of the firm's advanced training schools are likely to find that university graduates are overtaking them in salary at around the age of 25, and those who realize, around the age of 23 or 24, that despite their efforts to improve themselves they are not likely to gain admission to one of the advanced training schools are even riper candidates for a slightly embittered entry into union affairs.

But neither embitterment nor militancy is by any means a necessary qualification for union office. Most of the people who are elected as council members or workshop chairmen have not actively sought their position but have been invited into it. Offices rotate fairly rapidly at this level and it is the job of a workshop chairman to see that suitable people are persuaded to offer themselves as candidates at elections. Usually, the number of candidates exactly equals the number of places available and in place of a secret ballot election there is a secret ballot vote of confidence in the chosen co-optees. The same process takes place for the election of the three main officers and the rest of the executive. When they have decided between them how many shall stand down when their two-year term ends, they pick likely candidates from the general council to fill those positions. (In the confidence vote at Taga the various executive officers received individually between 3,250 and 3,350 favourable votes out of 3,800 cast in 1968. Voting ratios were close to 100% – the workshop committee rounds up voters. The results of the ballots are posted, but not now reported in the news-sheet which goes outside the factory, lest outsiders be too impressed by any minority expression of lack of confidence in the union leaders.)

Occasionally someone will resent not being invited to stand strongly enough to offer himself as an unsponsored candidate. This causes considerable consternation. When it happened in one of Taga's forty-six departments in the council elections in 1970 a contest was finally avoided. The outsider was persuaded to stand down on the promise of being sponsored the next time round. At Furusato, particularly in the bigger workshops, election contests do sometimes take place, and there have on two occasions in the last ten years been contested elections for the executive committee. One young executive member claimed to deplore the co-optation system and to have himself agreed to be a candidate for the council – the first step in his union career – only when he had persuaded six other colleagues to stand so that there could be a contested election. But the general view is that election contests are best avoided; they are liable to leave too much bitterness behind in a firm where the 'harmony' which appears in the founder's motto is not just a slogan but a regulating principle of social relationships, abandoned at one's peril.

AMBIVALENT COPARTNERSHIP

This does not, however, complete the story of how people get elected, as is shown in the following record of an interview with a man who had several years' experience on the federation executive.

'— Of course – and this applies throughout the company – it's just not possible for the union to sponsor whoever it likes for full-time official positions. The wishes of the company enter into the matter too.

— How?

— Well, we consult with the company – you see there's the question of the work situation where he's working. . . . I mean, for example, the union decides it wants to put up X; X is the union's first choice. But then you've got to look at what would happen in his shop if he were taken off the job. So the union goes along to the company and says: Look: we'd like to have X because he's such and such, but what does the company think of the idea? One always approaches the company first and one's got to make some kind of settlement, because sometimes the company might say: No, it would be very awkward if this chap were elected an official.

— Awkward having him to negotiate with, do you mean?

— Sometimes, yes, but not very often.

— Are people ever not put forward because of the Company's objections.

— Oh, yes. Sometimes it's because he's indispensable in the job he's in; sometimes there's no particular problem as far as the job is concerned but he's – well, ideologically speaking, his approach to things – the company will say: We see a bit of a problem there, and in the end the union has to give up the idea. It's understandable, really, that the company should look at a man and add up the pluses and minuses, and if the balance is on the minus side they shouldn't want him to be an official.

— But he could still stand as a candidate for election?

— Yes, but he wouldn't get elected. Nobody has got that much *personal* organized support.

— No, I mean that the union could still officially sponsor him as a candidate.

— Mm. But it wouldn't, you see.'

If one is looking for evidence that the Hitachi union is just a 'company union' one could find it elsewhere. Union leaders, particularly of the older generation of 'survivors' from the 1950 roll-back, make no bones about their intense dislike of communists – their opponents at the time of the great strike; men whose loyalty lies outside Hitachi, who would happily sacrifice the interests of the firm for political advantage. Plausible stories are told of co-operation between union and management in keeping communists out of the company, giving them punitive out-postings, or, if they show signs of repentance, giving them jobs on condition that they do not meddle in union affairs. Whereas in British factories the rule that union representatives should not meet management without a witness is often broken, in Japan it does not exist. Personnel officers sometimes invite union leaders for golf or for a boozy evening party at a Japanese-style restaurant. The reverse also happens with the union leaders playing host – but rather less often. (One estimate put company expenditure on such affairs at about double union expenditure.)

From the vantage point of the British trade union tradition, it is all extremely suspicious. And yet . . . it would be surprising if officials of the ETU – a union which had experienced factional bitterness between communists and their opponents similar to that generated in Japan in 1950 – had never co-operated with management to keep communist activists out of factories. And it can be argued that amiable social contacts are by no means necessarily corrupting. (Even before the roll-back, when the Hitachi union was in an undoubtedly militant phase, there was an annual baseball match and party between personnel officers and union leaders.) It could indeed be held that the absence of such contacts between managers and shop steward conveners in England is largely due to the social class gulf which often divides them – would they drink in the saloon bar or the public? – and which managements may seek to maintain on the assumption that intimacy weakens authority. (Liverpool managers were discouraged from drinking in the company's workers club just outside the factory gates.) Where equality of status is assumed – as between MPs of opposing parties in Britain – bouts of public contest can be interspersed with amicable social contacts – *provided* they belong to what used to be called the Butskellite centre. (It is doubtful, for example, whether there is much fraternizing between members of the Monday Club and the Tribune group.)

That last proviso is important. There must be a good deal of common ground. Such common ground clearly exists between managers and union leaders in Hitachi. They consciously share two major assumptions: first, that the prosperity of the firm is a precondition for all their other objectives; secondly, that a real mud-slinging stand-up fight (a *doro-jiai* – a phrase which came up frequently in conversation on these matters) would be extremely unpleasant and would in the end benefit no one. It is the second assumption which explains why the union leader quoted above – who was not naive and had not learned nothing on trade union tours to Europe and America – could describe the union's deference to the company's wishes in the matter of electing officers without a sense of making a shocking revelation. Given that assumption it makes sense to choose union leaders who will be able to get along with their opposite numbers. No one, after all, sends an ambassador to a foreign country without getting that country's *agrément* first.

But both the sovereign national power analogy and the gentlemanly beyond-ideology government/opposition analogy break down. They imply an equality of prestige and mutuality of respect, and that cannot exist unless, at least potentially, the two parties are in some ways equal in power *vis-à-vis* each other. But as between managers and union leaders the asymmetry of power is not likely to be reversed. To be sure, union leaders sometimes claim that they *do* have equality of power, that their possession of the weapons of the overtime ban and the strike severely limit the managers' power to make decisions. But they are very unwilling to push their luck and try using these weapons other than in the now institutionalized process of annual wage bargaining. (See later, p. 177.) For the most part, their power – their power, for instance, to impose a ceiling on the number of overtime hours to be worked or to secure the company's co-operation in collecting subscriptions by the check-off – rests on the company's tolerance or sense of long-term self-interest, not on the strength of the opposition they could put up. The union is a Finland to the management's Russia.

The gap between the assumption of equality which could justify their co-operative attitude towards management and the reality of power inequality explains why union leaders feel somewhat ambivalent about their position. The European trade union ideal of the militant, uncompromising embattled minority still has ethical force for most of them. That is why few would be quite so frank in revealing the company's role in union elections as the man quoted earlier, and few would like to admit that they are entertained at the company's expense.

The company does its best to diminish this gap by affording union officials at least formal equality of respect. A Hitachi union leader does not, like an English Electric shop steward, have to go along in person to ask the personnel manager's secretary if he can have an appointment. He picks up the telephone and calls directly. (To cite one incident witnessed: a union member phoned to complain that members of his shop who lived in a village where a mayoral election was to be held the next day were likely to be late even if they voted as soon as the polling booth opened. Their superintendent was proposing to count them as late-comers. With a quick telephone call the union official got a promise from the personnel office to broadcast a message immediately that lateness for this reason would be condoned.)

Union leaders, too, are at pains to make it clear that they are not the creatures of management, that within a context of general co-operation they reserve the right to differ sharply with managers over the distribution of rewards or about the extent to which the company

174

has a right to demand effort or the sacrifice of individuality from its employees. A personnel manager described the obvious delight with which union officials stamped 'not agreed' on overtime clearances he sometimes took along to them. (The Furusato Plant Union has an agreement that no one should work more than sixty-five hours a month of overtime except for matters of urgency. A central union official must agree to the exceptions, and a formal system whereby management can apply to the union has been worked out.) Similarly, if not in equal measure, union leaders insist upon *returning* hospitality to managers. They accept the convenience of the right to hold lunch-hour meetings in the workshop, but they build their own committee rooms and lecture rooms to secure the privacy of their discussions. They accept such information on wages as managers give them, but they carry out their own independent survey of wages by questionnaires. They accept the company's good offices for collecting union dues, indeed they consider the check-off as a right, but they use the money so collected to provide their own facilities – offices and telephones – independently of the company's good will (unlike the senior stewards at English Electric factories who have to rely on what the company sees fit to provide). A measure of the degree of 'stand-off' which the union feels necessary is given by the following 'agreed note' appended to the Furusato plant contract which fills out the details of the central contract between the Federation and the company:

'The union is not opposed to morning physical exercise before the daily commencement of work, but whereas the company requested the co-operation of the Union in ensuring that all employees take part, the union insisted on the principle of voluntary participation.'

To be sure unions differ, even within Hitachi, in the extent to which they insist on a 'legalistic' demonstration of their independence and reinforcement of their rights. The Furusato and the Taga unions – the latter with a much higher proportion of girls and young men, a 'clean' domestic appliance factory without the greasier, rougher skilled tradesman traditions of the Furusato plant – are different in this regard. Apropos of a similar Furusato plant 'agreed note' promising consultation before dismissals (see p. 186) a Taga union official was somewhat scornful.

'Those people at Furusato are fond of memoranda and notes of agreement and such. We laugh at them sometimes. We think there's often more to be accomplished by talking things over than by being legalistic over things. We take it for granted that the company will never dismiss anybody without consulting us. It's as much in their interests as in ours to keep to the custom and practice that's been developed. Very often you find that if you insist on getting things down in writing you end up with a much less favourable agreement than you had before.'

THE DIVISION OF FUNCTIONS: FEDERATION AND PLANT UNION

Within this structure of attitudes and organization, what actual transactions take place? The central function of the union, of course, is to raise wages, and this has been pre-empted by the central Hitachi Federation much more fully than, in England, by the central Confederation bargaining with the Engineering Employers' Federation. Plant negotiations have little importance. It is the annual central 'spring offensive' which settles wages (including those of managers who get pro-rated rises), the central summer and year-end bonus negotiations determine bonuses, and occasional *ad hoc* 'struggles', also at the central level, change the retirement payment plan which applies to everyone. The individual plant unions do not negotiate over such matters. Their function is to rally support for the central negotiators, by creating a situation in which the company would find itself facing a severe loss of morale among its work force if it refused to accede to the union's demands.

The spring offensive gets under way in February when the Federation of Electrical Machine Workers' Unions announces the minimum demands which it expects all its constituent unions to make – in 1970 mostly in the form of a new minimum wage scale for sample ages, together with a general average 'base-up' of 9,000 yen (over £10) per month. Then, in early March, the Hitachi Federation announces its own proposed demands – in the form of a detailed list of average per capita increases for each separate item of the wage (so much for the job-linked payment, so much for family allowances, etc.) totalling in 1970 an average of 9,950 yen per capita. These proposals are sent for discussion to each plant union. First, the plant executive issues a provisional statement of its views of these demands – always favourable, not usually requesting any changes, but perhaps making some suggestions about priorities. The plant executive's statement is then discussed within the plant at workshop meetings and at an emergency general congress, and there approved and sent off to the Hitachi Federation. The Federation executive then finalizes its demands in the light of plant union representations and presents them to the company at the end of March.

Meanwhile, in addition to these decision-making meetings (formal or real), March is a month for a multiplicity of meetings, rallies and study groups, designed to 'deepen understanding and heighten fighting determination'. There are general meetings for all union members, delegate meetings organized by the plant union youth section, by the Ibaragi Prefecture Liaison Committee of Hitachi Company Unions, or by the youth section of the Ibaragi branch of the Electrical Confederation. They consist usually of lectures, speeches and, in the case of the youth section meetings, community singing ending with a rousing three cheers for victory followed, sometimes, by a 'demo' through the streets. From March onwards all union members wear badges declaiming 'Victory in the Spring Struggle' and in mid-March a ballot is held to place the right to call a strike in the hands of the Federation executive. (At Taga, in 1970, there were some 200 out of 4,600 votes cast against.)

Eventually the company makes what is likely to be an unacceptable reply. Three times only since 1956 has an agreement been reached after further negotiations without recourse to a strike. But usually at a suitable stage, the union issues a declaration that it is breaking off relations. ('We have made no progress on x, y, and z. We can no longer believe the company's reiterated statements that they are genuinely seeking a settlement in good faith. . . . We have decided on direct action, relying on solidarity and the strength of our organization to force the company to reconsider. . . .') In 1970 this was reported to the Taga workers in a special bulletin. Underneath the Federation statement came a little panel formally reinforcing, in crisp military/bureaucratic style[1] the message of the banner headlines.

'Instruction (Taga Plant Union Order No. 48).

In accordance with Federation Order 31/4 (1970 Spring Offensive Order No. 1) the following instructions are issued:

1. All union members are to cease overtime and holiday work effective 16 April.

2. A strike will be carried out for 48 hours from 22 April.'

The flags and the red arm bands are brought out for the pre-strike evening rally, but on the day of the strike itself there is no fuss or bother. The workers enjoy their extra spring holiday and dig their

[1] The military flavour is characteristic of Japanese left-wing movements when engaged in 'struggles'. Militant students, as well as taking great pleasure in planning complex skirmishing tactics for their confrontations with the police, were given to distributing leaflets (to other students, unconnected with their organization) headed, e.g. *Struggle Order No. 6* (using the same military word, *shirei*, as was used in the Taga document).

177

gardens. Union officials dress up in red head scarves to do a little formal picketing, but they have no thought that there might be any strike-breakers to head off. The plant contract contains precise regulations as to who strikes and who does not, and like most regulations in Japanese factories, they are obeyed. After the strike, work resumes as normal without dispute. At Taga in 1970, in response to demands from union members, and after consultation between all Hitachi unions in the area, it was agreed to let every bachelor withdraw 2,000 yen, and every married man 4,000 yen from his individual strike-fund account.

In 1970, before a further planned one-day strike was held, the Company had made a somewhat better offer and (on 27 March) the Federation sent to all plant unions its recommendation for a settlement – at an average 8,550 yen per capita increase, compared with its 9,950 demand. (In doing so, it broke ranks within the Electrical Confederation and earned some opprobrium. The Confederation had been planning a further industry-wide one-day strike for the next day, and by recommending a settlement earlier – and for an amount barely above the 8,500 yen minimum that all constituent unions were pledged not to withdraw below – Hitachi, by its size and influence, had in effect set a ceiling to what lesser unions could now hope to get.)

The Hitachi Federation's recommendation for a settlement was discussed by the plant union's councils the next day at two-hour morning meetings. The delegates returned at lunch-time for workshop meetings in each workshop, at which they were instructed how to vote at the next plant council meeting on the 30th. This is the moment at which grumbles come to the surface. Some of the delegates have a rough time – particularly in the drawing offices when a high-school graduate delegate faces vocal young university graduates. But there has never been any doubt about the final outcome. With a few grumbling reservations the plant union telegraphs to Tokyo its support of the Federation's settlement. At Taga, in 1970, one out of fifty-three delegates on the council abstained and none voted against approval of the settlement in the final show of hands. At Furusato some 30% – a normal proportion for this slightly more contentious factory – voted against.

The spring offensive is the time of the year when the union comes into its own. As one union vice-chairman put it: 'during the spring offensive we are more careful about our behaviour'. Not only do the union leaders not give or accept (or indeed receive) social invitations from the personnel managers; in discussions they are careful to preserve sterner, graver countenances than in the more relaxed smiling encounters which mark negotiations at other times of the year. The interest of union members, too, is more likely to be aroused. At the Furusato factory, attendance at lunch-hour workshop meetings is not normally very high; 40 or 50% of members prefer to hide behind the machines, or sit out in the sun, chatting or playing Japanese chess. But when wage negotiations are in progress there is usually 100% turn-out, even though there might be two or three such meetings in a week.

Sub-group Interest and Differentials

One of the purposes of the workshop and council meetings in the weeks preceding a wage claim is, in addition to arousing support for demands, to discuss the union's policy with regard to the *structure* of wages – whether there should be greater or lesser differentials between supervisors and workers, or between younger and older workers. In some departments, the departmental committee, when persuading people to offer themselves for election to the general council, were careful to try to get a spread of ages. At the centre, essentially the same reconciliation of interest groups has to take place within the Hitachi Federation as takes place in working out a negotiating position within the Confederation of Shipbuilding and Engineering Unions in Britain. The differences are that in the Hitachi case the span of differentials concerned is broader (including supervisors and junior managers, for example), the relevant differentials are different (younger versus older, rather than skilled versus unskilled) and there is even less clear separate representation of separate interest groups.

Moreover, the structure of the wage system is such that changes in the distribution of rewards can be effected in all kinds of complex ways which do not lend themselves to clear-cut public discussion. Whereas in British negotiations, distribution is simply a matter of settling skill differentials, in Japan the relative fortunes of the main interest groups – age groups with no clearly defined boundaries – can be affected by adjustments of a very large number of variables whose effect can be calculated only by experts – for example:

the minimum and average ages for moving up the seniority grades (See Table 3.6);

the rate of increase in the annual wage increments as one goes up the seniority grades (Table 3.6);

the guaranteed average and minimum merit rating for each seniority grade and the steepness of the rise thereof (p. 102);

guarantees linking minimum job-grade payments to certain ages (p. 106);
the distribution of the total wage bill between basic salary element (favouring older workers), merit supplement (favouring older workers if the rise in the average merit rating is steep), family allowances (also favouring older workers) and job-related payments (favouring younger workers) (Table 3.4).

Given, therefore, the absence of any obvious cutting points on the age continuum which might clearly divide the interest groups involved, given that these vague age/interest groups are internally divided into those who are doing well with large merit increases and those who are not, and given the complexity of the issues, it is not surprising that the wage policies of individual plant unions tend to be based solely on their leaders' intuitive perception of where the major injustices and dissatisfactions lie.

It is true, however, that Japanese unions do have, as the British Confederation (being concerned only with manual workers) does not, the additional problem of reaching agreement on the appropriate differentials between the manual worker scale, the administrative worker scale, the supervisor's scale and the junior manager's scale (see Table 3.6). Here the relevant interest groups *are* clearly defined. For this very reason, open discussion of these differentials tends to be deliberately muted. The assumption that the existing differentials are an ineluctable given is a convenient one for the leaders of individual plant unions to adopt since it avoids conflict within the union ranks.

To be sure, when differentials are perceived as glaringly unfair, the union has to take some position. Thus, in the early sixties, the differentials in bonus payments were considerably greater than the differentials in wages. The following were the multiples in June 1962. (They are the multiples of the 'basic salary' element in the wage. Since this basic salary is already different for the different grades, the different multiples exaggerated differentials in monthly wages.)

'Junior managers and technologists (average) 1,554%
Clerical workers (averages). From 806% (8th grade) to 1167% (1st grade)
Manual workers (averages). From 730% (8th grade) to 981% (1st grade).'

The union consistently entered the annual bonus negotiations with the demand for a 'reduction of differentials' and indeed the differential between clerical and manual workers disappeared in the mid-sixties. But this was not so much because the union pushed hard as because the company, responding to the much greater scarcity of manual workers than clerical workers, wanted it that way. And the company has even succeeded in widening the differentials between junior managers and others. (Its negotiators believe that managerial workers deserve higher bonuses because they make a 'greater contribution' – and they themselves, of course, have a stake in maintaining this view since senior managers' bonus levels are linked to the junior manager percentage.) Bonus multiples in June 1970 were 1,049% for the average junior manager compared with averages for clerical and manual workers ranging from 378% to 693% depending on the grade. ('Average' because some receive a higher and some a lower percentage depending on their merit rating.)

Union leaders are simply not prepared to press hard on this issue. One remarked with some satisfaction that grumbles from the clerical and manual workers had diminished in recent years because of the size of annual increases – 'they compare with what they got last year, not with what other people get'. The reasons why union leaders do not press the issue are fairly clear. First, they face the danger of a split at the Federation level. Some unions – the head office union, the research institutes' unions, the sales branch unions – are composed predominantly of men in the junior manager grades who are doing well out of the present differentials. Those plant unions are prepared to subscribe to the ideal of greater equality provided it is not implemented – at least not implemented too radically or too soon. Secondly, if open disagreement did break out at the Federation level it would spread also to the plant level in those unions which have a majority of manual and clerical workers, but still sizeable groups of managerial workers. The bonus differential issue is, therefore, one of those fiercer dogs which every union leader concerned with union solidarity would prefer to let lie sleeping.

THE PLANT UNION

On any one of these matters of pay and conditions, there is in theory no constitutional obstacle to the plant unions' taking the bargaining initiative and seeking a plant agreement, irrespective of the Hitachi Federation's position.[2] A Furusato Plant Union official, for instance, said they had toyed, wistfully, with the idea of starting a campaign to increase the level of overtime premia (for rates current in 1970 see Table 3.3) but a plant union official who embarked on such an enterprise would be taking his life in his hands. He could fail completely, whereas the Federation's spring offensive never fails completely; it only achieves something closer to or further away from,

[2] The 1970 change in structure to a unitary union with plant branches will alter the situation, however.

what was demanded. Moreover, the likelihood of failing is very great, for the management normally insists on company-wide uniformity in major personnel matters, and the chance of arousing sufficient determination and solidarity within the plant to break that insistence would be low – given that people would be called on to strike without the comforting thought that all of Hitachi's 80,000 other workers were striking simultaneously.

What then is the plant union's function? 'That's a question that worries us somewhat', said the official who had spoken wistfully about the prospects of a plant strike over a plant union demand. As compared with the Bradford or Liverpool factories, the Furusato union had an organization neatly designed to deliver considerable power into the hands of union leaders. Nine full-time officials wholly devoted to the affairs of the Furusato plant are stationed immediately outside the factory gates. Every shop is represented at the council which meets every month, and the delegates report back to lunch-hour meetings of their department. There is one shop steward ('actually a member of the department union committee') for every twenty to thirty workers and they all have direct access to the full-time officials – all conditions contrasting with the British situation.

The plant unions are not inactive, but on the other hand they have considerably less impact on the running of the Furusato and Taga factories than the shop steward structure has in English Electric. This will become clear if we make a point-by-point comparison of the kinds of matters dealt with by shop stewards in an English Electric factory and search for the equivalent in Hitachi.

1. First, of course, a prime concern of a British shop steward is wage rates and piecework rates, and a good deal of his persuasive power is deployed against rate-fixers or against managers seeking to introduce new payment systems. The payment system in Hitachi has one opportunity for such bargaining in the piecework system which has some effect on the wage (see p. 107), and there is, indeed, a 'Standard Times Committee' of union and management, separate from the ordinary grievance procedure, to review piecework rates. In practice, however, it hardly functions.

There are several reasons for this. First, the effect which the piecework system has on wages is minimal (see p. 108). It is not particularly salient in the workers' consciousness. Secondly, the job of arguing with the rate-fixers if there is any danger of performance falling below the average 100% figure, is the job of the foreman. In English Electric, too, foremen who want to keep a happy shop may covertly try to persuade a rate-fixer to raise prices, but only covertly because the foreman is *supposed* to be on the firm's side – helping to get more for less. The differences at Hitachi are that in most departments bonuses are group bonuses so that the foreman himself is the man who handles all the group's tickets, secondly – as we shall see when discussing work organization – the Japanese foreman is more *expected* to play the role of protective leader of his men.

The union does get involved, however, in general policy matters relating to piecework. Union officials quoted one pertinent instance. Hitachi quoted very low prices on certain foreign contracts in order to break into the export market. In order not actually to lose money a general instruction went out to the rate-fixers that there should be a tightening of times all along the line. (The instruction was carried out with a certain lack of finesse. The original times were inefficiently blacked out on the ticket and new times, 10% shorter, were written in.) According to union officials they immediately short-circuited the normal grievance procedure and took the matter straight to the central plant negotiating committee, where they got the instructions countermanded.

Other wage matters in which the union might get involved are provisions for special allowances – heat and dirt money in the foundry, for instance. But this involves intra-union negotiations. The union representative of the foundry must persuade the other members of the general council to include such a demand in the next round of wage negotiations.

2. A second concern of British shop stewards is to ensure that no piece of work is classified below its proper skill level – i.e. allowed to be done by men earning a lower hourly rate than the appropriate one. Such questions obviously do not arise in Hitachi.

3. Nor does the other type of demarcation dispute (not particularly common at English Electric either) which does not necessarily involve 'letting the company get away with something' but is simply a conflict of interest between two groups of workmen – a dispute between plumbers and electricians, say, who might be receiving the same rate but each claim the right to do a certain job. An Hitachi man is not primarily typed as either a plumber or an electrician. He is an Hitachi employee, and while Hitachi employees have a stronger sense of an 'employment right' than their British counterparts they have little sense of 'job right'.

4. A fourth kind of case taken up by British shop stewards is that which arises from changes or proposed changes in production which

are seen as threatening existing job rights – new machines which either make the work harder, or reduce the number of jobs. Here a distinction has to be drawn. Innovations which merely reduce manning cause no problems because in the Hitachi system people are absorbed elsewhere with rarely any loss of salary. Innovations which lead in effect to an intensification of the pace of work sometimes do. We will deal with them below together with a similar category.

5. Fifth come working conditions – matters of safety, toilet facilities, draughts from unrepaired windows, preventable heat and grime and so on. In English Electric these are matters which may be dealt with by shop stewards but are also within the province of the works committee. In Hitachi they are the business of the union if they cannot be solved by direct representation to superiors. The grievance procedure is laid down in the contract between the company and the union. Each department has a committee made up of three union and three management representatives. Anyone with a grievance takes it to a grievance committee member in his department. The latter then either sorts the matter out directly with a manager or formally follows procedure by registering the grievance in quadruplicate on the prescribed form so that it can go to the committee. If no solution is obtained at that point the matter goes to a plant grievance committee. If that committee fails to resolve it, the matter becomes a dispute and is referred to the plant negotiating committee from which it may be referred to the local tripartite labour Commission for mediation, conciliation or arbitration. Strikes (with twenty hours' notice) may begin if there is failure in the plant negotiating committee to reach agreement, irrespective of whether approaches to the local Labour Commission are being made.

The complaints coming in this category which are lodged – about 300 a year – rarely even become matters for the negotiating committee. Only a small proportion of them even get to the first formal stage of quadruplicate registration. Many are taken first not to the grievance committee representative but to the full-time officials in the union office. (This is, in fact, recommended as an alternative procedure in the union diary.) The reason, clearly, is that one can more easily expect a full-time union official whose position is secure to take up a complaint, than a grievance committee member who is in one's own department and dependent on the same superior as oneself – the superior whose negligence or unfairness may be the cause of the complaint.

Perhaps English Electric workers, too, if they had a realistic choice between getting an outsider to take up a grievance or a

184

steward fellow-worker, would often prefer the former. But the preference of Japanese workers is likely to be stronger: (a) because the union representative in one's work place may be a foreman; and (b) because the adversary bargaining nature of management/worker relations – although perfectly acceptable at the company level – is not acceptable at the micro-level of an individual department in the way that it is acceptable in England. (Or at least has not been since departmental managers were subjected to kangaroo courts in 1951. And the *extreme* nature of the tactics in 1951 are in themselves an indication of the fact that they were a departure from traditionally deferential, rather than egalitarian-adversarial relations)

There is a generalizable point here which illuminates the discussion of British unions' hesitancy about adopting a copartnership stance. Where adversary opposition is institutionalized so that each man's position clearly falls either on the union or on the management side, individuals are not faced with agonizing personal choices even when conflict is endemic. The foreman does not hold it personally against his workers that they follow the shop-steward's lead in challenging him (though he may hold it against the shop steward for challenging too hard). Only in uncertain situations – like that of the draughtsmen section leaders mentioned on p. 135 – does personal strain of any high order appear. In Hitachi any conflict which does arise is more likely to cause personal distress[3] for two reasons. First, because in matters of production there is supposed to be co-operation, not opposition – and the union also explicitly subscribes to the values of hard work (though not unfairly excessive work demands), pride in skill, efficiency and productivity; secondly, because, with foremen and junior graduate superintendents belonging to the union, the line of division in the workshop between union man and non-union man does not coincide with the line of division between those who give orders and those who are expected to obey them.

6. The final category of matters negotiated by British shop stewards may be summarized as complaints about unfairness, distinguished from the last in that, although grievances in the last category *may* result from the negligence of superiors, a grievance in this category is always a direct challenge to some superior's decision. Examples which one can find in any British shop steward's diary include, for example, dismissals and other disciplinary penalties, unfair allocation of overtime, or attempts to force people into doing overtime,

[3] Rioting students at Japanese universities usually proved to have only two alternative modes of address to teachers – either tense abusiveness or quiet deference signalled by the traditional respectful term of address, *sensei*. The egalitarian stand-off was more than they could manage.

inequitable distribution of work tasks, the rude swearing at subordinates in a manner derogatory to their individual dignity, and so on, To this should be added a particular form of 'inequitable allocation of work'. mentioned earlier – intensification of work due to some change in technique, an intensification which is seen as inequitable in comparison to previous standards of what was normal and just.

The number of complaints dealt with by Hitachi union officials coming into this category is relatively small – 50 a year, compared with 300 a year in the last category and (according to a rough count through a chief shop steward's diary) about 80 a year in the Bradford factory with half the number of employees.

One possible reason for this difference in frequency – that Hitachi workers put less trust in their union representatives than British workers – can be disposed of first. When they were asked this following question, 38% of Hitachi workers said they would go to the union official first, compared with 20% in Babcocks' and 14% in Marconi.[4]

'When something's gone wrong for you personally and you want to complain about it or get it put right, do you go to a union official first, or straight to your foreman? I am not asking about what the procedure is supposed to be, but what actually happens.' [The last sentence was omitted from the Japanese version.]

One reason for the difference in volume of complaints is simply that the events which give rise to disputes at English Electric occur less frequently at Hitachi. Dismissals, for example, are extremely rare. Fifty-seven persons out of 85,000 employees in the course of a year (see p. 33) is a small proportion, a tribute to the care taken in selection procedures, and also to the 'totalitarian' nature of the workshop atmosphere where incipient delinquency/rebellion is a matter for such general concern that the incipient delinquent is either shamed or brainwashed back to the straight and narrow path or else leaves voluntarily because he cannot stand the moral pressure. (Compared with the English situation where the incipient delinquent/rebel may receive encouragement from his workmates since he acts out anti-authority fantasies which they make no bones about acknowledging.)

The dismissals which do take place are, however, clearly of more consequence in a lifetime employment system than in a system with much mobility. Again the rules are carefully laid down. The union contract contains within itself all the factory rules – a list of the fourteen admissible causes for dismissal, and of the other more

<hr />

[4] Replies may have been partly influenced by cultural preferences – in Japan for 'go-between' resolution of conflict, in Britain for 'having it out straight'.

venial sins which merit disciplinary warnings, fines or suspensions (see p. 242). In this way the union participates in framing and upholding the rules. Until 1951 it also had the decisive voice in applying them. But now that belongs to the prerogative of management. In the central contract there is a promise only that the union will be 'informed' beforehand of a dismissal or suspension, or of any intention to give publicity to a fine or a warning. The Furusato Plant Union's contract goes a little further with an appended 'agreed note'. 'Although the contract specifies only that the union will be informed . . . every effort will be made to ensure that harmony is preserved between company and union in all cases of disciplinary action.' And indeed the union does occasionally fight such disciplinary action. In a recent case at another Hitachi factory a driver who overtook on a blind corner and was responsible for an accident which cost two lives, was at first dismissed. The union objected and the company retracted the dismissal and allowed him to resign.[5]

Another item in the list of British grievances probably less common in Japan is the kind of bull-necked aggressiveness which earns some (nowadays a diminishing number) British foremen and supervisors such nicknames as 'big-'ead' or 'loud-mouth'. This is not a common feature of the Japanese supervisory style. Foremen may be curt and arrogant, but rarely blusteringly aggressive.

On the other hand, there is one source of personal grievance which is peculiar to Japan. Japanese workers are guaranteed – by law, quite apart from union contract – a rather generous number of holidays per year. These are to be taken in such a way as to cause least inconvenience to the work. The traditional Japanese concept of 'a holiday' is not a whole week or two weeks away at the seaside, but the two- or three-day trip to a hot-spring resort, to the mountains, to the capital or to a beauty spot. There is, therefore, no question of making a holiday schedule and apportioning the holidays in advance in weekly or fortnightly blocks. Instead, workers take their holidays one or two days at a time as the occasion arises. It is almost universally the practice to ask that days taken off for sickness should be counted as part of one's annual holiday. (That way one gets a perfect attendance record which automatically gets one some way towards a

[5] There is an interesting underlying factor here. British employers have a shared interest in giving honest appraisals of former workers for the benefit of future employers, since each wants accurate information about the employment record of those they employ. Hitachi, however, can afford to be considerate of individuals it dismisses and gloss over the misdemeanours in their record without any logical violation of the categorical imperative; it does not expect reciprocal honesty from other employers since it is not much interested in the market for experienced employees.

187

good merit rating.) The next, more or less legitimate, claim on holidays is for attending weddings and funerals. Those who do not use up their ten, fifteen or twenty days' holiday in these ways, may take other days off – with the foreman's agreement, though (see p. 25) it may be rather unwilling *ex post facto* agreement. Foremen are reluctant to have people take leave because they have a stake in a high attendance record and high production figures, and when order books are long they are likely to be under considerable pressure from enthusiastic managers. One can, of course, insist on taking one's holiday entitlement – and young people are more likely to take all their ten days than older people are to take twenty – but insistence on one's rights to a holiday *merely* for one's own personal pleasure when everyone else is working his heart out can well earn the foreman's displeasure – at the expense of one's merit rating and so of one's wage. The fact that the overall attendance ratio for the whole Hitachi company between April and November 1969 was in no month below 96·0% and in May was as high as 96·7%[6] is proof (since the holiday entitlement alone would amount to a good deal more than 4% of working days) that many workers do not take all their holidays. For many this self-denial is willing (there are many dedicated British managers, too, who believe themselves indispensable) for others, if not exactly willing, at least the product of a feeling that it *is* unfair to be away enjoying oneself when everyone else is working, but undoubtedly many are the not wholly willing victims of a work ethic enforced by stern foremen.

On balance, though, there *is* something to be said, in explanation of the lesser volume of individual complaints at Hitachi, for the view that it is partly because the system gives less frequent rise to complaints. The expectations of unfair dominance by supervisors, and recalcitrance from workers are sharper and more pervasive in Britain than in Japan because the workshop relationship is more generally defined as an adversarial one. Order in the Japanese workshop rests more on consensus and less on coercion or compromise. Consequently, there is less likely to be escalation in the resistance/even stronger reassertion of authority/greater resistance spiral, and less likely to be pre-emptive resort to authoritarian attempts to overbear in expectation of recalcitrance.

Another possible part of the explanation is that what would be perceived by a British worker as an intolerable infringement of his rights is not perceived as a cause of complaint in Hitachi. This is clearly to

[6] The reader may suspect, as I did at first, that this attendance record calculation must exclude the holiday allowance from the 100% of possible working days. This, however, is not the case.

some extent the case with regard to holidays. The obligations of one's work role hold higher priority in the values of Japanese than of British workers. Being told, therefore, to postpone long-cherished holiday plans to finish an urgent order might seem reasonable to a Japanese but not to a British worker.

Union officials, however, had a somewhat sharper sense of worker's rights and of what constituted a just cause for complaint. Or perhaps one should say *some* union officials. The young men who take full-time posts are to be distinguished in this regard from shop-committee influentials who are often much less preoccupied with rights than with duties.

One such was the chairman of the foundry's union committee. He had been blinded in one eye at an early age from welding with insufficient safety precautions. He was then made general tool keeper and safety officer, and in this position has advanced to the lowest of the three 'specially titled' ranks (see page 100). He took on his union job as an extension of his general role – which he had acquired thanks to his undoubted organizational and leadership skills – as organizer of safety campaigns, secretary of benevolent societies, travel clubs, etc. He spoke with enormous enthusiasm of his work. (And indeed the steady downtrend of the accident rate in the foundry was something to be proud of.) There was no doubt that he was a loyal Hitachi man. He was the proud drummer for the traditional dancing at the annual Hitachi Founder's Day Festival and his life revolved around work. 'If I thought that being in the union meant in any way disparaging work, then I wouldn't have anything to do with the union.' For him the *company* was often the innocent victim of un-scrupulous workers who chose to insist on their full quota of holidays even though essential work piled up in their absence. 'There's a lot of selfishness over this. You can take your holiday and because this is a big firm, it sticks to the Labour Standards Law, you can take holidays on false pretexts and get away with it.'

For this man, clearly, union activity was just another way of ful-filling obligations, the fulfilment of obligation being for him what life was all about. He it was, also, who showed great indignation at those who failed to attend lunch-hour union meetings and thought that an attendance register should be kept and a full record of attendance required before approval was given, for example, to loans from the workers, bank.

To be sure, when he spoke of cheating in the taking of holidays he had in mind not only cheating the company, but also imposing un-fair burdens on more conscientious fellow workers who might have to do unwanted extra overtime or work harder because of someone

189

else's insistence on his rights. Several union representatives spoke of their sense of guilt at putting extra work on others when they went to council meetings in working time.

The difference between the foundry chairman and the full-time officials was not so wide that they would consider his views outrageous and incomprehensible. The difference was one of degree. They were more likely to think in terms of workers' rights and certainly more likely to talk to outsiders in those terms. They spoke of the need, for instance, for more education of workers designed to sharpen their sense of what their rights were, and the union spent a great deal of money (on making up wages) for training courses for the 250 union councillors to sharpen their 'rights consciousness'. They speak in rather general terms, however. The union has never dared, for example, to mount a campaign in their newspaper positively *urging* union members to take all the holidays they are entitled to. By and large they have concentrated on trying to flush out into the open those who *were* resentful against what they considered an infringement of their rights but simply (in their phrase) 'cried into their pillow' – hesitated to complain because they feared the consequences of such complaint on their merit rating or their chances of promotion. Union leaders were clear that there *were* a good many workers in their factory who came into this category – a measure, said one, of the union's relative lack of effectiveness which caused *him* to raise the question as to whether the union could fairly be accused of being 'company-dominated'. They had adopted two 'listening devices' to bring complaints into the open – the works patrol (each workshop was visited fortnightly) and the complaints box in every department through which sealed letters, signed or anonymous, were delivered straight to union headquarters. (No answer to most individual complaints, of course, since names must be revealed if any redress was sought.) They suspected that most of the suppressed complaints were related to holidays, to overtime, or to resentment towards what was seen as an unfair merit-rating. As for the latter, real objective unfairness was thought by union officials to be rare. As for overtime, they had a fixed ceiling negotiated with the company. Up to fifty hours a month was permitted. A further fifteen hours could be permitted if there were special reasons and if the departmental union chairman gave his approval. (A certain amount of overtime, as in England, is seen as highly desirable. It is objectionable when too much is required and when it becomes difficult to refuse it on any particular night.) As for holidays, rather than seeking out an example and making a test case, they sought rather to persuade foremen *as union members* to be generous with requests for holidays. In one case, a foreman who was persistently offensive and inconsiderate to his subordinates (preventing one from taking days off when his wife was seriously ill, for instance) was made the subject of an official complaint. He was kicked upstairs, to a job in which he had no direct subordinates.

The only way that workers could be freed of the fear of speaking out against their superiors, of course, is by removing, as British unions have largely succeeded in doing, all occasions for supervisors to give extra rewards to favoured workers – i.e. by removing all merit-rating from the pay system, and making promotion as far as possible automatically dependent on seniority. Hitachi union leaders were aware of this, and in the annual bargaining process concerning the structure as well as the amount of wages, tried to reduce the merit element. They are prepared to accept the company's wish to enlarge the job-level supplement to cover about 50% of the wage bill if the merit supplement is removed (see pp. 98–104) but this will still leave the discretionary element in promotions and in bonuses, and it is apparent that the abolition of discretionary merit ratings does not occupy a very *high* priority in the union's objectives. Like most Hitachi workers (and, for example, like the British Clerical Workers' Union, and even with reservations DATA, which do not object to merit increases) union leaders accept the company's view that incentives to work well are a good thing, and that a good and conscientious worker *deserves* better wages than a poor worker.

The difference between Japan and England, however, is not so much a difference between workers' attitudes as between the institutionalized attitudes of union leaders. The following questions were asked in the survey. In the nature of the case they could not be exactly comparable.

Britain

The salary system for people on the staff works so that they can get a rise if their superior thinks they are doing a good job. Do you think that there should be the same system of merit increases for workers on time rates?

[*If answer Yes*]
People often object to this because it may lead to favouritism, and they insist on the principle of a fixed rate for the job. Do you think they are right or wrong to do so?

Japan

When salary increases are being considered, decisions are taken in the light of a man's superiors' assessment of his performance. Do you think this kind of merit system is necessary?

[*If answer Yes*]
Some people say that this kind of system leads to blatant favouritism by superiors and there ought to be a rule that everyone gets the same salary increase. Do you agree with this or disagree?

191

The proportion of the sample who said that they thought merit pay was desirable (or necessary) and who resisted the follow-up attempt to make them change their minds was 32% at Hitachi – *less*, in fact, than at Marconi (40%) and only slightly above the Babcock and Wilcox workers' figure (29%). Clearly public union attitudes do not necessarily correspond to private unionists' attitudes. (In the steel workers' sample, however, the comparable figures were much closer to what one might have expected – 61% at Yawata and 26% at Appleby Frodingham.)

One may sum up the situation roughly as follows. The union is not an instrument of management. Nor, on the other hand, is it an all-along-the-line opposition organization, maintaining the posture of the skirmish in every workshop. If the implicit model for the British factory is the two-party polity (so that one is surprised to find *in fact* that very often those who are most loyal to the union *also* harbour the strongest affection for the company) the model for a Japanese factory is the democratic centralist one. There is not assumed to be any fundamental discrepancy between the norms and goals of the company and those of the union. Such differences as exist are either matters of degree (how *much* of a man's identity should he sink in the company: *vide* the 'agreement to disagree' over morning physical jerks, for example) or of relative priorities (including the not inconsiderable disagreement, institutionalized in the annual spring offensive over the relative priority to be attached to wages, investment or shareholders' incomes – a disagreement which does not, however, penetrate to plant-level decisions or workers' reactions to them, as it does in English Electric). But apart from general, continuous pressure on these limited defined areas of disagreement, the union is there primarily to see that the managers do not make mistakes in the *way* they apply the norms or pursue the goals on which there is general agreement, particularly mistakes which adversely affect the fortunes of those with least power in the organization. They consider it possible to perform this monitoring ombudsman function – in fact easier to do so – if they maintain a general attitude of co-operativeness towards management, avoiding a mud-slinging stand-up fight. Thus, while the union newspaper's appeals for solidarity in wage negotiations criticize, both implicitly and explicitly, the obstinacy of 'the management' – the remote Tokyo managers and directors seen as an abstract entity – there is almost no direct criticism in the newspaper of the managers of the Furusato works; only, occasionally, of particular management policies. And even the central management is sometimes further depersonalized by being referred to as 'capital' rather than 'the management'. Certainly there is nothing in the union newspaper since 1951 as personally critical of managers as the attacks in pamphlets issued by English Electric shop stewards at the time of the merger – detailing the windfall gains to individual directors from the rise in English Electric and General Electric shares on the stock exchange, or criticizing the chairman for showing more concern for the shareholders than for the company's employees.

PLANT CONFLICT AND THE WIDER 'STRUGGLE'

At the same time the union has explicit organizational and ideological links with the Socialist Party, throws its weight behind Socialists in elections, and uses its newspaper to denounce the Japanese-American Security Treaty. (The 1970 New Year issue divided its back page into two halves, one on wages and the other on the Treaty under the general headline 'The Two Great Struggles of 1970'.) In brief it works militantly for a fundamental change in Japanese society. Since there is no obvious short-run chance of the Socialist Party winning an election – indeed chances have recently become increasingly remote[7] – the exact details of the fundamental change do not have to be formulated in any very concrete detail. There seems to be no particular expectation of an improvement in the legal rights of unions in private industry after a change of government (such as the TUC might hope for in Britain). The legal framework seems generally accepted (except with regard to public sector industries where the problems are different). In fact, it is quite unclear how, in any particular socialist scenario, the fundamental change would affect Hitachi at all, though it is a fair guess that it would be in ways uncongenial to Hitachi's senior managers (both as individual tax-payers and as beneficiaries of large expense accounts, and also as managers who want the maximum freedom of action for their company) – sufficiently so for them to view any such prospect with horror.

Generally speaking, however, the prospect has been remote enough for their horror of it to be nowhere equal in intensity to the union's enthusiasm for it. The local managers at the Furusato plant have until recently shown only indifference, not active opposition, to the union's political activity. The first break with this tradition was in the general election of 1969 when, for the first time, senior managers passed around the word that all right-thinking men would of course

[7] For nearly two decades the right-wing Liberal-Democratic Party has dominated Japanese politics with nearly two-thirds of Diet seats. The Socialist Party is still the biggest opposition party but no longer predominantly so. It has lost ground to the new religious party, the Kōmeitō, and to the communists. A fourth opposition party, the Democratic Socialists, has kept a roughly stable (and small) share of the votes since it split from the JSP in the late fifties.

vote for the conservative Liberal-Democratic Party. However, the word was passed only to non-unionists. Direct confrontation with the union was avoided. The company's vote-mobilization was effective in deposing one of the two socialists (ex-Hitachi unionists who had sat for years under the union's sponsorship) replacing him with a Liberal Democrat, but it was primarily directed at its sub-contractors whose (un-unionized) workers were fair game for pressure transmitted through their employers.

It was generally believed in the union that the company's change of policy was largely due to unusually heavy pressure on the directors from the Liberal-Democratic Party. Until then, Hitachi's management had not thought it worth antagonizing their unions in order to do a favour to politicians for whom they have a certain contempt. (They, too, are not excessively imbued with class consciousness.) In so far as they were more susceptible to such requests in 1969, this may have been related to the fact that the following year, 1970, was the anniversary of the 1960 Security Treaty crisis, the year in which the treaty became open to renewal, and the year in which the left-wing parties planned demonstrations on what they hoped would pass the 1960 scale. (And the student movement's rehearsals had shown that they well might.) There had been political demonstration work stoppages in 1960 and more were feared in 1970. An electoral weakening of the socialists might, therefore, help to minimize the damage to the firm. It was said to be with the same end in view that the company had, in 1969, promoted a number of younger men, likely candidates for leadership in political militancy, to foremen's positions. Union officials described this rather ruefully, but not with any great sense of indignation. This is partly because their feelings about the Security Treaty, though far from indifference, are still not quite as strong as their feelings about the desirability of an annual 20% increase in Hitachi's turnover. It was partly because they do not naturally see the situation in terms of a power struggle between company and union.

All the same, they do talk about their relative failure to raise 'union consciousness', they *have* built a splendid auditorium so that *union* stereo concerts can match every *company* stereo concert in the company auditorium. They do have a newspaper which vies with the company's newspaper, a savings and loans bank which vies with a scheme operated by the company, a union Chairman's Cup for softball, to set against the many prizes offered by the company for the athletic events on the Factory Sports Day, an anniversary hike on the Sunday closest to Union Foundation Day to set against the company's Founder's Day, a nicely graded set of medals, titles and citations for honour to set against the company's medals and citations, and (until it recently became too expensive to continue) a monthly literary magazine to set against the monthly magazine published by the company. Through these means they seek to keep the sense of belonging to the union as salient in the minds of their members as the sense of belonging to the company. They do so partly because their conception of the proper role of a trade union is coloured not only by the set of relations in which they are in practice engaged but also by the ideology which they have inherited from other countries. Britain's, America's and Germany's 'Socialist pioneers' are a model for Japanese union leaders as much as for British union leaders,[8] and foreign traditions of class-conscious unionism colour their conception of what the union should be. They also, perhaps, foresee the day when Hitachi's turnover will *not* be growing at 20% a year, and when the central wage negotiations will grow tougher, or perhaps a day when political conflict in Japan will grow tenser and management will try to reduce the entrenched power which the union does now have *vis-à-vis* the company, as part of a general offensive against the left-wing forces which the union supports.

The present 'frontier agreement', in other words, might not last forever. It requires restraint on both sides: restraint by the managers in not trying to hinder union activities, or in urging a vote for the Liberal-Democratic Party *only* on non-unionists, as much as restraint by the union in not making into spectacular confrontations matters which can be settled by quiet bargaining. Those restraints may one day break down and one side may begin pushing at the frontiers, just as in the traditional village community the intricate social techniques of coexistence sometimes broke down and there reappeared the ancient crime of 'secretly moving boundary markers at night'. The union leaders clearly feel that management is more likely to shake off the restraints, because in terms of the power balance there is no doubt who would win when the chips were down. That was made clear in 1950 when they were made to swallow the mass dismissals. Hence their concern for education and for 'consciousness'. At present, they can feel reasonably well supported. Only 8% of the Hitachi sample said 'no' to the question: 'If it wasn't for the union do you think that wages and working conditions would be worse than they are now?'[9] But they know that if the frontiers are ever chal-

---

[8] Okochi Kazuo, *et al.*, *Nihon No Union Leader*, 1965, p. 99. Sometimes even consciously so. A sample of union leaders were asked in the late fifties to name the person they most admired. Over a quarter of those mentioned were non-Japanese.

[9] The question in the British survey was not quite comparable: 'Generally

lenged again, the constellation of interest considerations on which they rely for support at present may not be enough to maintain a power balance. They will need to call on reserves of emotional loyalty – on the sort of class consciousness and 'union consciousness' which they rightly fear is more often a matter of rhetoric than of reality.

speaking would you say that there was any danger that individuals would get unfair treatment from management if there weren't any shop stewards to take up grievances?' The proportions who said 'no' were 25% at Marconi and 10% at Babcocks.

Chapter 7

Industrial Relations: A Summary

1. Hitachi's union admits only employees of Hitachi and the 'union shop' rule holds. Workers in English Electric are members of a variety of different unions, each specialized, usually, to a few skills or industries.

2. White collar technical and lower-ranking supervisory and managerial workers – including young university graduates destined for higher management – belong to the Hitachi union. A smaller proportion of the corresponding workers in English Electric belong to any union, and those who do nearly always belong to different unions from manual workers.

3. The grass-roots basis of the Hitachi union is the workshop department unit within the factory. British unions have a dual structure. The grass-roots unit is the local branch in which membership is defined by residence: there are also 'weed-roots' workshop units which often exhibit the sturdier growth.

4. The Hitachi union collects more money from its members than any of its British counterparts, and its superiority of resources is reflected in better union buildings and facilities, a higher ratio of full-time officials, and better means of communications between officials and members.

5. The Hitachi union has a more formal bureaucratic organization which provides for more contingencies with explicit rules than the British union which leaves more to custom and practice, or to *ad hoc* arrangements at the discretion of officials.

6. Wage bargaining is seen by their members as the main function of the unions in both firms, and the central bargaining of the Confederation of Shipbuilding and Engineering Unions with the Engineering Employers' Federation parallels the central bargaining of the

Hitachi Federation with the Hitachi management in that the negotiations are remote from the worker and his factory-level representatives who are called on only to be mobilized in strikes and other demonstrations of support. Differences are, however:

a. The mobilization calls go out for one major and two minor occasions (spring offensive, the summer bonus and the winter bonus) every year at Hitachi, where annual negotiations are institutionalized and expected by management; less frequently (and, despite recent attempts to negotiate three-year package deals, less predictably and therefore more challengingly) in the British engineering industry.

b. The nature of the conflicting sectional interests to be reconciled in a packaged wage demand are different (e.g. skilled/unskilled *v.* younger/older) and the means of reconciling them involve rather more public discussion at Hitachi.

c. But the reconciliation of sectional interests poses less of a problem for the Hitachi negotiators who represent 90,000 workers in the same industry in factories with homogeneous institutions, than for the CSEU negotiators representing a million and a half workers in a wide variety of industries and plants.

d. In neither case does the result of these negotiations by itself determine any individual's pay packet, but whereas, at Hitachi, almost the only other factor is a man's work performance and his supervisors' subjective assessment of that work performance, at English Electric there are two other factors – an individual or a group's quantitative output (under piecework schemes) and changes in bonus schemes, plus rates, and piecework rates which are negotiated at the plant level – the wage drift which in some periods contributes more to increases in earnings than do increases in wage rates.

7. The negotiations which lead to the last type of change in earnings provide frequent opportunity for the central concern of trade unions with wages to be translated, in English Electric, into overt conflict at the workshop level over local issues of bread-and-butter concern to small groups of workers. This does not happen at Hitachi. The only possible opportunity, provided by the piecework system, is rarely taken up because of its small consequence for earnings and because of the institutionalized practice of foremen, not union representatives, bargaining on behalf of workers.

8. Another cause of the greater frequency of overt workshop-level conflict at English Electric than at Hitachi lies in the fact that there is far less detailed contractual regulation at English Electric of

the extent to which union representatives are entitled to share in, or exercise veto power over, the making and enforcing of works rules. The Hitachi central and plant 'constitutional' contracts which specify the rights and duties of both sides and help to keep stable a *de jure* 'frontier' have no parallel at English Electric where the 'frontier' is seen as a mere *de facto* reflection of the balance of power, to be shifted if the balance changes.

9. The greater frequency of conflict due to the last two factors helps to keep the sense of a confrontational division between management and men more salient in the minds of British workers than in the minds of Hitachi workers. This in turn strengthens the expectations that 'they' (the management/the workers) will 'try to get away with something' and makes it more likely at English Electric than at Hitachi that a given act by managers or a given reaction by workers will be perceived on either side as an attempt by 'them' to harm or cheat 'us'. Hence more additional occasions for conflict are likely to arise at English Electric, so strengthening the sense of contestation, and so on in spiral fashion.

10. Partly for this reason, the workshop machinery of the Hitachi union, though efficient in dealing with matters of safety or work environment (usually equally amicably dealt with at English Electric though as much through the works councils as through the union representatives) is less often mobilized in protest against what is considered unjust exercise of authority by managers and supervisors.

11. Another reason is that the large element of merit-rating in the Hitachi wage system puts power over individual workers in the hands of their supervisors which in Britain has been taken away from them by the unions.

12. And another reason lies in the wide membership range of the Hitachi union which can make supervisors key men in, and often the formal representatives of, union workshop units.

13. The absence of institutionalized confrontation and the lesser incidence of overt conflict at Hitachi reflect also the greater degree of consensus which exists between managers and union leaders at Hitachi than in English Electric. This is hard to pin down in detail, but one might hazard the following assertions:

a. Hitachi managers and union leaders are closer together in the relative value they place on efficiency, on investment for later reward, and on the co-operative integration of different functions in a harmonious whole, than their English counterparts.

b. Where there is a clash between the values of harmony and obedience to superiors on the one hand, and individual dignity, freedom and equality on the other, English Electric unionists would take a stronger stand on the latter.

c. But quite apart from value placed on efficiency or productivity in the abstract, the major difference is that Hitachi union leaders share the managers' concern with the growth and prosperity of Hitachi as a corporation in competition with other corporations. Full-time British union officials may share with officials of the Employers Federation a concern with the future of 'the industry' in the abstract but they have no special concern with the prosperity of particular concrete firms within it. (Shop stewards are in fact likely to have such a concern, but the union ethos as set by the full-time officials, operates to discourage it.)

14. Joint productivity councils based on the assumption of shared goals exist at Hitachi, having been desired by union leaders and fairly readily accepted by managers. They do not exist at English Electric due to hesitancy shown by both sides to enter into moral commitments to the other that might limit their freedom of action in the 'contest' situation.

15. But whereas the Hitachi situation is institutionally static, the English Electric situation is institutionally fluid, partly under the pressure of external changes (Redundancy Payments Act, Training Boards, the Prices and Incomes Policy) but partly due to the initiative of managers seeking to move towards what might be called a Hitachi-type pattern of relations. Union leaders (who have rarely been initiators of change) have responded with a mixture of pleasurable surprise and suspicion.

16. Unions in both countries have ties to left-wing political parties. British unions support a party which is one of two alternative governments from which they expect, when it is in power, concrete benefits in the form of wage and taxation policies and legislation protecting union rights. The Hitachi union, on the other hand, supports a party which has never formed, and is unlikely in the near future to form, an effective government, and from which it can expect no concrete political benefits except the publicity of parliamentary protest if union rights are threatened by the government. That party is defined primarily as the party which seeks peace and independence in foreign policy – in support of which aims the union is prepared to consider – though hardly in recent years to go further than considering – striking as a form of protest action.

Chapter 8

The Enterprise as Community

The corporation buses come thick and fast outside the gates of the English Electric factories at closing time, though not always for the destinations that people most often want to go to. 'Improving the service on the No. 69 route' is a common item on the works committee agenda, and sometimes a welfare officer will actually remonstrate with the bus company. But by and large, once one is outside of the factory gates, one is a citizen. One rides on the corporation buses *qua* rate-payer, not *qua* English Electric employee.

From the Furusato factory, some of those who are not on bicycles walk out to bus queues, some to the train station. In the queue for each major route, in the group of workers decanted at each suburban station down the line, one is likely to see one man wearing a rather formal blue serge uniform. He is the communications committee member for the station. If he takes his job seriously he may make it his business to board the train last in the mornings, making sure that everyone is aboard before he nods to the porter who nods to the guard to blow his whistle. He it is, at any rate, who represents his fellow-commuters in any negotiations with the railways over changes of timetable. In strikes or breakdowns he really comes into his own, marshalling his patient team while he telephones to the factory to check on alternative transport.

In neither firm, of course, does one entirely cease to be an employee as soon as one walks through the factory gate. Both firms recognize in a multiplicity of ways that the employment relationship entails obligations and considerations beyond the mere exchange of labour service and cash. In Hitachi they go a good deal *further* than in English Electric.

This is certainly so, for *manual* workers, in the matter of fringe benefits of a conventional kind. Table 3.4 (p. 97) showed the difference in sickness provisions. It also gives some details of the pensions provided at direct cost to the firm. At English Electric these are supplemented by a contributory pension scheme, intended to be self-financing, which provides a supplement for staff and for skilled craftsmen, though the latter become eligible to join only from their *eleventh* year of service. There are no pension provisions for manual workers other than craftsmen who must rely on pensions from the state. In Japan, where a state scheme for contributory old-age pensions for employees began only during the war, and where universal non-contributory pensions began – and then on a very small scale – only a decade ago, firms have traditionally paid all permanent workers a lump-sum retirement gratuity based on grade, length of service and final salary. Recently, foreseeing the enormous cost of such a scheme when the big post-war intakes of workers begin to reach retirement age, the policy has been to hold constant the gratuity provisions and supplement them with a contributory scheme for which the firm contributes half the cost.

The big difference in retirement provisions, however, is that the working life at Hitachi is shorter. Retirement is at 56 (except for directors) compared with English Electric's 65. Increasingly, however, Hitachi 're-employs' the retired for an extra four or five years – but at a lower salary. A man may be cut back to the wage of a 30- or 35-year-old, but if his retirement gratuity pays off any remaining house mortgage and provides a little extra to launch his children into the world, he may be able to manage well enough. Others may be found jobs with the smaller sub-contractors of Hitachi where retirement comes later. Of the 79 men who retired from the Furusato factory in 1966, 10 stayed on and 45 were found other jobs.

These monetary provisions apart, in neither company need a long-serving member entirely sever his links with the firm when he retires. Both firms provide a certain amount of sociability for the retired – membership in clubs, annual dinners and outings for veterans. English Electric, through a fund set up in memory of the first chairman, provides a small number of old people's homes.

But the differences in other types of welfare provisions are greater than in the matter of pensions. Some of these differences, and the assumptions underlying them, are worth looking at in more detail.

THE SCOPE OF ENTERPRISE WELFARE

First, Hitachi's provisions are much wider in scope and more costly. Housing is the outstanding example. The Bradford factory has some twenty-seven company-owned flats and houses available, at more or less economic rents, for employees moving into the district. The welfare department also tries on occasion to help its workers to get into corporation housing. But this represents a supplementary reserve of assistance in a situation where the basic principle is that a man's housing is his own affair. Hitachi, by contrast, operates on the principle that the company must take the prime responsibility. At the Furusato factory, there are hostels enough to accommodate all the unmarried men and women high school and university graduates. (Middle school graduates are recruited locally and so are expected to live at home, though they can, if necessary, be accommodated too.) Then there are large company estates with rented accommodation which cater for some 40% of the married men employees. In principle, workers are expected to move out to their own house by the time they are 45. There is a special savings and loan scheme (with 4% mortgages) to help them to do so,[1] and the company also has a real estate subsidiary which is developing housing estates for the sale of plots. The company's estates of rented houses and flats are serviced with a chain of stores (subsidized until they were recently hived off to a separate subsidiary company – another outlet for retired Hitachi employees) and also bath-houses and barbers shops.

The difference in scale between the two firms can be indicated by the costs involved. Hitachi Company's total expenditure on housing, medical services, canteens, transport subsidies, sports and social facilities, and special welfare grants other than pay during sickness, amounted to 8·5% of total labour costs. English Electric figures are not available, but for the median British firm of a group surveyed in 1968, the corresponding figure was 2·5% *including* sick pay.[2]

VOLUNTARY CHOICE

A second difference is that more of English Electric's schemes are on a voluntary contractual basis. It had a convalescent home available for anyone who contracted in by paying twopence a week. The Staff Mutual Aid Fund was likewise voluntary. The Veterans' Association, too, was a self-governing association which received a small subsidy from the company. One could choose to pay or not to pay threepence a week at one English Electric factory to belong to the sports and social club. (The club was, in fact, started voluntarily by a group of workers independently of the management and later taken over and subsidized. According to local tradition, this happened only after it got into such a ramshackle state that it distressed the company

---

[1] At the moment this is good business. Reflecting the young average age of the employees, the majority of whom were still preparing for house purchase, the company had in 1969 deposits averaging £250 per employee and mortgage loans of £80 per capita.

[2] Industrial Society, *Cost of Personnel Services and Administration*, 1968.

203

n when he was one day invited there to present athletic

itachi factories, both the sports and social association (president, the works manager; vice-president, the union chairman) and the Mutual Aid Fund, are in theory independent organizations – and have been since the first embryo organization on these lines was created in 1919 – but even if there is, buried somewhere in the rules, a stipulation that membership is voluntary, no one knows of it. In practice everyone belongs. The degree of company subsidization is greater, too. For the Mutual Aid Fund, for example, the company pays 100 and the individual 30 yen a month.

THE FUNCTION OF WELFARE SERVICES

A third difference is that English Electric, unlike Hitachi, attaches no very great positive value to its welfare and fringe benefits. The firm is prepared, as part of its civic duty (in much the same way as it has co-operated since the war with government savings campaigns, arranges for mass X-rays and blood donations, trains apprentices who will leave the firm and permits deductions to be made from wages for charities) to provide facilities for its workers, provided that it is not too costly in money or managerial time. But the costs and benefits have to be nicely calculated:

'An insurance company came along the other day and asked if they could have a branch on the site. We've been talking it over. We can see the benefits, but where do you stop? You'd be getting untold numbers of agencies wanting to open on the site. And before you know where you are you get precious little production done. People on time rates would be in and out of them all the time. We've had requests from the welfare committees too for things like hairdressers and chiropodists. We asked the doctor about a chiropodist and he said that there was nothing in the nature of the work which would conduce to the need for a chiropodist. As for hairdressers, they say Marks and Spencers have one, but there hair's part of the job. Of course, during the war we even had one here in the factory, but during the war anything goes. We do have a dental surgery – after all, it *is* a time-saver; we'd lose more time if people went outside, but hair – they can have their hair done any time.

Anyway, I'm not so sure they'd really want it. There was an ice-cream seller used to come and set up outside the gates, so we set up a stand inside – same Wall's ice-cream, same prices, only we had coloured umbrellas and seats. And people walked straight past it and bought their ice cream outside. I asked one chap why. "You don't catch me putting a ha'penny into pocket o' this firm", he says. You've got to be careful about these things. We let the motoring club and the gardening club run shops in the lunch hour, for instance, but that's all right. By and large you can say it's production that decides. If you put the word production at the top and align everything to that, you can work the answer out.'

There is, to be sure, some recognition of the advantages of being a 'good employer'; at the most basic level, pensions and sick pay schemes have to be competitive with those of other employers; beyond that there is a feeling that some of the traditions of the more paternalistic past – the annual Gala Day with flower show, the annual dance, the foreman's dinner – are worth keeping up because they do, after all, help marginally to create good will towards the company amongst its employees. But if it turns out that the support for the sports club football team or for the male voice choir is so thin that both need reinforcement by outside 'associate members' no one is greatly disturbed.

At Hitachi, by contrast, the section of the general affairs department which deals with these matters is positively entrepreneurial. They are happy to offer interviewers an account of their philosophy – solemn little homilies about all work and no play making Jack a dull boy. In the mid-sixties, to increase participation in sports activities, they started nominating a *rekkuriidaa* (*rec*reation *leader*, of course) in each section and giving them a special weekend training camp. In other fields, too, their activity is impressive. The auditorium of the Hitachi factory, built to celebrate the firm's fiftieth anniversary, seats 1,200. It has been slightly overshadowed by the union's bigger auditorium built a few years later, but it fights back with some promotional skill. For every concert put on at the union auditorium by the Workers' Musical Society (a militant left-wing body, very keen on togetherness and audience participation) the company auditorium arranges a concert (albeit, to the welfare section's chagrin, a somewhat more sedate and unexciting concert) under the auspices of the capitalist-sponsored Industrial Musical Society. There is an athletics stadium, one large and one smaller baseball stadium, a gymnasium, a swimming pool and various tennis and volley-ball courts. To celebrate the firm's sixtieth anniversary in 1970 several thousands of pounds were spent on a spectacular fireworks display. The annual sports day is a grand affair, and the fact that preparations for the fancy dress parade which is one of its central features cause some loss of production in the previous weeks is thought to be an unfortunate but necessary cost.

TIMES OF TROUBLE

Fourthly, there is a difference in the handling of less formal welfare matters – personal contingencies not catered for in explicit rules. In Hitachi these are matters for the line supervisors. One's foreman or superintendent is the man one goes to if in trouble. If a man dies, the foreman tells a couple of the work team to take two or three days off to help the widow with the funeral arrangements, and the whole team would normally go to the funeral. The foreman has the responsibility for sick visiting, though he may delegate a workmate to do the job. In an English Electric factory, by contrast, these matters are taken care of not through the authority structure of the small work team, but in the first place by customs of spontaneous *collateral* assistance among workmates.[3] If a man dies, his mates will make a collection for the widow; the foreman may or may not take the lead in organizing it; it is more likely to be the shop steward, though the welfare office may see to ordering a wreath, from money collected on the shop floor, and some paid time might be allowed to attend the funeral. To that extent the event is officially recognized.

The second way such needs are met is through the impersonal mechanisms of the welfare department. Workmates may visit a sick man, but probably not his foreman unless they happen to be friends or nearby neighbours. There is a division of labour: sick visiting is a specialist job. In cases of lengthy sickness the foreman notifies the welfare officer and he or his assistant take care of the matter. They go to keep sick employees in touch and to provide human comfort on the one hand, to check up on malingering on the other, with the balance, one explained, being slightly on the latter. They are also available to talk over any private troubles. 'I always tell the girls in the induction talk', said one, 'that they can come along to see me in complete confidence if they are ever worried about anything that prevents them *getting on with their work*.' (My emphasis.) It was not clear whether she spoke in terms of work capacity because, in the managerial ethic which dominated her surroundings, production was the only justification for any expenditure of managerial time, or whether she felt that she needed this justification for presuming to offer what might seem to some workers a threatened intrusion on

---

[3] The following question in the survey showed no clear difference between Britain and Japan: 'If you were in trouble – a long illness or something – and needed help, whom do you think you could best rely on to help out? Relatives, neighbours or workmates?'

The answers did, however, reveal a difference between the Glasgow firm – where, as in Hitachi and the Japanese steel firm at the opposite end of Japan, some 80% said 'relatives' and only 17% workmates – and the 'new working class' Chelmsford firms where 50% said relatives and 25% workmates.

privacy. An energetic and kindly woman, she does in fact sometimes find herself mediating between parents and estranged daughters. The welfare officers may also, occasionally, make personal loans. But most problems are resolved by putting people in touch with outside public authorities – ministers of religion, probation officers, marriage guidance counsellors or solicitors. Somewhere between the direct collateral approach and the formal institutional approach was the Bradford factory's hardship fund. The money was raised from the interest on the holiday savings account (which workers draw out before their holidays). It was the workers' own money, but the firm provided the organization – though the actual distribution of the money was left to the chairman of the works committee who was usually the chief shop steward.

The differences in these matters in the role assigned to the small work team is paralleled in the patterns of sociability. Organized functions at English Electric factories are mostly on a factory-wide basis. The twice-annual dances are for anybody in the factory who likes dancing; the football club within the sports club exists for those, in any shop, who want to play football. The only example of a function organized for a section of the factory is the foreman's dinner – for a lateral *stratum* of employees throughout the factory. In Hitachi, by contrast, in addition to the factory festivals and the clubs for the like-minded, there is a good deal of sociability on a *segmentalized* workshop basis. Department outings are frequent and can claim subsidies from the company. Sections and small foremen's work teams organize trips and parties. They sometimes have their own baseball or softball or volleyball team. The implications of this deliberate policy of strengthening the cohesion of the small work group – with the leadership pattern of the shop floor carrying over into the social situation – will be considered further in the next chapter.

UNIONS AND WELFARE

A fifth difference lies in the union's role in welfare matters. At English Electric, by and large, the unions are completely uninvolved. A chief shop steward at the Bradford factory was also, as chairman of the works committee, responsible for making grants from the hardship fund mentioned above, but this was in his personal capacity. The combine committee has shown some concern with pensions and sick pay, but by and large unions have been concerned with matters of wages and work in their dealings with employers – though most unions, of course, also act as friendly societies and provide sick pay for their members, another form of collateral mutual aid entirely independent of the employment relationship.

The situation is different at Hitachi. In the 'soft' side of welfare the union is somewhat ambiguously involved. On the one hand the union chairman is vice-president of the sports and social association and *ex officio* member of the organizing committee for the annual sports day. On the other, the union is in competition with the company (see p. 194) offering its own auditorium, its own hiking clubs and its own loan schemes. On the 'hard' side of welfare involving monetary benefits, however, the union is actively concerned to make sure that the firm improves its provisions, pressing for better benefits as well as higher wages. One of the elected full-time officials is fully occupied with welfare matters. His job is partly to run the union's rival welfare services, partly to make sure that the company does not skimp its obligations in such matters as housing repairs, partly to prepare negotiating positions for demands for higher retirement gratuities. Company welfare is counted as part of the rights of employees to be guarded and extended.

VIRTUE

Another aspect of Hitachi's closer approach to being a 'total community' lies in its concern with its employees' morals. This has already been touched on in Chapter 2, apropos of the difference in training programmes. One English Electric factory did send some of its apprentices to Outward Bound for character training, but the scale of Hitachi's concern for moulding the values and attitudes of its employees is made much more openly evident – and for all grades of employees. Nor is the concern limited to the brief period of training. Under the influence of the former president of the company a number of Hitachi factories have branches of the Ethical Society, a body supported from the expense accounts of a number of Japanese companies, whose primary function is to publish a monthly magazine entitled *Kōjō*, which is best translated, perhaps, as *Aiming High*. The magazine's short stories and its articles on health in middle age, on gardening (the cultivation of flowers and the cultivation of the spirit), on the life struggle of a blind architect, on the persistence and intellectual enthusiasm of night-school students, its reminiscences of their youth by retired business men (including 'how I went to secret Marxist study groups but was held back by instinctive patriotism from total commitment – and didn't care if people called me a coward'), its advice to mothers on how to react when their 8-year-old sons get an erection and on how to get the most out of PTA meetings, its straightforward little homilies on kindliness in little things by the society's leader, promote virtues not dissimilar from those of Outward Bound – enthusiasm for work and vigorous play, healthy extraverted camaraderie, serious-mindedness, patriotism, honesty, clean living and high thinking. The society also arranges weekend outings to put clean living and high thinking into practice – getting up before dawn to stand naked under a waterfall intoning uplifting poetry, for example, or visiting the Ise shrine. The slogan which decorated more than one office wall in the Hitachi factory – 'a world without kindness is grim: a world without sweat is decadent' – is a part of the Ethical Society's initiation pledge.

THE FIRM AND THE FAMILY

A final and related difference: an English Electric man's family is his own concern and responsibility. Wives and girl-friends may be brought to the annual dance or to the Gala Day for the ambiguous pleasure of seeing the dim-witted or dastardly colleagues and superiors who figure in their husband's reports of his factory life. There is a widow's pension scheme for the very highest categories of staff, but even at that managerial level, hardly any obvious penetration of American organization man's belief that a wife's qualities intimately affect a man's performance. Welfare officers will, if necessary, help sort out serious family problems. But by and large the family of employees is of concern to the company as such only in so far as his work efficiency is manifestly affected by family problems, to his workmates only in so far as association breeds personal friendship.

In Hitachi the long arm of the company's concern reaches further. A man's family are peripheral members of the company family. The company, for instance, offers a system of educational loans for employees' children, and maintains a dormitory in Tokyo for the children of employees attending universities or cram schools preparing for university entrance. Perhaps the best indication of the scope of the company's concern is to be found in a list of the various uses of the Mutual Aid Fund. Each member of the firm receives, automatically and according to a standard tariff, varied only according to length of service (not, for instance, rank), gifts of money for a variety of occasions – his own wedding (with an additional present of the firm's electrical appliances for girls leaving the firm to marry), on the birth of a child, or when that child first enters primary school or when it gets married. Condolence gifts are made on his own death, or the death of a member of his family, or for flood or fire disaster. Gifts ranged in 1966 from £35 as condolence 'incense money' on an employee's death and £10 as an average wedding gift, to a standard £2.50 for a child's starting school. It does not matter that the fund is 20% contributory, 80% financed from the company's general funds; the principle is that the joys and sorrows of one are the joys and sorrows of all.

The family is involved at another level too. A foreman's wife may call on the sick wife of her husband's subordinates; and a man might send his wife round to a superior's house with a 'thank you' present when he has been shown some special consideration. The enthusiastic department chief at the foundry of the Furusato works got involved with his workers' families by another route. He was a great man for campaigns and in 1969 his current effort, supported by the eager lieutenantship of his safety officer was what was called an 'H.K. Campaign'. 'H' stood for *hirō*, fatigue; 'K' for KO or knock-out. The purpose of the exercise was to reduce fatigue (without, of course, resorting to such obvious devices as working less hard). This required the active co-operation of workers' families – allowing Dad to get his full night's sleep, for instance. Family co-operation was mobilized, *inter alia*, by offering prizes to the workers' children for slogans and posters supporting the campaign. This sense of family involvement is, of course, facilitated by and much heightened by the fact that a large proportion of families live cheek by jowl in the company housing estates.

The firm's recognition of the fact that their workers are not just individual sellers of labour, but also family men, is two-edged. The British system sharply separates the man's role as employee from his role as husband and father, and the firm disclaims responsibility for, or jurisdiction over, the latter. The Japanese firm, by contrast, admits a concern for both, but where there is possibility of conflict requires – to some degree at least – the subordination of the family role. The fact that a man had planned to take his children for an outing would be seen as a rather 'selfish' reason for trying to avoid overtime work on a Sunday if an order had to be finished. For a manager, a good wife is one who accepts that her husband's work must come first, and resigns herself to seeing little of him during the week – or even, should the need to sweeten the firm's clients or to express solidarity with his colleagues take him to the golf course on Sundays, at the weekends either. If the firm requires a man to go to a distant works he will accept the 'posting' and may, for the sake of the children's schooling or for some other reason, leave his family behind. (One young English Electric manager, by contrast, chose his firm because he wanted to live close to his Liverpool family and the Aintree racing ambience, then left it for another firm largely because he decided he would rather live in London.)

210

This is not *just* a matter of the demands of the organization. It is partly a reflection of the fact that for all the Japanese concern with 'the family' as a corporate group – its ancestry, its honour and its property – less value has been placed in Japan than in England on the actual quality of personal relations within the family, except on the relation of a mother with her children. There is in this something similar to the man's world/woman's world division found in some traditional British working-class areas.

But this is not quite the whole story; ethical traditions at a different level are also involved. One historical ancestor of the modern Japanese corporation (see Chapter 14) is the samurai band of the semi-autonomous fiefs into which Japan was divided during the Tokugawa period. This was more a hierarchical network of *family* groups than of individuals. The death of one family head and his replacement by his heir did not in theory alter the network of loyalties and obligations between families. The whole family was subordinated to the lord's family – from which it followed, for any particular individual, that the interests of his own family should be subordinated to the interests of the fief. That was the path of true virtue, true fief patriotism, true loyalty to one's feudal lord.

Using the categories of classical Chinese writers on politics, this was referred to as subordinating the 'private' interests (of one's own family) to the 'public' interest (of the fief). In the Chinese tradition the dichotomy was chiefly used to excoriate the sins of wicked rulers whose crime consisted in 'confusing the public and the private' – assuming that the empire existed for the benefit of their own family rather than vice versa. For the ordinary, non-official, citizen in China, filial piety – devotion to the 'private interests of one's family' – remained the supreme virtue almost until 1949. In Japan, however, the claims of the family on a man's loyalty were subordinated to those of fief, village community or state at a much earlier stage of history.[4] The main use of the 'public'/'private' dichotomy in Japan was to warn subordinates, not rulers, against the dangers of allowing 'private' concerns to take precedence over 'public' obligations.

This is not to suggest that a loyal Hitachi man is as ready to disembowel himself for his company as samurai were (or rather, some samurai were) for their feudal lord – only that these are the moral categories to the lengthening shadows of which the employment relation is assimilated. In Hitachi the official term for an injury sustained at work is, even today, a 'public injury'; an injury unconnected with work is a 'private injury'.

[4] See M. J. Levy Jr, 'Contrasting Factors in the Modernization of China and Japan', *Economic Development and Cultural Change*, 2, ii, 1954, pp. 161–9.

A 'national character' survey by a Tokyo Institute[5] provides a nice illustration of the state of overt public morality in these matters (and one, as we shall see in a later chapter, which well shows up the imprecisions of the sociological concept 'particularism'.) People were asked to suppose that they were president of a firm which ran formal recruitment examinations. Only one post was to be filled. The close runner-up is your relative. The section chief in charge comes to you and indicates he'd be happy to take either. What should you do? Only 18% said that one should push for one's relative – choosing the 'private' interest at the expense of the 'public' interest of the firm. Curiously, though, when the sample was next asked to suppose that the runner-up was, not a relative but the son of someone who had been good to one and to whom one owed an obligation, 39% were prepared to bend the rules in his favour. What one might call the 'contractual' bonds of obligation – those extra-familial bonds which, while still personal, half belong to the 'public' sector and very commonly (as in the case of a foreman or section chief who has helped one's promotion, a senior director who has got one on to the board) are found *within* the 'public' organization which claims first loyalty – have an ambiguous intermediate status.

To be sure, values are changing in this regard. The Japanese have come to need a word for 'privacy' which does not have – as all the possible traditional words had – overtones either of 'selfishness' or of 'loneliness'. They have adopted the word *puraibashii*, though it remains, still, somewhat an intellectuals' word, symbolic of a value which only those most influenced by Western individualistic ideas have come to attach importance to. Another, much more popular, recent coinage is *mai-hōmu-shugi* or 'my-home-ism'. This refers to the 'privatized' concerns of the man of small ambition – chiefly concerned to get a pretty little house and a pretty little wife and two model children, to have a colour TV and a cooler and to join the ranks of *maikaa-zoku*, the 'my car tribe'. The word has ambiguous connotations. The popular weekly magazines do in part encourage the my-home-ist. They feed his fantasies, extol the pleasures of the consumer society, treat it as natural to be in love with one's wife, and refer to my-home-ism as the trend of the times, the central modern tendency of the *homme moyen sensuel*. But at the same time they feed the older sensual fantasies of the world of bar-girl/geisha mistresses and lascivious weekends at hot-spring resorts – enjoyed in the company of one's *workmates* rather than of the wife one married from a sense of family duty, and thus a use of leisure which binds one more closely to one's work and workmates rather than drawing one away

[5] Hayashi Chikio, *et al.*, *Daini Nihonjin no kokuminsei*, 1970, pp. 318–19.

212

from them.[6] And there are many Japanese, too, for whom my-home-ism is an object of contempt. Radical students see it as a bourgeois renunciation of every true citizen's commitment to the 'public' world of political action. The articulate business leader sees it as a threat to social progress and national economic development. It is a renunciation of masculine ambition, a lapse into reprehensible hedonism, a menace to that capacity for vigorous dedication to causes greater than one's family which in the past made Mitsubishi great and in consequence made Japan great.

As long as the humourless radical students continue to transform themselves in the space of a few months, into the humourless dedicated corporation men, Japan is perhaps *fairly* safe against my-home-ism. But this is an area in which values are very much in flux, and structural changes are going to make a big difference. Sunday, for someone working six days a week really was a day of rest; a 'rest for the bones' as the Japanese say, a day on which one prepared oneself for the fulfilment of duty on the other six days of the week. Now, with a five-day week rapidly becoming the norm in large firms (in 38% of those with over 1,000 employees by 1971), one can afford to expend a good deal more energy on positively enjoying oneself. Again, an unmarried youngster can now afford to save less, to spend more on his leisure, acquiring tastes which give him interests – and sources of social prestige – outside his work. He is more likely to get married to a girl he is fond of rather than a girl his relatives or his foreman think would be a good match for him. In all these ways the supremacy of work and of the corporation is threatened.

But still it remains clearly true at the present time that Hitachi workers and English Electric workers differ markedly in the degree of their involvement in the firm; in the extent to which their work roles take precedence over other roles. Most Hitachi men of the rank of

---

[6] The distinction at issue is not the balance between devotion to work and devotion to pleasure, but the respective weights given, on the one hand to one's work role and membership in the firm (including the fun and games as well as the hard work entailed) and on the other to one's family role and relation to one's wife and children. To attach excessive importance to the latter is soft and un-masculine. (A girl-friend may call for a young man in his Tokyo office at the end of the day. When they marry he is likely to forbid her to appear. She now belongs to a different category: she is not part of the fun and games which fits into the masculine work role.) This way of viewing the world may be more intelligible to a *machismo*-preoccupied Mexican than to an Englishman who might expect the hard worker to be serious about his home and to disapprove of wild weekends with workmates. But this assumes that one works to make money to spend on the home. The Japanese ethic here described does not see work in that instrumental light – it is a natural performance of one's role as a member of the firm, just as making whoopee with one's workmates is.

foreman or above – and, indeed, a good number of ordinary workers – have calling cards on which they are identified by their firm, department and title. A Hitachi man often wears his Hitachi badge when he goes off for a holiday. An English Electric manager, by contrast, may show where his primary identification lies by wearing his Round Table or his Young Conservative ties to the works (though some foremen can be seen, at work, wearing a Foreman's Association tie). In our sample of Hitachi workers, 83% belonged to some sports or social club or hobby group organized exclusively for members of the firm or of the union; only 14% belonged to any outside social or political or religious organization. In our British engineering sample, although the balance was still in the same direction, the proportions were different – respectively 56% and 34%. Only 21% of the Hitachi workers had not been to any social function organized by the firm in the previous year; 73% of the British sample. 'I wouldn't have it any other way', said a British personnel manager, apropos of these differences between Japanese and British firms. 'It's much better that a man's work life should be separate from the rest of his life. I take work home in the evenings, but I don't ever do much. I hardly ever mix with my colleagues socially. I think it's better that way. It makes for a more rounded individual.'

THE FIRM AND THE INDIVIDUAL

Once again we come back to the lifetime employment pattern *v.* the market-oriented pattern as a precondition for the differences outlined above. Time builds up identification; not just time past, the familarity of long association, but also the prospect of time to come. And this is not just a matter of individual experiences. English Electric also has 50-year-old workers with a quarter of a century of service who expect to finish out their time with the firm. They too have *some* feeling for the firm. They are likely to tell you, with a tinge of sardonic pride, how English Electric never makes money because of its tradition of workmanship. ('Customer'll ring up and say he's got a generator we made in 1923 and still working but just needs a little spare part – and we'll waste hours digging out the blueprint and making it for him.') But still they feel themselves less totally and definitively English Electric men than their counterparts would feel themselves Hitachi men because personal experience is translated into sentiment and attachments only by refraction through the norms of the work community – the *shared* norms of their fellow-workers. It is overstating the case to say that one feels only what one is supposed to feel, but it is safe to say that one is more easily disposed to feel what one is supposed to feel – the more so the more oversocialized and conformist the society is. And in English Electric the relevant norms faithfully reflect the organizational assumptions underlying them – the limited commitment, the basic market orientation.

It is not just that the Japanese system enhances enterprise consciousness; it also – the other side of the coin – does less to develop individualism. Man-imbedded-in-organization has no great need to make personal moral choices; the organization's norms set guidelines; the organization's sanctions keep him to the path of virtue. It is the man between organizations, the man of limited commitment, who has the greater responsibility of choosing. 'When you buy a man over from a rival firm, you don't buy all that firm's secrets', said one English Electric manager. 'Of course, you couldn't help but be influenced by what you know about your old firm's plans and so on. But you don't give away confidences. Your people in your *new* firm wouldn't trust you if you did.' This kind of deliberate autonomous reserve, the acceptance of universal rules which is at the core of the integrity of man-in-the-market (whether it be in practice an operational norm or merely an ideal norm in the British business world) is something that the Hitachi worker has little need for, little chance to develop.

EXPECTATIONS

Institutions mould attitudes and they mould expectations. It is hardly surprising that the survey reveals differences in what employees expect from a company. One question asked:

'I am going to describe two different types of firms. If you *had* to choose between them, which would you prefer?

—One that paid very well, but didn't look after you when you were sick or in similar circumstances.

—One which was more human in its approach but paid lower wages.

Only 3% of Hitachi workers opted without qualification for the money, 94% for the security of being cared for. In the British engineering sample the proportions were 34% and 59%. What is perhaps more striking is the variation within the British engineering sample. The Marconi workers at Chelmsford were not so very different from Hitachi workers – 13% opted for the money, 83% for the care. The Glasgow workers, however, representing, perhaps, an older working-class tradition[7] (and, see p. 206, still relying much more

[7] Or it might have been Scottish rationality. 'You don't actually gain anything from a firm like the second one because he's reaping in the benefit of your labour

215

on kin for help in emergencies) showed a quite different balance of preferences – 53% chose the money, only 37% the security.[8]

Hitachi, it might be thought, is well adapted to its employee's requirements. But, and this may be a little more surprising, this does not mean that it succeeds in keeping them happy. The question preceding the one just quoted had asked:

'Generally speaking would you say that ... is a good employer? (The Japanese translation was more like 'a good firm to work for'.) The results were (in percentages):

	Hitachi	Marconi	Babcock
Yes	39	71	89
Yes, qualified	7	6	5
About average	24	4	3
No	22	7	1
Other, don't know	7	2	1

It is curious, first, to note that, in their further comments, although there were a number of references also to 'the money' being good, a large number of the Babcock and Marconi workers praised the firm for precisely those features which Hitachi workers have in fuller measure. 'Ay, the money's good and you could be there for a lifetime. If you're redundant they send you to another part of the works.' 'They've got a pension scheme. I pay 6s and the firm puts in 3s quite voluntary.' 'They do a lot for the workers – social activities if you're interested, and good facilities like the canteen and doctors and qualified sisters.' 'The way they treat retired men, for instance. They keep in touch – a monthly magazine goes out to all retired employees and they give them a summer outing.' 'I think they've got the best training facilities. If you're good they're willing to send you on in the world.' 'They're fair to the men. They're not strict. If you do a fair day's work, they're content.' The above replies were all from Glasgow workers, but many Marconi workers expressed themselves similarly. 'There's very little class distinction and they don't go around making people redundant at the least excuse.' 'They allow you to buy scrap for practically nothing, and you can buy everything from a washing-machine to a TV aerial for a discount.' 'They never really sack anyone unless they do something really wrong.' 'They've given me the opportunity to go to college and to be able to pass exams.' Even some of the criticisms showed similar sorts of criteria. 'There is no

and you're actually paying yourself. I mean, you're as well going out to some insurance company and saying "guarantee me £10 a week if I'm off sick" and paying them a pound a week for it. Better than having £5 a week less wages.'

[8] The British steel firm (44% and 47%) was half-way between the two. The Japanese steel workers showed a response practically identical with Hitachi's.

sense of loyalties about the place. You are just a number. You go unnoticed.'

To be sure the words 'good employer' in the question do have over-tones of nineteenth-century paternalism which might especially prompt this type of reply. One should be careful not to overestimate the prominence which such criteria have in British workers' judge-ments of their firm. Nevertheless, these replies do show that the kind of welfare benefits that Hitachi workers enjoy are of the kind that the majority of British workers very much appreciate too.

Given the full measure in which Hitachi workers enjoy them, they are singularly ungrateful. However, the replies to this question should not be interpreted to mean that Hitachi workers were seething with discontent and alienated from the firm. One factor in the dif-ference in the balance of replies may be that for an English worker in a time of relatively full employment to say that the firm he is working for is not a good firm is to invite the criticism that he is a fool for staying in it. ('Ay, it's no' a bad firm. I wouldna be there if it was.' was one reply.) A Japanese worker, on the other hand, could hardly be expected to take the drastic step of leaving if he became dissatisfied.

In part, though, the different responses to this question reflect the fact that the more you expect from your firm the more varied grounds you have for being dissatisfied. If all you expect is the chance to earn good money (the prime concern of the Babcock workers if the answers to the previously quoted question are to be believed) then if the money is good you can be satisfied.

This interpretation is borne out to some extent by the interview replies. Seven of the twenty-seven Hitachi respondents who elabor-ated on their answer and whose answers were recorded, did offer criticisms which reflect broader expectations than most British workers would be likely to entertain – 'They don't take enough account of the opinions of the people at the bottom.' 'You just have to do what you're told; there's no scope for independent work.' 'I want to use my skills more fully.' 'The foremen are too autocratic.' 'The foremen have out-of-date ideas.' In one case: 'The firm is just too relaxed, too complacent about its national prestige. Not go-ahead enough.'

The same differences in assumptions are reflected in the pattern of replies to the following question:

In most firms now management consults with the union on things like pay and working conditions and the handling of redundancies. Do you think workers should have a say in other matters too? For example, supposing the firm has to decide whether to lay out

£50,000 for a new machine. Do you think workers' representatives should take a part in that kind of decision, or do you think that is management's job?

At Hitachi only 32% thought it was management's job; 28% said in answer to further probes that the workers' representatives ought at least to have veto power. By contrast, at Marconi only 5% and at Babcocks only 6% thought they should be that much involved, 58% and 65% respectively thought this kind of thing should be entirely left to management.

This is not the whole explanation of the different answers to the 'good employer' question, however. Seventeen of the twenty-seven Hitachi workers whose reasons for their dissatisfaction were recorded complained about Hitachi wages. Evaluations of this kind are necessarily relative, and the implicit standard of comparison for the Hitachi worker is doubtless other comparable electrical engineering firms about which the chief thing they know is their wage levels – generally cited by the Hitachi union to strengthen its claims for an increase.

It still remains, perhaps, to be explained why Hitachi workers should take a gloomy view by comparing themselves with Matsushita workers, rather than count themselves lucky in comparison with workers in the other firms in the same district as themselves, than whom they are very considerably better off. The answer lies partly, as already mentioned, in the way the unions prepare their case, and this reflects the fact that in the lifelong commitment system there is no real local labour market of the kind the British workers – who compare the money they get with wages in other *local* firms – are involved in. A similar 'satisfaction' survey in a firm with the highest Japanese wage levels equally elicited a large number of complaints about wages. Their standard of comparison was the wage level of American workers – the only obvious yardstick available to their union in pressing for yet higher wages.

There is also involved, perhaps, a difference in culture or average personality, a difference on a dimension which has cheerfulness and good-humoured complacency at one pole and a worried earnestness and anxious questing for self-improvement at the other. That such national differences do exist seems clear from a comparison of the results of various surveys of professed 'job satisfaction' carried out in a number of countries. At all occupational levels from professional to unskilled workers, Germans are less likely to say that they were satisfied with their work than Americans or Norwegians.[9]

[9] Alex Inkeles, 'Industrial Man; the Relation of Status to Experience, Perception and Value', *American Journal of Sociology*, 66, July 1966. This may be in

At any rate there is little in the twenty-seven recorded replies to suggest that there is widespread dissatisfaction springing from the all-embracing demands which the welfare corporatist system makes of its members. Only four replies could be put in this category: 'The seniority wage system is bad.' 'You get moved around the factory from job to job too much.' 'There's favouritism', and the most sweeping condemnation: 'It's a feudalistic firm.'

The last reply bears a little further examination. Given the usual Japanese use of the word 'feudal' as a boo-word, the resentment it reflects is probably directed against superiors' high-handedness and the lack of consultation (made clear also in other replies quoted above) rather than against the holistic claims of the firm as community. The original pre-war version of the 'enterprise family' structure of firms like Hitachi combined corporatism with authoritarianism. The effect of the post-war 'social-democratic revolution' in industry was to modify the authoritarianism while retaining, indeed strengthening, the corporatist aspects reinforced by the ideology of the firm as community. But the changes in formal institutions – the sweeping reduction of status distinctions, the acceptance of the union's right to bargain – were not matched by an equally immediate democratization of the *informal* relations between superiors and inferiors in the work situation. Change in this regard has been slower. The complaints about autocratic foremen are symptomatic of the friction attendant on the still on-going adjustment from a highly authoritarian to a less authoritarian form of corporatism. The next chapter will look at the whole question of authority and status.

How much these frictions accounted for the general reluctance to call Hitachi a good place to work it is hard to say, but probably the other factors mentioned above were more important. Clearly, to be fully identified with the company family is not necessarily to love it. But it is doubtful whether the reservations which inhibited such affection were such as seriously to reduce efforts to make the firm prosper. For Hitachi workers, Hitachi is the best company they have got.

SUMMARY OF THE DIFFERENCES

1. Hitachi offers better sick pay provisions and (for manual workers) considerably better retirement pension/gratuities than English Electric, though the earlier retirement age somewhat reduces (despite

part the result of differences in the wording of the questions – in America, 'Are you satisfied or dissatisfied with your present job?'; in Germany, 'If you were fifteen and could start again would you choose your present job?' But this is unlikely to explain the rather wide differences in the results.

some opportunities for re-employment) the advantages of the Hitachi worker with respect to old age.

2. Hitachi provides a much wider range of other welfare services: housing, with all the ancillary services of housing estates; educational loans for workers' children; medical services; transport subsidies; and a wider range of more heavily subsidized sports and social facilities than English Electric.

3. Many of English Electric's welfare schemes are contributory and based on voluntary membership. Many Hitachi schemes are also contributory, but membership in them is automatic – like joining the union – on entering the firm.

4. There is a corresponding difference in managerial attitudes. English Electric managers tend to see these extra services partly as an expression of civic duty to be indulged in provided it does not interfere too much with profits and partly as dictated by the need to make employment in English Electric as attractive as elsewhere. Hitachi managers tend to place a positive value on these services as improving worker morale and identification with the company.

5. Personal crises are dealt with at English Electric either by the informal assistance of workmates or through a specialized welfare officer; at Hitachi they are the responsibility of the work supervisor.

6. There is a parallel difference in patterns of sociability. Hitachi puts more emphasis on organizing group outings and sports activities for smaller face-to-face work groups.

7. British unions are, except in some limited respects, generally indifferent to the welfare benefits provided by the firm: the Hitachi union, while seeking to rival the firm's activities in organizing solidarity-creating social activities, is concerned to press for increases in, and to share some control over, 'hard' material benefits like housing and medical services.

8. Hitachi is, English Electric is not, concerned with the morals of its employees.

9. An English Electric worker's family has very limited contact with the firm: an Hitachi worker's family are peripheral members of the enterprise family – a fact recognized in the system of congratulatory gifts, the work superior's assumption of the wedding go-between role, and so on.

10. But when the claims of the family on a man and the claims of the firm conflict, the latter more often take precedence at Hitachi

than in English Electric; though this is a field in which values are changing in Japan as 'my-home-ism' spreads.

11. All of which differences reflect, account for, or make possible, another difference – that an Hitachi man's consciousness of being an Hitachi man is a more salient part of his sense of identity than belongingness to the firm is for an English Electric worker. This is also a difference in degrees of individualism.

12. These differences are reflected in different expectations workers have of the firm they work for, Hitachi workers expecting to be 'looked after' rather more than British workers, though there is a significant difference within Britain between the more cash-oriented workers in a Scottish firm and the more welfare-oriented workers in a southern English firm.

13. These differences in expectations are probably partly responsible for the fact that Hitachi workers express themselves as less satisfied with their firm than British workers, though this is also to be accounted for by differences in the standards of comparison used, by differences in culture and personality, and by the frictions involved in the transition, within the Japanese firm, to less authoritarian forms of corporatism.

Chapter 9

Authority, Function and Status

The Japanese firm is seen as an organic community which admits selected recruits to life membership. The paradigm of employment in the British firm is the contract, specific in its obligations and limited in time by a specified period of notice. Despite this, British firms too do take on some of the characteristics of a community. Given the different points of departure, however, it is not surprising that as communities British and Japanese firms should have markedly different characteristics. Notably different are the patterns of authority, the way they are related to the division of functions, and the implications that both have for the status system.

DIRECTORS

To begin at the top of the authority system, in both firms the centre of the stage is occupied formally by the board of directors. Effectively, preponderant power lies in the hands of one or two individuals known in Britain as the chairman or managing director or their immediate deputies, in Japan as *shachō* ('head of the company', president), his deputy or *semmu* (senior managing directors). In both, the board derives its authority from the shareholders who in theory– increasingly remote theory – elect its members. In practice they are co-opted or, effectively, appointed by the leading executives.

But thereafter the resemblance begins to diminish. Of Hitachi's twenty directors in 1969, fifteen joined the firm (or another subsequently absorbed by Hitachi) immediately after graduating from a university or from one of the technical high schools which before the war had quasi-university status. All except one of the others joined within four years of graduating. (Some may have been waiting for an opening since there was a good deal of graduate unemployment in the twenties.) The exception was a former banker who left his bank directorship to enter Hitachi as a director at the age of 52. Apart from directorships of Hitachi subsidiaries or affiliates, the directors have no other institutional ties except as members of organizations in which they represent Hitachi.

English Electric's board at the end of 1967 had sixteen directors (six more than three years before). Ten of these were rather like Hitachi directors in that they had executive responsibilities, no major outside interests, and either had been promoted from senior positions in the firm or had been in charge of former subsidiaries absorbed into the group – though probably, between them, not much more than half their working lives had been spent in the group's companies. The other six were part-timers – a scientist, an ex-diplomat, bankers, chairmen of other companies – there to provide institutional links and advice which *depended* on the fact that English Electric was only one of the interests among which they divided their time.

Fourteen of Hitachi's directors were engineers; the others had qualifications in law and commerce; one of them was concurrently director of personnel. Of English Electric's directors six were chartered engineers and one was a scientist; the personnel director was not a member of the board. Hitachi's president was, at 69, the oldest member of the board whose average age was 61. English Electric's chairman was the junior of all except one of his board members. Their average age would have been slightly higher than Hitachi's but for the inclusion of one 38-year-old hereditary banker.

The Hitachi board, then, is something like a council of elders of the corporate community (whose closed nature is illustrated by the exclusiveness of the loyalty its directors must owe to the firm). The English Electric board is a collection of men appointed for their capacity to contribute to the direction of the company in the best interests of the shareholders. It is said[1] that the efficiency of top management in Japan suffers from the lack of broader perspectives that outsiders can contribute, from the internal stratification of the board which makes the most recent (and therefore necessarily the youngest) appointees too diffident to assert themselves, and from the likelihood of factionalism arising from the system of appointments – new appointees tend to owe their appointment to a senior 'patron' on the board and hence to be obligated to him. It is rare, however, that factional rivalries are strong enough to jeopardize seriously the interests of the firm as a whole. Hitachi managers do, at least, have an intimate knowledge of the details of the firm's operations; they have a more complete commitment to the firm, and they all have ties developed over long years of work in the company with colleagues and subordinates lower down in the hierarchy. It is unlikely that the

[1] See M. Yoshino, *Japan's Managerial System*, 1968, chapter 7.

Hitachi board would react as the English Electric board reacted initially to the Plessey takeover bid. A press release, posted on factory notice boards, concluded with a promise to keep shareholders fully informed. It made no mention of employees.

MANAGEMENT STRUCTURES

The difference in management organization between the two firms is immediately apparent in their organization charts. An English Electric chart is a chart of individual positions. The personnel and training manager at Liverpool, for example, had reporting to him men with such diverse titles as chief education officer, industrial relations officer, personnel superintendent, or head of staff grading and records. The chart on which the positions are drawn, however, warns against attaching any importance to the fact that these posts are drawn on the same level; this is done for convenience and has 'no significance so far as relative seniority is concerned'. A chart for the Hitachi factory, by contrast, shows as individual positions only those of the factory general manager and his four deputies. Below that, even for what are clearly staff as well as for line functions, there are only collectivities – some twenty departments, each divided into three or four sections. Thus, for example, there is a materials department with a purchasing section, a warehouse section, and a branch factory materials section; the general affairs department has a personnel section No. 1 (industrial relations), a personnel section No. 2 (welfare), an education section, a secretarial section, and so on. Each department has a department chief and each section a section chief. These levels *do* have significance in terms of authority and status and age-and-service seniority. Although some sections are clearly more important than others, apart from a general recognition that all section chiefs at Tokyo headquarters outrank section chiefs at the plants, all section chiefs are of equivalent status and roughly similar ages. Thus, of the head office staff in 1967, ten of the eleven department chiefs were over 50, and twenty-four of the twenty-nine section chiefs were below that age.

These differences have several implications. First, there are no ambiguities about relative status in Japan. Perhaps it is especially necessary that this should be so in Japan because of the general social concern with status rankings, whereas Britain can more easily tolerate ambiguities (does the personnel superintendent rank above or below the industrial relations officer, for instance), but these ambiguities are still of a not insignificant consequence. There are advantages, too, in the fact that the ranking system makes clear whether any particular personnel shift is a promotion, a demotion or a sideways motion. One English Electric manager refused a challenging post at an increase in salary, chiefly because it would have 'looked like' demotion in terms of the number of levels through whom he reported to the top.

Secondly, there are differences in flexibility. The Japanese system involves a less rigid and minute division of functions at the lower levels. A section might contain from one up to half a dozen junior graduate managers (it usually takes nine or ten years at least to get to the level of section chief), plus, of course, various grades of clerks and, in the production divisions, anything up to two or three hundred workers. The section as a whole has responsibility for the duties assigned to it, and a section chief can shunt duties around between individuals according to their capacities. At the higher levels, however, the Japanese system can be more rigid. A British general manager can alter the titles and specifications of posts at any level and the lines of authority which connect them. An English Electric manager, for example, explained how he had made his chief of engineering services report to the manager of one of the production divisions, not from any organizational logic, but because the latter was suitably development-minded and an amiable person not likely to be suspected of trying to steal the credit for new developments. In Hitachi, by contrast, while a department chief has some leeway to shift responsibilities between sections, the respective spheres of competence of different departments can be altered only in a major reorganization. Individuals have to be fitted to the posts rather than *vice versa*. On the other hand that is more easily managed than in Britain; personnel shuffles take place more frequently and without the danger that someone who thinks he has not got the right job will leave the company. There is, moreover, a wider choice because it is not necessary to match the salaries *for posts* to individual expectations. In Hitachi the manager's salary grade is overtly divorced from his functional post. In English Electric too, the salary attached to a post can also be tailored to the individual, but this is thought to be a deviation from proper, market-determined principles of payment.

In general, though, it is not organizational structures alone which make a management 'organic' or 'mechanistic'.[2] It is, rather, the motives and the objectives which underlie the way in which the system is operated. Among the factors which affect people's orientations to their work are the extent to which their assigned functions conform to their previous expectations and self-assessments; the extent to which they are secure in their job or are threatened if they

[2] To borrow the terminology of T. Burns and G. M. Stalker, *The Management of Innovation*, 1961.

perform poorly; the extent to which they think the criteria by which their performance is judged are fair; the recognition awarded for good performance and the likelihood of promotion and other rewards. All of these are crucially affected by the one great difference touched on in Chapter 2: Hitachi managers are in a civil service type career system; English Electric managers are recruited for and appointed to particular jobs, promoted from job to job by a system of applications and/or offers as opportunities occur, but with no clearly marked-out career expectations.

The Hitachi system of career promotion, blending the twin criteria of performance and seniority, ensures that there is not too wide a gap between expectations and appointments. By the time they were thirty, the '1950 class' of graduate recruits (as they are collectively referred to in the firm) already began, on the basis of crystallizing reputations as to who was 'outstanding' and who was 'ordinary', to have a shrewd idea as to which of their number would make the rank of section chief by the age of 32, and who would probably have to wait until after he was 36. By the time they are 40, only a small proportion of them will see themselves as likely future directors.

Moreover, in the job they occupy they are secure. An English Electric manager can feel threatened by a younger subordinate who is more intelligent and energetic than himself. A merger, a ruthless new top management, and he is likely to be replaced by his junior. By contrast, an interview at Hitachi with a 50-year-old department chief and one of his section chiefs aged perhaps 36 was instructive. The section chief made all the running, had all the statistics at his fingertips and had all the ideas. His bumbling superior gazed benevolently on much as a father might smile benignly at his child performing its party piece. The section chief may not have held much respect for his superior's abilities, but he was willing to defer formally to his office; he was unlikely (unless he had recently been reading American management books, or the new-wave popular Japanese management literature devoted to propagating what has become known as nōryoku-shugi – the ability-first principle) to resent his superior's existence and imagine that he ought to have his job. Loyal co-operation with his superior is his best chance of accelerating his own promotion – and given the lifetime commitment he is likely to be sufficiently socialized into the system to accept that such considerations *should* be the criterion for judging performance. The department chief, for his part, protected by the system from any threat of demotion, had every incentive to bring on his subordinate in order that the performance of his department can be improved – for it is the department to which functions are assigned and the department whose performance is assessed. The security of the career system thus facilitates co-operation between senior and junior.

In theory, in the British system authority is delegated and de-centralized to individual positions. In practice, managers are often uncertain as to the boundaries of their power and how far they should refer decisions to their immediate superiors. The Japanese system, by contrast, is in theory highly centralized. In matters of expenditure, it is not difficult to fix discretionary limits – expenditures of less than X yen can be incurred on a departmental chief's authority. Where the limits cannot be quantitatively set, however, the general rule is that all non-routine matters should be referred up. A policy proposal is drafted by a junior member of a section – it may be his idea in the first place or he may be acting under instructions from higher up. It then goes to the vice-chief of the section, the section-chief, the department chief, and may, even on quite minor matters, reach an executive director at head office, collecting a 'chop' of approval from each. (Every Japanese manager – indeed, every Japanese householder – has a carved name-seal and red-ink pad in his pocket the affixing of which is the equivalent of the British signature.)

Emphasizing the collective nature of, and the tightness of the boundaries around, sections and departments, lateral transmission of proposals should take place not below the level of section chief. The section chief who receives it sends it down to the bottom of his section to collect comment and approval seals on its way back to him for further upward transmission. In effect, however, this formality is usually preceded by direct personal consultation between junior members of the two sections involved.

This system, known as the *ringi* system (the system of 'proposal submission and deliberation')[3] is yet another aspect in which the organization of Japanese firms mirrors that of the Japanese civil service. The similarity is carried further in the use of the same terms as the civil service for different types of instructions. 'Regulations' come directly from the president. (One dated January 1970 was Regulation No. 1908.) 'Directives' come from the board; 'departmental instructions', 'factory regulations' and 'factory instructions' all have their separate uses and carry different degrees of authority. Similarly appointments are 'gazetted' and so on.

Reflected in the military-bureaucratic style of these instructions is the fiction of absolute central authority. The absolute obedience they

[3] See Yoshino, op. cit., p. 254 *et seq.*, and K. Tsuji, 'Decision-making in the Japanese Government, a Study of *Ringisei*' in R. E. Ward, *Political Development in Modern Japan*, 1968, pp. 457–76.

ostensibly demand reflects the degree of commitment to the organization required of a Hitachi manager as of an army officer. And indeed there is a very real difference in the degree of actual centralization. English Electric is much more like a federation of semi-autonomous product divisions; Hitachi more like a centralized empire. The uniformity of pay systems and the standardization of personnel and training policies in Hitachi contrast with great diversity between English Electric factories (see Chapter 3). It is hardly thinkable in Hitachi that a factory should choose to send people outside the firm for training in preference to one of the firm's own training courses (see p. 50). Managerial appointments in Hitachi are centrally controlled; so are production plans. The firm's operating budgets and investment budgets may be in practice collations of the budget proposals of the several divisions, but changes *are* made at the centre, and made even in sub-sub-items of expenditure. No rigorous effort is made to calculate the profitability of minor subdivisions, as became the practice in the post-McKinsey English Electric.

Nevertheless, a good deal of the *ringi* type 'proposal submission and deliberation' is more formal than real. A mere authorization of minor travel expenditure may sometimes have to collect, before it gets to the accountant, a dozen signature seals of men none of whom bothers to enquire whether the journey was really necessary. The function of the system is to diffuse rather than to centralize responsibility.[4] The superior, by affixing his seal, takes formal responsibility for the decision, though everyone knows that he cannot possibly acquaint himself with the details of every proposal to which he has to give approval in the course of a day. He may, when something goes wrong, 'take' responsibility (just as the head of the national railways will 'take' responsibility and resign when a ferry boat capsizes and drowns its passengers in a typhoon) but normally he would not be 'held' responsible. The need for ritual atonement by the titular head – resignation or grovelling apology – is seen not as a means of encouraging the others individually but of reawakening throughout the organization a proper sense of commitment and a determination not to make mistakes. So it is missing the point to ask exactly where, up the hierarchical line through which the proposal has come, the *real* responsibility lies. It is diffused through the organization.

The British system clarifies responsibilities much more clearly. It relies for efficiency partly, to be sure, on commitment and the desire

---

[4] See Yoshino, op. cit., p. 258.

to do a good job; partly on systems of management control (improved in English Electric on the advice of McKinsey) which provide measurements of performance as a basis for giving the rewards of advancement or merit increase and the punishment of demotion or dismissal. The principle of the scapegoat which deals with the whole group's guilt is rejected in favour of justice – pinning the blame precisely on the individual who was at fault. 'When things go wrong I want to know why – in detail, and what is being done about it and who is OK and who is not', to quote one top manager's circular. As between commitment and control the Japanese system puts a good deal more of its money on the former. There is no search for 'systems so perfect that no one will need to be good'. People are assumed to be sufficiently 'good' in the organization's terms – sufficiently committed to the organization's goals – that systems of individual sanctions are not all that important. Efficiency *is*, of course, promoted by the sanctions of faster or slower promotion, but more reliance is placed on creating the conditions for co-operative pursuit of the organization's objectives in an atmosphere of relative security.

Such a system has its risks. When it works well it works very well; when it goes wrong it can go badly wrong. As a Japanese political scientist has said of the pre-war political system in which in theory all decisions were taken by the Emperor, the system of Imperial responsibility was, in effect, a 'system of general irresponsibility'. As long as the attitudes of managers, reinforced by the 'culture of the firm' are such that their own internalized norms coincide with the 'public' norms of the organization, as long as they are genuinely committed to the firm's success, the system can work well. If, however, alienation sets in, or an increasing privatization such as might result from increasing affluence, or if the economic climate changes and the firm ceases to be able to deliver the 'success' which now so effectively reinforces loyalty – at that point the system might begin to function altogether differently.

'The feeling of security . . . tends to encourage indolence and thereby to depress the character of the service'[5] said the Northcote-Trevelyan Report on the British civil service, and, a century later, Fulton: 'The term "establishment" has acquired overtones of comfort and complacency, and damages the reputation of the service.'[6]

The Fulton Report recommended more thorough-going rationalization of British civil service promotion procedures – job specification,

---

[5] Quoted in HMSO, *The Civil Service*, vol. 1, cmd. 3638, 1968, p. 109.
[6] Ibid. p. 48.

performance assessments and promotion on the basis of aptitudes, skills and relevant experience, rather than of seniority which latter should count only 'in so far as it denotes valuable experience'.[7] Nowhere did it recognize that such a system might have some compensating drawbacks in provoking jealousies and rivalries which hamper co-operation, or in breeding insecurity which leads to ritualism and smoke-screen bustle. The Northcote-Trevelyan Report, by contrast, did recognize these difficulties.[8] The merits of thoroughgoing adoption of performance criteria at the expense of the most totally objective criteria possible – age or length of service – seemed more problematic in the England of the 1850s than they do today. Perhaps this is because Britain then was a society in which, as in modern Japan, sufficiently strong moral value was still placed on personal loyalties and patronage for it to be difficult for a performance-measurement system to have full legitimacy since no one would ever *believe* that subjective merit assessments would be unbiassed. Hence the need for safeguards, for a balance between different criteria, which ensured that performance measurements, while affecting a man's fortunes (in the Japanese firm, his merit supplement, his bonus, the speed of his promotion) could not entirely make or break them.

In modern Britain, a century later, 'performance norms' have achieved complete dominance in the ideology. Organizations are based on the assumption that interview boards will always choose, or at least seek to choose, the 'best man for the job'. To cast doubt on this assumption, to suggest as a general principle that men find it difficult to assess their colleagues impartially and uninfluenced by personal feelings, is to threaten the very principles on which organizations are based and to threaten the conception of 'integrity' on which British Establishment Man founds his self-respect. A British committee containing six knights and a lord could hardly permit itself the indelicacy of undressing the Emperor to that extent.

The difference between mid-nineteenth-century Britain and modern Japan, a difference underlying their similarity in respect to the place of patronage in public life, is that Britain was an individualistic, Japan was and still largely is a 'groupish' society. That is why a system which minimizes rivalry and maximizes co-operation and security could more easily lead in Britain to a comfortable 'I won't spoil your plans if you won't spoil mine' kind of conspiracy to *use* the organization for individual ends, while it can be more easily

[7] Ibid. p. 77.
[8] Ibid. p. 116–17.

directed in Japan to co-operative efforts in pursuit of the ends of the group as a whole. This, then, is yet another aspect of the functioning of the Hitachi system which cannot be divorced from the general group-orientation syndrome referred to so often in this book.

THE WORK GROUP

Hitachi's concern with the group, its integration and its collective performance, runs right down to the shop-floor work team. One can ask a Japanese worker 'what team are you in?' and he will answer either 'the erector team' or, if Suzuki is his foreman, 'the Suzuki team'. The only way to ask a British workman the same question is not in terms of group belonging, but 'where do you work?', or 'who is your foreman?' The British workman, particularly the skilled worker in engineering, is likely to see himself as an individual autonomous contracting party in the employment relationship. The fact that he owns a lot of his *own* tools is symbolic of his independence; so are his papers and his union card – certifications of skills which are his own proprietary possession. Demarcation disputes are not just economic disputes about scarce opportunities to earn money; they involve, also, something of the same ego-assertion as the black-bird shows when it drives another blackbird off its territory. In the Bradford machine erection shops the test-bed had to be temporarily extended. It encroached partially on an area in which an older skilled man was accustomed to work. It still left him all the space he needed to work in, but when he arrived and observed the encroachment he was incensed and stalked off to the foreman to complain. It was some time before he could be mollified.

Japanese workmen do not have their own tools; they wear the firm's uniforms (although after the first issue they pay for replacements). They still develop proprietary instincts about places and jobs (some girls on the assembly line at Taga, for instance, had written their names on their chairs – as far as one could see identical to all the other chairs) but to a lesser degree. For most of them, output bonuses are for group performance, not individual performance. They appear to have less autonomy in the work situation. The answers to questions in the interview surveys which asked whether people could work at their own pace perhaps tell us as much about people's perceptions of themselves, or about the dominant cultural definition of the work situation as about the actual nature of technological or supervisory constraints. 78% of the British engineering sample, compared with 25% of the Hitachi sample, said that they could work at their own pace. (Or course, the actual technological constraints were also important, and we cannot rely enough on randomness and the general similarity of products and methods to be sure that the mix of work situations was in fact broadly similar, but the difference is wide enough to suggest that organizational differences must have been important.)

These differences clearly have implications for the role of the supervisor. Let us start with information from the interviews. Samples in both countries were asked whether they thought that the following characteristics were: (a) very important; (b) of average importance; or (c) not important for foremen to have.

Table 9.1

| Characteristic | Percentage considering this 'very important'/'not important' | | | |
| | Britain | | Hitachi | |
	(a) very	(c) not	(a) very	(c) not
He should have a good knowledge of the job and be able to organize it properly	97	0	86	0
He should help out with the work on occasion	30	32	62	7
He should be ready to stand up to his boss for his own men	81	4	66	4
He should be tough enough to tell people off when necessary	81	3	60	9
He should be pleasant and considerate to the people under him	73	5	64	4
He should be something of a psychiatrist – skilful in handling people	66	9	62	7

Allowing for a greater Japanese tendency to avoid extreme committal and to prefer 'average' answers, one major and one minor difference appears. Marginally the British workers were more likely to admire the tough man who will not let his subordinates get away with anything. 'Too easy-going', 'can't handle the men' were criticisms which cropped up several times in the answers of the British sample to another question whether 'the foremen at your factory are generally good at their job'. The much bigger difference was over the question whether the foreman should help with the work. The Japanese, to whom the foreman is a team leader, are more likely to think that he should. British workers, seeing the work group as a collection of individuals with differentiated functions, are more likely to think not.

The role of the British foreman is (to use the specific/diffuse distinction) specific. He is to organize the work, give or transmit orders as to what should be done, check on performance and apply sanctions if necessary. But if he is in charge of skilled workmen he has to tread carefully when he ventures beyond saying what should be done and presumes to prescribe how to do it. 'I've seen some of our foremen try to tell the men how to do a job. "All right", they say, "here's the spanner. You do it."' The range of competence of the supervisor has been gradually restricted in recent decades, and the sanctions at his disposal to reinforce his authority have been further whittled down. One manager's statement is typical of many.

'It's a far cry from the old mill-master type – the bowler-hatted whip-cracking foreman of the old days. Even if they didn't wear bowler hats the foremen used to be the be-all and the end-all in most works. They took decisions on material. There was a lot less detailed design so they had a lot of discretion left in telling workers how to do a job. They had to be planning engineers, rate-fixers *and* progress chasers. And they could hire and fire, and they needed a good deal of moral fibre to use that whip they held properly. Now it's different. The supervisor is almost superfluous in most areas. He's backed up by better services and direction all along the line. Most of his decisions are taken for him. Now he can't be a disciplinarian, because he has no whip. Nobody's afraid of the sack any more and in any case we can't afford to sack people. I can't risk leaving my foremen with the power to turn a man off. They're not always right. There's a good deal of familiarity on the shop floor; foremen could get into a slanging match and send a man off and we'd lose a good man when we can't afford to. I suppose we don't really choose the right foremen. We tend to use the worst principle of choosing someone who's "good at his job". But it's really organizing ability and especially leadership that counts. You've got to get somebody who inspires respect.'

The assumption, in McGregorian terms, is the X-theory assumption.[9] Workers are naturally lazy or delinquent. Sanctions are necessary to correct these tendencies. Now that the sanction of dismissal had lost much of its force and in any case has to be used very sparingly, there are only two kinds of substitute – the positive sanctions of bonus incentives to improve work efficiency and, to ensure that rules are obeyed, having a supervisor of sufficient strength of character that his disapproval or anger is itself a deterrent to minor infringements. It is also a negative precondition that he should not arouse

9 See D. McGregor, *The Human Side of Enterprise*, New York, 1960.

dislike among his subordinates by inefficiency or unfairness. (Elaborate rosters for the fair distribution of overtime opportunities or favourably rated piecework are a common further limitation of the supervisor's discretion.)

Hitachi operates on principles different in two respects, both related to the group/individual difference already noted.

1. The supervisor's function and the scope of his authority are much less specific – they extend diffusely over a larger segment of his subordinates' lives.

2. Supervisory relations are based on the assumption of original virtue rather than original sin. It is assumed that workers share the same goals as management. Ill-discipline is thus back-sliding which it is expected that workers will be suitably ashamed of if they are properly chided.

A DIFFUSE RELATIONSHIP
The first point can be illustrated very simply from the Furusato factory's elaborate job description for foremen. Item 4 in the list of his activities concerns his personnel function, the first sub-item of which is 'education and training'.

1. He should, at morning assembly, at other meetings of his work team and in personal contacts take every opportunity to make sure that his workers fully understand safety precautions and all the factory rules and instructions, thus contributing to the maintenance and supervision of a safe and disciplined workshop.

2. He should always be aware of the personalities of his workers, their family circumstances and their friendships; he should, as circumstances require, have private talks with them, and so do what he can to raise individual morale (in Japanese: *morāru*) and to maintain and improve the level of teamwork (*chiimu-wāku*).

In short, the foreman's role is intended to be much more like that of any army sergeant's than like that of a British foreman. And it is. The foreman is usually referred to at Hitachi as 'the old man' (*oyaji* is also a common way of referring to one's own father). He is the natural person for a young man to ask to be ceremonial go-between at his wedding (or perhaps the master of ceremonies for an ambitious young man who aspires to have the section chief as go-between). The foreman might, indeed, play an even more important role and actually find a bride for a young man. He would be the natural person to ask to be master of ceremonies at a parent's funeral if one were a responsible eldest son and did not have any convenient uncles around. One might consult him over any other kind of personal trouble.

Similarly, as paterfamilias, the foreman presides over the team's communal leisure activities – outings and/or drinking parties for the spring cherry-blossom viewing, a mid-summer 'cool-in' (an evening river-bank party, preferably with municipal firework display), a new year's party, farewell parties for someone going to erect a generator abroad, victory parties when the group's team wins a soft-ball competition, celebrations of some notable work achievements – completing the first production model of some long-planned machine, getting a record production total, etc.– or just straightforward 'social parties'. Apart from such set-piece occasions, bachelors may make up a group of three or four to buy a bottle of rice-wine and go to 'assault' the foreman at home – i.e. boisterously demand that he invite them in to share their (and subsequently, in larger measure, *his*) wine. (This piece of borrowed culture – believed in Japan, at least, to be an authentic German method of expressing genial affection for superiors – is known as a *sutōmu*, from the German *Sturm*. It reached the factories via the universities and elite high schools. It is hard to imagine – another illustration of the relatively much greater homogeneity of Japanese culture – that Bradford workers might organize a 'rag'.)

The money for this sociability comes partly from regular contributions to a work team social fund (out of which are also paid collective condolence and congratulatory gifts of cash for births, marriages and deaths) occasionally by gifts from the firm – for work achievement celebrations – and partly out of the foreman's own pocket – as his own wedding and funeral gifts and expenses for entertaining individuals certainly do. To be a foreman, as to be the patron in any kind of patron-client relationship in Japanese society, is not inexpensive. This is recognized by the firm in a little something extra on the mid-summer and year-end bonuses; otherwise the only other compensations are the flattery the system offers his ego, and the gifts he may receive from his subordinates when they come to pay their new year respects. (New year is generally a time for a hectic round of gift-giving, calling particularly on anyone – superior or colleague – on whose goodwill one depends. The standard greeting formula is: 'during the last year you have been very good to me. I hope I can count on you again this year.')

The ego-flattery is clearly considerable. Foremen will talk with rather solemn pride of the need in their job for skill in what they are apt to describe nowadays as '*human rirēshonzu*'. One described, for example, how he had sharply cut a young man's merit rating, not exactly as an act of justice, as punishment for poor work; he had, to be sure, been working badly, but the point was rather to administer a salutary shock for the young man's own sake. Another explained how he could usually sense when one among his subordinates was in some personal trouble, but he would usually make no move himself. If the troubled worker was himself too diffident to come to him, frequently one of his workmates would volunteer the story of what was wrong and ask the foreman to help. Only at that point would he take the man aside for a heart-to-heart talk.

It is hard now, though, to say what, even at the single Furusato factory, is a typical work team. The foundry has work groups fully functioning in the manner described. It has a higher proportion of older workers, and foundries are noted for the comradeship that is strengthened by the toughness of the work, by the thirst that it generates and by the fact that all suffer equally from a low social evaluation of their dirty and unpleasant tasks. In other parts of the works, relations are, as the Japanese say, 'drier'. Young men, interested in motorbikes and girls, and now with more money and leisure to develop and indulge these tastes, do not much look forward to boozy parties at which they are expected to listen deferentially to their elders' reminiscences. Some of them have a conception of themselves as individuals, capable of looking after themselves, which precludes their taking their troubles to their foreman. Some have learned from the new ethics of post-war Japan to look on the taking of new year gifts to foremen not as a properly moral recognition of a relation of indebtedness, but as an attempt to curry favour. But the transition is gradual, much more so in the provincial-town setting of Hitachi than it would be in one of the metropolitan centres. Curiously although it does generate a certain amount of friction – as was evident in a small minority of replies about job satisfaction discussed in the last chapter (p. 219), the transition seems on the whole to be a smooth one – much as the big changes in ideas about the family and parental authority have been accepted without too much friction[10] – and for the same reasons. The older generation too is prepared to admit the validity – even in theory the superiority – of the new values. They do not so much vigorously and righteously defend the old ways as stick to them in so far as they can because they are more comfortable, and where they cannot to adapt. Adaptation means, generally, seeking to retain the *solidarity* of the work group while minimizing hierarchical and authoritarian elements. Pre-war fore-

[10] See E. F. Vogel, 'The Democratisation of Family Relations in Japanese Urban Society', *Asian Survey*, 1, iv, 1961, pp. 18–24.

men would address their younger subordinates simply by their sur-
names. Now they add the semi-polite suffix *-kun* and are careful to
use the politer suffix *-san* to those who are their own age or older.
One Furusato superintendent (who had, in fact, served for several
years as a full-time executive of the company union federation) was
trying a new way of increasing solidarity which, he said, depended on
effective communications. He got his foremen to convene discussion
groups which he also attended. These started in the lunch hour and
often ran on into working time. Sometimes they discussed company
policy or their work organization, sometimes social problems like
traffic accidents. A main purpose was to get the younger workers to
speak their minds.

What is not clear is whether the situation is still constantly changing in the direction of 'drier' personal relations, or whether the
apparently stable kind of compromise reached in the driest work
groups (fewer parties, less open intimacy, less deference, but still a
fairly strong sense of identification with the group and a fairly faithful performance of formalities at weddings and funerals, etc.) will
prove lasting.

One interesting indication that it well might is given by a national
sample survey of Japanese 'national character'. One question which
has been asked in four repetitions of the survey between 1953 and
1968 (using very carefully constructed samples) runs as follows:

'Imagine you worked in a firm where there were two section
chiefs different in the ways described on that card. Which of the
two would you prefer to work under?

A is a man who would never try to get extra work out of you to
the extent of breaking the rules, but at the same time would never
look after you in matters which had nothing to do with the work.

B is a man who might occasionally make extra work demands,
even in breach of the rules, but on the other hand would always
look after you, even in matters outside of work.'

The striking thing about these replies is their constancy. First, the
total balance has been constant over time – consistently, over
fifteen years, 12–14% have chosen A and 82–5% have chosen B
except for a curious drop to 77% (when there were more 'don't
knows') in 1958. Secondly, the pattern of age differences has held
constant, with the *younger* age groups being more likely to prefer the
paternalist – reflecting, presumably, differences in individual life
cycles and not at all secular changes in attitudes. The only other
discriminating factors are that among university graduates 6–7%

237

more, and among supporters of the Communist Party 10–12% more than in the sample as a whole expressed a preference for the 'drier' section chief.

It is worth, also, summarizing the responses to a further probe question which asked a subsample how they imagined these respected chiefs of section. Those who approved of the paternalist saw him as warm, full of human feeling, flexible, a man with some 'bottom' (literally 'big-bellied'), a boss (*oyabun*) type, somebody who trusts his subordinates, a man with social sense, a kind, human person, a man with leadership powers, a man who thinks of others, considerate, responsible. Those who disapproved of him saw him as arbitrary, small-minded, lacking in principle, and inclined to confuse the public and the private (see p. 211), while their own preferred type, the 'drier' man, not only kept private and public properly separated, he was reasonable, rational, modern, straightforward, honest, responsible, serious-minded, just. To those who disapproved of him, however, he was cold, lacking in human feeling, inflexible, bureaucratic, obstinate, individualistic, introverted, self-centred and opportunistic; he thought that everything could be settled by rules, had a slide-rule for a heart, thought of nothing but work, and lacked social sense.[11]

THE ASSUMPTION OF ORIGINAL VIRTUE
Consider the styles of the following two documents:

'To all employees:
The amount of lateness and absenteeism is causing us growing concern and has reached a level which cannot be tolerated. On an average day no less than 1,600 people are late for work and in addition 10% of employees are absent for one reason or another. It is an established fact that an absenteeism rate on account of sickness and normal certifiable absence should not exceed 5%.

You will see from the foregoing that the situation at Liverpool Works has become very serious and it is essential that all employees should make a strenuous effort to be punctual, and employees must not absent themselves from work unless they are sick or have other causes which must be explained to their supervisor.

From now on a very serious view will be taken if employees are persistently late for work or absent themselves without due reason.'

'To foremen: For use at morning assembly:
As already announced the Workshop Discipline Enforcement Campaign for the 1970–1 first half-year will take place for the two weeks 13–24 July.

[11] Hayashi Chikio, *et al.*, *Daini Nihonjin no kokuminsei*, 1970, pp. 90–3.

The purpose of this campaign is to ensure that the essential rules which we all take for granted in our everyday activities are fully observed. It is to make those who have recently joined us aware of what the rules are, and to get those who have been here longer to reflect for a moment so that we can establish even better workshop discipline. . . .

For the first week the two themes will be more efficient use of time and the elimination of lateness. The slogans will be:

"Use every minute: use every effort!"

"Ingenuity and creativity bring higher productivity!"

"The elimination of lateness depends on your attitude of mind!" '

The minatory tone of controlled anger in the first document contrasts with the earnest cheer-leader tone of the second. The 'very serious view' taken of lateness and absenteeism was translated in one Liverpool department into a formal set of sanctions. Six times late or three times absent without a certificate was counted as bad time-keeping and merited in the first instance a verbal warning in the presence of the shop steward. The next stage was a written warning handed over in the presence of the senior shop steward. Then finally came dismissal. Over a period of five months, eighty-five were dismissed from the department of a workforce of 1,600.

Furusato had rather higher standards than were implied by Liverpool's definition of bad time-keeping. For example, on the second day of the campaign fortnight, foremen were expected at the morning assembly to explain the slogan: 'Use every minute; use every effort!' One of the points to be made was about the lunch hour.

'When the warning siren goes five minutes before the end of the lunch break, make sure that you are ready to start again immediately the next siren goes. You should, for example, stop your ping-pong or other sports and wipe the sweat away, or leave your *shōgi* chessboard. In other words your mind and your body should be already turned towards the next job of work to be done.'

The next day the subject was lateness. Statistics (analysed by entry gate) were given for one particular day. Of the 8,000 employees at the factory site, 917 had arrived between 7.50 a.m. and 7.55 a.m. Thirty-eight had arrived after the physical jerks had begun at 7.55 a.m., and seven, even, had arrived after work had actually started at eight oclock.

'The beginning is important, as in all things. Staying up late the night before, just taking the relaxed holiday mood too far on a Sunday and forgetting the next day is Monday – if we can lead more

239

regular daily lives this kind of lateness can be reduced to zero. We should all think about this, because it is our problem, the problem of every one of us.'

Apropos of creativity, ingenuity and productivity, foremen were to tell their workers:

'Ours is the oldest factory in the company, with the longest tradition. Compared with other newer factories we have a stronger organization, a richer stock of skills and experience. The underlying strength of our tradition is something we can be proud of. But, on the other hand, is there not a danger that we are losing flexibility, falling into the trap of ritualism?' [*Manneri*, translated here as 'ritualism' is none other than the English word 'mannerism'.]

Unfortunately, we did not have a chance to observe with what valiant urgency the foremen (who wore yellow arm-bands with the slogan 'Discipline!' for that fortnight) did carry out their denunciation of ritualism at their morning assemblies. Perhaps they did not show quite the same enthusiasm as was apparent in the hand-outs drafted by the personnel department. 'Apparent', however, was the operative word. The young man who drafted them was not wholly committed. As he said, using one of his favourite words, *manneri*, 'doing this kind of thing regularly every six months, it tends to become just ritualistic. I suppose it's better than not doing anything at all. But you know, I'd have thought, wouldn't you, that the foremen would have been embarrassed to go around with those arm-bands on. In fact they quite seem to take a pride in wearing them.'

The Japanese ability to listen to portentous solemnity with a serious face is not, of course, confined to factory life. It affects politics and education just as much. The slogan is a ubiquitous phenomenon. Seeing, say, the little admonition hung in gracious calligraphy in a Hitachi committee room: 'Dark is the life where there is no kindness; decadent is the society where there is no sweat', a good many Japanese might be moved to indignation at this insidious embodiment of a pernicious capitalist ethic. But few would be moved to giggles.

Even allowing for this cultural factor, there remains the basic difference that Japanese managers can and do operate on the assumption that workers fully accept the values and the goals of the firm; British managers operate on the assumption that their workers' commitment is a very limited one. This is apparent, for example, in the factories' suggestions schemes. Both firms try to mobilize creative ideas from the shop floor, partly to improve productivity, but partly to increase the sense of involvement. (Though according to the manager in charge of the scheme in one English Electric factory, more the former than the latter. 'It brings better worker-employer relations, some firms say. I've never heard such cut and tuff in my life.') The basis of the reward system varies considerably, however. In the English Electric factories, suggestions are made on a prescribed form. In one of them the name of the suggester is detached and the proposal given a number so that there can be no suspicion of favouritism in the judges. Engineers assess the practicability of the proposal, and if it is acceptable estimate the annual saving which would result from adopting it. The reward is based on that saving (but with some flexibility: a very bright idea may not bring great savings because it applies to a product produced in very small batches). The Bradford leaflet explaining the scheme allows for appeals against the value of the award. In Hitachi, by contrast, suggestions are judged into three grades, but there is no attempt at costing. Grades A and B receive prizes – gift tokens of a quite modest standard value for use in the firm's co-operative shops. There is no question of appeals.

The basis of the British scheme, in other words, is the reciprocity of the contract. An employee who contributes *his* (his own individual, private) ideas to his employer can expect to share proportionately and is entitled to complain if he does not get his rights. (The frequency with which he does so was the reason why the manager quoted earlier doubted the scheme's contribution to better worker-employer relations.) An Hitachi worker, on the other hand, is just doing his natural duty a little more conscientiously and enthusiastically than normal and deserves commendation, but this is hardly a matter of rights and the commendation is more symbolic (in the language in which these matters are discussed in socialist societies, 'moral') than material.

A parallel difference may be found in the disciplinary regulations. The Bradford factory had a published set of rules issued to each worker. Apart from information about hours of work and wages, it consists of a few simple prohibitions – against bringing liquor or unauthorized strangers into the factory, against taking company property or secrets out, against holding unauthorized meetings or posting unauthorized notices. Apart from the scale of automatic pay deductions for lateness, the only sanction mentioned is summary dismissal for breaking the rules – i.e. termination of the contract, one part of which is acceptance of the rules. In practice, suspension is also used on occasion, but fines and other disciplinary measures belong to the paternalistic past of British industry.

In Japan, however, the corporation is a micro-polity. As the traditional Chinese political classics used to say, the secret of good government is the judicious use of rewards and punishments. Punishments, according to the Hitachi regulations, are graded. A reprimand requires the offender to write a *shimatsusho*, a formal admission of guilt combined with an apology and a promise to reform. (Rather like writing lines in an English school.) A fine may be for up to half a day's pay and suspension for up to thirty days. In both cases a *shimatsusho* is also required. The final sanction is dismissal. The offences which might meet with reprimands, fines or suspension are listed under fifteen heads and include most of those specified in the Bradford rules, but also such sins as slandering members of the company or having 'seriously disgraced oneself as a member of the company'. Causes for dismissal include theft, accepting bribes, sabotage, violence, unauthorized moonlighting, convictions for a criminal offence and wilful disobedience of a superior's instructions.

But, as the Chinese treatises all went on to say, the mark of *good* government was its more frequent recourse to rewards than to punishments. It is significant that in the Hitachi rules the section on 'Rewards' precedes the section on 'Punishments'. Suggestions for improvements in working methods come here as just one occasion for reward. Others are saving life in danger, preventing disaster, outstanding results in training schemes, bringing honour to the company by social and national achievements, general excellence in the performance of duties, and 'being a model to one's colleagues for devotion to one's work'. Rewards are graded, from letters of commendation, gifts in kind, and gifts in cash to extra holidays. Exact statistics were not available, but the general guideline was to award – apart from the long-service and suggestion awards – some five commendations or prizes annually per thousand workers. These were mostly in the 'model of devotion' category, awarded to people who 'also serve' in dull and unexciting jobs. More rewards were in fact meted out than punishments.

WORK STYLES
How far do these differences in assumptions and organizational methods reflect in the actual methods, pace and style of work? Our opportunities for unobtrusive watching of people at work were too limited to treat the subject exhaustively, but some comparisons can be made.

Work started more promptly at Hitachi and lasted until the appointed time. There was frequently a slackening off in the last half hour; sometimes, but not always, an assembly line belt would be slowed down in the last ten minutes, but one did not see, as one saw in one shop at Liverpool, a queue of men, their overcoats on and lunch bags in hand, already lined up across the gangway from the time clock at 4.52 p.m., ready to leap forward as soon as the bell rang three minutes later.

The difference in lateness and absenteeism is clear from the earlier discussion, though the Liverpool factory was particularly plagued by absenteeism and is far from typical of English Electric factories. In a department of 200 at Bradford which had what was considered a good record, absence without permission accounted for a smaller loss of 1·6% of working days over one half-year. In that half-year, though, lateness averaged ten times per worker for an average of ten minutes each time. (A less serious view of lateness is taken than at Hitachi, however. Up to twelve minutes lateness a week is allowed without loss of pay. One man received a severe warning only after he had been late sixty-seven times in a few months.)

The actual pace of work was probably not very different. Work study men at English Electric who used the MTM system said that, as was common in British factories, they added 15% grace time to the standard times for operations used in the United States. Furusato used the WF system and added 20% to American times, but expected that to cover waiting time and other contingencies for which no extra allowance was made. The Taga factory manufactured auto-mobile electrical equipment under licence from Joseph Lucas. A Taga manager who had seen a Lucas film of the process said that his girls worked a little more slowly than the British girls did – at least when the film was being made.

Work at Hitachi was more minutely organized. The bureaucratic procedures of formal regulation and recording penetrated further down the system. There was more use of pencil and paper, of written rather than verbal communication. Workmen erecting machines at Bradford had blueprints to which they referred only when they struck something which was unfamiliar. Their opposite numbers at Hitachi had not only blueprints but also a detailed work-book specifying the operations and the order in which they should be done. They also had a log-book in which they recorded each operation as they did it, noting, for instance, that a hole had been wrongly drilled in a flange and had had to be redrilled. After morning assembly described in the first chapter, one worker began his day by writing in his log-book the three tips and hints about the job which the foreman had offered. Another example of formal written communication at Furusato where in Britain a verbal discussion would be likely: the erectors had complained that a cooler casing was too hard to get on and asked that the design should be modified. The prescribed form for request-ing changes in design required a detailed verbal description plus drawing, and had no fewer than nine spaces for signature seals of approval – for the head foreman, superintendent and section chief of the erection shop and for their opposite numbers in both the design and the inspection departments. Again, the Furusato safety roster was a feature which had no counterpart in Britain: one man in each work group was made safety officer each week. He was required to do routine checks and record the results in a log book as well as give a verbal report to the foreman. It was pointed out in Chapter 2 how much more *literate* apprentice training was in Japan than in Britain. It is not surprising, perhaps, that an American psychologist who carried out comparative experiments in persuasibility with groups of students from several different countries found that Japanese students were unlike all others in being more influenced by written than by verbal communications.[12]

In English Electric factories regulations and procedures were in the first place less fully prescribed. For example, only the Bradford factory had a published set of rules to be given to every employee; at Liverpool a copy was available in the personnel office for anyone who had the temerity to ask to inspect it. One manager explained that spelling these things out only gave points away to the barrack room lawyers. You wanted security officers for instance, to have the right to search people whom they suspected of walking out with several pounds of copper wire wrapped around their waists, but people start shouting about human rights if you put that down in black and white, so it was better just to exercise the right and keep quiet about it. Again, the elaborate job description for foremen at the Furusato factory contrasted with the situation in one Liverpool shop where a manager and a foreman seemed to have different opinions as to whether foremen had the right to sack or not. Secondly, the procedures prescribed were taken less seriously. On a Liverpool assembly line, the foreman had an official weekly report form in which he was supposed to report all interruptions of the work flow. It showed no entry for several days. 'But this is the one you want to look at', he explained, fishing out of a desk a school exercise book in which his pool leader had kept detailed jottings. This unofficial record could be turned into an official record later when they had decided what was to be their bargaining position in the weekly haggle over the allowance for waiting time (bargaining both *vis-à-vis* their workers and *vis-à-vis* managers). Furusato foremen when they had to fiddle the books to get a 100% average and couldn't do it by borrowing tickets from other foremen, at least went along to the rate-fixers and got

[12] E. McGinnies, 'Cross-cultural Investigation of Some Factors in Persuasion and Attitude Change: Written *v.* Oral Presentation', Tech. Rpt. No. 6, Contract No. 3720 (01) University of Maryland.

an *official* retiming for one or two big jobs. The same Liverpool foreman, a highly intelligent young man, who was making his way successfully up the night-school qualification ladder and was clearly destined for higher things, spoke ruefully of some of the dilemmas he had to face. There was, for instance, a rule that no one who came to work late should be given the chance of overtime that day. But he had to meet his production targets, and if he could not persuade those who were entitled to work to stay on, the rule just had to go by the board.

Other features reinforced the impression of a greater neatness and disciplined formality at Hitachi; a looser, even sloppy, informality at English Electric. At Liverpool a dented and hence unusable washing-machine casing had been going round the supply conveyor belt for weeks, collecting a layer of dust and the odd cigarette packet. It was no one's job to take it off and no one bothered. At Furusato, the foundry had surrounded itself with some rather splendid flower beds which workers tended in their lunch hour – thus they tried to compensate for the foundry's dirty low-status image, and to soften the arid masculinity of the one shop in the factory where no women worked. (The explanation of the safety officer.) At Furusato one was allowed in the engineering shops to break off for a cigarette, but not on the assembly lines; at Liverpool and at Bradford one could smoke while one worked. So, too, in dress and speech. Hitachi workers wore safety helmets issued by the company in every shop where there were cranes: assembly line girls had uniform head-scarves. English Electric workers wore a variety of clothes; they were urged to buy protective boots and they were offered for sale at a cut rate, but they were not compulsory. A foreman in Hitachi was addressed by his title – 'Foreman!' He addressed his subordinates by their names plus the polite suffix appropriate to his addressee's age. In English Electric foremen and their workers mostly used Christian names, occasionally for the foreman a 'Mister', but there was generally greater informality. The young foreman quoted above described how 'the first time I heard Jimmy [the pool leader] say to one of the women "what the fuckin' hell do you think you're doin'?" I looked hard in the other direction. But I found they just answered back, "Oh, fuck off", and now I find myself talking the language.'

PRIDE, WORK ETHIC AND AUTHORITY

It is not unreasonable to summarize these differences as differences in the intensity of the work ethic. People work for a variety of reasons, but among them is a kind of nagging inner urge that leaves one uncomfortable at the non-fulfilment of *duty* if one denies it. It is

245

highly probable that the average Japanese feels this more strongly than the Englishman. The only true test of this would be outside the *employment* situation – among the self-employed. Certainly, the standards of cultivation on Japan's minute agricultural holdings both now and a century ago, suggest a quite high level of this 'pure' dutiful work ethic in a large segment of the population.

But people also sometimes work for the instrinsic satisfaction of the work, or the anticipated pleasure of completion and achievement, Consider the following:

'I've pretty well been all over the department now. I can do welding and I've been on the coils long enough to have a good knowledge of the electrical side, and I can put one of those generators together in my sleep. The company likes to have a number of us all-round men to send off for outside work – for erection jobs – especially abroad where they can't send too many people. We're getting a lot of foreign orders now. Apparently Hitachi is getting a good reputation in the world.'

'I suppose us chaps in the tool-room are about the tops, though talking about this job evaluation business, I'm often having friendly arguments – well, sometimes not so friendly – with Joe Burks the boilermakers' steward as to which job needs the most skill. It'll be awkward if they come out with more points. But I don't think they will. You need such a variety of skills in a tool-room. A tool-maker gets some satisfaction out of his work too – making something that depends on him. That's one reason why they're not militant. I could never stand a production job – turning out bits of metal the same shape every day. . . . Hm. Seems funny, doesn't it, to be talking about getting satisfaction out of your work. Or taking pride in it. If I were to go down to the local and admit that I take a pride in my work I'd be laughed at.'

What are the cultural differences which explain the differences between the Bradford worker's ambivalence and the Hitachi worker's lack of inhibitions about expressing pride in his work? In the first place, those who have the kind of routine jobs in which it is hard to take any kind of pride have probably made up a more dominant majority of the working class over more generations in Britain than in Japan, so that their natural view of work as purely an unpleasant means of earning money has become the dominant cultural assumption of working class society.[13] Secondly, as will be discussed in the

[13] Though the extent to which it dominates may vary depending on the type of work a man does. See J. H. Goldthorpe, *et al.*, *The Affluent Worker: Industrial Attitudes and Behaviour*, 1968, Ch. 7, especially p. 161.

next chapter, there is a more separate 'insular' Hitachi culture. His Hitachi workmates, rather than the chaps at the local, are more likely to form a Hitachi worker's reference group. Thirdly, a Hitachi worker has no inhibitions about conflating his own individual pride in his own skills and his collective pride in his company's achievements. An English Electric worker, on the other hand, is more likely to see the employment relation as essentially one of exploitation – hence to express pride or satisfaction in one's work is to show a naive complicity in one's own enslavement, a pitiful susceptibility to the boss's propaganda.

An important source of the difference in work styles and behaviour, then, lies in a difference in attitudes to authority. In Hitachi it is accepted that the company has the right to 'post' a man around the factory as needed – and even to send him out to work for a sub-contractor. In English Electric one expects to be consulted and given a choice; in one case where, with a switch from an individual to a group bonus system, a work force had to be cut down, managers in effect renounced their pretensions to direct and let the shop stewards decide which three 'poor earners' would be transferred out of the shop. Very minor changes in work allocations can, if not preceded by consultation, cause a walk-out in a British factory; in Hitachi, as Chapter 6 made clear, managers' authority in work matters is rarely challenged. In one shop there were complaints at an excessive work load which was causing far more overtime than men wanted to do – complaints (met with an explanation of the urgency of the order) but no suggestions of refusal. Overtime, in an English Electric factory is spoken of chiefly as an opportunity (which the employer has a duty to provide) to earn extra money. Only 30% of a national sample of workers said that they had ever done overtime under pressure, when they didn't positively want it.[14] In Hitachi (although many people are apt to complain if there is *less* than thirty hours a month of overtime) overtime work is still spoken of as a burden and the union is concerned to limit the number of hours which a man may 'be required' to do overtime – because, by and large, the culture of the factory expects a man to do overtime when he is told to. We have already seen in Chapter 6, that Hitachi workers accept – albeit, some of them, with some resentment – that they should not insist on taking their entitlement of holidays.

At least three alternative explanations might be offered of this important difference:

1. That the Japanese are basically more submissive.

[14] A National Board for Prices and Incomes report, summarized in *The Guardian* (7 October, 1970) but apparently never published.

2. That they consciously identify with the success of the firm and accept the authority of superiors as legitimate and functionally justified.

3. That they do not subjectively identify, but they are the victims of subtle psychological and organizational manipulation which prevents their (conscious) anti-authoritarian impulses from being expressed.

The first explanation should by no means be ruled out. That there are differences in 'national character' – in the average personality – which contribute *something* to the differences in behaviour described seems fairly clear. In the interview survey this was reflected consistently in the greater cautiousness of Japanese workers. When offered a range of alternatives, Japanese workers were more likely to choose intermediate 'more or less' answers: British workers more likely to opt for definite ones. A small, but perhaps significant difference came out in answers to the question: 'What sort of thing do you like especially about your present job?' Among the variety of (unprompted) answers, 8% of Japanese, compared with 3% of the British said that their present work was 'easy' – i.e. they were not likely to make mistakes and 'get in trouble'. The formal use of titles to address superiors; the vestigial nod-like bows which sometimes accompanied acknowledgement of an order, are both manifestations, and reinforcements, of a general syndrome of authority-acceptance which doubtless has its roots in the family and the school.

In both companies people spoke of a diminution of submissiveness. Thus a Hitachi foreman:

'I don't know what would happen if I talked to the men in my team the way my old *oyaji* (old man) used to bawl at me when I was learning the job. The ideal worker then was somebody who never answered back even if he was told to do the impossible. Nowadays – I like people to be co-operative, of course – but you've got to recognize that people have their own ideas – and I prefer it that way. I like a man to speak up when he doesn't think what I've told him to do is the right way of going about it.'

And an English Electric manager:

'Youngsters today are better in some ways than they used to be. They *are* better educated, there's no doubt about it, and they're not prepared to accept the dogmas of their fathers and forefathers. They're no respectors of authority, either. Why, people in the thirties touched their forelock – literally. Partly that was fear of the sack. Partly it's the difference growing up in the average decent working-class family then and now. They never had any money to spare. You couldn't indulge the children if you wanted to. Where money was short, so were tempers. People were irritable. Discipline was brusque. Children had more respect for their parents and when they went to work they were already conditioned to accept authority.

Now – well, first there was the war with lots of fathers away. Smaller families. Full employment. More money about. Parents can indulge their children now. They keep them quiet by buying them things rather than giving them a clip round the ear. The parents have more money to go off to dances and bingo, leaving the kids at home with somebody who doesn't care tuppence about disciplining them. And so you get the "I want it" attitude. These lads are no worse fundamentally. In fact they learn more at school and their education is more designed to encourage them to think and ask why. So in the factory they tend to resent authority – not only what I'd call pseudo-authority, all puffed-up hot air, but also, unfortunately, real necessary authority, too.'

The secular trend has been similar in both societies; Britain has gone a good deal further.

But clearly, Japanese workers are not by any means without any feelings of resentment against authority. There must be quite a number whose Walter Mitty fantasies centre on The Day I Told the Boss to Jump in the Lake. According to one young man:

'A friend of mine had been to high school and was here welding with me. Work was slack at one time and he was given the order to go to the Totsuka factory which is all light stuff. It so happened that he'd broken his leg skiing and was off for two months, and in that two months orders picked up again. So he was told he didn't have to go to Totsuka. So he came back one day and right there, on the shop floor, he went for the section chief and bawled him out: "What the hell do you mean by playing people around like a game of chess every time the order book changes? I came to this company to do welding. What do you mean by telling me to go on to low voltage stuff?" He'd taken the precaution of getting his national welder's certificate before he did it so he was preparing for this. We could all hear every word, because he did it right here on the shop floor. I thought, "My God! He's quite a lad!" I can remember his words now. They're burnt into my ears. I'd like to think that I could walk out just like that any time I wanted. If I was put off welding on to some other work I rather think I would.

Why do these resentments not crystallize into open and *concerted* rebellion? It is partly because they don't seem to be all that strong –

because the managers' assumptions (see the earlier discussion) that workers share their own goals and values are not all that mistaken. This in turn can be ascribed to certain features of the micro-organization of the shop floor:

1. The density of supervision. The Hitachi factory has one foreman for every sixteen workers. Even the Taga factory with a number of large co-ordinated assembly lines has one for every nineteen. The Liverpool factory had one for every thirty-five – one for every forty-four in the domestic appliances division. One of sociology's better-attested generalizations is that, other things being equal, the higher the authority level a person occupies in an organization, the stronger is likely to be his commitment to that organization's goals. Foremen are more likely than their subordinates to share the goals of management, and their stronger commitment is more likely to spread to and influence sixteen workers than thirty-three.

2. The chance of his exercising such influence is enhanced by the emphasis on the work team as having collective responsibility for tasks assigned to it, and on the foreman as a *member* of the team, not as someone set above it. The fact that the foreman very often *is* the union representative, and even where he is not it is an accepted part of *his* role (not the union representative's) to negotiate with senior management to reduce excessive work loads, enhances this.

3. Especially in the more traditional type of work groups (less so in those where the authoritarian element has been reduced while retaining solidarity and the sense of belonging) the foreman is the nodal point of relationships. For each of his subordinates their relation with the foreman may well be of more importance to them than relationships with fellow workers. Each worker relates to the foreman as an individual rather than collectively.[15] The situation can be diagrammed

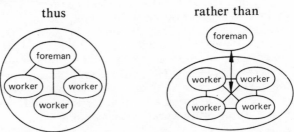

thus   rather than

[15] On the structure of groups in Japanese society see Chie Nakane, *Japanese Society*, 1970.

and certainly rather than

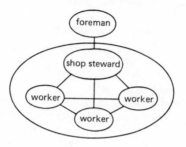

There are very good institutional reasons why this should continue to be the situation even in groups where the foreman has moved a long way from the traditional authoritarian *oyaji* style. The foreman decides a man's merit-rating. His recommendation will determine his chance of promotion on the one hand, or uncomfortable transfer on the other. Generally, it seems that, except for young workers least identified with the firm and the work team, men rarely discuss their merit-rating with their colleagues in their *own* work team. Both the discovery and the revelation could be embarrassing; one might incur either dislike as an unduly favoured 'blue-eyed boy', or wounding commiseration as someone justly marked down. It is much more comfortable to assume (as in fact seems very generally to be the case) that everyone is around the average. The merit-rating, therefore, is a secret which each man shares only with his foreman, not with his fellow workers. Divide and rule is too familiar a principle for the situation to need elaborating.

4. Since the union pretends to only a very limited degree of control over the work situation it is only in rare situations in Hitachi – where the union representative is not the foreman, where he is exceptionally independent-minded, and where the foreman is either inept in dealing with his men or too compliant with excessive demands from his superiors – that there ever emerges any rival leadership, comparable to the shop steward's function in Britain, which provides an alternative focus of solidarity for the work group. (See the diagram above.)

THE STATUS SYSTEM
The microstructure of the work group thus explains something, but it does not explain everything about different propensities to resist authority. Underlying the English Electric worker's resistance is often a resentment against a superior management based on the

251

belief that they: (a) are overprivileged; (b) are inefficient; and (c) owe their jobs to influence rather than merit. Thus a shop steward:

'Japan eh? They showed us some films about Japanese industry in the lunch hour. Marvellous organization it was, the way all those materials come in on the conveyor belt. What's it like over there? Do they have the same class distinctions as we've got?'
— What do you mean by class distinctions?
— I mean the fact they won't give the workers staff status. There're men have been working here for forty-five years, and they still get only two weeks' holiday, and then some youngster comes in as a storeman and in no time he's got three. I consider anybody can copy out a lot of figures. . . . Well, anyway, do you want to ask me questions, or shall I make a statement?
— Why don't you make your statement first.
— Well, this factory, to start with, isn't run proper at all. It's bloody disorganized. Management at the top don't know what they're doing and the reason is they've brought in a lot of people who don't know their job. Take C for instance. He was brought in by his brother eight years ago and now he's a flaming superintendent. Then there's E in charge of production control. Straight out of the army, and when he came in here he didn't know a Whitworth bolt from a DSM.
   The result is that we can't put four components together that they will fit. Sometimes it's the fault of the drawing office, sometimes they can blame the outside suppliers, but then these parts ought never to get past Goods Receiving.
— Don't the drawing office people come down when you complain?
— Oh, they come down all right. Sometimes they stand back and have a jolly good laugh about it. Oh, they're honest enough. Admit the drawings are wrong. They just say it's too expensive to change them. They're blurred, you see – reproduced from old negatives, often they don't have the essential measurements written in and you've got to work them out yourself. I can tell you there's strong feeling about this. I've been here nine years and if it goes on much longer this place will close down.
— But don't you have shop stewards meetings with the managers now so that you can make these points?
— Oh, yes. Mr D started that, but you know these meetings don't get you far. I suggested they ought to alter the layout of the floor so that we could make better use of the space. But Mr F told me: "We are the managers. We have to manage and you're hired to do the work." F's improved a lot, though. The story is that he cost the

firm £50,000 at Preston, so they gave him six months' leave on full salary and then gave him a job here.

— Don't you get the impression, though, that he's told the foreman to allow a bit extra on the bonus scheme for the fact that the work has fallen off.

— I grant you that, but what good's that doing us? I've been forty-five bob a week down overall since Christmas whereas the cost of living has gone up and up. F says he's very sorry; there just isn't the orders to provide the work, but *he*'s not getting a cut in his five thousand a year. I think managers' pay ought to be tied to production. When the machine gets on that wagon there you get paid and not before.

— I was looking at the attendance record and the late register. . . .

— You probably saw my name down there too. I admit I'm a poor getter-upper. Discipline used to be a lot stricter when they could get skilled men easily. Also the place was better run. There was only one superintendent and three foremen and three managers. Now there are fifty-four managers. The reason is not because the work has got complicated but because they are working a fiddle. They're giving people what's supposed to be a new job so as to get a wage increase past the Prices and Incomes. There are thirty-five managers in this firm who've got cars supplied free and all petrol free from the company. Jaguars, Rovers, right down to Corsairs for the little chaps. And down here on the shop floor when we've got to tighten big six-inch nuts we have to do it with a hammer and a plug because the firm won't buy spanners to fit.

This may not be an accurate picture of the firm (in one or two ascertainable facts it is not – the salary of the manager referred to, for instance) but it is an accurate reflection of this man's disaffection, and of the general character of the factors responsible for it. Such disaffection is less likely in an Hitachi worker because the stratification system is different in three respects.

First, status differences are more likely to be seen as legitimate. In so far as there *are* clearly defined strata – managers, middle-level technicians and supervisors, and workers – recruitment is quite rigorously geared to educational qualifications, and in Japan there is sufficiently widespread respect for education in general for superior qualifications to make superior authority seem legitimate. Moreover, whatever sociologists might discover about the advantages middle-class Japanese children do enjoy in practice (though few Japanese sociologists are in fact concerned with the question), the educational system is believed to be an open, competitive one, offering equal

253

opportunities to all: there is no privileged sector equivalent to the British public schools.[16] Disaffection is likely to occur only when there is ambiguity about the relative worth of different kinds of qualifications – as in the case of the products of the firm's own technical high school who are not accorded the same career opportunities as graduates of outside schools. (See the discussion of the recruitment of trade union officers on p. 170.)

In default of education, age, too, can be a legitimator of authority, more effective in Japan than in England. (In answer to one of the interview questions, only 20% of the Hitachi sample, compared with 52% of the British, said that they saw no 'objection to having foremen of 22 or 23 giving orders to workers twice their age'.) Hitachi foremen were not always the oldest members of their group, but they were nearly always older than the majority of their subordinates. The Furusato factory's job description for foremen specifies appropriate appointment as being after fifteen to twenty years' service. The exceptions, chiefly at Taga, are younger foremen chiefly supervising women.

Secondly, the meritocratic elite of Japanese industry – like the elite in other spheres, politics, education, etc. – is a new post-1870 creation. The old feudal upper crust of the warrior class lost its power, its land and its cultural dominance in the Meiji transformation. The life-style created by the new, westernizing, lower samurai elite had no direct continuity with that of the previous rural aristocracy. In England, where change was slow and non-revolutionary, the cultural traditions of the land-based aristocracy, and the political and educational institutions which embodied and preserved them were only gradually modified, not sharply broken. Hence styles of authority still reflect a society in which superior status is demonstrated by conspicuous leisure and merely amateur engagement in pursuits which to lesser mortals are real and earnest. Still, in the era of Weinstock and Marks, many feel that authority is most authoritative when it seems, Macmillan-like, languid and effortless. *Surtout pas trop de zèle.* When a Japanese manager asks a visitor from Britain, 'Don't you think that we Japanese are *kosekose shite iru* – that we fuss too much?' he is implicitly expressing his admiration for the languorous confidence he meets in many foreigners, their cool

[16] There are, of course, private universities, entry into which can be bought, but they do not act as bearers of a distinct, class-specific culture in the same way as the British public schools, and they do not have as high a reputation – either educationally or as being the place to make influential connections – as the best of the open, state-subsidized universities. Private education acts to favour the well-to-do chiefly through the private middle and high schools which provide better coaching for the state universities' entrance examinations.

254

étonnes-moi scepticism about new technology or new scientific management gimmicks, contrasting with his own earnest determination never to fail in the duty of self-improvement, never to be left behind in the race to keep up with the onward march of science. What their self-criticism[17] does not take into account is that while their more earnest fussing style may not so effectively overbear, it does run less risk of causing resentment among subordinates than mannered, cool, aloofness. Japanese managers work hard, are seen, wish to be seen and must be seen, to work hard. Whether this results in greater efficiency or not is a debatable question (by and large it probably does, though see the remarks about the complications of the wage system in Chapter 3, p. 106) it certainly seems to make for more willingly co-operative subordinates. Status in Japan is not correlated with the time one gets up or has dinner or goes to bed. Managers and men keep the same hours in Japanese factories.

This brings us to the third difference. Japanese managers are less privileged in fact, and less attention is drawn to such privileges as they actually have. Table 3.3 (p. 96) showed the wide difference between managers and manual workers in English Electric in matters of holidays, hours of work, sick pay and pensions. In Hitachi, managers and workers work the same hours; holidays depend only on service not on rank, and in practice managers are likely to take fewer holidays than workers; sick pay and pensions are based on the same criteria, though they differ in amount, in the case of sick pay paralleling, in the case of pensions exaggerating, differences in monthly salaries.

The Liverpool factory had a directors' dining room, another superior dining room where the top category of managerial staff gathered for free drinks before free lunches, a slightly less well-appointed dining room with waitress service where the next category of staff paid for their own meals, and a canteen. Formerly there had been two canteens for junior staff and manual workers separately, but a building

---

[17] To be sure, success has somewhat diminished the frequency with which one meets this kind of self-criticism (though it is too much part of the Confucian self-improvement syndrome – utilized also in China's cultural revolution in the intellectuals' self-flagellating renunciations of their errors – to disappear completely). Japanese are now more likely to be proud of their serious earnestness, and a little scornful of the aristocratic decadence of the countries they are overtaking. A famous Japanese *littérateur*, giving a Press conference before a British Council-sponsored tour of Britain perhaps set the tone when he said (making it clear that although he was accepting the trip he was no British stooge). 'Somehow the British seem to me to be typified by Lord Chatterley. We Japanese are the gamekeeper, but the difference is that we've now got both the virility *and* the money.' (*Shūkan yomiuri*, 6 June, 1969.)

reorganization meant that they had to be amalgamated, with roped-off sections. This caused some embarrassment because the workers could see the white tablecloths and HP sauce bottles on the other side of the rope. So everyone had white cloths. Eventually the rope was removed. Segregation at this bottom level then became a less rigid, more voluntary matter between the table service and self-service sections. Toilets were likwise segregated. 'How silly can you get?' said one shop steward relating an incident which resulted when a rather superior hourly-rated worker toilet was installed in one shop. The workers' steward had 'got his own back' by lodging a formal complaint when drawing office staff came down to use it.

Since the Japanese do put flowers in their home toilets one presumes that they are not wholly insensitive to lavatorial aesthetics, but Hitachi does not ration such pleasures according to status. There is no formal segregation of toilets and there is only one kind of canteen – though senior managers do get frequent occasion to entertain visitors at the firm's expense in the factory clubs which are generally used by manual workers only for weddings or other formal celebrations. The only comparable form of segregation is in housing. For young men there are separate dormitories for university graduates and for high school and middle school graduates. In the housing estates there are what are known as a superintendent's row, a section chief's row, a department chief's row and so on, graded according to size, though the actual correspondence between size of house and rank is not exact.

As important as real privileges are symbolic distinctions. (Starting times, for example, are as much a matter of symbolism as of real privilege; some English Electric managers may, in fact, put in more hours.) The pay system presents another contrast. Everyone in Hitachi is paid by the month: there is no distinction between wages and salaries. (And perhaps, incidentally, the need to plan the spending of exiguous wages a month at a time has contributed to the general prudence and longer time-horizons of Japanese workers, compared to weekly-paid British workers, the majority of whom would be likely to resist payment by the month. It has thus contributed – along with many other factors such as the integrated national school system – to a minimization of the actual *cultural* differences between managers and men, to the production of a more homogeneously 'middle-class' society.)

Dress is another outward and visible sign of differentiated self-perceptions. One 'places' a man easily in an English Electric factory; blue overalls for manual workers, brown overall coats for labourers and storemen, white for foremen, red for inspectors, green for apprentices – and suits, collars and ties for superintendents, rate-fixers and above. In the production shops of the Furusato factory all ranks wore the same denim battle-dress type of clothes with helmets. In the offices some wore the same dress; others, especially young graduates, either for aesthetic reasons or as a gesture of noncon-formity, wore ordinary clothes. Everyone had an identifying name badge at Furusato (see p. 24) whose only obvious indication of status was a number indicating seniority. At Taga there is no such number; the rim of the badge has a different colour according to rank – one colour for a foreman, another for a section chief and so on. When the badges were introduced at the Furusato works in the early sixties ('the place was getting too big; nobody knew anybody any more') the management there also wanted to have differentiating rim colours as well as numbers, but the union objected and sustained its objections. In the production shops, however, foremen, super-intendents and section chiefs are distinguished by stripes around their helmets.

The union's concern to eliminate status discriminations based on any other ground than seniority, is symptomatic of the fact that this deliberate underplaying of status distinctions – contrasting with quite rigid distinctions in pre-war Japanese companies – is very much a product of what was called earlier Japanese industry's social demo-cratic revolution (see Chapter 4). But it would not be accurate to characterize the differences simply as a difference in the degree of egalitarianism. In English Electric factories deference is, to be sure, shown to some degree. There is some asymmetry in terms of address. A shop steward is likely both to address and refer to a manager as Mr B; the manager to use a Christian name, or if he is a top manager the surname unadorned by Mister. But in general relations are less formal than at Hitachi; foreman and worker are more likely to be on first-name terms, whereas in Japan the foreman is addressed more deferentially by his title.

The difference, then, is not that Hitachi is devoid of hierarchy. The hierarchy is of a different kind. Consider the diagrams below:

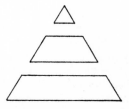
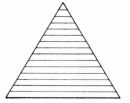

The contrast, dichotomizing sharply in what is, in fact, a matter of degree, is between a class system and a system of infinitely divisible strata. English Electric employees have a conception of the status system of their factory (and, for that matter, of their society) in terms of a few more or less homogeneous layers separated by marked gaps. The extent to which people are conscious of the gaps depends on the *variety* of differentiating criteria which *coincide* on the same lines of division – income, method of payment, toilets, canteens, holidays, pension rights, dress, accent, union membership, etc. – in addition to functional authority positions.

In the Hitachi system, by contrast there are:

1. Far fewer discontinuities – toilets, canteens, etc. do not demarcate status groups. Pay scales are a *single* continuum.

2. Such discontinuities as do exist do not coincide on the same lines of division. Thus the most important middle school/high school/university division which most affects career chances and is reflected in the housing provision, does not coincide with the management/union division: graduates are likely to spend the first decade of their career as union members.

3. Sometimes they not only do not coincide: they cross-cut. Thus, the seniority criterion of status frequently cross-cuts both the educational criterion and the structure of functional authority. The functionally superordinate superintendent, a university graduate aged 26, will use the more deferential equivalent of Mister when he is addressing a subordinate foreman, and he will certainly be getting *less pay*. The dirty/clean criterion of status which puts the head office staff at the top, the engineering shops in the middle and the foundry at the bottom, likewise cross-cuts rank. So does departmental membership. Such is the strength of identification with one's department that the graduate superintendent in, say, the turbine shop, may well conspire with his non-graduate foreman against the other graduates in the head office. Similarly, the special titles of master craftsman, etc. for manual workers and the ranking system for managers (see pp. 68 and 100) provide other systems of status ranking which may not coincide with actual authority positions.

4. Finally, the hierarchy of 'functional' authority positions is much more finely graded, so that no single superior/inferior line of division puts too great a distance between one position and the next. Even among directors, there are deputy presidents, senior managing directors, managing directors and just plain directors. For every title to which the word 'chief' applies – foreman (which is literally in Japanese 'team-chief'), section chief, department chief – there is also

AUTHORITY, FUNCTION AND STATUS

a vice-chief, frequently also an assistant chief, and sometimes an assistance vice-chief as well. Between foreman and assistant section chief there is always a superintendent and probably a senior foreman and a supervisory senior foreman. Add to this the smaller size of the work group and the higher proportion of foremen, and it will be obvious that although Hitachi does not go so far as Dentsū, the advertising company, 70% of those employees are said to possess a title, it does not have a large mass of workers, untitled and un-honoured and destined to remain so all their working lives. Where the 'functional' authority system is in this way so finely graded, sharp discontinuous breaks are less likely to be seen to exist. And that is the purpose. 'Function' has been put in quotes in this paragraph since the proliferation of posts is, of course, far beyond any actual needs for mobilizing experience or intelligence in the taking or implementing of decisions. Japanese organization builders have been aware of the fact that the latent function of organizational structures to distribute *prestige* can have just as much ultimate importance for the organization's effectiveness as the manifest function of distributing *authority*.

The consequences of these differences in perceptions of the factory status system are fairly obvious. In the Hitachi system, an encounter between a department chief and a shop-floor worker is an encounter between X the manager and Y the worker *tout court*. Where there are clearly demarcated status groups, on the other hand, it is assimilated to, it becomes an instance or a development of, relations between 'managers' and 'workers'. Any resentment which might be generated between 'him' and 'me' illustrates and confirms the general assumption of an antagonistic relation between 'us' and 'them'. The process is a familiar one: in Marxian terms it is the process by which a class 'in itself' is transformed into a class 'for itself'.

THE BASES OF AUTHORITY

It is now time to summarize with a tentative answer to the question raised on p. 247. How does one explain differences in the propensity to resist authority? Apart from basic cultural differences in attitudes to authority in general, can one say that the Japanese worker rationally accepts authority which he perceives to act in his own general interest, or that he is exploited but manipulated?

In terms of dignity, or prestige status, Hitachi workers *are* less deprived than their English Electric counterparts. There are, there-fore, fewer occasions for resentment on that score. There are, also, fewer occasions for resentment on grounds of managers' calm in-difference either to the needs of efficiency or to the needs of the workers. There might seem to be *more* occasion for resentment in the greater scope of managerial authority in Hitachi – the limited degree of choice allowed to individuals, but given the difference in the general values of the societies, this in fact is less irksome to Japanese workers than it would be to their British counterparts. Whether there is a more exploitative relation in terms of money will be considered more fully in the next chapter; the answer seems to be: if so, only marginally.

Overall, then, given the respective orientations and expectations they bring to the factory in the first place, the Japanese worker is less likely to have occasion for resentment against authority than his British counterpart. But that is not the whole story. In so far as he does experience rebellious impulses the organization is such that his resentment is less likely than in Britain to be shared, echoed, magnified and crystallized into category antagonism. In British factories the differences in privilege, etc., which create the framework in which the resentments are magnified also helps to create the resentments themselves.

To say that the Japanese system is manipulative and the British is not, is presumably to suggest that while both Japanese and British managers would like to diminish distrustful antagonism among their workers, the Japanese do it better. It might also be, of course, that British managers care less whether they arouse resentment or not. Some ideals of 'strong' leadership, after all, require opposition in order to prove themselves, and some people cannot get the maximum enjoyment from their power unless others visibly suffer from it.

SUMMARY OF THE DIFFERENCES
1. Hitachi directors have nearly all graduated to their position after a lifetime of work in the firm; they are at the top of a civil-service-like career structure, the most senior of them being chairman. Some English Electric directors have also reached their position via internal promotion, some are outsiders who contribute certain specific kinds of expertise or influence. The Hitachi directors are more likely to see themselves as elders of a corporate community rather than as men responsible to the shareholders for wringing the maximum profit out of the shareholders' property, the firm.

2. Hitachi's management organization is fitted into a pyramidical arrangement of teams, sections and departments, much in the manner of a civil service organization, or of any army divided into platoons. companies and battalions. In English Electric managerial staff have titles which directly specify their functions; in Hitachi responsibili-

ties are assigned to groups and can be shunted around among individuals within them (another contrast on the individualism/groupishness dimension).

3. Hitachi's organization relies on maximizing co-operation between managers. Co-operation is enhanced by: (a) the career security of a seniority plus merit promotion system (so that seniors are not too threatened by more able juniors); and (b) the system of diffusing and sharing responsibility. English Electric relies rather on the clarification of responsibilities, performance checks and sanctions on individuals – yet another aspect of the group/individual contrast.

4. Hitachi's management organization is in many other respects similar to that of the Japanese civil service. English Electric's is dissimilar from the British civil service. The civil services of the two countries also differ along the same dimension as suggested in the last paragraph, but much less so than the two industrial firms.

5. On the shop floor, British workers are more individual workers: Japanese workers are more members of a team.

6. Foremen in Hitachi are leaders *of* their team, expected to take a direct part in the team's work, rather than supervisors set *over* a work team.

7. Their role is less specific, more diffusely extending to concern with the general well-being of members of their team. There is a good deal of sociability between the foreman and his subordinates outside of the work situation.

8. But there is a tendency for the extent of a Hitachi foreman's concern with his subordinates to narrow and for his assertion of that authority to be less assured and autocratic. How far the solidarity of the work team will be retained with less authoritarian leadership remains in doubt.

9. English Electric work discipline is based on rules reinforced by formal sanctions; Hitachi work discipline is based on rules reinforced by exhortation designed to recall workers to the path of their original virtue.

10. Work effort at Hitachi is more disciplined and sustained than at English Electric, though the work pace is probably not very different.

11. Work at Hitachi is more minutely prescribed and regulated and there is greater reliance on formal written communication and records

261

BRITISH FACTORY—JAPANESE FACTORY

than at English Electric where less is formally prescribed, there is more reliance on verbal communication and human memory, and the formally prescribed procedures which exist are treated with a lesser respect.

12. Hitachi workers are more likely to express a sense of pride in their work. One among several reasons for this is that Hitachi workers more easily accept the firm's legitimacy: English Electric workers are more likely to see it as a system of exploitation, to express pride or satisfaction with any aspect of which would be to show a naive complicity in one's own enslavement.

13. This relates to a generally greater willingness on the part of Hitachi workers to accept, a greater tendency on the part of English Electric workers to resist, managerial authority. This can be ascribed to several factors, among them:

a. Cultural differences, a generally greater 'submissiveness' in the average Japanese (though in both Britain and Japan such submissiveness as a general cultural trait is diminishing).

b. Certain features in the structure of the work team which inhibit the expression, and hence the magnification of such rebellious urges as Hitachi workers do sometimes feel, viz.,

  i. The greater density of supervision; the higher ratio of foremen to workers than in English Electric.
  ii. The fact that the foreman is in Hitachi seen more clearly to be *of* the group and to represent its interests *vis-à-vis* superiors than in English Electric.
  iii. The fact that the foreman tends to become the centre of the team's network of personal relations, whereas the collateral relations of workmates are more important in the English Electric work group.
  iv. The fact that the union does not generally seek control of the work situation.

c. Differences in the status system generally.

  i. Positions in Hitachi depend more on the objective characteristics of formal educational qualifications and age, and the ranking of status and authority is therefore seen as more legitimate than in English Electric where it depends more on subjective assessments.
  ii. Styles of authority are less influenced in Hitachi by aristocratic traditions. Japanese superiors are supposed to set an example by working harder, not to emphasize their superior status by demonstrating that they have less need to work.

262

iii. English Electric has a 'class system', a hierarchy of fairly clearly demarcated strata: Hitachi has a status pyramid of more finely graded divisions. In contrast with the English Electric system in which staff and hourly-rated are sharply separated by pay methods, fringe benefits and holiday entitlements, by canteen and toilet segregation, by dress and often by type of education and family background.

Hitachi has fewer such clear differences in either material or symbolic privileges;

such differences as exist do not coincide, as at English Electric on the same lines of division and sometimes cross-cut (as with seniority and functional rank); and

Hitachi has a greater proliferation of hierarchically ranked job titles, the function of which is more related to morale-building than to effective division of labour.

As a consequence, therefore, there is,

a lesser tendency for individual subordinates to experience resentment against the authority and privileges of superiors; and

a lesser tendency for such resentments as are experienced to crystallize in and to be magnified by, a sense of membership in a particular stratum and collective antagonism between strata.

Chapter 10

Two Employment Systems

'System' is an insidiously fashionable word among social scientists, and it is a healthy instinct, on hearing it, to reach for one's dejargonator. Nevertheless, the preceding chapters will, I hope, have made it clear that there is a sufficient *consistency* in the differences between Hitachi and English Electric for one to speak with some reason of different employment systems. Lifetime employment, a seniority-plus-merit wage system, an intra-enterprise career system, enterprise training, enterprise unions, a high level of enterprise welfare, and the careful nurturing of enterprise consciousness, are all of one piece; they fit together – as do the contrasting features of the British firms: considerable mobility of employment, a market-based wage and salary system, self-designed mobile rather than regulated careers, publicly provided training, industrial or craft unions, more state welfare and a greater strength of professional, craft, regional or class consciousness.

How, most conveniently and illuminatingly, can one characterize these differences? We are not concerned here with the viability of the two systems and their futures. That will be the subject of Chapters 12 and 13. Nor are we concerned with explaining the origins of these differences, which will be the subject of Chapters 14 and 15. Here we are concerned with rationales, underlying organizational principles – and finally moral evaluation.

One way of characterizing the differences is to say that the Japanese system is one which differs from the British chiefly in that it accords to manual workers those privileges – fringe benefits like pensions and sick pay, considerable security of tenure, a rising curve of earnings consonant with the increase in family responsibilities – which in Britain are restricted to middle-class workers and almost entirely denied to those who work with their hands. With the slight qualification, before one applauds the equality of the Japanese system too enthusiastically, that what is here called the Japanese system should

264

be properly called the Japanese large-firm system (see Chapter 12) and that the majority of Japanese manual workers are outside a full version of the Hitachi-type system, there clearly is a good deal of truth in this characterization. It is clearly not the whole story, however. It explains – or summarizes rather – what were called in Chapter 4 the post-social-democratic-revolution aspects of Japanese industry, but it does not, as a characterization, embrace the fact that British managers also differ from Hitachi managers in being mobile and market-oriented, less enterprise conscious and so on.

A second characterization commonly encountered (and one not wholly, perhaps, lacking a whiff of ethnocentrism) is that whereas the British system is open, honest and contractual, frankly recognizing conflicting interests and reconciling them in an adult and masculine way, the Japanese system is a hypocritically devious form of exploitation by paternalism. One possible objection to that characterization is to ask: who, exactly, is conning whom? Are the directors of Hitachi fostering false consciousness in order to enrich themselves and their friends the shareholders at the expense of the ordinary workers and the underpaid junior graduate? And were they themselves equally the victims of exploitation when they, too, joined the firm as junior graduates from fairly humble middle- and lower-middle-class homes in the 1920s? One could suppose that they are and were, and that over the years they have shed their false consciousness and come to see, and manipulate, the system for what it really is. Alternatively one could reject such vulgarian notions in favour of the view that exploitation does not require conscious deceit on the part of the exploiter; he *usually* believes the ideology which bolsters his power.

It might be more profitable, however, to ask of the Japanese system *is* it exploitative, and secondly is it paternalistic?

Exploitation is the first difficulty. Let us evade all scholastic economic metaphysics about surplus, and make the simple assumptions that (a) everyone's definition of exploitation involves some kind of inequality (b) as between situations which are structurally similar in terms of the social functions people perform, exploitation in almost anyone's definition is likely to correlate with inequality of material rewards, and (c) that one can therefore use inequality of material rewards (on the measurement of which it is fairly easy to agree) as a proxy for *all* the various things that various people mean by exploitation. Be that as it may, inequality *is* what the following discussion is about.

First, let us look at company accounts. Because of different ways the firms make up their accounts, particularly different ways of treat-

265

ing the costs of services, it is not possible to arrive at comparable figures for 'value added' as conventionally defined in either country. One can, however, find the total of the following items, components of value added in both definitions, and show their relative shares.

Table 10.1   *Relative weights of certain components of value added*

Shares	Hitachi (Fiscal 1968–9) (%)	English Electric (Calendar 1967) (%)
To Labour		
Wages, salaries and directors fees	47	76
To Capital		
Dividends	6	6
Interest	10	5
Total	17	11
To the State		
Corporation tax	14	5
To the Company		
Depreciation	12	7
Retained earnings	10	2
Total	22	9
Total	100	100

Dividends made up the same proportion in both firms and amounted, as it happens, to 11% on the ordinary shares in both firms, representing in each case something like a 4·4–4·5% return on market values. As for the shareholders' capital gains, in the seven years up to 1967 English Electric shares had appreciated by 48%, Hitachi's in the seven years up to 1969 by 37%. Discounting by the consumer price index for inflation these percentages become 18% and −7% respectively. The much larger difference in the other element of the returns to capital – interest payments – reflects primarily the much more rapid pace of capital investment at Hitachi and the greater reliance on bank rather than equity capital which is common in Japanese firms. (English Electric's share capital in 1967 equalled 30% of the total funds employed: Hitachi's only 15%.) The banks also plough back their profits so that the interest payments are not necessarily available as anybody's consumption, but lead instead to an expansion in credit.

When we come to look at the *relative* shares of labour and capital, however, the difference is striking. Since the rewards to capital seem similar in terms of the total amount of resources to be distributed, it is perhaps more true to say that labour gets *less* in Japan than in England, than to say that capital gets *more*. Labour gets less chiefly because (a) the state gets more, and (b) more money is invested in the further growth of the firm. It can be argued that employees as a group gain more from the government services bought with their taxes than do the owners of capital (if only because there are more of them) and that they will also benefit, as well as shareholders and banks, from the increased productivity resulting from capital investment. Hence, if one includes transfers and takes a long-term view, the gap between the shares of the British and the Japanese worker is somewhat narrowed. A big difference still remains, however, and in spite of the general scepticism of economists about the potency of institutional factors in altering the labour share, it seems plausible to attribute a large part of that difference to the tighter union squeeze at English Electric. This is not a true measure of comparative union strength, however. The Hitachi union was able in the 1960s to gain regular annual 10–18% increases in wages, compared with English Electric workers' 2–5%, thanks to Hitachi's growth and increase in productivity. (Turnover at English Electric nearly doubled in its last four years, but chiefly through mergers: Hitachi's doubled in three years without benefit of mergers, though helped, perhaps, by a slightly faster rate of inflation.) Only if Hitachi's growth rate and rate of growth in labour productivity fall to British levels would the respective bargaining strength of their unions really be tested.

The above table by no means tells the whole story, however. 'Labour costs' includes all wages and salaries and directors' fees. The inequality of income *within* this category is nowadays a more generally important determinant of overall inequality than the Ricardian categories of labour and capital shares. Comparisons here are somewhat complicated by the wide age differentials at Hitachi, but the following table gives a fairly good idea of the magnitudes involved. The manual workers' wages include bonuses, but exclude overtime.

These figures need some qualification. Directors on both sides may have had some other sources of income. In the Japanese case, since there are published lists of upper-bracket tax payers, it is possible to some extent to check. The average return of pre-tax income for Hitachi directors was approximately £16,000 compared with the £11,500 given in the table below which was derived (like the British figures) from the information about directors' salaries and bonuses given in the company accounts.[1] Some of the difference may be due to salaries received by some of the directors by virtue of

[1] The total declared as directors' bonuses and salaries was divided among the 15 directors not listed as having another salaried post within the firm. Some of these fifteen were also probably receiving executive salaries, however. See Okurashō, *Yūkashōken hōkokusho sōran 69-3, Hitachi.*

Table 10.2   *Indexes of Comparative Earnings Levels*

	English Electric (1967)		Hitachi (1969)	
	£s p.a.	Index	Yen 1,000s p.a.	Index
Manual workers				
aged 25	850	101	540	63
aged 35	845	**100**	850	**100**
aged 55	840	99	1,500	177
University graduates aged 24–6	1,400	166	852	100
Works manager of factory with 4–5,000 employees	4,000	470	4,500	529
Full-time director (average, including chairman, president)	14,140	1673	11,500(?)	1,353(?)

executive positions in the firm or from the accounts of the Hitachi subsidiaries they also direct. Only a small part of it is attributable to extra income from dividends on Hitachi shares. The Hitachi president owned enough to bring him a dividend of £3,200, less than a tenth of his gross income. The holding of some directors was such as to yield annual dividends of not much more than £200. Unfortunately it was not until English Electric had ceased to exist that the law required British companies to disclose at least some of the information which Japanese companies have long since had to provide to the public, but using the accounts of the post-merger company's first year, if the chairman's share-holding remained unchanged he would, in 1967, have received from an 11% dividend an addition of some £1,500 to his salary of £35,000 (before tax). The Hitachi President's declared gross income before tax for 1968–9 was, at the prevailing exchange rate, approximately £35,200.

Other fringe benefits need to be taken into account, but unfortunately there is no easy way of estimating them. Both companies would provide a factory manager with a car; Hitachi with a car and personal driver. A Hitachi factory manager would be certain to have more meals and more lavish meals on expense accounts. He, and even more directors, would also have a wider variety of other emoluments smuggled into the firm's accounts. Altogether, according to the Japanese tax authorities, during the 1969–70 tax year the tax-deductible expenses in the average engineering firm amounted to 5·4% of gross turnover – midway between the agricultural enterprise average of 2·8% and publishing's 12·5% [sic].[2]

It is hard, therefore, to reach a clear verdict. There are complications in the middle ranges – with a 35-year-old manual worker getting as much as a 25-year-old graduate in Hitachi, for instance, but

[2] *Asahi shimbun*, 13 January 1971.

considerably less in English Electric. In terms of the distance between top and bottom, inequality of pre-tax incomes is probably slightly greater in Hitachi, though the difference is not large. In terms of post-tax income, however, the gap would be much greater since the top income tax and supertax rates are higher in Britain than in Japan.

Another aspect of the matter is how the workers *view* the distribution of rewards. Do Hitachi workers show signs of having been brainwashed by the 'Hitachi family' ideology into accepting a larger measure of income inequality more docilely than their British counterparts would be? It does not appear so. The respondents in our sample were asked of various grades of employees whether, on balance, they considered them very, or somewhat, overpaid or underpaid, or paid just about the right amount. About directors, the chief difference was that 57% of the Hitachi sample compared with 44% of the British sample said they didn't know. Exactly the same 32% of both samples thought directors were overpaid (though in line with their general tendency to give more cautious answers, the Hitachi respondents were rather more likely to say 'somewhat' rather than 'very much' overpaid). A mere 1–2% of each sample felt that directors were underappreciated, leaving 24% in Britain and only 9% in Japan generally approving of the *status quo*. 'Managers other than directors' were viewed a little more favourably in both countries, but not very much more so at Hitachi. Of the British sample 42% and of the Hitachi sample 20% thought they got too little or just the right amount. More Hitachi workers than British workers (29% compared with 20%) thought them overpaid.

To sum up, then, the degree of inequality in the distribution of the proceeds of the companies' operations may well be greater in Hitachi than in English Electric, especially if taxation is taken into account, but the difference is not very great, and it does not seem that the effect of Hitachi's greater 'paternalism' is to brainwash the Hitachi workers into a less critical acceptance of the inequalities which exist.

PATERNALISM

But is it correct to describe the Hitachi system as 'paternalistic'?

Paternalism is usually seen as typical of industry in societies still predominantly agricultural. It represents an adaptation to industry of the kind of face-to-face patronage relations typical of many peasant communities. Paternalistic employer/employee relations can be characterized using Parson's set of dichotomies in the way that, for example, Hoselitz has done,[3] in the following manner.

[3] B. F. Hoselitz, 'The Development of a Labour Market in the Process of Economic Growth', *Trans. 5th World Congress*, International Sociological

1. *Ascribed* characteristics (of kinship, caste, hereditary 'estate') affect the relationship. Employers may derive their authority from superior hereditary positions; they may recruit people because they are their kinsmen or co-religionists – these are all *ascriptive* deviations from the *achievement* principles which would require the employer to seek only the best performing workers, and would require the worker to seek only the best-paying employer.

2. The employment relation is not *specific* (as an exchange of labour and cash) but *diffuse* – affecting the whole man. The employer 'takes care of' his employees and they respond with a general loyalty which might extend to voting for his nominees or performing domestic chores for him.

3. The employment relation is not based on any *universalistic* principle such as the duty to stick to promises, to perform contractual obligations, or to maximize one's profit or to earn one's living. The only obligations acknowledged are *particularistic* – the duty of loyalty to one's employer or supervisor, the duty to look after those who are loyal to oneself.

4. These relationships are *affective* rather than *affectively-neutral*. There are warm human ties, not just the impersonal cash nexus of the market place, between master and man.

How far, in these senses, is the Hitachi system paternalistic?

Ascription/achievement

On the first count, hardly at all. Let us begin with recruitment. Positions in Hitachi are achieved, not given on the basis of ascriptive characteristics. Entrance is regulated by very strict qualification standards which might be bent only very marginally in favour of someone with kinship connections – and rather less easily at the graduate level than in the case of middle-school leavers. (Some Japanese firms explicitly ban all children of employees from entry. One firm known for recruitment by influence practices rational profit-maximizing nepotism on a large scale – it is an advertising agency which recruits the sons of the family firms whose accounts it handles.) It is English Electric, not Hitachi, whose chairman got his job in direct hereditary succession to his father – and that in what was by no means a family firm in any conventional sense. It is worth recalling, too, the discussion of 'public' and 'private' in Chapter 8 and the

Association. Similar approaches may be found in other standard works on labour and vol. 2, economic development, e.g. the editors' preface in W. E. Moore and A. Feldman *Labor Commitment and Social Change in Developing Areas*, 1960, and C. Kerr, *et al.*, *Industrialism and Industrial man*, 1962.

results of the national opinion poll in Japan largely condemning any bending of rules in favour of a relative.

Nor is the authority of the manager in Hitachi substantially dependent on the aura which attends birth in an hereditarily superior class. Hitachi managers are mainly of fairly humble middle-class origins (middle in the sense that they belonged to that proportion of the population – perhaps 40%–50% in the twenties, 50%–60% in the thirties – who could afford to let their children go to a selective state middle school if they proved to have the necessary talent). They went through exactly the same curriculum at exactly the same kind of primary school as their workers; they are not easily distinguishable in accent or vocabulary or bearing. It is in English Electric factories, not in Hitachi factories, that these things clearly mark off some managers – the public-school-educated managers – from their workers.

Position within the firm is also achieved, by job performance, though here the ascriptive characteristic of age acts as a qualifying factor. Certain minimum ages are necessary to occupy certain positions. (The same is also true in English Electric, though in a much less formalized way and within broader limits.) One might almost say that educational qualifications become another form of ascribed characteristic in Hitachi since they limit the range of posts which one can achieve in a more absolute and formal way than in the case of English Electric and do not have a clearly obvious relevance to job performance. Educational qualifications are achieved, however. All of which shows up the limited usefulness of the achievement/ascription dichotomy.[4] Let us leave *that* question to be pursued in a footnote by those whom it interests. Here it will suffice to note that the

[4] Metaphorically one can say that entry into the firm is a kind of rebirth; a process of permanent reascription in terms of achievements up to that date, but this hardly gets round the problem. In fact, of course, there is not one dichotomy but a multiplicity. If one sets up at one pole the ideal of allocating positions 'solely on the basis of assessed capacity to perform the duties attaching to those positions', one has to distinguish various different directions of deviation from it – allocating positions in the light of: (a) characteristics of a man's family ('birth ascription') being careful to distinguish birth ascription *per se* from performance criteria which are highly correlated with birth – for example, the power to command which may be much more likely to be bred in upper class families; (b) irrelevant acquired discriminatory characteristics – a convert's religion, membership in the Free Masons, marital status, to some extent educational qualifications; and (c) irrelevant egalitarian characteristics – like age, the Buggins' turn principle – which are egalitarian in the sense that everybody reaches the age of 50 in exactly the same number of years after he was born.

Even after one has drawn these distinctions one is not finished. First, there is a difficulty inherent in the ideal-typical 'filling of positions solely on the basis of assessed capacity to perform the duties attaching to those positions.' How can

271

Hitachi system is very different indeed from the 'ascriptive-orienta-tion' of the paternalistic small employer taking on hereditary serfs or co-religionists and promoting his kinsmen to the major positions of trust.

Moving now to the second dimension – specificity and diffuseness – it is clear from Chapter 8 that the relations between an employee and the company is seen as a very diffuse one – considerably more so than in English Electric. But here again there is a wide difference between the diffuseness of Hitachi and the diffuseness of the typical early-industrial small employer. The latter assumes a responsibility for his employee's general welfare which he exercises at his personal discretion. How long he looks after him when he is sick, whether he will lend him money to pay a debt, depends on how loyal the worker has been and how grateful the employer feels for his loyalty. In Hitachi, by contrast, the 'diffuse' side of the relationship, the ar-rangements to look after the employee's welfare, are institutionalized and contractual. So many weeks of sick pay are guaranteed. When one's wife dies one receives a condolence gift according to the tariff set out in the Mutual Aid Fund rules. Only in a very limited degree is there any personal discretion involved in the conferral of benefits: first, within the official system a supplementary retirement bonus is, like the merit element in pay and in the annual bonus, based on an assessment of one's contribution to the firm; secondly, the foreman or section chief's visiting of sick employees or acting as go-between at their weddings, is a direct continuation of older forms of per-sonal paternalism on a small workshop team basis, sanctioned and encouraged by the firm.

The development of trade unions in nineteenth-century Britain was one factor helping to destroy earlier forms of paternalism. Unions, concerned with the specific matter of bargaining over the market price of labour, destroyed the efficacy of early forms of paternalism as a means of keeping the employment relation diffuse and thereby

capacities be assessed in advance? Perhaps the best one can do is to look for characteristics which have, in the past, proved to be highly correlated with superior performance. Thus considerations of a man's age, educational qualifica-tions, or his class of origin (if, for instance, upper class people are generally bred to give orders effectively) may be a reasonable way of predicting performance. These 'ascribed' characteristics thus become proxy measures of unmeasurable achievement.

Secondly, the 'duties attaching to those positions' may include in some or-ganizations being willing, for example, to lie vociferously to the income tax authorities to cover up for one's superior. Such loyalty may be found only in kin: again an ascribed characteristic can have a direct connection with per-formance.

keeping the workers docilely underpaid. At Hitachi, by contrast, the unions have sought to *reinforce* the 'diffuse' elements in the bargaining relationship, to extract bigger and better fringe benefits from the employers and to secure some say in their operation.

In short, although there may be a similarity between the way a traditional paternalistic employer looked after sick workers and the way Hitachi looks after its workers when they are sick, while the first may be seen as evidence of a 'diffuse' relationship, in Hitachi these elements have been incorporated into the specific contractual definition of the employment relationship. Diffuseness proper, in a more limited form, characterizes the relation between superiors and inferiors in face-to-face work groups.

The third point (universalism/particularism) concerns the definition of duties. In traditional forms of personal paternalism, the worker's overriding obligation is loyalty to his employer, or perhaps, in larger firms which retain these patterns, to his particular manager or supervisor. In Hitachi, on the other hand, the emphasis is all on loyalty to the company as a total entity: the employee's chief duty is to foster the interests of the firm as a collectivity.

Again, in the more traditional firm, because one reacts to other people in terms of a total relationship, one behaves differently towards a co-religionist on the one hand and to some unrelated stranger on the other. (It was generally accepted, for example, in an Indian factory studied by a sociologist, that Marathi foremen gave extra favours to their Marathi workmen and Gujurati foremen did similar favours for fellow-Gujurati speakers.[5]) In Hitachi, by contrast, the performance of duties within the firm is not expected to be influenced by any other consideration than the pursuit of the goals of the firm – higher profits, bigger markets, a glowing reputation. The one commonly acknowledged deviation from this in practice is the tendency of graduates of the same university, or of Hitachi's own training school, to favour each other. This seems to enter only as a marginal factor, however, when on the merits of the case there is only a small margin of doubt.

Particularism and universalism are tricky concepts. Devotion to Hitachi's interests is still a more particularistic obligation than devotion to Japan's interests, but it is a good deal less particularistic than the wholly personalized social relations of the traditional paternalistic firm. It is, moreover, an obligation which the individual is expected to fulfil from his own inner sense of commitment and according to his own notion of how the firm's interests can best be

[5] N. R. Sheth, *The Social Framework of an Indian Factory*, Manchester, 1968.

273

promoted; acceptance of superiors' authority is part of one's obligations, but so is the duty to remonstrate if one thinks they are wrong.
Loyalty does not mean an unswerving obedience to persons.

The final point concerned affectivity. In the personal paternalism
of the traditional firm, 'warm human relations' are maintained
between employer and employee not only by care for the sick, but
also by social contacts outside of work – the Christmas party, the
employer's garden party, the annual works outing – and by the
employer's expressions of personal concern; the stroll through the
works with a nod to everyone: 'Hullo there, Joe, how's the missus?'
The Hitachi worker's affectivity is split in two directions. First, he
has a sense of belonging in the firm as a community, and probably
some sense of prideful attachment to it. This emotion (akin to
patriotism) contrasts with the traditional worker's sense not of working *in* a firm, but of working *for* Mr X. Secondly, face-to-face relations at the workplace are indeed made into something more than
mere instrumental relations by the cultivation of social contacts and
expressions of concern, and to some extent the superior – the foreman, the section chief – acts as the focal point of the group in much
the same way as the traditional employer did. However, in Hitachi,
solidarity is horizontal as well as vertical. The work-group might
have a soft-ball team in which the foreman is not involved. Affective
relations between equals are encouraged in the official ideology of the
firm as much as those between inferior and superior: they help to
reinforce the sense of membership in the firm as a community.

It is clear enough that this is a different kind of animal from traditional types of personal paternalism. 'Managerial paternalism' is a
term coined by some writers[6] uneasy about calling this sort of
organization paternalism *tout court*. Even that is not right, however.
It conjures up an image of the managers benevolently handing out
favours and buying a personal loyalty by their expressions of personal concern. But this is not the case. The personal paternalistic
tradition (still very much alive in Japan, of course, in the small
non-unionized family firm) still exists in Hitachi only in the inter-
stices of its organization – in the personal 'looking after' of the section chief who acts as his subordinate's marriage go-between. The
favours that count materially – the welfare benefits, the housing, the
educational loans and the dormitory accommodation for one's
children studying in Tokyo – are all specified and contractual: their
distribution rule-bound and institutionalized as employee 'rights'.
And the loyalty which is bought by these favours is an institutional,

[6] e.g. Clark Kerr, *et al.*, *Industrialism and Industrial man*, 1962.

not a personal loyalty. Perhaps a better term for this kind of organization would be, on the analogy of 'welfare statism', 'welfare corporatism'. The personal paternalism of the foreman and section chief – which as we have seen is already somewhat attenuated in some workshops – could disappear entirely without having any effect on the main institutions of 'welfare corporatism'. It might be, too, that its disappearance would have no necessary effect on the individual worker's sense of identification with the firm either, though that is a matter for enquiry. *A priori*, one would think it might make a difference. As long as the norms and values of a sub-group faithfully mirror those of a larger group of which it forms part, affective solidarity in the sub-group can strengthen attachment to the larger group: friendship and solidarity within a British Legion branch can enhance its members' sense of patriotism. Hitachi would, one suspects, lose that reinforcement of the Hitachi spirit if work-group relations become more specific and less affective; but the organization need not thereby be threatened; British patriotism survives outside the British Legion.

BUREAUCRACY

Another characterization of the differences between the two systems to be considered has already been hinted at in the discussion of managerial organization (p. 68). It is this: Hitachi's form of organization is by no means foreign to Britain. It is very much the pattern of the British army or civil service. Japan's peculiarity lies in the fact that a type of organization which in most Western countries is considered suitable only for the army or the civil service is adapted in Japan to industry. Consider, for example, the following notes on points of resemblance between a Japanese firm and the British army in the days of national service, offered by a former British officer.

'1. Intelligence and dexterity tests on entry, which determine to a great extent a man's allocation to an army trade, etc., and therefore the whole of his subsequent career.

2. The great difficulty of transfer from one army corps, such as Signals, to another, such as Engineers, once a man has been conscripted.

3. The curious stigma attaching to the very few men that have made such a transfer. For example, a Signalman who has been at one time in REME, is regarded in his new corps with a mixture of awe, suspicion, wariness and even contempt, which never quite fades away. In some way, his mates always think of him as a REME soldier.

4. Primary identification with the corps rather than the trade. A man is much more likely to say 'I'm in the Signals' than 'I'm a wireless operator.' This attitude persists after his release from service.

5. Great importance attaches to seniority. Many pay increases are automatically linked to length of service, and it is possible, for this reason, to find poorly qualified privates who are better paid, say, then highly qualified corporals.

6. This affects not only pay, but deference accorded to soldiers. The men respect young officers far less, say, than old corporals. In fact, they don't respect young officers at all, in my experience. Similarly, among themselves, differences in length of service are closely observed. In my experience, men who had served six weeks longer than others serving the same two-year period looked down on their juniors. I knew men who could instantly calculate from comparing numbers, such as 22428321 with 22433435, that there was, say, a seniority of six weeks involved.

7. Familism. This applies more to regular soldiers. But the army guaranteed the same sort of security as the Japanese firm, also guaranteed retraining, etc., reallocation to a new job in case of redundancy, and so on.[7]

The reader will recall several other points at which the word 'bureaucracy' was used in earlier chapters of the book – apropos of the greater formalization of training in Hitachi; the greater reliance on explicit written instructions and records; the formal classification of circulars and instructions of different levels of authority; the emphasis on formal qualifications; the structuring of careers and the management of promotion by a mixture of seniority and merit criteria, the existence of a system of personal ranks separate from, but related to, the hierarchy of functional offices – and so on.

Whether Japan is suffering from premature bureaucratization, or whether Britain is suffering from delayed bureaucratization – and whether, as both these terms imply, there is in fact a trend towards greater bureaucracy as industrial organization becomes more complex – is a matter which will occupy us again in Chapter 13.

THE BALANCE SHEET

Most of these characterizations – 'paternalistic', 'bureaucratic' imply some covert evaluation. But evaluations are better done explicitly. Every man will have his own balance sheet in the light of his own values. My own runs as follows.

[7] David Phillips, personal correspondence.

In Hitachi's favour is the basic equality of condition of employees and the minimization of differences between workers by hand and by brain.

Also the fact that manual as well as middle-class workers can enjoy steadily rising incomes matching the curve of steadily increasing family responsibilities.

Also the fact that (reflecting the difference between the doctrine of original virtue of the dominant Mencian form of Confucianism and the Christian doctrine of original sin) Japanese factories operate, by and large, on the assumptions of McGregor's Y theory rather than the X theory assumptions (that people can be weaned away from idleness only by a judicious mixture of direct material incentives and punitive sanctions) which operate in British factories.

Also the fact that the work atmosphere in Japanese factories is such that people are pleased (not, like the British shop steward quoted on p. 246, embarrassed) to acknowledge that they get some satisfaction out of their work and some feeling of pride from the exercise of their skills. Where the norms encourage the expression of such satisfaction they are likely also to stimulate its actual experience, so that even those performing humble operations with very little independent discretionary control over them can enjoy some sense of their own worth and are less prone to alienation.

Also the fact that the Japanese system seems to be more productive and better capable of delivering to all concerned in it a steadily rising level of real income.

On the other side:

The instrumentalization of work in the eyes of the British worker; the insistence that the building of generators or washing-machines is not necessarily the supreme end of man, does permit a greater attachment to private pursuits and to the private virtues (as well, of course, as to the private vices). The cultivation of personal relationships outside work, political, recreational and artistic pursuits are allowed a higher place in an Englishman's scheme of things.

The British system, by not offering security of tenure in a cosy niche in a particular organization, teaches men that the only thing they have to rely on is their own individual capacities, the competences they can offer for sale in the market – or, if the market does not work to give them their due, the egalitarian solidarity of the union or class seeking to change the system. As such it fosters a spirit of independence and a willingness to resist arbitrary authority. 'Sturdy individualism' is not something the Hitachi system fosters: in Britain it is not just a mythical ideal. Quite a few, particularly older,

277

workers could match the experience of a former shop steward, reminiscing about his earlier life, who recalled in these words the outcome of a dispute with his employer in 1930:

'It was horse-whip days, were those days. I went in the following morning into the shop and the old man started shouting and bawling at me. They had no respect for the human being – you were all more or less hired hands: you were slaves, and you did what you was told to do or get out. I said: "Don't shout at me. I'm not a dog so don't shout at me." "Well, if you're not satisfied with it, you know what to do." "Well," I said, "I'm not satisfied with being made into a dog. So you'd better get me me money ready." So I were paid up there and then. And things looked very bad in Bradford, and that were the start of unemployment for me. And a long spell it was too.'

SYSTEM?

At this point one should, perhaps, enter a modification of the assumption which began this chapter – namely that the differences should be seen as differences between two integrated and internally consistent systems – the market-oriented and the organization-oriented. This would imply also that the virtues and vices listed above are intimately and inevitably linked. To some extent this seems clearly true. Organizations cannot guarantee security of tenure *and* maintain relative efficiency unless they can require their members to make some sacrifice of individual choice and accept 'postings' from one factory to another. But there are other elements of the differences between English Electric and Hitachi which are not so clearly related to the market-oriented/organization-oriented syndromes and are more a product of differences in the two countries' cultural traditions – which suggests that there *can* be other mixes of organizational features besides the two described here as the typically British and the typically Japanese. For example, the relatively greater meekness of the Japanese worker towards constituted authority, and the greater propensity of the British worker to rebel is an example of such a culturally-rooted difference. It is not wholly obvious that the Japanese system would collapse if general attitudes towards authority changed in Japan. Nor is it obvious that the work ethic has to be as strong as it patently is in Japan for the Japanese system to survive. (Though it does seem highly probable that it is a necessary condition for the system to operate at the high production levels and high investment levels now attained. Although a sociologist, ever anxious to subvert the easy platitudes of the received wisdom, must blush to admit it, there would appear to be some truth in the idea that one

278

major reason why Japanese factories produce more is because Japanese workers work harder.)

Some of these considerations will be more obvious when we come to discuss the origins of the Japanese and British systems in Chapter 15. They are of some importance since they affect one's assessment of both the desirability and the feasibility of transferring institutions from one country to another. Is a Japanese-type organization-oriented welfare corporatism feasible in a society which does not have Japan's group-oriented culture? If one tried to borrow Japanese forms of industrial organization would one inevitably curtail individual freedom and individuality? These are questions to which we shall return.

The question of transferability apart, however, these considerations of the cultural and institutional setting of the two systems make it clear that one cannot evaluate them in isolation. It is necessary, too, to look at their interrelations with the other institutions of their respective societies. That will be the concern of the next chapter.

Chapter 11

Some Implications

Employment systems do not exist in a vacuum. They relate to the rest of society in at least two major ways. First, they fit into (articulate with, in the jargon) other institutions in the sense that what happens in the employment sphere directly affects what happens in other spheres. Workers and managers are also members of *families*. The demands which their working life makes on them, and the money they earn, affect the kind of husbands and fathers they are. *Politically*, the more the state regulates the economy, the more work relations are likely to affect men's perceptions of their political interests and the shape of political groupings. One function of the *educational system* is to measure and certify individuals in ways that affect their chances of competing for various jobs; another is to prepare them vocationally for their working life.

Secondly, in a more general way, the attitudes and principles, and patterns of social relations found in the workplace are likely to have a certain *congruence* with those shown in other social spheres, simply because of the tendency towards consistency in individual personalities and sets of values. It is hard (though not impossible) to behave in different spheres of life according to entirely different criteria as to what constitutes proper self-respect or a legitimate basis of authority or a fair distribution of rewards. The way in which managers and workers talk to each other in the workplace is bound to affect the way they see each other as neighbours or as political animals in a political context.

Some of these connections will be explored in this chapter under the four headings indicated above – the family, politics, education and general attitudes. It seems fairly clear that their respective employment systems are significantly related to other differences between British and Japanese society.

'Related to' is a suitably vague term which leaves the exact causal relationship unspecified. And so it must be. About the present state

280

of relations between employment and education, the most one can say is that they mutually reinforce each other; if the employment system were to change, the educational system would probably change also. One can speculate a little as to (a) which reinforces the other more – i.e. if the employment system were to change would it force a change in the educational system more rapidly or more completely than a change in the educational system would affect employment? and (b) which is the more independent variable – which has the greater possibility of changing by its own internal development or through extraneous influences independently of the status-quo-reinforcing effects of the other. As to the further historical question – did the nature of the family or the attitudes and patterns of social relations generally prevalent in society *cause* the employment system to develop this way in the first place, or was it vice versa – we shall return to this theme in a later chapter.

THE FAMILY
Studies of family life in Britain have frequently emphasized differences in the family relationships of different social classes. Middle-class family life may be more individualistic and a less all-embracing source of emotional support than working-class family life, and kinship relations have less relative importance as compared with friendships in shaping an individual's recreational social life, but middle-class families tend to maintain relations with a wider range of relatives than working class families, and these relationships have for the middle-class family rather greater economic importance.

More germane to the present discussion is that the children of middle-class families tend to marry later, and to remain more economically and perhaps more emotionally dependent on their parents to a later stage of life than working-class children. Secondly, the likelihood is that, following their parents into middle-class occupations they will be receiving in their early twenties an income very considerably smaller than the income of their fathers. Parental capital can help provide the down-payment on a house when they marry. Working-class children, on the other hand, who follow their parents into working-class occupations, can be receiving at the age of 17 or 18 – and even if they take an apprenticeship at least by the age of 21 – a wage little different from that of their fathers. There are no prospects of economic advantage to reinforce affection as a motive for maintaining family ties.

The Japanese sociological literature on the family, while very much concerned with differences between urban and rural families, or between families where the family group is still a producing unit

281

and families whose income is derived from wages and salaries, shows little concern with differences within the wage and salary group comparable to differences in England between the middle and working class. Such differences are not perceived to exist, or are not perceived to be sociologically interesting.

In the absence of such studies one can only speculate on the basis of casual observation, but the fact does seem to be that differences in family relations between the manual working class and the middle class are not very marked. The age at marriage is not very different, nor is the relative incidence of 'arranged' marriages and free enterprise marriages. Nor – and this is the crucial point of connection with the employment system – is there so much difference in the extent to which working children have economic expectations *vis-à-vis* their parents. In Japan the young manual worker also has a father receiving two or three times his own income no less than a white-collar or managerial worker. He would not expect regular allowances to supplement his smaller income, but, his capacity to save being limited, he could expect financial help from his parents when the time comes to marry.

Another difference between British and Japanese families lies in the extent to which there is a sharp differentiation between the feminine and the masculine sphere, and this too has connections with the employment system – in particular with that aspect of it discussed in Chapter 8, the extent to which the firm can lay claims to a man's time and emotional resources at the expense of his other attachments.

To be sure, Britain is far from homogeneous in this respect. A Durham coal mining village, studied some twenty years ago, very clearly had a sharply divided man's world and woman's world.[1] But this is an extreme case. Generally speaking the differentiation between feminine and masculine roles is a good deal more marked in Japan than in England. The most common polite word for 'wife' in Japan is 'okusan' – 'the lady inside' – a word which reflects the fact that in the traditional family, either warrior or peasant, the wife's role was to look after the home. The man was the one who took part in outside activities, not so much in the matter of earning a living (for the farm family, work, in which men and women shared, was part of what went on at home) as in the business of maintaining correct social relations with other families and playing a full part in the community – village or retainer band – to which the family belonged.

There are two points about this tradition to be noted. The first is that it implied a sharp differentiation between the roles of men and

[1] N. Dennis, F. Henriques, C. Slaughter, *Coal is Our Life*, 1956.

women and their expectations as to what they could properly hope to get out of life. Second, that the husband's *obligations* to the wide community – village or retainer band – were expected to take precedence over his *sentiments vis-à-vis* his family members. If his son stole a neighbour's carrots, breaking village rules, he might have to disown him, conquering natural affection. If, when his turn came to provide the *sake* rice-wine for the boozy (all-male) parties which followed village meetings, he could only manage to do so at the expense of the family budget, then his wife and children went without their weekly treat of a slice of dried fish and were not expected to complain. It has been suggested, indeed, that the fact that in the later feudal period, the Japanese family succumbed to, was subordinated to, the micro-polity whereas the similarly structured Chinese family never so succumbed, helps to explain why Japan could more easily make the transition to a modern nation state.[2]

Both features have their modern legacy. Husbands and wives tend to have different sets of friends – the husband's network being exclusively male except for a few bar girls, the wife's exclusively female except for the milkman and perhaps a teacher of flower arrangement. Feminine speech and masculine speech still remain clearly distinguishable in verb forms and vocabulary. Although the ratio between the average years of education received by men and by women is not much different in Japan from in Britain, the majority of girls go to special *girls'* high schools and universities. Japan is full of little Roedeans with no particular class associations, designed to ensure that girls can get the kudos of a higher education and so improve their marriage chances without at the same time endangering their femininity. The bringing up of children is primarily a woman's affair: men are not frequent attenders at PTA meetings. Nor are married women as frequently represented in the labour force as in England.

Women are, consequently, rather more prepared than English women to accept the fact that they share very little of their husband's lives and can lay claim to little of his time. And if it is now the company and the office rather than the village or the retainer band that claim his primary loyalty, the difference in principle is not so great. When he comes home at midnight from a drunken sales party she will help him to undress and put him to bed, perhaps with not *quite* the same respectful admiration as her great-great-grandmother helped her husband off with his armour, but at least with almost as little sense of being the victim of an unfortunate marriage.

[2] M. J. Levy Jr, 'Contrasting Factors in the Modernization of China and Japan', *Economic Development and Cultural Change*, vol 2, iii, October 1953, pp. 161–97.

POLITICS

There are many reasons for expecting class consciousness to be more attenuated among Japanese workers than among British workers. Some of them are in no sense consequences of the employment system – the fact, for instance, that the feudal period of relative *cultural* homogeneity was so much more recent in Japan than in England, or the fact that simultaneously with the end of the feudal period Japan created an almost completely universal school system in which bureaucrats' sons and fishmongers' sons absorbed a uniform curriculum in the same schools. The result was naturally rather different from the results of the British system of public, grammar and elementary schools differentiated not just in intellectual level but even more consequentially in the cultural content of the training they offered. If not a consequence of the employment system, however, this greater degree of cultural homogeneity – the fact that both manager and worker shared a common culture, knew from their school readers the same stories about Benjamin Franklin and the heroic trumpeter of the Russo-Japanese war, could sing the same songs and recite the same poems, had the same interests in baseball, the same tastes in liquor and amusements – may have been one of the facilitating factors which made Japan's employment system possible. And at the same time the other cultural similarity noted above – the similarity in patterns of family relations which is in part a *consequence* of the similarity in the economic constraints imposed on the parent-child relationship in both manual and managerial families as a result of the employment system – has helped also to preserve that cultural homogeneity.

But the difference in British and Japanese employment systems is more directly relevant to an explanation of different degrees of class consciousness. The way people perceive the structure of the individual factory – the social microcosm in which they work – inevitably affects the way they perceive the society at large. Chapter 8 examined the various features of an English factory which served both in fact and symbolically to separate the 'status' of worker from that of 'manager', and tried to show how the absence of some of these differences and the de-emphasizing of others serve to attenuate the basis for strong us/them feelings within a Japanese factory. And if Japanese workers are less likely to see their factory in terms of the bosses and the workers, they are less likely also to see their society in terms of a boss class and a working class.

Again, where the membership of each union transcends the boundaries of the individual enterprise there is obviously more likelihood of union membership inducing a sense of working-class identity than in Japan where workers typically belong to an *enterprise* union which serves rather to reinforce a sense of identity with the enterprise and a sense of difference from other workers in other enterprises — strengthening vertical, segmental loyalties rather than horizontal class solidarity.

At first glance there is a certain formal similarity between the relationship in Britain of the TUC and the Labour Party, and the relationship in Japan of the national union federations and the Socialist Party or Democratic Socialist Party to which they are linked. But the differences are great. In Britain the unions are affiliated to the party and union members pay personal party subscriptions. In Japan a number of trade union leaders have become party members, but party membership is extremely rare among the rank and file, and contributions to the party are discretionary *ad hoc* contributions made from time to time from union funds at the initiative of union leaders.

More importantly, the perception of the purpose and nature of the relation is also different. Sōhyō does not look on its relation with the Socialist Party as fated and organic, determined by a consonance of aims. In 1970, when a weakened Sōhyō was seeking a realignment and strengthening of the trade union national organizations, it readily accepted a resolution which, while maintaining Sōhyō's general support of the Socialists. gave a free hand to any constituent union which wished to support some other party. And the leader of one major industrial federation said that he saw no harm in a union supporting the Liberal Democrats if they wished. The road to a totally apolitical business union seems wide open.[3]

The differences in British and Japanese union – party relationships are obviously rooted in history. In Britain the unions and the Labour Party grew together. The party was seen as a means of achieving through the national political process some of the objectives of union members which could not be achieved through industrial bargaining. The focus of the Labour Party's activities has traditionally been on nationalization of industry, on taxation policies and social welfare policies designed to redistribute income in favour of manual workers. Goldthorpe *et al.* found that their Luton workers, though far from exhibiting any traditional form of class consciousness, still voted for the Labour Party as being 'inclined to do that bit more for the working man'.[4]

In Japan, by contrast, although there was a beginning in the

[3] Asahi, 11 August 1970.

[4] J. H. Goldthorpe, *et al.*, *The Affluent Worker in the Class Structure*, 1969, p. 177.

285

twenties of a similar development of intimately linked union and party activities, the repression of the thirties nipped these developments in the bud. Left-wing – primarily Marxist-oriented – parties suddenly burst on the scene again in the first free flowering of political activity of 1946, more or less simultaneously with the sudden and widespread development of trade unions. But these were separate developments not organically linked. Only a small number of those elected to the Diet as Socialist Party representatives had had trade union experience; their concern in the immediate post-war period was more with the democratization of the political structure, with land reform and the reform of education, than with income redistribution or state control over industry. Links between unions and parties were soon formed; they were closest in the highly disciplined Communist Party where, however, rather than the Party being a means for achieving union aims through the political process, the unions were seen as mere instruments for the Party to consolidate its strength in the country in order to capture power and bring about revolutionary changes. There was little interest in promoting half-measures designed to redistribute income in the interval before the revolution came.

The link which developed after 1950 between the Socialist Party and the largest labour federation, Sōhyō, was not of the same means-end kind; Sōhyō kept its independence. In fact, although both have lost strength steadily through the sixties, the Party has been more dependent on Sōhyō than vice versa, both for money and voting support. This dependence has been reflected in a steady growth in the proportion of ex-trade unionists among its parliamentary members. (In the 1969 elections they accounted for 37 of the 90 Socialists, a proportion (41%) very close to that of TU-sponsored MPs in the British Parliamentary Labour Party (39%)). This should not, however, be seen as an attempt by the trade union movement to control the political movement. The prestige of a parliamentary seat has been one way of 'paying' for the political contributions union leaders have made. Union leaders can make good candidates with a high chance of success because of their ready-made organizational support. And – a third factor – the supply of ex-officials, university professors, lawyers, etc., who flocked to the party in the optimistic days immediately after the war, has almost entirely dried up; there are fewer attractive alternative candidates.

As a consequence, the changing character of the Party's parliamentary group has had little effect on the character or ideology of the party. As a permanent opposition party which has never in more than twenty years faced an election with the remotest hope of forming a government, it has had little use for detailed legislative blue-prints for reform of the existing society. There has been no need to translate its ideology into practical legislative proposals and this is one reason why the party's fundamentalists have been able to keep the ideology in the same schematic Marxist mould as when it was originally imported. When the party gains power, so the doctrine goes, capitalism will be ended and socialism established. Meanwhile its effective role has been to act as watchdog, exposing the darker and more scandalous aspects of the Government's rule, secondly to attack such aspects of the government's policy as offend against – not so much socialist principles as principles which have fairly wide support among public opinion. On major issues it has mounted massive campaigns of parliamentary obstruction and extra-parliamentary demonstrations. It is noticeable, however, that these major issues have all involved either (a) issues of foreign policy, or (b) the constitutional structure and attempts by the ruling party to reverse some of the post-war occupation-period reforms in ways that might limit freedom and concentrate more power in the hands of the central government.

A fair sample of the Party's policy statements, and one which shows fairly clearly where the balance of its concerns lies, is contained in the Party's official analysis of what it acknowledges to be its 'great defeat' in the December 1969 election from which it emerged with only 90 – compared with its previous 120 – seats. The reasons were:

'The fact that the Liberal-Democratic Party and monopoly capitalism gradually gathered strength through the sixties and in diverse ways consolidated their system of control; the fact that by means of a hypocritical joint Japanese–American community [concerning the return of Okinawa to Japan], the American government indirectly assisted the Liberal Democrats, the fact that, in order to remove all obstacles to their plans for the seventies all their attacks were concentrated on our Party [rather than other opposition parties].

The fact that the LDP could choose its own time to dissolve also played its part, but we must admit to grave inadequacies in our conduct of the propaganda battle, in our effort to link the problems of the Japanese–American Security Treaty and Okinawa to the people's perception of their everyday problems, and in our efforts to explain in simple terms what we mean by opposition to the Security Treaty and a policy of unarmed neutrality.

As for the policy of the Party it must be particularly pointed out that on important issues – the university and student problem, the problem of the Youth Committees Against War, the problem of restoring relations with China, the Czechoslovakia issue, the Sino–Soviet conflict, the Great Cultural Revolution, issues on which some expression of opinion on our part was required, we had no clear and unified view, our wavering attitudes lost us support among the people, and we left the impression of a "don't know" party, a "can't quite be certain" party.

Also important was the fact that we were slow in trying to grapple with the issues which have developed during the period of rapid capitalist growth in the sixties – issues for which the nation is urgently seeking a solution, such as urban problems, agricultural policies, prices, pollution and housing, and also social and cultural problems – the demand for a "recapturing of humanity", for escape from alienation in the midst of what is called the administered society or the information revolution. We did not face these issues squarely enough or propose sufficiently concrete counter measures.'[5]

The order in which problems are listed is significant; so is the absence of any specific redistributional problems – welfare services, taxation burdens, education. The Party has, in fact, shown a great deal of interest in education, but its concern has mostly been with covert attempts at 'thought control' implicit in the Government's centralization policies, hardly at all with problems of equality of opportunity.

In view of what has been said so far, the voting figures in Table 11.1 which show the Japan Socialist Party's lack of roots in any real 'working-class movement' will perhaps come as no surprise. They

Table 11.1 *Opinion Survey Estimates of the Proportions of Different Social Classes/Occupational Groups Voting for the Labour Party/Japan Socialist Party*

	Labour Party (Election of 1966)[a]		Japan Socialist Party (Election of 1969)[b]
Middle class	15·5	Managers of large	
Lower middle	29·9	enterprises	28·6
Skilled working	58·5	Clerical and	
Unskilled 'very poor'	65·2	technical workers	24·2
		Manual workers	21·8

[a] D. G. Butler and A. King, *The British General Election of 1966*, p. 264.
[b] Mainichi Newspapers, Survey of 5–7 December 1969.

[5] *Gekkan Shakaitō*, June 1970, no. 160, pp. 21–2.

may not be accurate, but they confirm what other studies have shown (including some which find a high positive correlation between length of education and propensity to vote Socialist) namely that there is a higher proportion of Socialist supporters among middle-class than among working-class voters.

A related difference is that the Japanese Socialist Party has no real grass-roots base except for a thin structure of local politicians. Whereas a Labour Party Conference is flooded with resolutions from constituencies and unions which the agenda committee takes days to combine and select, the 1970 Socialist Party Congress received exactly four. Two were concerned with expressions of support for people involved in court cases arising out of demonstrations, one concerned the expulsion of an extreme left youth group, and only one – from Hokkaido concerning the coal industry – was of the type which make up the bulk of British Labour Party Conference resolutions.[6]

To sum up, although paradoxically the JSP so far clings to traditional European rhetoric as to call itself a 'party of the working class' in a way that the Labour Party no longer does (the brief rhetorical declaration of the 1970 Congress speaks of the party 'responding to the hopes of the entire working class'), it is as devoid of class feeling of the classical British kind, as the most intellectual middle-class radical group in European or Latin American politics. And the reason for that seems clearly to be that few of the leaders of either party or union have grown up in *milieu* suffused with that kind of class feeling, and few of the Party's members or voters have enough class feeling to make policies which appeal to it evoke a wide response. There are, indeed, many Japanese who consider the Prime Minister and his colleagues as personifications of evil, there are many who hate their own superiors, and there are many who have learned, intellectually, to conceive of the object of their resentment as an organically coherent 'capitalist ruling class'. But there is little of that passion for equality and individual dignity and of the sense that the social distribution of wealth and status offends against those principles – the elements which, mixed with sheer envious resentment at the privileges and the complacently superior airs of the rich, go to make up class consciousness of the British kind. Once again one comes back to Japan's relative cultural homogeneity as a reason for this – the fact that the nation's top universities are middle-class meritocratic institutions, not inheritors of an ancient aristocratic culture, and the fact, consequently, that Japan's Tokyo Imperial University-graduate establishment does not bear and never has borne

[6] *Gekkan Shakaitō*, June 1970, no. 160, pp. 160–2.

anything like the same distinctive marks of an exclusive privileged culture as the public-school-Oxbridge elite of, say, Britain in the 1920s. But the social structure of factories and trade unions must also have played its part – promoting a sense of membership in the enterprise rather than class membership, making a Hitachi welder willing to believe that he has more in common with a Hitachi manager than with a Mitsubishi welder. And the relative absence of class feeling can be seen in turn as one precondition for the success of management policies in the factory: because they were not conditioned to see society in terms of a class of rulers and a class of ruled, workers have been more susceptible to policies which sought to blur their perceptions of clashes of interest within the firm and to give them a stronger sense of identification with their own firm's managers than of any community of interest with workers outside. Causal influences run both ways.

But, it might be objected, there *are* some militant unions in Japan. They, surely, must have roots in – or at least serve to foster – a sense of class feeling. It does not seem that this is necessarily so. The results of a survey carried out at the Oji paper works are interesting in this regard. It took place at a time of bitter struggle between a militant original union and a second 'company union', and asked members of both unions a wide range of questions. There was no discernible difference between members of the two unions in the replies they gave to a range of questions about politics and class and the way that saw the employment relation. The only significant difference was that workers who had stuck to the original militant union showed a stronger sense of peer-group loyalty; those who had shifted to the new union showed a sharper perception of which side their own personal bread was buttered.[7] It seems legitimate to see at work here a 'general propensity to develop strong organization loyalties'. (It is this factor which explains the 'dual loyalty phenomenon'; sociologists have found an even stronger tendency in Japan than in other countries for the more loyal and conscientious union members to be also loyal and conscientious servants of the firm.[8] It is the strength of this propensity rather than class feeling proper which *supports* militancy in Japanese unions, but it is the personalities of union leaders or situational factors (such as the desperate economic situation of the declining coal industry) which initially *produce* it.

One ought not to exaggerate differences between Britain and Japan

[7] Nihon Rōdō Kyōkai Chōsa Kenkyūbu, *Rōdō Kankei ni kansuru saikin no shinrigakuteki kenkyū no gaikan*, *Chōsa kenkyū*, no. 60, p. 55.

[8] K. Odaka, 'Industrial Workers' Identification With Union and Management in Post-war Japan', *American Journal of Sociology*, Spring 1954.

however. To be sure, as Table 11.2 shows, there is a difference (in so far as our samples are representative) in the extent to which British and Japanese workers are likely to give themselves the label 'working class', but when it comes to more concrete questions like the following, the differences within each country are in fact greater than the differences between the national sample.

Table 11.2 *Self-identification in Class Terms*

'People often talk about belonging to such and such a class. What class would you say you belong to?'

	Hitachi	British engineering sample
Working class, lower class, labouring class	22	65
Lower middle class	4	1
Middle class, intermediate class	27	20
'Human class', refusal to classify, joke answers	6	7
Can't say	42	5

Japan. 'Do you think that, even if it should go against your own interests, you ought to support "joint struggles" with workers in the small subcontracting firms and subsidiaries? Which of the following represents your views? [Show card]

(1) Workers ought always to stick together on class lines.
(2) They should in theory, but in fact it has to depend on the time and situation.
(3) There are all kinds of differences between large and small firms and so inevitably there are differences in union activities.'

Britain. 'What do you think about sympathetic strike action? Take this kind of case, for example.

Let's say, in a factory the transport people come out on strike. The firm brings outside contractors to move materials in. The Transport Union declares the material black – OK? What do you think the operators' union ought to do? If they refuse to work with the blacked materials, they are sticking by the other union. But this may also mean that all work stops and everybody loses money. What do you think you should do in such circumstances?'

The Glasgow firm in an old long-established industrial district, employing traditional skills in tough 'man's-work' boiler-making, does show a very different pattern of response from either of the

Table 11.3 *Sympathy Strikes*

England	Japan	Japan Hitachi	Japan Yawata	England Marconi	England Babcock
Support the other union	Alternative (1)	30	13	30	66
Give moral support but no direct action/it depends on the issue they are striking over	Alternative (2)	27	39	33	14
Should not give support	Alternative (3)	36	43	31	13
Other answers		2	4		
Don't know		5	2	6	6
		100	100	100	100

Japanese firms. But in the newer Essex industrial area, at the bright, clean, modern Marconi factory, the more *embourgeoisés*, or more 'privatized', workers drawn from the 'respectable' southern English working class show a distribution of attitudes very similar to that at Hitachi.

That there has been a change in attitudes among British workers, particularly those in southern England, seems undeniable. Even those most concerned to challenge the embourgeoisement thesis conclude that the workers they studied in southern England saw trade unions and the Labour Party as 'instrumental' to the attainment of their own 'privatized' concerns, rather than objects of loyalty such as they presume were characteristic of 'traditional' working-class communities.[9] But despite these attitude changes, the formal institutions of the trade unions and the Labour Party and the relations between them have changed very little.

One can, therefore, sum up the discussion more or less as follows. There is a congruence between the British pattern of industrial relations and the British political party structure (including party–union relations and the focal concerns of left-wing politics). Both seem to reflect a fairly widespread consciousness of class among manual workers. There is a similar congruence in Japan, both sets of institutions reflecting the absence of such consciousness. Attitude studies bear out the weakness of class consciousness in Japan, but much less consistently display its presence in Britain. It is highly likely, though, that there would have been more consistent evidence of class consciousness in Britain if the survey had been carried out in the early years of this century at the time when the institutions were *being created*. The better fit between attitudes and institutions in Japan is due to the shorter history of the labour movement in that country.

[9] J. Goldthorpe, *et al.*, *The Affluent Worker: Political Attitudes and Behaviour*, 1968, p. 177.

EDUCATION

The points to be made about education and the employment system are simple and obvious.

1. For recruiting purposes Japanese large enterprises place more emphasis on formal educational qualifications than do British firms. (Among the chief reasons for this are: (a) Japan was a late-developer and late-developers facing a large technological gap depend much more on academically-learned knowledge than a slowly developing early developer where work experience is more important; (b) by the time Japanese large-scale-industry developed Japan had universal primary education. Since the large firms took only a small proportion of the available labour and preferred to recruit at the beginning of an occupational career, they could, and did, use school results to 'cream off' the available labour force. Similarly, with the vast expansion of higher education since the war, the largest enterprises have been able to 'cream off' each year's crop of available university graduates by the same criteria.)

2. Because of the life-time employment system a man's first job has a much greater determining effect on the whole of his subsequent career than it does in England. It decides the enterprise to which he belongs, and the education status with which he enters that enterprise enormously influences his subsequent promotion chances within it. (This tendency is stronger in Japan than elsewhere partly because the bureaucratic promotion system, which inevitably results when there is little mid-career inflow and outflow of personnel, works with least friction when the field of candidates is narrowed by use of some objective criterion such as educational qualifications, and partly because those who operate the system are university graduates – i.e. men with the highest grade of educational qualifications who have a strong interest in upholding the idea that initial educational qualifications are of overriding importance.)

As a consequence the educational system in Japan bears practically the whole burden of occupational allocation – a function which in other countries is shared between the educational system, apprenticeship patterns, and the mid-career labour market. Any child with ambition cannot afford not to try to go to high school or to a university. The pressure of demand for education is clear from the figures. Forty-two per cent of those reaching school leaving age went on to another three years of high school in 1950; 77% in 1968. The percentage of the relevant age group going to university increased from the pre-war 2% to nearly 10% by 1950 and to 20% (of men, nearly 30%) in 1968. Public provision has more or less kept up with

293

the expanding demand for high school education, but at the university level the growth in demand has been met by a big expansion of private universities which charge high fees and over the quality of which there has been only very loose public control.

All that universities have in common is that they teach youths between the ages of 18 and 22 and send them out into the world as university graduates. In reputation they vastly differ. Reputation in this case partly reflects age of foundation, partly real differences of quality in facilities and teaching staff. The gradient of these prestige differentials is gradually steepening as a result of the selection system – each university runs its own competitive entrance examinations. This means that universities of high reputation can ruthlessly prune their entrants and ensure that they have students of a uniformly high quality, who further enhance the reputation of the university by their subsequent careers. The other tail of the distribution is affected by the fact that there are no minimum standards for university entrants beyond mere completion of high school. Hence many children of relatively low intelligence but anxious or ambitious parents find their way to universities who in other societies might not get there. Hence the differences are wide. At one end of the spectrum are the older state universities of high prestige whose stiff entrance examinations cream off a tiny percentage of each age group and whose graduates can more or less choose among a variety of attractive jobs in the nation's elite firms.[10] (Almost irrespective of their university performance: the fact that they got into these universities in the first place is seen as an adequate guarantee of their worth.) At the other end are the mass-production private establishments, charging vastly higher fees than the subsidized state universities for a very inferior education, taking those who could not get in to better universities, in numbers which permit only the most mechanical and depersonalized of teaching methods, but which are necessary for the university to make ends meet. Graduates from such universities cannot look forward to anything much better than a firm of the second rank.

Given this range, for that 50% or more of each age group whose parents entertain some hopes of sending their children to a university, it is not so much important to get into a university as important to get to the right university. Thence spring all the phenomena so often pointed out as pathological features of Japanese education[11]–

[10] For an account of these mechanisms, see K. Azumi, *Higher Education and Business Recruitment in Japan*, 1968.

[11] See OECD, *Reviews of National Education Policies: Japan*, Paris 1971, pp. 87 ff.

the distortion of the curriculum in high schools due to their pre-occupation with coaching students for the university entrance examinations; the distortion of the curriculum in middle schools due to their preoccupation with getting their graduates through the entrance examinations of those high schools which have the best record for getting graduates into the high-prestige universities – and so on down the line to the pre-kindergarten; the bias of all examinations towards factual memorization tests which are more objective (objectivity being such an overwhelming requirement because so much is at stake and such large numbers are involved); the economic waste involved in the maintenance of flourishing industries manufacturing mock tests for use in the final years of middle and high schools, or running cram schools for those who try in successive years to get through the entrance examinations for 'good' universities rather than accept a second-rate one – and the personal distress bred by repeated failure; the blighting of young lives by 'educational mamas' who focus all their frustrations and status strivings into anxiety about their children's progress, and reduce their children to nervous wrecks – and so on.

None of these phenomena are absent from Britain either, of course, and there is good reason to think that as the qualification requirements of the professions continue slowly to escalate, and as a higher percentage of the age group proceeds to tertiary education with a consequent sharpening of the prestige differentials between different tertiary institutions, the situation in Britain may come to resemble that in Japan. But at present Japan is ahead in this scale of progress. These 'pathological features' – as the Japanese see them – of the educational system are neither so common nor so extreme in this country. They go practically unremarked – in contrast with Japan where they are the subject of constant commentary and debate in the mass media.

It may well be that differences in cultural traditions – the fact that Japan is a Confucian country where education, learning and scholarship have traditionally been given a much higher place than in a more philistine culture such as Britain's – have something to do with the fact that these elements of educational neurosis are a good deal more pronounced in Japan than in England – even allowing for the British preoccupation with selection and 11-plus. But the difference in the finality of the consequences of one's type of schooling for one's life-chances is surely a more important reason.

GENERAL ATTITUDES

It is fairly obvious that some of the differences between our firms –

and some of the differences in other social institutions set out in this chapter – find their consistency in differences between the 'average' Englishman and the 'average' Japanese in the preferences they have for some values and patterns of social relations over other values and patterns, or in their general disposition to anger, to laugh, to sympathize, to compete, to co-operate, to achieve, to affiliate, to dominate, etc. This is no place to embark on a general disquisition on the respective 'national characters' or 'modal personalities' of Japanese and Britons. The field is mined with all kinds of traps for the unwary, not least the danger of assuming a cultural homogeneity in a nation of a hundred million Japanese and the even greater danger of assuming a similar homogeneity in a population of sixty million Britons (recall the wide differences in attitude revealed by the questionnaire survey between workers in Essex and Glasgow – differences much wider than between Japanese sub-samples).

Nevertheless, provided that when one says the Japanese are more polite one is not taken to mean that the average Japanese bank robber is more polite than the average British waiter, only more polite than the average British bank robber, there is clearly something meaningful to be said about average tendencies and dispositions. Unfortunately not a great deal of it can be said on the basis of hard research. A series of 'national character' surveys has been carried out in Japan,[12] but there is no strictly comparable British counterpart. In any case a survey which is to be meaningful must pose behavioural choices in concrete institutional contexts (see, for example, the question quoted on p. 212) and a good deal of interpretation is still needed to specify general qualities and predispositions. However, the Japanese survey did contain one question at that very general level which is perhaps worth quoting.[13] The sample was asked to pick out from lists the adjectives which they thought generally characterize the Japanese people. The adjectives they chose from the approving list, in order of the frequency with which they were chosen, were (in 1968, but there was no great difference in earlier years) diligent (chosen by 61%), persistent, capable of 'sticking it out' (58%), polite (47%), kind (45%), idealistic (23%), cheerful (13%), open, matter of fact (13%), respectors of freedom (12%), rational (11%), and creative (8%), while from the list of boo-words they chose short-tempered (49%), quick to enthuse, quick to cool off (47%), insular (39%), imitative (27%), vindictive (26%), stingy (20%), cunning (19%), arrogant (9%), insincere (9%), cruel (5%). Unfortunately, no one asked them 'more diligent, etc. than whom?'

[12] Hayashi Chikio, *Daini Nihonjin no kokuminsei*, 1970.
[13] Ibid., p. 391.

Even a relative consistency in the stereotypes the Japanese have of themselves, is, however, no evidence that these stereotypes are correct. In this field one man's stereotype is almost as good as any other's. My own list of the main differences between the average Japanese and the average Englishman is given below. As an exercise in the detection of ethnocentrism, I express each difference in two ways.

The Japanese are lesser individualists, are more inclined to submerge their identity in some large group to which they belong, and more likely to be obsessed by a sense of duty.

The British are more selfish, more irresponsible, more inclined to tell Jack that they personally are all right.

The Japanese are less self-confident and more neurotically preoccupied with retaining the good opinion of others.

The British are more apt to be dogmatic and aggressive, being less sensitive to the feelings of others.

The Japanese are more introverted.

The British are less hesitant about imposing their views and feelings on others.

The Japanese are less men of principle than the British.

The British are less willing to forgo the pleasures of self-assertion in the interests of social harmony.

The Japanese are imitative.

The British complacently fail to take opportunities to learn from others.

The Japanese are more ambitious.

The British, again from their greater complacency, have less concern with self-improvement.

The Japanese are more submissive to superiors.

The British are more inclined to resent authority by virtue of its very existence and irrespective of its functional necessity.

The Japanese are more slavishly diligent.

The British are more afraid of hard work.

297

The Japanese care less about what happens outside their own group, and have less sense of social responsibility to correct abuses in their own society.

The British are more given to busybodying, less willing to live and let live.

The Japanese are more childishly naive.

The British are more suspicious and cynical, less good humoured and cheerful.

This, of course, is a game which anyone can play. Most people's lists, however, would contain some reference to at least the three dimensions of difference which have been referred to in one guise or another on frequent occasions in earlier chapters: the individual/group dimension; the submissiveness/rebelliousness dimension, and the strength or otherwise of the work ethic/sense of duty/earnest self-improvement syndrome. We shall return in Chapter 15 to a discussion of the role of these factors in *producing* a distinctively Japanese system.

PART TWO

Convergence?

Chapter 12

The 'Japanese Employment System' and Recent Trends of Change

The practices of one firm do not make an industrial relations system. I propose to take it for granted that the reader is capable of assessing roughly in what respects English Electric was, and in what respects it was not, typical of British firms. But he is perhaps entitled to some discussion of how far Hitachi can be considered typical of Japanese large enterprises. That will be attempted in this chapter. To give the conclusion first. Hitachi *is* reasonably typical: the features which make up what we shall call the 'Japanese system' – low labour turnover, wages determined more by seniority than by function, enterprise unions, high levels of welfare payments – are generally shared by all Japanese *large* corporations – as will be demonstrated as far as possible from national statistics.

This chapter has a second aim. No industrial relations system is wholly static. It is very commonly assumed – equally by visiting Western businessmen and trade unionists as well as by those Japanese scholars who have written voluminously on the subject – that the Japanese system in particular is changing fast. It is seen as the aberrant product of a temporary phase. Everybody knows, runs the argument in its naivest form, that paternalism of one kind or another is characteristic of labour relations in immature industrial economies. It was more marked in Japan because a fully fledged feudal past was so recent. And for the same reason it has persisted to a more advanced stage of industrial development. But eventually – since it flies in the face of all the canons of bureaucratic rationality on which capitalism is founded – it is bound to give way to a 'proper' system of an Anglo-American kind – one which is impersonal, market-determined and fluid, a system in which the concept of loyalty has little place and the notion that it should override material interests has none, a system which is wholly achievement-based and ignores such irrelevant ascribed characteristics as an employee's age, a system in which workers are committed to a craft, a way of life, a labour market, not 'over-committed' to a single firm, and a system in which trade union loyalties transcend corporation boundaries and acquire some essential class overtones.

Plausible, perhaps, but by no means self-evident. The chapter which follows will attempt, while giving an overall picture of the labour economy and the state of labour relations in Japan around the years 1969–70, to indicate what trends of change *have* been visible over the last ten years and to guess how reasonable it would be to extrapolate them. In the next chapter I shall consider trends in the British situation over the same period, and argue that there is more evidence of the British system becoming more like the Japanese than vice versa.

LARGE AND SMALL: THE UNIVERSE OF DISCOURSE

First, a clarification is needed of the reservation implied at the beginning of this chapter. 'The Japanese system' is typical of the *large* firm sector. There is, indeed, in Japan, a marked difference between large firms and small; although the concept is hard to define precisely, no other advanced industrial economy is as aptly described as a 'dual economy'[1] as Japan's. In the manufacturing sector dualism takes the form of a division (in reality, of course, a continuum) which can be schematically represented in the following list of contrasts

The 'modern' firm	The 'traditional' firm
Larger	Smaller
Larger amount of capital per worker	Smaller amount of capital per worker
Bureaucratic corporate structure	Looser personalized management structure
Has union and formalized wage structure	No union: wages result of individual bargains
Contracts out a lot of work to small firms	Frequently dependent on subcontracting from big firms
Has research department	No research
Higher labour productivity	Lower labour productivity
Higher wages	Lower wages
Lower labour turnover	Higher labour turnover

The interrelations between these various dimensions of difference are fairly obvious. It is equally obvious that a formalized pattern of recruitment, training, remuneration and promotion of the Hitachi

---

[1] See S. A. Broadbridge, *Japan's Dual Economy*, London, 1967, and review of same by K. Taira in *Economic Development and Cultural Change*, 18, ii, Jan. 1970.

type requires a fairly large labour force to be viable. Smaller firms, less able to control their market, less able to weather the storms of business fluctuations, have a greater mobility of labour. They tend, particularly the firms small enough for the employer to know his workers individually, to be paternalistic in a traditional sense. Good workers are rewarded by discretionary increases in salary, sick workers are given sick payments not according to formal published scales, but at the discretion of the employer.

Until the end of the fifties, when Japan still had a labour surplus, it almost looked as if dualism might be a permanent feature of Japan's manufacturing industry. The large firms offering superior working conditions, better prospects and higher wages could take their pick from the labour market; workers who failed in the competition for employment had to settle for second best and man the smaller enterprises. By contrast, the boom conditions of the sixties have made for rapid change. The large enterprises, with expanding markets, have sought rapidly to increase their labour force. Their demands alone could absorb almost all the new entrants to the labour market. Small firms had to raise their starting wages if they were to recruit at all, even for replacement purposes. The result was rapid structural change; first, as shown in Table 12.1, a narrowing of differentials in wages as between firms of different sizes; secondly, an increase in the proportion of the labour force in larger firms as the smaller firms were weeded out by a process of natural selection – some which were able to raise their prices or finance capital expansion managing to survive with higher wage costs, some modernizing and reaching a viable, though still small, size in branches of production where economies of scale diminished rapidly; some expanding to become big firms themselves; some going bankrupt.

Table 12.1   *Wage differentials in manufacturing by size of firm*

	Japan			
	1959		1970	
No. of workers	Monthly wages	Monthly wages plus bonuses	Monthly wages	Monthly wages plus bonuses
500 or more	100	100	100	100
100–499	73	70	83	81
30– 99	63	56	76	70
5– 29	52	44	71	62

Source: Rōdōshō, *Shōwa 43-nen rōdō keizai bunseki*, Appx, tables, p. 62, and Rōdōshō, *Shōwa 46-nen rōdō hakusho*, Appx, tables, p. 338.

Table 12.2 *Employees by size of firm in manufacturing, 1960–70*
(10,000s)

| Firm size | All workers | | | Men only | | |
	1960	1970	Incr. 1960–1970 (%)	1960	1970	Incr. 1960–1970 (%)
500 or more employees	243	413	70	174	295	70
100–499	131	224	71	90	145	61
30– 99	142	202	42	95	124	31
1– 29	235	304	29	160	189	18
Total, private sector	787	1144	45	538	754	40

Source: Sōrifu, Tōkei chōsa kyoku, *Rōdōryoku chōsa hōkoku*, 1968 pp. 80–1, and monthly volumes for 1970.

Table 12.2 shows the consequences of this process in the manufacturing sector. In other fields, too, though less markedly, the same change took place; chain stores and department stores encroached on the preserve of the small retailer; large corporate developers invaded the real estate world; the small builder found it harder and harder to survive; insurance companies merged, and so on. The total change in the pattern of employment is shown in Table 12.3.

Some of the implications of this change will be explored in later sections of this chapter. Here the main point to establish is the universe of discourse. Generally speaking, employment institutions characteristic of the 'Japanese system' are found in (a) government employment, (b) firms with more than 500 employees, (c) a fair but not easily estimated proportion of enterprises with one to five hundred

Table 12.3 *Employees by size of firm, all industries, 1960–70*
(10,000s)

| | All workers | | Men only | |
	1960	1970	1960	1970
Total labour force	4511 (100)	5105 (100)	2673 (100)	3098 (100)
Total employees	2208 (49)	3298 (64)	1537 (58)	2202 (71)
Government employment	423 (9)	394 (8)	319 (12)	282 (9)
Private firms with 500+ employees	448 (10)	867 (17)	332 (12)	619 (20)
Private firms with 100 to 499 employees	229 (5)	463 (9)	163 (6)	309 (10)
Private firms with 30 to 99 employees	287 (6)	482 (9)	199 (7)	316 (10)
Private firms with 1 to 29 employees	744 (17)	1055 (21)	472 (18)	660 (21)

Source: Sōrifu, Tōkeikyoku, *Rōdōryoku chōsa hōkoku*, 1968, and monthly volumes, 1970.

employees, especially in the white collar industries – insurance companies, small banks, private universities – and in those manufacturing establishments, perhaps about a quarter of the total,[2] which have trade unions.

This means (Table 12.3) that at least ten million workers – half of the total number of employees (though a good deal more than half of non-manual and a good deal less than half of manual employees) or about one-third of all those gainfully occupied in the Japanese economy – are involved in a full version of 'the system'. And it will be seen that both in the economy as a whole and in manufacturing in particular their proportion has grown by about 5% since 1960. This, moreover, is the elite ten million. It includes almost all of Japan's university graduates except non-salaried doctors and free-lance lawyers, and it includes the most skilled of Japan's manual workers. Though 50% of the employed labour force it is a fair guess that it receives 60–70% of employee income. And since income per capita in the self-employed sector is lower than in the employed sector it is equally probable that, though only a third of the labour force it receives a half or more of total earned personal income.

The importance of 'the system', therefore, is to be measured not only by its gradual absorption of a larger proportion of the Japanese labour force, but also by the influence it has as a normative model for the rest of society. The smaller enterprises do not have an alternative set of institutions to which they cling with tenacity, the virtues of which they would be prepared to defend against all comers. They are simply firms whose employers cannot manage to emulate the big corporations although (except perhaps in the matter of having to deal with trade unions) they would probably wish to.

So much, then, for the pervasiveness of 'the system'. To return now to the central question: is Hitachi a typical exemplar of it, and is it changing?

RECRUITMENT

One fact illustrates better than any other the preference for virgin labour straight from school which Hitachi shares with other employers. The Japanese Ministry of Labour's annual report on the

[2] The total number of trade unions with between one and five hundred members in 1967 was 7,366, and the total number of establishments (not firms) with 100–500 workers in 1966 was 27,741. One has to make allowances both for establishments which are part of larger enterprises and for unions which are (as at Hitachi) nominally independent but closely tied to an enterprise federation. Rōdōshō, Tōkeichōsabu, *Shōwa-42-nen Rōdō kumiai kihon chōsa hōkoku*, p. 72 and *Rōdō tōkei nempō*, 1967, p. 15.

labour market produces two quite separate sets of tables in recognition of the existence of two separate labour markets. One concerns the demand for and supply of school-leavers of various types: the other the 'mid-career' market. The figures of Table 12.4 give some of these figures which show clearly where employers' preferences lie.

Table 12.4 *Number of advertised places carrying permanent employee status offered for men, per male job seeker in relevant categories*

| | Job offers limited to | | | Jobs open to mid-career workers |
	15-year-old new middle school graduates	18-year-old new high school graduates	New University graduates	
1960	1·9	1·8	n.a.	0·6
1966	2·6	3·2	8·8*	1·1
1968	4·3	6·0	14·1*	1·6
1970	6·2	9·7	n.a.	1·9

Source: Rōdōshō, *Rōdō shijō nempō*, 1965, 1966, 1968, 1970.

* These figures have meaning only to the extent that an increase almost certainly reflects a real increase. The number of job offers is a summation of all the requests sent to university appointments offices from all firms. But, for example, Hitachi might request some 200 universities to recommend anything from 2 to 50 suitable candidates – making a total perhaps of over 10,000 when its actual plans call for recruitment of 1,000 new graduates – and then perhaps find only some 600 who measure up to its standards. The high school and middle school figures are also inflated by the same factors. They are calculated from each labour exchange's lists of offers (plus those sent directly to schools) and the number of local graduates.

The effects of the increasing labour shortage of the sixties can be seen in these figures. As the demands of industry have grown the fall in the birth rate from 1949 onwards simultaneously reduced the supply of new graduates. The ratio of vacancies to applicants in the school-leavers market has risen, and employers have had increasingly to turn to the other market, either attracting experienced workers from other firms, or drawing on the diminishing supply of under-employed workers in the primary and tertiary sectors. For the latter purpose – since there are no longer any spare younger sons of farm families to be drawn from the countryside to the cities – some firms have located new factories in rural areas to attract the heads of farm families who can commute to the factory from home, looking after their fields on Sundays, or leaving them to their wives.

But still, for most jobs employers prefer to recruit new graduates if they can get them, and, although the wage differentials between small and large firms have been narrowed (Table 12.1) – and particularly the differentials in starting wages – it is still the bigger firms which succeed in attracting them. In the first half of 1969, a half of establishments with more than 500 workers recruited more than 60% of their new workers from the school-leavers' market, compared with only one-fifth of establishments with fewer than 30 workers.[3] The following Table 12.5 shows that in the early sixties the larger enterprises were able to fill an increasing proportion of their vacancies with school-leavers (or were developing a stronger preference for school-leavers) and have been able almost to maintain that proportion since – in contrast to the smaller firms.

Table 12.5 *Numbers of school and university graduates entering large and small manufacturing establishments 1959–70*

| | Size of establishment (in 1970, enterprise)[a] | | | | | | | |
| | More than 500 workers | | | | 30–99 workers | | | |
	1959	1964	1968	1970	1959	1964	1968	1970
Number of new graduates recruited (thousands)	107	224	245	306	128	136	105	65
New graduates as % of total recruits in the year	30	45	43	37	28	24	20	12

[a] Note that the figures up to 1968 refer to size of establishments, not enterprises. Some establishments of very large firms will also have less than 100 workers.
Source: Rōdōshō, Tōkeichōsabu, *Koyō dōkō chōsa hōkoku*, 1964, pp. 111, 115; 1968, p. 68; 1970, p. 41; and *Rōdō idō chōsa hōkoku*, 1959, p. 62.

If one may rely on the Japanese Ministry of Labour's employment trends survey – and it has been operating for some fifteen years and has acquired a considerable degree of sophistication in the process – one can say a little more about the recruitment patterns of large firms. These figures refer to males only:[4]

Total male entrants into manufacturing enterprises with 1,000 or more workers, 1970	100
Of these, the proportion just leaving school or university	36
Others who had not been employed in the previous twelve months	6
Those who had been gainfully occupied elsewhere in the previous twelve months	59

[3] Rōdōshō, Tōkeichōsabu, *Koyō dōkō chōsa hōkoku no gaiyō*, 1969, first half year, p. 23.
[4] Rōdōshō, Tōkeichōsabu, *Koyō dōkō chōsa hōkoku*, 1970, pp. 43, 63.

Among the latter (as a percentage, still, of total entrants):

Those who had been *employees* in secondary industry	25
Those among the latter employed in other firms with more than 1,000 employees	10

Not many people move from one big firm to another – a mere 10% (12% if one adds those who came from firms with 500–999 workers) of total new male entrants in 1970, equivalent to 1·3% of all men employed in manufacturing enterprises with over 1000 workers. This is less, in fact, than the number of men who moved into establishments within these same large manufacturing enterprises, not from other firms but on 'posting' from a different establishment in the same firm. In 1970 their number was equivalent to 4% of the total male labour force in these firms.[5]

One more indication of the effects of labour shortage is to be found in the reduction in the number of temporary workers. In manufacturing establishments with more than 500 employees they made up nearly 9% of the labour force (both sexes) in 1958[6] and nearly 12% in 1959 (reflecting the expansion of the economy in the latter year). In 1969 the figure had fallen to 6%, and during the year 1% were transferred to permanent status. For men only the fall was from 11% in 1959 to 4% in 1970.[7]

But the interesting question is whether the pattern of mobility is changing. Many have been predicting that mobility – and in particular mobility between big firms – would increase and that the 'life-time employment system' would be one of the first features of the Japanese pattern to crumble. There were some plausible grounds for this view:

1. Labour shortage means that the big firms simply cannot meet all their labour requirements from the school-leaver market; therefore they get used to a pattern of mid-career recruitment.

2. Now that the big firms are capable of absorbing the whole output of schools, only the most prestigeful firms can insist on recruiting from the top 10% or the top 20% in academic achievement of graduating classes. Most firms, therefore, do not now have a select body of hand-picked workers whom they are anxious to keep and whom they find it worth while to offer, in the form of seniority increments, special inducements to stay with the firm. (On the other

---

[5] Rōdōshō Tōkeichōsabu, *Koyō dōkō chōsa hōkoku*, 1970, pp. 22, 27.

[6] Though these figures are plausibly argued by Kōji Taira to be underestimates. See *Economic Development and the Labour Market in Japan*, 1970, p. 181.

[7] Ibid., 1969, 1970, and *idem*, *Rōdō idō chōsa kekka hōkoku*, 1959.

hand, the absolute shortage of labour more than compensates for this.)

3. The shortage of labour and the diminution of wage differentials between large and small firms makes employees more willing to cast their bread upon the waters and take a chance on leaving the security of a Big Firm.

4. Shortage of labour is likely sooner or later to prompt employees to try seducing skilled workers away from other employers.

5. Shortage of labour reduces the availability of temporary workers. Deprived of this element of flexibility employers have an enhanced incentive to hire and fire permanent workers according to the fluctuations of the market.

6. The increasing pace of technological change is likely to produce critical shortages of skills which require relatively prolonged training, and employers facing such a need will have to raid other firms.

7. The post-war education system and general changes in society are thought to be breeding more independent and individualistic people, too 'dry' (to use the Japanese phrase) to be easily susceptible to traditional 'wet' appeals to loyalty.

A certain amount of superficial evidence seems to support the prediction of greater mobility. There are more advertisements for skilled workers in the newspapers. New private placement agencies have appeared. The thriving 'how to get ahead' book industry, in addition to the traditional compendia of good advice for the salary-man who seeks to improve his chances of promotion within the firm, now produces the occasional book entitled *Change Your Job!* or *In Praise of Mobility*. Perhaps more significant, a Tokyo survey[8] in September 1970 found that under the age of 25 new mid-career entrants were, for the first time, receiving *higher* wages than their 'conventional' contemporaries who had been in the firm since leaving school. Previously, in many firms, agreements with the unions had limited wages of such late entrants to a fixed proportion – 80% to 90% – of the wages of 'loyalists'. The change to paying a *premium* for deserters from other firms is therefore a considerable one.

It is hard, though, as yet, to evaluate the significance of these changes. It has been mentioned already that Hitachi has recruited a number of graduate technicians from smaller computing firms. On the other hand, the example of the gas turbine development has also been quoted: a team of technicians was recruited from within the

---

[8] Tōkyo-to, *Chūto-sayōsha no shoninkyū*, 1970.

firm to spend a year retraining for the new task. That is perhaps the more typical way of coping with expansion. Larger new developments are planned well ahead, and the lead time for manpower retraining is not often longer than for physical retooling.

The increase in mobility is primarily, as the figures of Table 12.6 show, increasing mobility of the young. In every industrial society mobility declines with age.[9] 'Lifelong employment' could come to mean, in Japan, just that the tendency is more pronounced and the settling down, after a few years wandering, is more definitive. Whether increasing shopping around in one's early years before settling down to 'lifelong employment' can happen without affecting the subsequent permanence of the employment is as much a moot point as whether premarital sexual experimentation affects the stability of marriage.

At any rate, as the figures of Table 12.6 suggest, if the system is changing the change is taking place very slowly. It is noticeable, too, that although no satisfactory measurement of the trend in the movement of graduates is possible, the 1968–70 figures are very low. This is important since graduate employees are the high-prestige pacesetters, and the most likely to be the object of poaching if it becomes common.

The movement remains predominantly a movement of the young, but the Japanese Ministry of Labour points out in its 1972 White Paper[10] that in the late sixties the increasing relaxation of the institutional barriers to mid-career recruitment was bringing an increase in separation rates for older workers – from something below 3% for workers in their forties in 1960 to 7% in 1971 – still well below the figure for younger workers (see Table 12.6), but nevertheless a not negligible figure.

Most of the movement, however, remains a movement of young people and there is, indeed, every reason to expect that as the tertiary sector expands, particularly the small-scale agencies employing graduates and offering specialized services to industry – there will

[9] Making one of the few statistical comparisons of mobility by age which are possible, Robert Cole shows that as between a national sample of Japanese job-changers in 1967 and a sample of workers in Detroit, mobility differences between age groups (the settling down effect) were *less* marked in Japan. At ages up to 35 the Japanese rate was around one-third of the American rate; thereafter it rose to one-half. This is probably, however, due to the fact that the older Japanese workers were heavily over-represented in the small and medium firms where mobility rates are, of course, much higher than in the large firms which have predominantly youthful labour forces. Robert E. Cole, *Permanent Employment in Japan: Fact and Fantasies*, mimeo.

[10] Rōdōshō, *Shōwa-46-nen rōdō keizai no bunseki*, 1972, p. 80.

Table 12.6   *Annual separation rates*

Year	All males in establishments (in 1970, firms) of more than 500 employees (%)	Males under 25, manufacturing establishments (in 1970, firms) with more than 500 employees (%)	Male university and college graduates in manufacturing *establishments* of more than 500 employees (1968–9), *firms* of more than 1,000 employees (1970)[a] (%)
1964	10·3	19·3	
1965	9·4	16·0	
1966	8·4	14·3	
1967	10·6	18·7	
1968	11·0	20·2	3·4
1969	11·3	21·3	3·8
1970	12·2	21·4	4·0

[a] These figures cannot be derived directly from the *Koyō dōkō chōsa hōkoku*, since although the survey provides a breakdown of leavers by educational background, there is no information on the educational composition of the total labour force. For the latter one must resort to the annual wage survey: *Chingin kōzō kihon tōkei chōsa hōkoku*. For 1970 the two surveys refer to the same category – enterprises with more than 1,000 employees, but for the two earlier years it was necessary to make the assumption that the proportion of graduates in firms with over 1,000 employees (between 12 and 13%) was the same as their proportion in *establishments* with over 500 employees.

Source: Rōdōshō, Tōkeichōsabu, *Koyō dōkō chōsa hōkoku* various years.

be an increase in the fall-out from the big corporations. And capital liberalization and an increase in the number of foreign firms with different employment traditions will accelerate the trend. But one cannot properly speak of a substantial break in traditional practices until the number of employees in the big firm sector who move from one firm to another – at present about 1½% of total employees each year (see p. 308) shows a noticeable increase. The tradition that one does not raid other firms in the same league as oneself remains an effective barrier to mobility of the British type. It rests only in part on an unspoken 'do-as-you-would-be-done-by' understanding. The other part of it is the sense that to raid one's competitors would be to weaken the bond which binds one's own employees to the firm – it would be to abandon the assumption that entry into a firm is a kind of once-and-for-all-rebirth that fixes one's group membership for the rest of one's life. For Hitachi to raid a small parts-maker is one thing; even to take someone from a large steel corporation might be acceptable; but to raid a comparable direct rival like Toshiba in the same league is quite another. Not many Hitachi men would have anything to gain by transferring to a small parts maker, but once one rejects the convention that once a Toshiba man, always a Toshiba man, then Hitachi men too might begin thinking of themselves as potential Toshiba men, and then the sense of loyalty to the *Gemeinde*, devotion to the collective Hitachi goal of wresting another

Table 12.7   *The composition of wages and salaries in large manufacturing firms (5,000 or more employees)*

Type of wage element	Proportion of firms whose wage system contains that element		Weighting of that element in the total wage (average all large firms)	
	1966 (%)	1969 (%)	1966 (%)	1969 (%)
Person-related payments				
Basic personal wage (depending entirely on age, service, experience or education)	14·2	25·4	19·3	9·8
Mixed criteria combining the above with some assessment of performance (as at Hitachi)	72·1	68·5	56·6	47·7
Family allowances	95·9	96·8	2·7	2·5
Local cost of living allowances	23·1	26·6	0·6	0·3
Commuters' transport allowances	85·3	91·4	2·1	1·8
Housing allowances (in lieu of housing provision)	44·1	50·5	0·8	0·6
Other personal allowances	20·7	24·6	0·6	0·6
Function-related payments				
General pay scales depending on worker's *job* classification	30·2	28·5	2·7	12·4
General pay scales depending on worker's *skill* classification	40·5	44·9	8·2	14·0
General pay scales depending on broad work categories	2·8	7·9	0·4	0·2
Special skill bonuses for particular individuals	14·7	20·2	0·1	0·1
Special bonuses for holders of supervisory and managerial positions	71·6	75·2	1·6	0·9
Heat, danger, etc. allowances	81·3	70·5	0·9	1·2
Performance-related payments				
Individual piece-work	4·1	4·4	0·8	0·3
Group piecework	15·4	10·4	1·8	7·3
Merit assessment (based on attendance, punctuality, diligence, co-operativeness, etc.)	18·2	27·5	0·7	0·2

Source: Rōdōshō, Tōkeichōsabu, *Chingin rōdō jikan seido sōgō chōsa*, 1966, pp. 65, 88; 1969, pp. 41, 56.

1% of the market share away from Toshiba, might start to be seriously eroded.

WAGES

The first of the next pair of tables, derived from Ministry of Labour surveys (Table 12.7), shows that the structure of wages at Hitachi is not untypical. The second (Table 12.8) shows, further, how general

Table 12.8 *Average male earnings (overtime included) at various ages: manufacturing establishments with 1,000 or more employees*

				Manual workers				
	17	18–19	20–4	25–9	30–4	35–9	40–9	50–9
1955[a]	36	52	72	100	122	142	157	168
1964	42	61	79	100	128	151	169	175
1968	44	63	78	100	118	134	151	157
1971	49	66	80	100	116	125	138	141

	White collar workers: graduates of pre-war middle, post-war high, schools						
	18–19	20–4	25–9	30–4	35–9	40–9	50–9
1955[b]	54	71	100	133	157	169	180
1964	58	72	100	136	167	213	233
1968	60	78	100	125	148	182	199
1971	59	76	100	122	144	168	197

	University graduates					
	20–4	25–9	30–4	35–9	40–9	50–9
1955	80	100	145	172	190	179
1964	81	100	139	190	259	317
1968	78	100	129	163	222	278
1971	78	100	132	160	213	258

[a] The 1955 figures for manual workers are for selected trades only (foundryman, lathe mechanic, press operator). These are weighted according to the numbers in these jobs at the time to give an overall figure for manual workers. The appearance of these figures for selected trades, and indeed, the title of the survey in 1955 – 'a survey of wages by *occupation*' – reflects the Ministry of Labour's lingering attachment to traditional Western notions of what a labour market is like (notions which had, after all, still considerable relevance in the pre-war and immediate post-war period). In recent years, however, the title has been changed to 'basic statistics on wage structures' and classifies workers by general job and educational categories.

[b] The 1955 figure is for administrative workers only – i.e. technical personnel are excluded.

Source: Rōdōshō Tōkeichōsabu, *Shokushubetsu chingin jittai chōsa kekka hōkoku*, 1955, and *Chingin kōzō kihon tōkei chōsa hōkoku*, 1964, 1968, 1970.

is the Hitachi pattern of a rising lifetime curve of earnings even (though to a somewhat lesser degree than for university or high school graduates) for manual workers.

The wage system is another crucial point from which one might have expected a general crumbling of the Japanese employment system to begin. Basically, the expectation rests on the belief that age differentials in wages do not accurately reflect differentials in skill and experience, nor, therefore, in the market value of services rendered. Hence, it might be thought, they are likely to disappear as rational profit-maximization becomes a dominant principle of industrial organization.

Indeed, quite apart from academic theories arguing that the system *will* disappear, there have been many influential voices urging that it *ought* to disappear. Thus, in 1955, a report issued by the main employers' federation, the Keidanren, is categorical in its recommendations. Its phraseology, echoing Robert Lynd, is clearly influenced by sociologists' formulations of the rational performance oriented criteria which are supposed to characterize modern industrial society.

'In most industries the base pay system involves payment according to the employee's age, sex, marital status and length of service. The base pay is paid according to 'who a person is', not according to 'what job does a person do'. This committee believes that if Japan is going in future to make efficient production a major objective, the nature of an employee's work should become the determining element in his reward. We recommend that the base pay should not be affected by such personal characteristics as age, sex, marital status or length of service.'[11]

In 1967, a committee of the Ministry of Labour is equally categorical:

'It is necessary to move from the traditional wage system heavily weighted with personal elements such as service, to a functional wage system based on the quality and quantity of services rendered.'[12]

Nor are these views confined to employers. The statements by various union organizations in preparation for the 1970 spring wage offensive contain some equally clear expressions of the same view. For example, the Japan Council of the International Metalworkers'

[11] Nihon Keieisha Dantai Remmei, *Shokumu-kyū no kenkyū*, 1955, quoted in Nishimiya Teruaki, *Shokumukyū: Kangaekata, susumekata*, 1967, p. 3.
[12] Rōdōshō, Chingin kenkyūkai, Rōdō seisansei kankei shō-iinkai, *Rōdō seisanseikōjō to chinginseido ni tsuite*, 1967, p. 30.

Federation, a body formed to embody the principles of non-political economic unionism, has this to say:

'The wage system must be based on the foundation of a guaranteed minimum, to which are added fair and appropriate differentials based on the principle of equal pay for equal work. Wage rates should not be determined by such personal characteristics as age, education, length of service. . . .'[13]

Again, the right wing socialist Dōmei, also in its 1970 statement:

'As is well known the age-and-service wage system is a wage system peculiar to our country, originally developed as a means of keeping wage costs down. . . . It creates a multiplicity of status systems and is intimately linked with the lifetime employment systems . . . reflecting the nature of our closed labour market in which each enterprise is an isolated island to itself. An age-and-service wage system of this nature cannot adapt to present day conditions of work in an age of rapid technological change – to changes in the content of work and in the nature of the skills required, to changes in workers' attitudes and to the increasing fluidity of the labour market. . . . It is our task to take the lead in reforming the pre-modern characteristics of the age-and-service wage system – its low-wage character and its perversion of the principle of equal pay for equal work. It is necessary to develop a modern wage system suitable for a new age and conforming to the new outlook of Japanese workers.'[14]

However, the spring 1970 statement by what is still the most powerful body in the organization of the wage offensive – the Spring Struggle Co-ordinating Committee led by the left-wing socialist Sōhyō federation – is rather more ambiguous. Although in the early fifties Sōhyō was a powerful advocate of the principle of 'equal pay for equal work', its attitude has changed since the principle of job-related payments became accepted by employers and began tentatively to be implemented. The 'equal pay for equal work' slogan appears nowhere in its 1970 statement. After a long review of the movement of differentials in the sixties, the closest it comes to a general conclusion is the statement:

'There remain a large number of socially unjust wage differentials – between firms of different size, between men and women, or

[13] Kokusai kinzoku rōren, Nihon kyōgikai, *45-nendo chingin tōsō no tame ni*, reprinted in Nihon rōdō kyōkai kyōikubu, *1970-nendo chingin hakusho*, p. 136.
[14] Zen Nihon rōdō sōdōmei, *Atarashii hiyaku e no ōhaba chin-age*, reprinted in ibid. p. 94–5.

between men doing identical work who merely happen to be of different ages. It is necessary to use our spring struggle to correct these differentials.'[15]

It then goes on, however, to refer back to earlier calculations of the minimum cost of living requirements for men at different ages and speaks of the need to 'secure the wages necessary for each age group to cover household expenditure'.

'Equal pay for equal work' is so eminently reasonable a slogan that to oppose it is like being in favour of sin. Nevertheless, when it comes to the crunch, a large number of workers and trade unionists do oppose it. Despite its ambiguities of expression the position of the left-wing federation is fairly clear, and even the more right-wing Dōmei, despite its resounding clarion call for a 'modern' wage system, when it comes to give concrete recommendations for formulating 1970 wage demands suddenly begins to urge 'a minimum wage of 30,000 yen at the age of 18, and of 50,000 for male production workers at the marrying age of 27. . . . In working towards a minimum living standard guarantee line, the emphasis should be placed on protecting the living standards of middle-aged and older workers.'[16]

The ambiguities in attitudes are revealed, too, in the questionnaire survey. In answer to the question: 'Do you think that a man with long service should receive higher wages than a man with short service, even if they are doing the same work?' only 18% of the Japanese sample (compared with 67% of the British) said 'no'. Then, when the Japanese sample was asked what should be the relative proportions respectively of the job-related element and the personal element in wages, 67% said that the job-related element should make up half or more of the wage, but only 11% thought that it should account for the whole wage.

These replies seem to reflect a preference for the kind of compromise between conflicting principles of wage determination which Hitachi has in fact introduced. If the system were to be changed at all, of course, some kind of gradual compromising change is the only possible policy – as is recognized clearly in the recommendations of the Ministry of Labour committee quoted above, and, indeed, in the Dōmei document. Compromising gradualness is necessary because it is extremely difficult in any country at any time to introduce changes which give some individuals lower wages in absolute terms than they had before. Change has to be accomplished by strategic distribution of wage increases.

[15] Shuntō kyōtō iinkai, *1970-nen chingin hakusho*, reprinted in ibid, p. 45.
[16] op. cit. p. 94.

This, many companies have done. Table 12.7 shows the number of firms whose wage system included job-related elements. In the majority, it is a safe bet, they were newly introduced, as at Hitachi, in the course of the late fifties or early sixties. It is an equally safe bet that, although their introduction undoubtedly did affect the age-distribution of wages, many of these job-related payments are, as at Hitachi, calculated in such a way as to include within themselves a substantial seniority element. It is significant, for example, that (Table 12.7) there were more firms in 1966–8 which had a payment element explicitly related to skill – i.e. to the quantity and quality of work a man is *capable* of doing – than had one related to job – the work a man is *actually* doing. Hitachi's system (see p. 105) though titularly a job classification system, was implicitly based on skill classification.

It is, in fact, very much to be doubted whether many Japanese employers introduced job-related wage elements in a spirit of hopeful anticipation, confident that they had found a solution to a longstanding and bothersome problem of finding some means of enhancing work motivation. It has already been argued that the Japanese wage system embodies a manifold variety of subtle, not to say insidious, incentive payments.

How then is one to explain the fact that changes in the wage system have in fact taken place?

The first part of the explanation seems to be that Japanese managers take very seriously the recommendations of the expert committees quoted above. If they are not convinced by the theoretical arguments, they *are* convinced by the plain fact that such indisputably *modern* countries as America and those of Western Europe do base their wage systems on function, not on personal characteristics. Although they may appreciate intellectually that Japan's 'pre-modern' wage system has not prevented Japan from becoming the world's third largest economy with the highest growth rate among the developed economies, they find it hard to accept the fact emotionally. Ten years of manifest success are too short entirely to obliterate the century-old assumption that 'modernity' (which is seen as intrinsically desirable) is embodied in Western institutions. (And, of course, the continued patronizing attitudes of many of the Westerners they meet who also share this assumption tend to confirm these older attitudes.)

The trade unionists who belong to the groups which are in favour of a movement towards job-related payments share essentially the same attitudes – see, for example, the use of 'modern' and 'pre-modern' in the Dōmei statement quoted above. The chairman of the Hitachi Federation, when asked why the union was in favour of increasing job-related payments until they made up 50% of the wage bill could only say that as the Japanese economy is becoming increasingly internationalized it is necessary to bring Japanese wages up to international levels *and* to conform to international practices.

Nevertheless, those who hold this view are often rather like the sinner who recognizes where the path of virtue lies, but, the flesh being weak, prefers to wallow in his sin for a little while longer. *And*, of course, there are a few people who do explicitly reject received notions of modernity and argue that since the Japanese wage system has performed well enough, it could well be left alone. In these circumstances a tentative move *in the general direction* of a job-related payment system represents the least contentious point of compromise.

But there are also several other reasons for making such a move. The first is that in Japanese management circles a high premium is placed on *innovation* (as distinct from modernity). Young graduates in management are nowadays much more commonly given planning tasks than ten or fifteen years ago when, for the good of their souls, they were made to sweat through several years of routine administrative work which was well within the skill range of high school graduates. In personnel offices an obvious planning exercise, and one which can earn one some distinction, is to devise a new form of wage payment. And where innovation is generally considered to be a good thing (unless it strikes too hard against existing interests or prejudices) there is a good chance of the plan being adopted.

A subsidiary calculation – never, of course, made explicit – may well be that complication of the wage system is a good thing because it makes the wage system harder for the average worker to grasp. In answer to the question: 'If there were a mistake in the calculation of your wages, would you immediately spot it?', 30% of Japanese workers said that they probably wouldn't and 13% that they might not, compared with only 7% and 5% respectively of the British sample (despite the fact that many of the latter were on quite complex systems of piecework). The point is not that the addition of an extra complexity makes it easier to cheat workers; it is, rather, that it diffuses complaints. It makes it harder for the worker to identify what might seem to him unfair about the system, and it adds to the number of variables which can be gradually altered over the years to bring about a change in the distribution of rewards – a change which arouses less opposition because the direction in which it is tending is not always clear.

Finally, a more powerful and probably decisive motive for introducing a job-related payment element lay in the increasing competition for labour in the school and university leavers' market. It was necessary to compete by raising wages at the younger ages, and it would have been far to costly too jack up the whole age-wage scale by a comparable amount in order to maintain existing age differentials. Between 1960 and 1968, average male wages in manufacturing firms with 1,000 or more employees rose by 107% (nominal).[17] The starting wage for male middle-school leavers increased by 177% and for male high-school leavers by 154% in the same period,[18] thus in effect flattening the gradient of the age-wage curve – as is already shown in Table 12.8. This effect could have been achieved by altering the differentials on the seniority scale itself, but it could be accomplished with less opposition by introducing a new payment element under the banner of the impeccable slogan 'equal pay for equal work'. (For a more detailed discussion of the effect at Hitachi, see p. 106.)

As a rule of justice, the market principle of 'equal pay for equal work' does, after all, command respect in Japan. This is reflected too, in the reasons given by the 72% of the Japanese sample who said 'yes' to the question: 'Do you think that a man with long service should receive higher wages than a man with short service, even if they were doing the same work?' A subsequent open-ended question asked why the long-service men should get more, and the most common response was 'because they have more experience and are better at the work' – a justification which still falls within the scope of the 'equal pay for equal work' principle. The other reasons and the proportions offering them are shown below. (Some offered more than one justification: if the question had been explicitly in terms of *age* rather than service the 'family responsibility' answer might have been more frequent.)

	%
Because that's the Japanese tradition	8
Because they've given more of their lives to the company and therefore deserve more	26
Because they are older and have heavier family responsibilities	14
Because they have longer experience and are better at the work	32
Can't think of a reason	5

In so far as the 'longer experience: better at work' justification for the present system is a real one, the fact that experience does count

[17] Rōdōshō, Tōkeichōsabu, *Year Book of Labour Statistics*, 1960, pp. 198, 200; 1968, p. 154.
[18] Rōdōshō Shokugyō Antei Kyoku, *Rōdō shijō nempō*, 1968, p. 126. The starting wage figures actually refer to enterprises (not firms) with 500 or more employees.

for much less in an age of rapidly changing technology, and that older workers have less adaptiveness and less energy – and less schooling – than younger workers becomes, therefore, an argument at least for reducing, if not abolishing or reversing, age differentials.

Abstract principles of justice apart, if the wage system is looked at simply as a pattern of long-term incentives, one can see how Japanese managers might recognize a lesser need to extend the rising curve of wages into the later ages. There *is* some point in giving even older workers the hope of an increase the following April to spur them to greater efforts. But the other function of the incentive system – to reinforce the lifetime employment pattern and prevent workers from drifting away – has less relevance; the worker in his mid-forties, even in modern days of labour shortage, is not likely to receive tempting outside offers. And, aware of their lack of alternatives, they are less likely to allow disaffected thoughts to surface in their minds. Hence, justice apart, personnel managers are likely to feel that they *can* safely reduce (relatively) the wages of older workers.

But an examination of the forces at work on the wage system has to take account of two other factors besides the pursuit of modernity, the tightness of the labour market for new school-leavers, the appeal of the justice of the 'equal pay for equal work' principle or managers' calculations of incentive effects. The first is the strength of the other justifications of the present system mentioned above – 'it's the way we've always done it'; 'loyal workers deserve more'; 'older workers with more family responsibilities *need* more'. The second is the bargaining position. Older workers who have most to lose from a change in the payment system are, though not a majority, influential out of proportion to their numbers in trade unions. Attempts to flatten the age-wage gradient consequently meet with opposition in the bargaining situation.

These factors explain why the total effects of the changes have been limited. In the first place the job-related payments themselves have in effect been modified to include a large seniority element. Secondly, recent years have seen a roll-back effort: the unions have pressed harder the claim that 'it is now time to do something for the older workers', and to some extent the claim has been granted – sometimes, as at Hitachi, by increasing family allowances, sometimes by adjustments to the seniority scales.

The consequence is that the total shift in the age distribution of wages has been of less than startling proportions. The figures of Table 12.8 provide the best indication. It will be seen that the gradient of the age-wage curve, which by 1964 was a good deal steeper than it was in 1955, had been reduced by 1968 to something a little below the

1955 level. But still, in 1971, for manual workers, the final wage was nearly three times the starting wage, and the average wage of men in their fifties was still nearly double that of men in their early twenties. The pattern is still markedly different from the age distribution of wages in British factories.

It is conceivable that the trend of change visible between 1964 and 1971 could continue in the future until, over a decade or two, a British-type pattern is reached. The institutional obstacles to an

Table 12.9   *Composition of labour costs: Britain and Japan*

	British manu- facturing firms with 1,000 or more employees 1964	Japanese manufacturing firms with 5,000 or more employees	
		1965	1968
Regular wage/salary payments	89·4	82·7	82·3
Monthly wages		53·7	51·9
Overtime		9·4	10·4
Bonuses[a]		19·6	20·0
Statutory insurance contributions	3·4	4·5	4·9
Private social welfare payments	3·6	5·6	5·9
Contributions to insurance/ pensions	(3·3)[b]	0·1	0·1
Marriage gifts/condolence money		0·1	0·1
Family, housing, travel allowances		2·2	2·2
Retirement allowances	(0·1)[b]	3·3	3·5
Provision in kind	0·1	0·7	0·9
Subsidized services	1·6	4·6	4·1
Housing		2·5	2·3
Food		0·8	0·7
Cultural, recreational		0·4	0·4
Health		0·8	0·6
Recruitment and training	1·7	0·9	1·0
Other expenses	0·2	0·4	0·5
Total	100·0	100·0	100·0

[a] British employees also received profit-sharing bonuses amounting to 0·7% of their wages and salaries (average amount for firms of all sizes). This sum is not included in labour costs.

[b] Calculated on the assumption that the breakdown of this item for firms of all sizes (*Ministry of Labour Gazette*, December, 1966, p. 810, table 6) applied equally to firms of 1,000 or more workers.

Source: *Ministry of Labour Gazette*, December, 1966, p. 810; Rōdōshō, Tōkeichōsabu, *Rōdō hiyō chōsa hōkoku*, 1965, 1968. For both countries, the wages and salaries of specialized personnel are included in expenditures for 'subsidized services' and 'recruitment and training'.

indefinite continuation of the trend are considerable, however, and most firms have set a limit to the proportion of the wage bill which – according to present plans – they propose eventually to allocate to job-related payments – a limit which is frequently well below Hitachi's 50%.

ENTERPRISE WELFARE

The next feature of 'the system' can be dealt with summarily by means of Table 12.9 which suffices to make the following points:

1. Japanese firms devote a larger proportion of their labour costs to the provision of various forms of welfare service, and a smaller proportion to cash wages than British firms.

2. Assuming that the bulk of the British contributions to 'insurance and pension schemes' are in fact for pensions, and thus equivalent in function to Japanese retirement allowances, the biggest difference lies in the firm's provision of concrete subsidized services.

3. There is no indication in the two sets of Japanese figures of any substantial change in the distribution of labour costs, despite a considerable increase (of 35%) in total labour costs during the three-year interval.

One further relevant comparison can be made. It is possible, using Japanese and British statistics, to arrive at a rough estimate of the relative importance of the role played respectively by the state and by the employer in providing social security to employees in manufacturing industry. The comparison works out as follows. (See page 323.)

TRADE UNIONS

Most enterprises like Hitachi have trade unions with approximately the same membership coverage. According to a survey in the early sixties,[19] 76% of all employees in manufacturing firms employing 500 or more workers were in a union, compared with 96% in Hitachi if one excludes temporary workers, apprentices and post-retirement re-employees from the definition of 'employees', 86% if one does not. The difference is likely to be due to the complete absence of unions in a number of small firms with not many more than 500 employees, rather than to firms excluding a markedly greater proportion of employees from union membership than does Hitachi.

The overall rate of unionization is much lower, of course. In the peak year of 1949, 55% of all Japanese employees belonged to trade

[19] Rōshi kankeihō kenkyūkai, *Rōshi kankeihō unjō no jitsujō oyobi mondaiten*, 1967, p. 161.

Table 12.10   *State and enterprise as sources of social security: Britain and Japan*

	Britain 1964 (%)	Japan 1967 (%)
Total income received during the year per wage or salary earner in manufacturing industry	100·0 (£937)	100·0 (638,000 yen = £748)
Discretionary income, including freely disposable income as normally defined and also those elements of taxes, etc. not attributable to the cost of social services[a]	76·4	78·4
Receipts in cash and kind from central and local government social services and insurance schemes (excluding education)	18·7	9·6
Receipts in cash and kind from the enterprise other than as direct payment for labour	4·9	11·9

[a] That is to say, cash receipts from employment – including holiday pay – *less*: 1. Contributions to enterprise or governmental insurance schemes; 2. That part of central and local government taxes attributable to the cost of social services (other than education); 3. That part of the wage paid not directly for labour but with regard to personal contingencies (sickness payments, family allowances, housing subsidies, etc.). Full details of these calculations are given in R. P. Dore and Machida Toshihiko, 'Shakai hoshō no ninaite: kokka to kigyō', in *Kikan shakai hoshō kenkyū*, 8, iii, Dec. 1972, pp. 46–57.

unions. At the end of the 'roll-back' period, 1953, that percentage had fallen to around 36%. It continued to fall slightly for the rest of that decade, but then rose again with the beginning of the boom (and the growth in the average size of enterprise) and has stood at around 35% throughout the sixties (38% in manufacturing), the number of unionists growing *pari passu* with the number of employees.

The British rate, by contrast, is something like 45%. The difference, of course, springs from the complete absence of unions in large numbers of small firms in Japan. That the obstacles to union organization are greater the smaller the firm is a principle which applies as much to England as to Japan, but the difficulties in small firms are much greater in Japan where workers in small firms cannot count on aid from fellow-unionists in large firms, where workers do not – indeed, given the enterprise pattern of organization cannot – carry their union membership with them from firm to firm, and where the remaining traditions of personal paternalism in small firms, together with the traditional reluctance to avoid open conflict, make it more difficult than in England to translate underlying resentments into overt and controlled adversarial bargaining.

Organizational Pattern

The vast majority of Japan's trade unionists belong to unions which, like Hitachi's, embrace exclusively the employees of a single factory or a single enterprise.

There are two kinds of exceptions. First, there are a number of 'general unions' which serve workers in firms which are too small to achieve the 'normative pattern' by creating their own union. According to a survey of 1964, none of these unions had more than a regional coverage, their average membership was 200 and they made up 2% of the total number of unions.[20]

The second notable exception to the enterprise union pattern is the All-Japan Seamen's Union with nearly 150,000 members from many companies. It has port branches, not enterprise branches, though each company does have a bargaining committee, rather similar in powers to an English joint shop stewards' committee. It has succeeded, too, in maintaining a pattern of collective bargaining, at least with the larger ocean-going shipowners. The reasons why it should be exceptional are not hard to guess. Seamen were the Japanese workers who were most continuously in contact with foreign workers and trade unionists and were among the first to develop a strong union organization in the 1920s.[21] The circumstances determining a seaman's sense of identity are quite different from those of a worker in a Hitachi factory. When a Mitsui boat and a Mitsubishi boat are the only two Japanese boats in a Guatemalan port their crews have far more in common as Japanese seamen than they have to divide them as Mitsubishi men and Mitsui men. And with the bulk of the membership abroad the importance of a strong Tokyo-based executive of full-time officials is increased.

There are one or two other unions which take the same form as the Seamen's Union as far as paper organization is concerned – the National Movie and Theatre Workers' Union is an example. But lacking the special circumstances which contribute to the solidarity of the seamen, their actual operation is rather different. Company branches do the actual bargaining, and central officials merely sit in on, and assist, negotiations in individual companies. They are, in fact, little different from the industrial federations which will be considered later.

As for the enterprise unions which account for the bulk of Japanese

---

[20] Ibid. p. 173.

[21] For an account of the early history of the seamen's union see, G. O. Totten, 'Collective Bargaining and Works Councils as Innovations in Industrial Relations in Japan During the 1920s', in R. P. Dore (ed.), *Aspects of Social Change in Modern Japan*, 1967.

union membership, their formal structure varies from firm to firm. Some multi-plant enterprises take the Hitachi form of a union in each plant, and a federation at the centre. Others have a single union with plant branches. But the actual division of functions is similar whatever the formal situation. (The Hitachi pattern has, in fact, been changed since Chapter 4 was written. The Federation has become a unitary union and the plant unions are now its branches, but the change was generally acknowledged to be much more one of form than of substance.)

Most of the big unions include both white collar and manual workers. About 20% of all unions are for white collar workers only, and slightly more for manual workers only, but these are usually in small-scale establishments – the former in banks, insurance offices, etc. where the only manual workers are porters and cleaning staff, and the latter in small manufacturing and trading establishments where there are only a small number of white collar workers who are expected to exhibit a personal loyalty to the employer. It is very rare to find a large enterprise which has both a blue collar and a white collar union.

Again like the Hitachi union, most Japanese unions exclude temporary workers. According to a survey of 1961, some 10% of unions admitted temporary workers in practice. (Of the rest, some excluded them in their constitution, but rather more *agreed* to exclude them in a contract with the employer. It is safe to say that the positive desire to keep temporary workers as a separate unprotected buffer force comes from the employers, and that unions, with some quirks of conscience, see that it is in their members' material interests to comply with the employer's wishes.)

Bargaining over the central issue of annual wage increases is almost never devolved to individual plant unions in multi-plant firms and it is almost as rare to find a British-style national agreement which transcends the individual firm. The notable exception of the seamen's union which has both an industry-wide organization and an industry-wide bargaining pattern has already been mentioned. Some other industrial federations have managed to insert themselves into the bargaining process with varying degrees of effectiveness. The Federation of All-Japan Metal Mine Labour Unions (32,000 members) is a rare example of an industrial federation which has firmly institutionalized a pattern of industry-wide bargaining. Each constituent enterprise union has a clause in its contract with the employer recognizing its right to transfer its bargaining powers to the Federation as it sees fit. The spring offensive begins with each union putting forward uniform demands which are uniformly rejected. It proceeds through a stage in which representatives of each union together with Federation officials meet with representatives of each company together with Employers' Federation officials, and ends, usually, in a closed bargaining session between the Federation president and a single employers' representative. The Federation of Private Railway Workers' Unions (253,000 members) has tried to achieve a similar pattern since its inception in 1947, but usually negotiations run the other way. They begin with collective bargaining, but end with firm-by-firm settlements. Other industries in which bargaining has to some degree transcended the enterprise are textiles, synthetic chemicals, taxis, beer and coal. In nearly every case, however, arrangements are only tenuously institutionalized. Neither employers, nor unions are willing to surrender negotiating rights other than on an *ad hoc* year-to-year basis, and both sides are likely to break ranks and make a separate settlement if the prospect is that it will be more favourable than the likely industry-wide bargain.

Even where industry-wide bargaining does take place it often, as in the coal industry, sets only the basic minima, leaving the bargain over precise amounts to the enterprise level, and the bargain over the distribution of wages (as between age groups and skill levels) to the pit level. Moreover the negotiated minima are usually only minimum *increases*, not minimum *rates* – thus leaving interfirm differentials much as they were before – as far from the European notion of a negotiated national market rate as ever.[22]

The next step down the scale of Federation involvement is for officials of the Federation to sit in with enterprise union negotiators to strengthen their hands and to fortify them against employers' sentimental appeals to loyalty to the firm. According to one survey, they did this in 16% of unions in 1960–1, but only in 5% of unions with more than 1,000 members.[23]

But for the most part, as with Hitachi and the Federation of Electrical Machine Workers' Unions, the federation's role is to work out a 'braking line'– a minimum set of demands below which each union promises not to be pushed. For the rest, as it was scornfully put by the president of one federation which does play a strong bargaining role, federation officials are 'lieutenants behind the rock'– they stab the maps with their forefingers and wave the troops on with their sabres, but themselves are out of the line of fire.

Why the differences between industries? Generally, the industries where collective bargaining transcends the enterprise share certain unusual characteristics, e.g. an unusual pattern of social contact

22 Ibid. p. 194–5.
23 Ibid., II, p. 48.

between employees (seamen, taxis); a relatively high degree of labour mobility between firms (particularly in both coal and metal mining where the running out of seams ineluctably causes closures); lesser disparities in size between large and small firms and lesser interfirm differentials in wages (textiles, beer, taxis); fairly strong employers' federations induced by: (a) the need for solidarity unrelated to labour problems (e.g. the coal industry crisis precipitating government intervention, the taxi firms' need for a solid front *vis-à-vis* traffic authorities), and (b) the absence of fierce price competition (metal mines' prices are determined by world markets, shipping rates by international conferences, taxi fares by municipal authorities, beer by cartel arrangements between a small number of firms).

The pattern of industrial conflict, too, is predominantly of the kind described apropos of Hitachi – strikes are usually half-day, one-day or two-day strikes, used as pressure tactics in the annual round of wage negotiations over wage increases or bonus rates. In 1968, for example, of the 2·8 million working days lost as a result of strikes and lock-outs lasting more than 4 hours, 74% were lost in the 'spring offensive' months of March, April and May, and another 12% in the year-end bonus negotiation months of October to December. The average number of days lost by the workers involved was 1·6. Of the 1·4 million workers involved, additionally, in strikes lasting for four hours or less, 32% were involved in the peak month of April, and 54% between October and December. (The less aggressive tactic is preferred for the less crucial bonus issue.)[24] Again, of the total number of recorded disputes, 79% were primarily concerned with wages or bonuses (in a rough proportion of two to one) with the next largest category in the official classification – questions of dismissal and reinstatement – making up 3%.[25]

As to the extent to which trade unions can be judged truly independent, it is hard to give other than an impressionistic judgement. There certainly are, as the Japanese say, *goyō-kumiai* ('unions by appointment', as in 'by appointment to His Majesty') – unions whose leaders receive continuous and even lavish hospitality from the company, or even direct money payments, and where union leaders do not make formal wage demands until they have been assured in private consultation that something close to these demands will be met without a strike. These are particularly common among the so-called 'second unions'. The birth of a second union usually follows a standard pattern. A left-wing union under militant leadership, associated with the left-wing Sōhyō federation, makes demands

[24] Rōdōshō, Tōkeichōsabu, *Yearbook of Labour Statistics, 1968*, p. 322.
[25] Ibid., p. 324.

which the employers find it difficult to meet, or which they consider that they can claim to be exorbitant enough to give them an opportunity to scotch their opponents once and for all. (Frequently these are not wage demands, but attempts to encroach, in matters of job control, on areas which management considers, and which more 'moderate' unions grant to be, within the scope of management prerogative.) The managers dig their heels in. A prolonged strike ensues in an atmosphere altogether more tense than the 'ritualized' strikes during wage negotiations. Extreme bitterness is generated which leads to, and is in turn exacerbated by, sporadic violence. (No quarrels are as fierce as family quarrels; the greater the expectation of loyalty and co-operation, the greater the emotional tension generated when that expectation is disappointed.) Dissension breaks out in the union ranks and a second union is formed with the covert assistance of the company. It may also receive assistance from the right-wing national federation, Dōmei, though again covertly since while Dōmei and Sōhyō are rivals competing for membership, Dōmei is reluctant to appear to be traitorously splitting the ranks of workers engaged in a life and death struggle. As the strike becomes more painful and costly to the workers, the second union gains support, receives official recognition by the company, concludes a compromise agreement and work restarts. The rump of the original union gradually drifts back to work. Its leaders leave the company, and in the course of time most of its members join the second union which later affiliates with Dōmei. There have been a number of famous instances of this 'second union phenomenon',[26] notably at Nissan Automobiles, Oji Paper Works and the Mitsui Miike mine. At Miike the two unions were locked in bitter and often violent struggle for several months in 1960 – and still, ten years later, a minority remain in the vestigial original union, clinging stubbornly to their earlier loyalties (and what may seem stranger in British terms, clinging stubbornly to the company) despite the fact that they were generally discriminated against in matters of promotion, bonuses, etc.

The 'second-union phenomenon', of course, is only an extreme case of what was described as the 'roll-back' at Hitachi. At Hitachi, thanks to the additional means of coercion available under the American occupation, the very severe deflationary conditions and the very high level of militancy of the communist leaders who laid

[26] See Fujita Wakao, *Daini Kumiai*, new edition, 1967, for an account of some of these cases. One does not have to agree with Professor Fujita's views (all first unions are good and all second unions and their members are traitorously wicked) to find the book a useful source of information and ideas.

themselves open to criminal charges, a more moderate faction took over without the need to destroy the original union.

Generally speaking, by either route, 'militant' trade union leaders have been giving way to 'moderate' ones, and the trend has been reflected in a steady growth in the membership of the Dōmei Federation, at the expense of the Sōhyō Federation during the 1960s. In 1970 20% of all trade unionists in private industry were in unions affiliated to Sōhyō, 22% affiliated to Dōmei and 16% to the Independent (Neutral) Federation, compared with 26%, 20% and 14% respectively in 1960.

'Militancy' and 'moderation' are relative terms, however. There is a whole spectrum at one extreme of which the wholly collusive 'union by appointment' is to be found. A little further along comes the highly co-operative union whose leaders happily accept managers' hospitality as part of the prerogative of office and will sometimes discuss their union members with managers in terms they would not like to have repeated, but would still dig their heels in and fight genuinely against some act of management (a dismissal of a union member, say) which by the standards of their members was flagrantly unfair. A little further along still comes a fairly co-operative union of the Hitachi type which seeks to avoid confrontation but whose leaders feel obliged at least partially to requite managers' hospitality, are somewhat guarded in their conversation with managers, and are prepared to call a strike if necessary to achieve high wage demands. And finally, at the other extreme comes the militant union whose leaders never accept managerial hospitality except on the most public and formal of occasions, and who feel cheated if a spring offensive passes without a strike since they assume that they have thereby missed an opportunity to raise the level of political consciousness of their members.

These, of course, are only ideal types: there are many intermediate positions on the spectrum and the posture adopted by any particular union may vary from time to time depending on changes in leadership and fluctuations in circumstances which increase or diminish the occasions for friction. 'Increasing moderation' in the sixties certainly means a decrease in the number of unions taking the last, most militant, position, but not necessarily a shift to the other, wholly collusive, end of the spectrum. Even the second unions formed through the defeat of militant leadership, may settle down in a pattern of limited co-operativeness of an intermediate kind. Certainly, if the propensity to strike to force through wage demands be taken as an index of independence, the trend of change is not entirely clear. There have been fewer strikes in the later sixties, but the trend is neither strong or consistent. The following index figures (1958–60 = 100) refer to the number of days lost through strikes and lock-outs per union member in manufacturing industry:

Table 12.11

Year	Days lost	Year	Days lost
1961	175	1967	46
1962	100	1968	60
1963	61	1969	77
1964	85	1970	88
1965	130	1971	130
1966	64		

Source: Rōdōshō, Tōkeichōsabu, *Rōdō tōkei yōran*, 1969, 1970, and *Rōdō sōgi tōkei chōsa nen-hōkōku*, 1970, p. 71.

As for the effectiveness of trade unions in maintaining or enlarging the workers' share of the product, the following two tables are the best measure one can offer. The first, drawn from national income estimates shows that the size of the wage bill (a function, of course, of total employment as well as of wage rates) has at least grown faster than dividends, but a good deal less rapidly than corporation income. The stockholders, too, have not managed to press their income claims very effectively, though they have doubtless been quite content with the appreciation of their stocks. The major beneficiaries have been the enterprises as entities, and the holders of bank capital. Japanese companies, as is well known, rely a good deal more on bank capital and a good deal less on equity capital than in most other industrial societies. (The total of interest payments was nearly four times the total of dividend payments in 1968.) But probably only a small part of interest payments find their way into individual pockets; they largely go to swell bank reserves. Hence, whether banks or industrial corporations, it is the organization, rather than individuals, which has succeeded in gaining disproportionately from the boom period of the sixties. (Therein, of course, lies part of the secret of Japan's rapid growth.)

Table 12.12, of course, refers to all enterprises, not just to the large ones where one would expect unions to be strong. Table 12.13 deals exclusively with larger establishments. Although, of course, the actual growth percentages conflate increase in the labour force on the one hand with the rise in wage rates and in productivity on the other, the relative movements of these growth rates, and the labour share, do give an indication of the relation of earnings to productivity. The figures suggest three things: (a) it is hard to discern any

Table 12.12   *Growth of some elements of national income*

(Billions yen: index numbers 1958–60 = 100)

	Composition 1958–60		Index figures of growth				Composition 1970	
			1958–60	1963	1968	1970		
Employees' compensation	5655	(72)	100	189	393	477	26993	(69)
Corporation income	1303	(17)	100	183	459	565	7356	(19)
Dividends	168	(2)	100	233	353	406	683	(2)
Taxes	509	(7)	100	205	402	529	2692	(7)
Reserves	630	(8)	100	146	523	621	3889	(10)
Transfers to persons	19	(0)	100	180	353	483	93	(0)
Interest	449	(6)	100	214	503	636	2854	(7)
Rent	408	(5)	100	192	374	433	1765	(5)
Total n.i. excl. self-employed incomes etc.	7833	(100)	100			439	34349	(100)

Source: Nihon Ginkō Tōkeikyoku, *Shōwa-44-nendo keizai tōkei nempō*, p. 287, Sōrifu, *Kokumin shotoku tōkei nempō*, 1971.

secular trend in the fluctuations of the labour share over these years (the high level in 1957–9 was partly due to a sharp drop in value added in the recession year of 1958); (b) in years of rapid growth wages grow less quickly than productivity; but (c) in years when

Table 12.13   *Wages and Salaries and value added: manufacturing establishments with 1,000 or more employees*

	Wages and salaries		Value added		
	Index figures	Growth over previous year (%)	Index figures	Growth over previous year (%)	Labour share (%)
1957–9	100		100		35·3
1960	143	+24	164	+38	30·7
1961	178	+24	205	+25	30·6
1962	195	+10	215	+5	31·9
1963	215	+10	230	+7	33·0
1964	250	+16	282	+22	31·3
1965	268	+7	275	+2	34·4
1966	297	+11	321	+17	32·6
1967	353	+19	415	+29	30·0
1968	430	+22	489	+18	31·0
1969	529	+23	625	+26	30·4
1970	634	+20	739	+20	30·3

Source: Sōrifu, Tōkeikyoku, *Nihon tōkei nenkan*, various years.

productivity increase slows down wages tend to catch up. In other words, unions do not, or cannot, push hard enough to get for themselves all the gains of boom periods, but they can push hard enough to draw something from the accumulation of previous years in times of falling profits.

Prospects for change in union organization

How permanent is the present pattern of trade union organization? Are there any signs of movement towards a European-type industrial or general union structure in which the focus of bargaining will be not the total size of the wage bill in particular firms, but the national market price for particular kinds of skills? Clearly the present unions are sufficiently well entrenched for it to be unlikely that they will simply dissolve themselves into craft unions transcending company boundaries. The only possibility of movement would seem to lie in a gradual strengthening of the powers of the industrial federations vis-à-vis their constituent enterprise unions, and a gradual reorganization of the bargaining system towards an industrial framework.

Such an evolution of the trade union movement is, in fact, a *positive objective* of the movement if one is to believe the formal statements of its leaders and the declarations of its congresses. In part, to be sure, this is because the Japanese labour movement is a late-comer movement whose leaders tend to see the Euro-American pattern as a model of 'proper' organization. But there is more to it than that. Thus, the 1964 policy statement of the left-wing Sōhyō Federation says the following:

'The enterprise union system, combining in a single union all the workers of a single enterprise – workers in the favoured sector of a dual economy who are employed under a life-time employment contract sustained by enterprise welfare facilities and a seniority wage system – inevitably tends to make 'employee consciousness' stronger than 'trade union consciousness' and so weakens the union's ability to fight. . . . Let alone in times of depression, even in boom periods the desire to see one's firm not lose out in commercial competition holds back the desire to improve wages and working conditions and so sets a limit to the union's strength. Hence it is essential to strengthen the industrial federation structure as a means of overcoming these limitations.'[27]

[27] Quoted in Rōshi kankeihō kenkyūkai, *Rōshi kankeihō unjō no jitsujō oyobi mondaiten*, vol. I, p. 93.

Similarly the right-wing Dōmei federation said in its 1965 policy statement:

'In seeking to strengthen and expand the organization of the Federation, one important focus of activity must be the strengthening of industry-by-industry organization. . . . Naturally the major impetus in this direction must come from the national industrial federations, but Dōmei itself, and its regional branches, can from time to time assist in the process of realignment of the labour movement on industrial lines.[28]

The same views about what *ought* to happen prevail not only among trade unionists, but also in the academic world – even among scholars who in Japan count as sufficiently neutral, or sufficiently sympathetic to officialdom, to be nominated to government committees. A commission appointed by the Minister of Labour to consider the need for reform in labour law (it contained nine jurists, one civil servant and two other experts on labour relations) left no doubt where its collective heart lay when it reported in 1966. After listing various 'problems' associated with the enterprise union structure – the fact that union officials retain their status as company employees, thus compromising the independence of the union, the fact that unions are very liable to upset from company mergers and reorganizations, the weakness of the industrial federations, the frequency of 'second union' type splits, and so on – it sums up:

'Generally speaking one may say that the enterprise union structure has the advantage that since the focus of industrial relations rests between a particular company and its own employees, it is possible to improve and stabilize relations in a manner best adapted to the true circumstances of that company. On the other hand, however, there is a tendency for the sense of membership in the company to be much stronger than loyalty to the union and for union activities to be circumscribed by that fact. Even in companies where the union and management are said to 'co-operate' the truth frequently is that the union's attitude could be more correctly described as 'compliant' than as 'co-operative', and there is always the danger of the union degenerating into a mere 'union by appointment'.[29]

There seems no doubt, then, that everyone concerned with union activity (except, of course, employers) consider 'breaking out of the enterprise chrysalis' – to quote a common union congress slogan – a

[28] Ibid.
[29] Ibid. vol. 1, pp. 168–9.

consummation devoutly to be desired. Sōhyō, the left-wing Federation, is apt to claim indeed that progress is being made, particularly through the Spring Struggle Co-ordinating Committee in which it plays a dominant role. Thus, the committee's final review of the 1969 offensive claims, as point 7 of the achievements of that year's struggle that 'co-ordinated industry-by-industry struggles were intensified', and held up a number of federations as examples of 'sustained and tenacious leadership' and cited others which had for the first time agreed to a minimum 'braking line' set of demands less than which individual unions promised not to accept.[30]

As some federations have got stronger, however, others have got weaker, and taking the picture as a whole it would be hard to sustain the claim that the industrial federations were stronger in 1970 than in 1960. The liaison mechanisms and bargaining techniques have undoubtedly improved as the Spring Struggle Co-ordinating Committee has gained in experience, and this has certainly helped weaker unions to secure larger concessions from employers. But there is little evidence of any significant transfer of bargaining powers from the enterprise union to a higher level.

Industrial activity apart, the gradual depoliticization of the union movement during the 1960s has also reduced the extra-economic bonds of ideological solidarity which helped to provide a *raison d'être* for the industrial federations, particularly those belonging to the most politically oriented national congress, Sōhyō. It was primarily those enterprise unions at the extreme end of the spectrum of militancy in industrial matters which were also most willing to follow the lead of the federations in political activities. During the sixties the formation of second unions and changes of leadership have reduced the responsiveness of the enterprise unions to the political rallying calls of the industrial and national federations. Federation leaders have often failed to accommodate to the change and have tried to force political activities on their member unions which they were not prepared to undertake, thus generating friction and further weakening the federations. There is a marked contrast between 1960 when the Sōhyō leaders were able to mobilize large numbers of workers in strikes and demonstrations in protest against the revision of the Security Treaty with the US, and 1970 when Sōhyō planned a similar protest campaign against the continuation of the treaty. These plans had to be gradually whittled down because of the lukewarmness of constituent unions and eventually produced only a few whimperish half-hour work stoppages. It seems certain that this failure (which prompted the resignations of the main Sōhyō

[30] Ohara shakai mondai kenkyūjo, *Nihon rōdō nenkan*, no. 40, p. 291.

leaders) together with the failure of the Socialist party which Sōhyō supported in the December 1969 elections, will rapidly accelerate the depoliticization of the union movement. And this will further weaken the possibility that any considerations beyond their members' material interests could be mobilized to help strengthen the enterprise unions' willingness to sacrifice their individual sovereignty for the sake of a wider cause.

Perhaps it is best to leave the final summing up of the situation to the 1966 report of the Commission on labour law. The Commission concluded its discussion of the enterprise union structure with the following (given its declared views, pessimistic) judgement:

'It is possible to discern some features which might be thought gradually to reduce the strength of the economic and institutional factors [which have created the enterprise union system] – the increasing division of labour skills with technological innovation, and the corresponding equalization of the *levels* of skill required, the gradual revelation of the contradictions of the seniority wage system and the changes in the balance between supply and demand in the labour market. . . . Nevertheless, those economic and institutional factors which were responsible for creating and entrenching the enterprise union system still remain deeply rooted. To take as an example the factor of workers' attitudes, it may indeed be possible to point to a weakening of the sense of loyalty to the firm on the part of some younger workers, but given the plain empirical fact that the whole development of the union movement since the war has been within the enterprise framework, and given that in an increasingly decontrolled and deprotected economy the intensification of competition between enterprises is likely to lead to a redoubling of employers' personnel relations efforts, it is hard to forecast any trend for the workers' strong sense of identification with the company to fade away. We are forced to conclude that although there is a possibility that union activity and the pattern of labour relations in the individual firm may be considerably altered by the efforts of the superior federations to promote trans-enterprise bargaining and co-ordinated bargaining, there is little prospect of any change in the enterprise union structure itself in the near future.'[31]

SUMMING UP

It should at least be clear by now that there is no evidence of 'the Japanese system' changing rapidly towards a British-type pattern. It still remains possible to argue that it *is* so changing, if slowly. Labour

[31] Rōshi kankeihō kenkyūkai, op. cit. vol. 1, p. 166.

turnover in the big firms does seem to be, however slowly, on the increase; the gradient of the age-wage curve is slightly less steep than it was. And one can think of factors which might in future accelerate the change.

1. Continuing full employment and greater security and a growing tendency to take security for granted may induce greater adventurousness and a greater willingness to change jobs.

2. The labour shortage might get worse and lead to stronger competition for new graduates and increasing pressure to raise wages for younger workers.

3. The gradual equalization of the two parts of the dual structure may make a difference. It is not possible to argue that because the privileged position of the workers in the big firms rests on the exploitation of the sub-contracting firms, the disappearance of exploitation will necessarily change the system. There can be an equalization of wage *levels* as between big firms and small without the system itself being altered. But it is true that if the relative advantages of employment in a large firm diminish, the large firms will no longer be able to 'cream off' the labour market as they do now, and will so have a lesser incentive to maintain employment practices necessary to keep the workers they have. Even in the oldest of developed economies, however, larger firms do offer their workers better wages and conditions than smaller ones and retain a competitive advantage in recruiting.

4. If there is a recession new elements will enter the situation. It is not hard for an employer to renounce the right to sack redundant workers when the manufacturing sector as a whole is expanding at between 15% and 20% a year. But the path of virtue becomes much harder if the figure changes to 0% or −5%, particularly if it is no longer possible to absorb the effects at the expense of expendable subcontractors. To be sure the unions would fight tenaciously against dismissals. But they fought tenaciously at the time of the Dodge deflation and the 'roll-back' in 1949–50 – and lost. (If it comes to an all-out struggle management has many powerful weapons – the withdrawal of facilities, particularly of the right of union officials to return to jobs in the firm – in reserve.) And if employers did abandon the lifetime employment principle the whole system might crumble. On the other hand a recession would have the counter-effect of destroying the growing sense of security which (see point 1, above) seems to be a factor in the present slow increase in labour turnover. Those who were not dismissed would cling even more dearly to their

jobs. It should not be forgotten that many of the modern features of 'the system' were established as a result of union pressure in the period of intense hardship and insecurity after the war

These are clearly imponderable factors, and the fact remains that the trends of change so far visible do not amount to a serious subversion of the system. The gap which remains between the British and Japanese employment systems after a decade of rapid growth and increasing labour shortage is large enough, and the union structure and the pattern of enterprise welfare seem sufficiently firmly entrenched, for one to hazard the guess that in 1980, and even in 1990, Japanese workers will still be hired and promoted and paid and trained and socialized in a distinctively Japanese way.

Chapter 13

Britain Catching Up?

The Japanese employment system is not standing still. But the changes are not such as to make it more like the English employment system. So much, some would say, for the fashionable sociological doctrine of 'convergence' – the view that the constraints of high technology are gradually making industrial societies indistinguishable from each other. But what about convergence from the other direction? Are there, perhaps, signs that the British system is becoming more like the Japanese?

There are, and it will be the business of this chapter to enumerate them. The best starting point for the argument is the comparison noted earlier – the great similarity in organization and career structure between Hitachi and the British civil service. It is not that the Japanese employment system is unknown in Britain. Something very like it exists in the civil service, the army and the police. What is different about Japan is that this employment system is also normal in industry, whereas in Britain the application of such organizational principles to industry seems eccentric.

Or, rather, *has* seemed eccentric hitherto. Now, as large industrial corporations like ICI or Shell or British Leyland begin to approach the police or the civil service in (a) scale[1] and in (b) security of prospects, they too are becoming bureaucratized and are taking on many of the characteristics shared by the Japanese corporation and the British civil service.

The following, then, in its broadest outline, is the thesis which will be developed further in Chapter 15. The Japanese employment sys-

---

[1] There are no available figures on changes in the size of company workforces in Britain. Figures for *establishments* (which break up multi-plant firms) have been collected three times since 1935 and show the proportion of workers in establishments with over 1,000 workers increasing from 21% to 35% between 1935 and 1961. See the Table in J. H. Dunning and C. J. Thomas, *British Industry, Change and Development*, 1963, p. 58.

tem is (apart from certain features stemming directly from Japanese cultural traditions) simply one national manifestation of a pheno-menon characteristic of all advanced industrial societies – namely the adaptation of employment systems to:

1. The emergence of the giant corporation.

2. The extension of democratic ideals of a basic 'equality of con-dition' for all adults at the expense of earlier conceptions of society as naturally divided into a ruling class and an underclass.

The Japanese have got there ahead. They made that adaptation earlier than Britain did, first because – a characteristic of late de-velopment – the larger corporation set the pace in industry from the *beginning of industrialization*, and second because the great post-1945 flood of egalitarian ideas hit Japan (backed with the full authority of an occupying army) *before* union-management relations had acquired any institutional rigidity.

In Britain, by contrast, the giant corporation emerged as the culmination of a century of slow industrialization, long after a labour-market-oriented employment system adapted to a fluid small-firm pattern of industry had become highly, indeed rigidly, institutional-ized in the existence of national trade union organizations beyond the power of any individual employer to reconstruct. Equally, there are marked differences on the other score. Traditional pre-industrial ruling class/underclass perceptions of society became in the nine-teenth century adapted to and entrenched in industrial Britain (in contrast to Japan where a more far-reaching political revolution before industrialization gave industrial Japan a meritocratic rather than aristocratic pattern of political and economic power). Egali-tarianism has not fully succeeded in altering these perceptions partly because they were institutionalized in an employment system which acquired great rigidity, partly because egalitarianism in Britain has always been creeping egalitarianism; there has been no cataclysmic event comparable to Japan's post-1945 experience signalling the dawn of a new age of equality and offering a 'charter' for wholesale changes in institutions. Even today influential sociologists deny the popular journalists' view that the affluent British worker is a middle-class worker, and insist that he continues to see himself as, and to behave like, a member of a subordinated (though far from docile) underclass.

But, to return to the main thesis of this chapter, the institutional luggage acquired by Britain as the pioneer of industrialization, may slow down the adaptation of institutions to the existence of the giant corporation and to the growing strength of egalitarian ideas, but it does not entirely prevent it. The changes are taking place in the British employment system, many of them largely unnoticed because of the neurotic national preoccupation with unofficial strikes. The changes which might reasonably be characterized, however loosely, as 'in a Japanese direction', can be grouped under the following heads: changes in the structure of bargaining and in union organizations; changes in pay systems; changes in the enterprise as a community; changes in the degree of bureaucratization; and changes in ideology.

THE STRUCTURE OF BARGAINING AND UNION ORGANIZATION

The key theme of the Donovan Commission's diagnosis of the British situation in the mid-1960's was the progressive 'transfer of authority in industrial relations' from the national-level bargaining units – national trade unions and employers' associations – 'to the factory and the workshop'. Perhaps the blessing which the Commission gave to this trend has since helped to accelerate it, but clearly it was strong enough not to need much help. One of the members of the Commission remarked that during the long months in which the report was being written:

'I was increasingly disturbed by the way in which the Commission was being scooped by events.

The rubber and chemical industries made framework agreements for company negotiations. Then the engineering employers proposed the same thing. The Confederation of British Industry, formerly lukewarm, came down in favour of plant productivity bargaining. . . .'[2]

One short-run factor which probably did more than the blessing of the Donovan Report to promote the trend towards plant bargaining was the Prices and Incomes Policy. The productivity bargain (by its very nature a plant bargain) became a popular means of circumventing the limitation on wage increases. But the trend towards plant productivity bargains as a means of genuine restructuring of pay systems and work organization dated back to the Fawley agreement of the early sixties and had a momentum of its own which continued despite the collapse of the incomes policy. Even more lastingly significant is the increasing number of large companies which have set up regular machinery for negotiating normal periodic wage adjustments. Most decisive of all was the disintegration, during 1971

[2] Eric Wigham, *The Times*, 14 July 1968.

and 1972, of the last-ditch attempts by the smaller firms and the smaller unions to retain the traditional system of national bargaining in the engineering industry. By the summer of 1972 both sides, though with some misgivings, seemed prepared to accept plant bargaining as the pattern of the future. As a factor both supporting and reflecting these trends, evidence accumulated that rank and file union members were little interested in their union *qua* formal structure though much concerned with and prepared to support the 'informal' activity of their stewards on the workshop floor.[3]

These changes are the combined consequence of several trends:

1. The growing importance of the workshop as the basis of union organization rather than the residential district.

2. An expansion in the functions of workshop representatives (shop stewards elected directly by the work group they represent) and of their (often multi-union) factory committees, partly at the expense of 'managerial prerogative', partly with a corresponding contraction of the functions of the formal trade union structure of full-time officials and union district committees.

3. The increasing frequency of formally negotiated agreements between the management of a particular factory and committees of workshop representatives – with or without the involvement of full-time union officials.

4. The emergence of 'combine committees' (also multi-union) linking the workshop representatives across the whole of a large multi-plant enterprise.

5. The parallel development in large enterprises of *official* negotiating committees (also multi-union) formed by national union officers to negotiate company agreements limited in scope to a single firm. (Ford's National Joint Negotiating Council, for instance.)

6. The tendency for unions to amalgamate and to become more general in their membership, and for the division between white collar unions and manual worker unions to be eroded.

Evidence of these trends in English Electric was noted in Chapter 5. In both factories the 1960s saw the gradual formalization of the functions of chief shop stewards, and the first rounds of formal negotiations, with minuted meetings and a written agreement, between factory shop steward representatives and managers.

[3] W. E. J. McCarthy and S. R. Parker, *Shop Stewards and Workshop Relations* 1968, Royal Commission on Trade Unions and Employers' Associations, Research Papers 10, and J. H. Goldthorpe *et al.*, *The Affluent Worker in the Class Structure* 1969, p. 170.

As for the fourth and fifth of these trends, it is hard to say whether the combine committee in English Electric (which dates from the forties) increased its influence in the 1960s, but certainly the merger gave it greater prominence, and led, also, to the creation, in the new company which resulted from the merger, of a company consultative committee containing representatives of the national executives of the chief unions involved in the firm.

In other firms this trend has gone much further. Fords and ICI, for example, have company agreements rather than factory agreements, very similar in scope to the contracts reached by Japanese enterprise unions. One union leader criticized the Donovan Report for not having spoken out more strongly in favour of such company agreements.[4] Company agreements, understandably, are more attractive to union officials than factory agreements. They are normally negotiated by committees of full-time union officials appointed by the union executives, not by shop stewards' committees. They are, therefore, more firmly under the control of the union hierarchy.

It is precisely at this level, however, that the clash between the 'formal' and the 'informal' system becomes most obvious. The 'stalagmite' organizations – the combine committee at the pinnacle of the pyramid of workshop representation – naturally claims to share power with the 'stalactite' official negotiating body appointed from above by the union executives.[5] Where they do work together it is only on the basis of the official body deferring on many important matters to the combine committee – as at Fords where, in February 1971, it was the conveners of the shop steward's committees, not the (official) union side of the National Joint Negotiating Council which called the men out on strike.

What chance is there that the two systems, the formal and the informal, will merge to produce a Japanese-type structure – the present combine committee, elected from the bottom up, becoming the effective negotiating body with its own full-time officials, and the national unions becoming just the next layer up in the hierarchy, responsible to its members *through* their workshop–factory–company organization?

---

[4] *The Financial Times*, 26 August 1968.

[5] See S. W. Lerner and J. Bescoby, 'Shop Steward Combine Committees in the British Engineering Industry', *British Journal of Industrial Relations* 4, ii, 1964, p. 161. 'This relationship whereby management and the union ignore the existence of the combine [committee] is the one most commonly found. This relationship is analogous to the Englishman's way of quietly ignoring remarks or actions which are not approved by polite society, but which are nevertheless not illegal.' For later developments in combine committees, especially at BLMC, see J. Bescoby, 'A Combination of Strength', *Personnel Management*, January 1961.

Hardly any chance, is the obvious answer for anyone who knows anything of the institutional inertia of the trade union movement. And if the unions are unlikely to change themselves, it is hard to see who else can change them. The law can dictate the structure of voluntary associations in Ghana under Nkrumah or in the immediate aftermath of war in Germany, but hardly, in peacetime, in a country with Britain's entrenched traditions of voluntarism – even if there were total consensus among politicians as to what was desirable. Nevertheless, it is possible to affect the situation by legislative pressure, and the direction in which that pressure is being exercised in the 1971 Industrial Relations Act is fairly clear. The formal institutionalization of the workshop representation structure is to be accelerated. 'We want shop stewards to be more involved, more clearly, within their authority and status as the agents of their unions', the Minister of Labour is reported as saying. 'Rather than crippling the shop stewards' operations, we are seeking to give them a new confidence in their role and status.'[6] The statutory requirements that union rules should formalize shop steward elections and specify their powers are very much in line with the Donovan Commission's recommendations: the mechanisms for giving formal status to factory committees (joint negotiating panels) through the bargaining agent recognition system go a good deal further. Mr Wilson's charge, in the House of Commons, that the agency shop provisions, allowing 20% of the workers to challenge a recognition agreement, made the bill a 'Trots' charter' (a somewhat curious charge in view of the energy with which Trotskyites opposed the bill) showed him to share Mr Carr's forecast of the structural effects of the legislation; though he was, apparently, less sanguine about the extent to which workshop democracy would result in a greater sense of responsibility.[7]

If, as seems likely, the workshop representation system becomes stronger, the unions will clearly be forced to make their formal organization snuggle up to its contours. The big obstacle to the ingestion of the factory committee fully into the formal union structure, is, of course, the fact that the factory and company committees are usually *multi-union* committees, and so cannot become part of any single union's framework. It is notable that the closest approach to a 'Japanese pattern' exists in the mines, and on the railways where, if not exactly single-union situations, at least the unions involved exist only within the single enterprise. In engineering, Pilkingtons, where there is a permanent company-wide committee responsible for

[6] *The Times*, 28 January 1971.
[7] *The Times*, 16 December 1970.

343

bargaining company agreements, does have on the union side of the committee fifteen workshop representatives sitting with seven full-time officials, but this is exceptional in that a single union organizes nearly all the workers at Pilkington factories.

There are two routes by which a one enterprise/one union situation could be reached. One is through a series of horse-trading deals between unions carving up their respective 'spheres of influence'. One recent study of trade union structures notes some of the tentative standing arrangements between unions intended to facilitate such moves. It concludes that the transition from the *status quo* emphasis of the Bridlington rules to 'the positive handling of a multilateral "rationalization" policy would obviously be a long one. It is not necessarily an impossible progression.'[8] The leader of one of the largest unions, Lord Cooper of the General and Municipal, came out strongly for the idea in the union journal in 1968.[9] It is possible that the process might be somewhat accelerated by the agency shop provisions in the Industrial Relations Act. (It is clearly expected that the CIR should when necessary act as honest broker in helping to work out such exclusive spheres of influence – at least initially as between different categories of workers within companies.[10]) It will also be accelerated by factory bargaining. Plant negotiating committees can only be fully incorporated into national trade union structures if their members belong to a single union.

The other route is through union mergers. These proceeded apace in the 1960s. What started in the nineteenth century as a union of skilled engineering craftsmen and had since absorbed a majority of semi-skilled and unskilled workers, successively absorbed the foundry workers union, and then, marking a greater change, the white-collar draughtsmen's union, to become the AUEW. Talks were proceeding for a further merger with the second biggest engineering union, the ETU.[11] 'As the unions grow larger by amalgamation . . . they will become increasingly general in their scope of membership . . . this trend will continue, since under conditions of rapid technological change the boundaries of any particular industry are likely to be continuously shifting, so too are definitions of occupation and skill.'[12]

The craft union recedes into history as skills become more fragmented and specialized. In the nineteenth century a man could come

[8] John Hughes, *Trade Union Structure and Government*, Royal Comission on Trade Unions and Employers' Associations, Research Papers 5, part 1, p. 53.

[9] See *The Times*, 8 August 1968.

[10] Industrial Relations Act, Clause 48 (7) (b).

[11] *The Sunday Times*, 2 April 1972.

[12] B. C. Roberts, *Minutes of Evidence*, 33, Royal Commission on Trade Unions and Employers' Associations, p. 1401.

out of an apprenticeship, a fitter like thousands of other fitters, and the general skills he had acquired might carry him through practically the whole of his working life. Now, the detailed knowledge and knack that he acquires with the particular work of his particular company is more likely to outweigh his general craftsman's expertise in the total quantum of his abilities. The relaxation agreements, the provisions for interchangeability of jobs as between men of different crafts which regularly formed a part of the productivity deals of the 1960s can be seen:

1. As a recognition that the connection between the craft training a man receives as an apprentice and his subsequent work has become more tenuous.

2. As resulting from a diminished fear on the part of, say, the carpenter, that he or a fellow-carpenter might be put out of work if he condones electricians' boring holes in skirting boards – a diminution attributable partly to changes in the general labour market situation, partly to changes in company policies – avoiding redundancy except as a last-ditch resort, and sometimes giving guarantees of security of employment as part of a productivity deal.

3. As a result of lower turnover, and of the fact that craftsmen generally have lower turnover rates than semi-skilled workers. A carpenter who stays in firm X and expects to stay in it is more open to the argument that he has more in common with the electricians in firm X than with other carpenters in firm Y.

And, of course, the flexibility agreements which reflects these trends also strengthen them. They change consciousness and self perceptions. As one writer commented on an agreement at Port Talbot:

'. . . under the new terms, all the maintenance men are of a similar grade, and they are called Steelworker – Grade 7. At the moment few of them would accept that as an accurate description of themselves. They see themselves still as drillers and turners and machinists. But Steelworker – Grade 7 may herald the time when industry loses its schizoid appearance and maintenance men and process workers merge.'[13]

This change in self-perceptions aids the trend towards union mergers, and as the general union becomes the dominant form the greater the likelihood of single unions coming to embrace the vast majority of the workers in a company – in the way that the GMWU had organized most of the manual workers in Pilkingtons, with a closed shop agreement, a check-off for paying union dues and so on.

[13] Jeremy Bugler, 'The Maintenance Men', *New Society*, 20 June 1968.

The significance of the AEF-DATA merger is that the general union is likely in future to embrace, also, white collar employees (a matter we shall return to later in this chapter). When that happens the possibility of all the employees in a firm below managerial rank being (as in Japan) in the same union will be that much greater. That possibility would be enormously increased, of course, if there were to be a merger between two or three of the big general unions. That possibility has been considered in the past,[14] and there is no obvious reason why it should not be considered again.

The sort of structure which, if this analysis of trends is correct, may be said to be struggling to get out of the chrysalis of nineteenth-century traditions, is certainly similar to the Japanese enterprise-union, enterprise-bargaining structure, but it is by no means the whole of it, nor would it necessarily, by itself, bring about the smoother pattern of industrial relations which those who seek to accelerate the trend hope for. A recent study of the Pilkington dispute – an outstanding recent example of conflict which escalated beyond the control of those who began it – illustrates this. Pilkingtons *was* a firm which had a single union for its manual workers, and a Joint Industrial Council containing shop floor representatives as the body responsible for negotiating company agreements. There are, however, big differences between industrial relations in Pilkingtons and in a firm like Hitachi.[15]

1. Pilkingtons had one full-time secretary for 7,400 workers. A Japanese union would have six or seven.

2. Pilkingtons had a central company negotiating council, but no similar plant-level bodies of the kind found in Japanese companies (though this omission is since being corrected).

3. Japanese unions rely much more on the distribution of written bulletins and news-sheets to keep members informed, the GMWU at Pilkingtons (with less funds at its disposal) relied more on distortion-prone verbal communication.

4. Japanese unions have regular channels for reporting back to shop-floor level during negotiations. When agreements are referred back to the shop floor they are discussed in small workshop groups; crucial decisions are not taken, as they were at Pilkingtons, at mass open-air meetings which, as the union side said at the court of enquiry, 'were not the most appropriate settings for discussing detailed arrangements'.[16]

14 Hughes, op. cit., p. 51.
15 See T. Lane and K. Roberts, *Strike at Pilkingtons*, 1971.
16 DEP, *Report of a Court of Inquiry under Professor John C. Wood into a*

5. Union meetings take place at work in Japan, usually in the lunch hour; not off the premises, in the evenings, and consequently with lower attendance, as at Pilkingtons.

6. Japanese companies have more unified wage structures which makes for less difficulty than at Pilkingtons in applying company agreements at the plant level.

7. Japan has a system of regular annual wage bargaining which involves routinized processes of consultation and preparation. Wage demands are consolidated in these annual rounds. At Pilkingtons they could be presented at any time with the greater likelihood of finding the system unprepared to cope with them.

Some of these features will be touched on in the sections which follow.

CHANGES IN PAY SYSTEMS

The connections between the trends towards factory-based or company-based bargaining procedures and union structures on the one hand, and changes in pay systems on the other is not altogether obvious, but a connection exists. The change in union structures represents a move away from a market-based conception of employment towards a conception based on a notion of a more generalized attachment – of a relatively stable kind – to a particular firm. Piecework, as the most thoroughgoing means of applying straight market principles to wage determination, is likely to decline in consequence, particularly since the assumption of relative stability of employment (a) makes more relevant more long-term types of incentive and (b) creates pressure for 'career-type' employment structures with regular promotion grades.

The growing disenchantment with piecework systems,[17] rests primarily, as is made clear in the PIB report on the subject, not on the grounds just mentioned, but on the realization that piecework systems tend to get outside of management control, contribute to wage drift, and thus constitute, in the words of another PIB report, 'one of the main reasons why the growth in incomes tends to outstrip the growth in productivity – namely, the struggle engendered by what are regarded as inequitable, irrational and arbitrary pay structures.'[18]

Dispute Between Pilkington Bros. and Certain of Their Employees, HMSO 1970, p. 13.

[17] National Board of Prices and Incomes, Report 65, *Payments by Results Systems*, Cmd. 3627, 1968. See also D. Pym, 'Is There a Future for Wage Incentive Schemes?' *British Journal of Industrial Relations*, vol. II, pp. 379–97, and F. R. Bentley, 'Piecework: Drop it', *Works Management*, January 1963.

[18] National Board for Prices and Incomes, Report 83, Cmd. 3772, 1968, p. 15. Other reasons are summarized in a report for the Royal Commission: 'the impact

Nevertheless, the trends in bargaining systems and in wages are congruent; they do serve to supplement each other. There is, indeed, a widespread recognition in practice that the kind of motives evoked by conventional piecework may inhibit co-operative instincts of the sort which managers try to appeal to when they enter into productivity bargains. This is explicit in the most celebrated experiment in abandoning piecework at the Glacier Metal Company,[19] and it is explicit also in the new long-term strategy of British Leyland in which, according to a report in *The Times*, the 'replacement of piecework is one of the key points', together with a new form of negotiating machinery at company and plant level which 'will aim at securing a greater involvement of workers in company objectives'.[20]

It is easier to discern swings of opinion about the value of piecework than to give a statistical assessment of the extent to which it has been abandoned in practice. British Leyland is one outstanding recent example of a painful attempt to move away from piecework (which Ford and Vauxhall had long since abandoned) and Imperial Tobacco, Rolls-Royce, Pressed Steel Fisher, and Raleigh are other recent examples. There are also, however, some examples of the reverse trend – at Lesney toy works, for example, where as part of a scheme for job enlargement assembly lines were broken up, individual workers were allowed to assemble complete toys, and the former group bonus system was replaced by an individual piecework system.[21]

The Ministry of Labour statistics show that the incidence of payment by results systems was slowly increasing from 1938 to 1961 taking industry as a whole. Between 1964 and 1967 surveys on a different basis showed a very slight decline for adult men in engineering with increases in shipbuilding, chemicals and steel partly cancelling out decreases in other branches of industry. The two new-style earnings surveys in 1968 and 1970 would seem to show a decline in piecework, however. The contribution of PBR systems to the average

of new technology with less opportunity for increasing output; the growth of control systems enabling management quickly and accurately to monitor worker performance; the growing importance of the indirect segment of the work force with the need to motivate this group in concert with other groups in the organization'. R. B. McKersie, *Changing Wage Payment Systems*, Royal Commission on Trade Unions and Employers' Associations, Research Papers 11, para. 160.

[19] See W. Brown, *Piecework Abandoned*, 1962. The dust-cover reproduces the key quotation: 'wage incentive systems . . . stimulate envy and greed, whereas equilibrium between personal capacity, level of work and pay, stimulates co-operative behaviour.'

[20] *The Times*, 26 October 1970.

[21] *The Times*, 23 November 1970.

adult male wage in manufacturing fell from 13% to 10% between the two years.[22] The surveys of the early sixties showed sharp regional differences; the older industrial north had between a half and two-thirds of workers on PBR schemes; the London and South Eastern district with its newer industries only one-third.[23]

Complete abolition of PBR systems apart, even where some kind of output-linked incentive pay remains, it is probable that many firms have shifted from the conventional individual piecework system towards some kind of group bonus or even factory-wide bonus system – of the kind designed to evoke co-operative, rather than individualistic effort. Such a trend, away from what he calls 'stimulation bonuses' to 'participation bonuses' is seen by Marcel Bolle de Bal as a dominant tendency in French and German industry too, a common solution to the universal 'crisis in old piecework systems'.[24] Examples of such changes in both the Bradford and Liverpool factories were given in Chapter 3. It is unlikely that these factories were exceptional, and such changes may account for the increase from 2% to 4% in the contribution of the category 'bonus' in the average male manufacturing wage between 1968 and 1970 as shown in the DEP's surveys.[25]

The other fashionable theme in contemporary discussions of pay systems is the virtue of a careful system of job evaluation – the grading of pay rates according to measurements of the intrinsic nature of jobs, the degree of skill, responsibility, etc. they require. (This is not *necessarily* related to the trend away from piecework, since basic piecework rates can also depend on job evaluation, but the relation is strong in practice: firms which undertake a wholesale job evaluation exercise generally go over to time rates in the process.) The spread of the job evaluation doctrine from America simultaneously to Britain and Japan during the 1950s and 1960s is an interesting illustration of the diffusion of ideas and institutions which is perhaps more likely than the inevitable 'functional requirements' of technology to bring about an eventual international uniformity in industrial systems. But whereas in Japan it was accepted as an additional refinement of, and a convenient means of making adjustments to, a basically seniority wage scale, in Britain it was seen as a means of introducing order and rationality 'and equity' into the complex varieties of rates which had grown up in particular firms.

[22] *Employment and Productivity Gazette*, 1969, p. 728; 1970, p. 1139.
[23] National Board of Prices and Incomes, Report 65, pp. 78–9.
[24] Marcel Bolle de Bal, 'The Psycho-sociology of Wage Incentives', *British Journal of Industrial Relations*, 7, iii, 385–96.
[25] *Employment and Productivity Gazette*, loc. cit.

There are some grounds for counting the introduction of job evaluation schemes as a 'move in the Japanese direction' (quite apart from the fact that their introduction often in practice accompanies the switch from piece rates to a time rate and hence implies the shift in orientations discussed above). In so far as the principle of equity it embodies starts from the principle of 'equal pay for work of equal worth'[26] it is, of course, still some way from the 'person-related' wage system of a Japanese factory. Nevertheless, it does mark a significant step away from the traditional market-oriented wage systems, in so far as jobs are evaluated relative to other jobs in the *same* factory or firm, not equated with similar jobs in other factories in the same district. It therefore can be said to be predicated on the assumption that workers are oriented towards permanent employment in a particular firm and take their co-workers as their reference group, rather than being oriented to a local labour market and taking their market competitors as their reference group. The PIB report on job evaluation recognizes that difficulties can arise when that assumption is not borne out. When there are shortages of skills in the more mobile white collar occupations, firms may have to attract, say, computer programmers, by offering more than a strict application of their job evaluation techniques would suggest. But the report also suggests that this may not be such a serious drawback as one might think since there is evidence that, in fact, for manual occupations it is already 'difficult, if not impossible, to place any meaning on such phases as "the going rate" or the "local level of wages" '[27] – a judgement which subsequent research has clearly confirmed.[28]

A second feature of job evaluation schemes is that they are usually accompanied by the introduction of a promotion and grading structure which, to quote the PIB report again, may help 'manual workers . . . to enjoy the incentive, satisfaction and security of a career progression of a kind which has hitherto been mainly the white-collar workers' prerogative.'[29] And this, once again, increases the incentives to workers to 'throw in their lot' with a particular firm. Even without

[26] See National Board for Prices and Incomes, Report 83, p. 3.

[27] Ibid., p. 22.

[28] Derek Robinson, *Local Labour Markets and Wage Structures*, 1970. Robinson found 'that there is very little uniformity between the standard hourly earnings of members of the same occupation in different engineering plants in the same locality. Indeed there is a very wide range of average standard hourly earnings' (page 263). This applies both in areas where the labour market situation is very tight, as well as in areas where there is considerable unemployment. Moreover, the addition to the wage of the quantifiable fringe benefits received by different workers serves not to equalize the differences but to exaggerate them.

[29] National Board for Prices and Incomes, op. cit., pp. 16–17.

a strict job evaluation scheme the same effect can be obtained. We quoted in Chapter 3 the Liverpool factory's consolidation of a multiplicity of rates for time workers into five job grades with formalized promotion criteria between them.

Thirdly, at the enterprise rather than the factory level, job evaluation can be called on to rationalize management salaries and to move closer to a Japanese, civil service type of career management. As the PIB report puts it:

'Larger companies increasingly move managers, sometimes internationally, to broaden their experience and fit them for increased responsibilities, and find they need some control over the payment systems of their member units in order to be able to do so. A manager cannot be promoted from job A in subsidiary X to job B in subsidiary Y if his salary is reduced in the process.'

This requires evaluation of managerial, professional and technical jobs so that 'whilst subsidiaries retain discretion to award salary increases, they do so within a broadly uniform framework.'[30]

The discretionary salary increases for managers are, of course, based on superiors' assessments of merit. Are there any signs of the extension of the same principles to manual workers' salaries, as in Japan? We certainly saw no such sign in the Bradford and Liverpool factories. In the south of England, merit-rating has been a good deal more common than in the north but the best guess seems to be that older merit-rating schemes are being abandoned more often than new ones adopted. In two of the four case studies of the introduction of job evaluation quoted in the PIB report, merit pay was replaced by a seniority increment – which in practice was what the merit pay system had degenerated into being, anyway.[31] On the other hand, an Industrial Society survey of 140 firms in 1970 found that 30% of them said that their manual workers were eligible for wage or salary increments 'by merit' and another 31% said that they got them by 'annual review' (23% said they were awarded on a predetermined scale and 44% 'by negotiation').[32] Unfortunately neither the representativeness of the survey, nor the precision of the questions are such that one can attach too much importance to these results, and there is no easy way to get more general information. The PIB's request that it should be given a reference on merit-rating systems was never granted.[33]

[30] Ibid., p. 14.
[31] Ibid., pp. 44–5.
[32] Industrial Society, *Status Differences and Moves Towards Single Status*, 1970.
[33] See Reports 65, p. 74 and 77, p. 53.

Merit-rating is not a dead issue, however. It was the subject of a TUC booklet, *Job Evaluation and Merit Rating*, published in 1964. Somewhat surprisingly, the tone of the discussion was cool.[34] While the objections were seen to be strong, stronger than those against job evaluation (it can 'lead to favouritism and patronage on the one hand and obsequiousness and jealousy on the other'; 'it tends to destroy group loyalties that, if anything, are strengthened by job evaluation') the conclusions were not entirely hostile. 'It is a fact that some men are more competent, more adaptable, more conscientious than others.' Inevitably subjective assessments *are* made, if only for promotion and job allocation. 'To the extent that merit-rating systems provide corrections to . . . tendencies [for favouritism and patronage to creep in] they represent an improvement.' Trade unions were not advised to discountenance any such schemes but to insist that their introduction should be negotiated and that the scheme should be subject to trade union audit.

THE FIRM AS COMMUNITY

Under this head one can subsume a number of related features which all bear on the way in which a worker conceives of his attachment to his firm and the strength of that attachment. They are:

1. increasing welfare and security benefits,

2. increasing recognition of seniority,

3. changes in the status system, particularly an erosion of the manual/white-collar divide.

1. *Welfare and Security Benefits.* Chapter 8 has already noted changes in English Electric in the last decade – notably the introduction of a sick pay and pension scheme for manual workers. The number of firms with such schemes has certainly increased in the last decade. They were a feature of many of the productivity deals concluded in the early sixties,[35] and an industrial society survey found that 75% of its sampled firms had such schemes in 1970, compared with 69% in 1966.[36]

The trend towards workshop or company bargaining – especially company bargaining – is almost certain to heighten this tendency.

[34] It is said, however, that the reaction of some unions to the TUC's 'soft' line on merit pay was far from cool.

[35] Royal Commission on Trade Unions and Employers' Associations, Research Papers 4, p. 25.

[36] Industrial Society, *Status Differences and Moves Towards Single Status*, 1970, and *Survey of the Comparative Terms and Conditions of Employment of Manual and Non-manual Workers*, 1966.

Company combine officials – usually senior men with a stake in 'their' firm – have much stronger motives for pressing for expanded fringe benefits than national union officials whose primary concern tends to be wages. Thus Lerner and Bescoby noted already in 1964 that 'virtually every company combine investigated in the past 6 years has become preoccupied with the question of fringe benefits. . . . The increase in the number of companies which have introduced fringe benefits schemes in the engineering industries may be, to some extent, a by-product of pressure from the combines.'[37]

Another feature of many productivity deals was an explicit guarantee of security of employment.[38] The most notable innovation in the package recently offered to British Leyland workers was a scheme for guaranteed payments during lay-off periods.[39] On a national scale, the Redundancy Payments Act of 1964 has affected security of employment more generally. While being designed, on the one hand, to *increase* mobility of labour – by providing an inducement to trade unions to drop opposition to reorganization schemes which involved redundancy – it also has a contrary effect. First, by recognizing that someone dismissed for redundancy is entitled to compensation, it implicitly recognizes that workers, once employed, have a right to expect to continue to be employed. Secondly, since only a part of the redundancy payment is paid from the general fund and the rest is a direct charge on the firm, it does act as a deterrent to casual hire-and-fire policies. Employers have an added incentive to try to keep workers on by redeployment and if necessary retraining. One side effect has been to introduce into British industry the Japanese-type distinction between ordinary workers and 'temporary' workers who waive their claim to redundancy payments. To be sure, there is no evidence that turnover is decreasing as one would expect if employers are becoming more reluctant to dismiss. Overall separation rates were if anything higher in 1970 than in 1960. It could well be, however, that stability rates in large firms are increasing even though there is a general increase in separation rates. On that there is no easily available information.

2. *Seniority.* As the expectation of continued employment with the same firm grows stronger, it is not surprising that seniority should come to count for more. Already in the nineteenth century it was the

[37] S. W. Lerner and J. Bescoby, 'Shop Steward Combine Committees in the British Engineering Industry', *British Journal of Industrial Relations*, 4, ii, 1966, p. 164.
[38] Royal Commission, Research Papers 4, p. 27.
[39] *The Times*, 20 October 1970.

unions in industries like the railways,[40] where most workers did not have a choice of employers and consequently hoped for permanent employment with one firm, which first showed a concern to get seniority formally recognized as the criterion for promotion and for the order of dismissal in the case of redundancy.

At the national level several pieces of legislation recognize length of service as conferring special rights. The Redundancy Payments Act makes entitlements dependent on length of service. The Contracts of Employment Act of 1963 varied the period of notice required from one to four weeks depending on length of service, and these provisions were extended in the 1971 Industrial Relations Act to make 8 weeks' notice necessary after 15 years' service. In individual firms, extra days of holiday for length of service are not uncommon – we saw in Chapter 8 that such a scheme was introduced in the Bradford factory in the 1960s.

The seniority principle has not made any great inroads into the wage system, though there are firms which pay service increments to manual workers. The PIB report on job evaluation schemes quotes two instances of such pay scales being introduced to replace earlier merit-pay.[41] A related change of more general consequence, however, is the negotiation of age-based minima by the draughtsmen's union. During the 1960s DATA first secured recognition of a set of minimum annual increments up to the age of 25, and later got this extended to 30.

Seniority is a tricky concept. There is both age seniority and service seniority. The chief justifying principle of service-linked benefits is that years of loyal devotion deserve recognition. It is a principle which can apply both in traditional kinds of personal paternalism where the service is to the employer as a person, and in modern forms of welfare corporatism where the service is to the corporation as a collectivity. The justification of age-linked benefits on the other hand, is partly that experience grows with age and therefore makes a man's work more valuable (a market principle), partly that family responsibilities increase with age (a welfare principle), and partly that prospects of a regular career progression increase satisfaction and hence commitment to the job (also partly a welfare principle in so far as delivering satisfaction to its employees is implicitly counted as one of the purposes for which the corporation exists). Age seniority and service seniority become practically indistinguishable in the Japanese

[40] See P. W. Kingsford, *Victorian Railwaymen*, ch. 8, and for developments in the US see F. Myers, 'The Analytic Meaning of Seniority', Industrial Relations Association, *Proceedings of the Annual Winter Meeting*, NY, December 1965.

[41] PIB, Report No. 83, p. 44–5.

system where there is permanent employment with standard entry ages. In Britain they are more distinct, but both are of increasing if slowly increasing, importance.

On present showing, however, the likelihood is that if there is a general shift in the age/wage curve for manual workers (at the English Electric factories, see p. 109, it was almost flat; men reached their earning peak at around 25) it will come not so much from explicit service-based or age-based increments as from the establishment of promotion grades, with wage increases resulting from promotion from one grade of job to the next and seniority playing a large part in the criteria for promotion. Such promotion grades have long since existed in, for example, the railways or the steel industry. It was noted earlier that a common feature of many productivity deals in the 1960s has been the introduction of such job gradations. Another manifestation of the same trend can be seen in the handling of promotions of a more traditional kind. We saw in Chapter 2 how in one case of a managerial appointment at English Electric a balance was held between on the one hand the market principle of getting the most qualified man for the job, and on the other the organizational requirements of being seen to reward diligent service, and of providing for career development. Although it is hard to find quantitative evidence (it *could* be found in principle in statistics of the proportion of appointments made by internal promotion in given firms) it seems that the latter considerations are given increasing weight. One isolated piece of evidence of union pressure in that direction can be seen in the fact that the 1969 annual conference of the Transport Salaried Staff Association passed a resolution condemning the appointment of outsiders to managerial and technical positions in the transport industry. 'We want', said one of the delegates, 'recognition for faithful and loyal service and experience.'[42]

3. *The Status System.* Sick pay, pensions, service increments, a career progression – all these features now entering into the conditions of employment of manual workers in some firms have been, of course, characteristic features of middle class, white collar employment in Britain. These changes, therefore, tend to diminish differences between staff and manual workers, and this has, indeed, frequently been one of the *objects* of such measures, rather than their incidental effect. The PIB report on productivity deals, noting this

[42] *The Financial Times*, 16 May, 1969. It *could* be that the union's concern was provoked by an actual increase in the appointment of outsiders rather than by a change in the union's expectations. Only statistics on managerial mobility could resolve the question.

underlying objective of many agreements, points out how firms such as ICI, the Electricity Supply Industry and Mobil Oil have tried symbolically to emphasize the change towards equality of status – by expressing manual workers pay in the form of annual wages or annual salaries (though still paid weekly), by allowing for short periods of approved and urgent absence without loss of pay, by replacing payment for overtime with extra time off, and in some cases by abolishing time clocks.[43] The Industrial Society surveys quoted earlier found 11% of the sampled firms giving time off instead of overtime in 1970, compared with 1% in 1966, and only 64% using time clocks for manual workers compared with 93% in 1966.[44]

The author of a popular Penguin in the early sixties which traced a good many of Britain's ills to the persistence of class divisions and class resentment in industry expressed his disappointment with the Donovan Commission's report by saying that 'industrial relations would not be got right until every worker was given a "manager-type" contract and the security that went with it.'[45]

This still seems a long way off in Britain in 1971, but at least the *idea* that it is a good thing to 'put everybody on the staff' has become a familiar one. The new *Code of Industrial Relations Practice*, 1972, says that all 'differences in the conditions of employment and status of "white collar" and other employees' which are not 'related to the responsibilities of the job . . . should be progressively removed'. Many managers say that they would dearly love to remove them but cannot afford to. It is hard to say how long it will be before a sufficiently large proportion of workers expect such treatment that managers will no longer be able to afford not to.

GREATER BUREAUCRATIZATION

Bureaucracy is a protean world. I leave the sense in which it is used here to be inferred from the discussion in Chapter 9 and from the following list of trends which for convenience can be grouped under this head.

The first is the growing professionalization of management, reflected in the proliferation of business schools and management training institutes. This involves three elements in the classical Weberian formulation of bureaucracy. The first is the emphasis on

[43] National Board for Prices and Incomes, Report 36, p. 10.

[44] The same warning should be entered as before concerning the unreliability of the sampling. The questionnaire was sent to 250 of the society's members in 1970 and to 300 in 1966. The numbers responding were 140 and 180 respectively. Since all biases appear to be the same in both cases, however, the trends are probably significant of real trends.

[45] Michael Shanks, quoted in *The Financial Times*, 21 June 1968.

formal qualifications produced by formal planned training (as opposed to traditional methods of 'standing by Nelly'). The second is the increasingly rationalized specialization of functions. Of particular interest to this discussion, since it breeds further innovation of organizational structure, is the specialization of the personnel function. The Institute for Personnel Management doubled its membership from 6,000 to 12,000 between 1963 and 1970. The third element, largely the work of personnel specialists, is the current vogue for 'management development' – the design of organizational structures to provide (on the assumption of permanent employment) for individual career progression.

The second, related aspect of this process of rationalization is the increasing emphasis on formal planning – not only for production and financial control, but also deliberate planning of organizational structures, the planning of manpower requirements[46] and the attempts, as in the large-scale productivity deal, to plan wage systems, introducing some kind of rational consistency into what are often jungles of rates each the result of separate *ad hoc* decisions.

The third aspect, also related, is the increasing use of formal written communications and explicit rule-books and codes of procedure replacing verbal communication and 'custom and practice' – most notably in industrial relations at the factory level where minuted meetings and written agreements are becoming common. In his study of shop stewards McCarthy noted the multiple reasons why written agreements have hitherto been rare at the factory level.[47] Many of these remain of unchanged validity: in matters of substance, for example, both sides can hope to reinterpret unwritten agreements in their favour if the balance of advantage changes. Nevertheless, in the first place, if the status of shop stewards is to be increasingly formally regulated on the union side it will be harder for managers to resist the desire of shop stewards to have *procedural* agreements which specify their negotiating positions formalized in writing. Secondly, as substantive agreements become more a product of committee negotiation rather than of an understanding between individual shop stewards and supervisors, they are more likely to be formalized. Thirdly, the experience of formal factory productivity bargains has created precedents, and, as McCarthy suggested, both

---

[46] A DEP survey of 1968 found that half of some 300 large and medium firms had some kind of manpower plan. *Company Manpower Planning*, Manpower Papers 1, HMSO quoted in *The Financial Times*, 9 October 1968.

[47] W. E. A. McCarthy, *The Role of Shop Stewards in British Industrial Relations*, Royal Commission on Trade Unions and Employers' Associations, Research Papers 1, p. 26–9.

managers and stewards may well have discovered the advantages of having more secure, stable and predictable relations.[48]

CHANGES IN MANAGERIAL IDEOLOGY

It has always been in the interests of employers to hold that there was fundamentally no division of interest between employers and workers. And it has always been the mark of a refusal to be misled by hypocritical propaganda, of the ability to see reality *en clair* for a trade unionist to insist that 'there are two sides to industry' whose interests are inevitably opposed.

The issue, once clear in the context of the family firm with a recognizable personal, profit-taking boss, has become more complex as a result of several trends:

1. The increasing divorce of ownership and control.

2. The increasing size of companies which means that in some firms middle managers are now to be counted in their hundreds or thousands, with the result that the man who represents 'management' most directly to shop floor workers is increasingly a man who is very conscious of his own subordinate employee status, feels himself to have very little direct influence on the making of policy within the firm, and also – *vide* the apparent success of ASTMS' recruiting drive among managers – little chance of securing his own position through personal ties with superiors, and a consequent need for collective support.

3. The change in authority patterns in society generally. Partly as a result of increasing affluence (individuals, accustomed to guaranteed economic security give more strong expression to the need for self respect) partly as a result of the continuing influence of egalitarian ideas, Britain has moved further from being an ascriptive, deferential society, and authority patterns in a variety of institutions have had to adapt – between officers and men in the army, between parents and children, between university teachers and their students, no less than in industry.[49]

[48] McCarthy, op. cit., p. 29.

[49] See for example, the report of a paper on the shipping industry read at a British Association meeting in Dundee. 'The basically nineteenth-century system of shipboard authority is finding it more difficult to cope with [social] change. . . . The assumed organizational requirements of the ship at sea [come] into conflict with changing conceptions, derived from the wider society of what [is] considered legitimate within an authority relationship.' *The Financial Times*, 24 August 1968.

4. The specific change in the bargaining situation resulting from full employment, higher social security benefits and greater personal savings. The 'fear of the sack' is no longer a potent weapon of management. Authority which can no longer rely for support on *coercion* has to seek a basis in consent.

The changes in the prevailing ideology of management have mostly been responses to the last two (closely interrelated) trends, rather than to the first two.

'We have got to recognize, whether we like it or not, that real power now resides in the workshop and on the office floor. It has, if you like, returned to the grass-roots whence it came. We have got to accept, again whether we like it or not, that workpeople have a veto which they are increasingly prepared to exercise; in other words, that management these days can no longer function by the arbitrary exercise of traditional "prerogative", but only by winning the consent of its workpeople.'[50]

The directors to whom Mrs Castle was talking did not have to be told. They, too, had become accustomed, as a matter of course, to talk of 'buying out' piecework systems or restrictive practices. Few of them had not developed the automatic habit of asking, as the first question when any reorganization was proposed, 'What will be the unions' reaction?' Few of them would have been surprised by the PIB's finding on overtime that, despite the fact that the average worker does seven hours of overtime a week, more than 70% of the sample interviewed had never worked overtime when they were not personally inclined to.[51] Few of them have not, under the pressure of circumstances, surrendered some jealously guarded bit of 'managerial prerogative', though they might well feel morally guilty about such back sliding, and be somewhat ashamed to admit it.[52]

Slowly the move towards 'constitutional management' is taking place. Unions are accepted as part of the scenery. In a survey, 'only 2% of managers held that shop stewards were unreasonable, 95% taking the view that they were either very reasonable or fairly reasonable. . . . Nearly a third of them thought that shop stewards were a lot of help to management, and most of the remainder that

[50] Speech by Mrs Barbara Castle to the Institute of Directors, 6 November 1969 (DEP press notice).

[51] *Guardian* report of a study which was apparently never published. See *Guardian*, 7 October 1970.

[52] A point made by Alan Fox *Industrial Sociology and Industrial Relations*, Royal Commission on Trade Unions and Employers' Associations, Research Paper 3, p. 12.

shop stewards were of some help.'[53] It is now common for management to give shop stewards paid leave to attend shop stewards'
courses. 'Communications' are now seen as all-important. The obligation to disclose information which trade unions need for negotiations will eventually be included in the new Code of Industrial
Relations Practice (when a committee has succeeded in specifying
what information that should be) and the new Industrial Relations
Act makes it possible to enact regulations which will enforce the disclosure of information.* The Industrial Society energetically proga-
gates the idea of 'briefing groups', regular talks by superiors to their
immediate subordinates to tell them what is happening in the firm,
rather similar in function to Hitachi's morning assemblies.[54]

From communicating to consulting is a delicate step, but more
firms are taking it. The National Coal Board scheme for works conferences at which *whole* work groups periodically spend a day not
working but discussing the organization of their work and how it can
be improved, is an outstanding and apparently successful example.[55]
The need for consultation is now discussed in more realistic and
practical terms than it has ever been since the last war when external
circumstances produced a sense of common aims and Joint Production Consultative and Advisory Committees were started and proved
effective all over industry, only to linger on[56] in the moribund condition described in an earlier chapter once external circumstances had
altered again. Now productivity bargaining usually starts from the
assumption that workers' representatives have to be fully involved in
the reorganization of work, not just in changes in the pay structure.
'We call this participative management', declared a representative
of the pioneers of productivity bargaining, 'because the employee is
part of the whole concept and effort and is likely to be proud of his
achievement and participation, which will continue.'[57] On a wider

[53] Royal Commission on Trade Unions and Employers' Associations, *Report*,
para. 124.
[54] See the article by the director, 'Briefing Groups Help Work Relations', in
The Times special supplement on 'Involvement at Work', 23 November 1970.
[55] Michael Thomas, 'When it Pays to Give Men a Say in Their Jobs', *The
Times*, 23 November 1970.
[56] In about 40% of British factories according to a 1962 Industrial Society
Survey. See A. Marsh, 'Joint Consultation Revived?', *New Society*, 16 June 1966.
[57] Mobil Oil, quoted in Royal Commission on Trade Unions and Employers'
Associations, Research Report 4, 1967, para. 169.
* The report of the committee, when it came, proved so anodyne and un-
specific that no amendment of the Code and no regulations under the law were
necessary – or, indeed, possible. The committee did, however, *resoundingly* declare that the disclosure of information was a good thing. (CIR, Rept. No. 31,
Disclosure of Information.)

360

scale, firms introducing job evaluation schemes, now as a matter of course, put worker representatives either on the evaluation panel or on an appeals panel.

The pattern of constitutional management which seems to be becoming the new norm is still predicated on the 'two sides' perception of the industrial situation, two sides with different though not necessarily (and this makes the difference from traditionally militant views of either trade unionists or union-bashing employers) incompatible interests. Thus, two leading trade unionists had similar things to say for *The Times* symposium on involvement in industry.

'If we, in fact, recognize that there are two sides in industry, it becomes perfectly possible to hammer out agreements that injure neither but benefit both.

If we confuse the position by arguing that there are not two sides then we reach a position where instead of negotiating intelligently we lecture each other to no purpose at all.'[58]

'The first essential is recognition by the employer of the simple truth that there are two sides of industry, not one. . . . Once the manager takes that view it is clear that shop stewards should be properly trained to do their job, should have adequate facilities to carry them out, should have access to relevant information about the firm they need, so that they can effectively represent their side in response to and in co-operation with the management side.'[59]

This version of the 'two sides' view is a modification of traditional views in response to the changes in authority relations discussed earlier. It implies that, while people are to be treated with respect and should not be asked to take orders without explanations; while they can and should contribute to decision-making about the organization of their immediate work, beyond that it is 'the managers' responsibility to manage' – to take the bigger policy decisions and to ensure that there is work to be done. The unions are there to squeeze the maximum advantage for the workers they represent, while doing all they can co-operatively to increase production so that there is more to squeeze. But beyond that they do not want the responsibilities, or the inhibitions on the ability to squeeze, of participation in management. On these matters the views of managers are not very different. They merely wish that the unions would make their lives easier by squeezing less and think that perhaps more talk of 'common

---

[58] Jack Jones, speech reported in *The Times*, 24 November 1970.
[59] Victor Feather, *The Times* supplement 'Involvement at Work', 23 November 1970.

purposes' and less of 'two sides' might help to direct more attention to production and less to the division of the spoils.

The consensus which has developed around this, what one might call the 'reconcilable and co-operative two sides', view is now of considerable weight. The older, 'irreconcilable class opposition' view is becoming a minority view shared by the Trotskyite left-wing groups, some of the Communist party, and the numerous business leaders who still make 'one happy family' speeches reflecting what Fox calls a 'unitary' view of the industrial firm, in which union autonomy can have no place.[60]

1. The older view sees industrial relations as a zero-sum game; the newer view suggests that *both* sides can gain from co-operation.

2. The older view assumed an inequality of power; the newer a rough equality of power in the bargaining system.

3. The older view assumed that if ever the inequality of power were corrected or reversed, the *system* would change; the workers would 'win'. The newer view assumes that the system is in equilibrium.

4. The older view, consequently, saw industrial relations as a struggle for supremacy; the newer as a permanent source of recurrent but curable and manageable conflict.

5. The older view assumed that inequality of power was reflected in inequality of status. Managers were naturally either arrogant or patronizing; representatives of 'the men' either deferential, prickly, or aloofly hostile. The newer view rests on the assumption of equality of status.

These differences are not sharp. That is why a good deal of ambiguity can persist, and why practice can still lag so much behind rhetoric, with managers talking co-operation but behaving in an authoritarian and secretive manner and unions responding with the assumption that it is exclusively the boss's responsibility to make sure that productivity covers wage increases.

One source of ambiguity lies in the fact that the other changes mentioned above – in the pattern of ownership and control in large corporations and the increase in the number of employee managers – have in fact blurred the identity of the 'two sides'. The point was nicely illustrated in a debate in the House of Commons in 1968 on the role of foremen, the men who most obviously upset any attempt to divide industry into two sides claiming mutually exclusive loyalties.

[60] A. Fox, *Industrial Sociology and Industrial Relations* (Royal Commission on Trade Unions and Employers' Associations, *Research papers* No. 3) 1966, p. 3.

A private bill was introduced to outlaw rules in the Foreman's and Staff Mutual Benefit Society which had formerly made the receipt of insurance benefits (to which employers also contribute) conditional on *non*-membership of a trade union. A Sheffield MP who declared himself a supporter of a strong trade union movement, was nevertheless deeply disturbed by the prospect of foremen joining ASTMS in large numbers:

'It is my view, based on my experience . . . in active management, that a man once he becomes a manager ought to identify himself with management. . . . Hon Members are surely not suggesting that there is no need to encourage a man to begin to dissociate himself from the shop floor once he has been promoted off the shop floor.

I ask, where are we going? Is it proposed that the managing director of any industry, as a result of this should ultimately become a member of a trade union? If he is a member . . . who is in charge of the company? Are there to be no employers?'[61]

The answer, of course, is that in small firms there are and in large firms there are not. In small firms the 'two sides' are still the traditional two sides: employer and employee; profit-taker and wage-earner. In large firms there remains an authority relation, a division between the vast majority who are on the receiving end of orders, and the minority who give more orders than they receive. Most conflict, and all effort-wage bargaining divides the organization across these lines of authority. All bargaining is *bi*lateral between organizations of workers and 'management', the organization of the minority. These are the facts which give the 'two sides' view its continuing relevance and viability. But in large firms that minority is now infinitely graded in the degree of their autonomy and responsibility, and their role in profit-taking is obscure. The weak point of the 'co-operating two sides' paradigm is its assumption that in the bargaining situation 'the interests of the shareholders', 'the interests of the company', and 'the interests of management' are identical.

This suggests an alternative view – that there are not two sides but many sides to a large corporation. This view underlies a paragraph in the Donovan Report subscribed to by five of the Commission's dozen members. Arguing the need for workers' directors they point out that 'the interests of the shareholders themselves can conflict with the *interests of the company* as much as can the interests of the workers' (my italics). Shareholders, for example, might well vote to sell a company to a competitor who would close it down, totally ignoring the workers' interests in their jobs, a move which a director

61 Mr John. H. Osborn, *Hansard*, 24 October 1968, cols 1703–4.

specifically representing the interests of workers might forestall.

Implicit in this view – what one might call the 'corporatist' view – of the firm are the ideas (essential parts of the Japanese management ideology):

1. That 'the company' as a collectivity corporate, can be said to have interests in much the same way as one talks of the 'national interest' – either as something 'over and above' sectional interests, or as the sum of those interests.

2. That 'membership' in, or 'having a stake in' the company can take many forms including both investing in it and working in it (*in* it, not for it).

Essential to this 'multi-sided' conception of the corporation and industrial relations is the idea that while on the one hand there is a functional division of responsibilities in the *productive* process which requires some people to specialize in giving, some in executing orders, this authority relationship can be logically separated from the division of the spoils (including investment decisions). As to the principles which should underlie the latter, there are two types of solution.

The first, the Japanese solution and the solution of, for example, the John Lewis Partnership,[62] is to see the managers as the benevolent guardians of the interest of the company as a whole (including the interests of the workers as well as the shareholders). Their 'broader' view, and more long-term view, entitles them to adjudicate the claims put to them by individuals or by various interest groups within the company. One might call this 'hierarchical corporatism'.

The alternative, what one might call 'democratic corporatism' is some kind of conciliar process in which all the main interest groups are represented – the shareholders, the managers who also own shares, and various other groups of employees from managers down, grouped according to their own perceptions of the boundaries of their common interests. In such a system bargaining becomes multilateral not bilateral. It also becomes reciprocal: workers' representatives would have a say in determining managerial salaries as much as vice versa.

It is, of course, not easy even in theory to separate decisions about

[62] See A. Flanders, *et al.*, *Experiment in Industrial Democracy*, 1968. The fact that the top managerial positions are formally elective does make a difference to managers' – and for the most part workers' – definition of the object of the enterprise, but still pay is a matter for unilateral managerial determination in the light of market conditions. In some sectors of the company where workers are unionized, the structure of relations is not, in fact, very different from the 'co-operating two sides' pattern.

production from decisions about the division of the proceeds (the effort part of the effort-wage bargain can be as much a matter of dispute as the wage part), and it is not easy in practice – given, particularly, the 'two sides' traditions of capitalist society – for managers to divide their roles between the productive sphere in which they assume functional authority, and the bargaining process in which they are on an equal and reciprocal footing.

They come close to managing it in the civil service and nationalized industries. The fact that the staff side in the Whitley Council before they come together to present a common case have to reach a reconciliation of the claims of different groups across a wide spectrum of the hierarchy seems not to affect functional authority relationships.[63]

The pattern of the civil service may be the basic pattern of the future corporation in this as in other respects. In principle, although some would disagree,[64] there seems no reason why what would be akin to a Yugoslav type of self-management system should not develop within a capitalist framework. (Or would it be evolve *out of* rather than within? If shareholders' powers were reduced by legislation would the system still be capitalist?) Frank Tannenbaum in the early fifties saw something like this as the pattern of all our futures. The whole history of trade unionism, in his view, is to be interpreted as an attempt to re-create the sense of community destroyed by the collapse of feudalism; its culmination will be the merging of the union and the firm in the democratic corporation as community.[65]

The prospect certainly seems still remote from contemporary Britain, though there is a certain edging towards it. 'Participation' is very much in the air. Even the CBI set up a committee to discuss it in 1968. The Liberal Party has expressed itself in favour of the workers

[63] Note, though, the curious way in which the Donovan Commission referred to this fact: 'Appropriate arrangements can be made . . . to prevent any conflict of loyalties.' 'Conflict of loyalties' shows how deep the 'two sides' conception runs. Managers, the implication seems to be, by organizing collectively to ask for higher salaries naturally invite the suspicion of 'disloyalty' (i.e. behaving like a 'mere worker' not expected to have any commitment to the firm). *Report*, p. 63, para. 205. See also the discussion of this question during the evidence of B. C. Roberts, *Minutes*, 33, p. 1417, para. 5229.

[64] See, e.g. Allan Flanders 'The Internal Social Responsibilities of Industry', *British Journal of Industrial Relations*, 4, i, 1966, pp. 1–21. Commenting on the idea of George Goyder that articles of association should explicitly define the objectives of the firm to include the promotion of its employees' interests, he suggests that this could have no effect on managerial behaviour because of the structure of the situation. Unfortunately he gives no reasons.

[65] Frank Tannenbaum, *The True Society*, 1964. The English edition is published with an introduction by Lord Robens.

having equal rights with shareholders in the election of directors.[66] The Donovan Report devoted a chapter to the subject and a minority of its members came down in favour of schemes to appoint workers' directors somewhat on the German model. The John Lewis Partnership now has a number of imitators. Some like the Scott Bader company, move further towards the democratic model with, for example, a constitutional provision setting a $1:7$ ratio between minimum and maximum salaries. Such experiments are all small, however. Scott Bader, which emphasizes its community character not only with a good deal of real workshop decision-making, but also with social outings, gifts for births and marriages, etc., in much the same way as in a Japanese firm, has only 360 members. Membership is still an individual matter; size has not created a need for sectoral representation.[67]

By and large, though, it is the 'hierarchical corporation' which at present seems most likely to get effective support – largely by default: because those who would count themselves 'on the left' and who might be expected to urge that the new corporatism should be democratic are hostile to the whole corporatist idea. The moderate left objects because it would weaken trade unions and delay the establishment of a fully fledged 'co-operating two sides' situation, and also because they see the corporation's 'totalitarian claims . . . either alone or in conjunction with the trade union . . . to provide the worker with his "society", one that will satisfy all his basic social interests outside the family' as threatening individual independence, privacy, and the integrity of national politics.[68] Those further left such as the proponents of 'workers control' vigorously reject corporatism as a fascist plot and mean by workers control extension of the workers power to hamstring capitalists with collective sanctions until people realize that capitalists are unnecessary. A few favourable references to Yugoslavia (before the system was corrupted by the introduction of free market elements) give the only clue to their preferences in the way of management organization after the revolution has occurred.[69]

Let us conclude with a rough schematization. Implicit in this discussion is a broad typology of perceptions of industrial relations. One, not discussed here, is the 'divine right of management' view

[66] See the report of its Industrial Partnership Committee, 'Partners at Work', described in *The Financial Times*, 11 September 1968.

[67] See Society for Democratic Integration in Industry, *Industrial Democracy in Practice*, 1970; R. Hadley, 'Common Ownership in Practice', *Factory Management*, January, February 1965.

[68] Allan Flanders, 'The Internal Social Responsibilities of Industry', *British Journal of Industrial Relations*, 4, i, 1966, p. 1–21.

[69] K. Coates *et al.*, *Can the Workers Run Industry?* 1968, p. 234.

accepting complete managerial autonomy (either benevolent or coercive) as part of the order of nature. The others are the 'conflicting two sides' view, the 'co-operating two sides' view, the 'hierarchical corporatist' view and the 'democratic corporatist' view. One might plot the progression below, following the thesis outlined at the beginning of this chapter, of an evolution effected by (a) the increasing size of the corporation and (b) egalitarianism.[70]

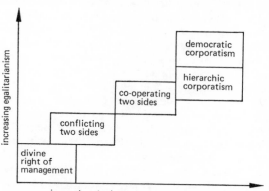

In Britain the rhetorical consensus now lies in the 'co-operating two sides' zone; practice still reflects a good deal of the 'conflicting two sides' perception. In Japan managerial, and sometimes even union, rhetoric reflects the corporatist view (not very clearly either hierarchic or democratic) while practice hovers between the 'co-operating two sides' and the 'hierarchical corporatist' zones. Which, to repeat the main thesis of this chapter, is to say that both societies are moving in the same direction, with Japan, for historical reasons, further along.

OTHER COUNTRIES

If what is said about British trends is true, and true for the reasons suggested, one would expect similar trends to be observable in other countries too. They are. Few other countries, however, started as far

[70] Note that these are meant to be *consensual* perceptions – assumptions shared by both workers and employers/managers. Thus it is the workers' rejection of the 'divine right' principle which marks the transition to the 'conflicting two sides' perception, though managers can still (while sharing this perception of the situation *de facto*) continue to believe in the 'divine right' principle *de jure*. That, indeed is an important source of the conflict, and the reason why it takes so long to evolve the mechanisms for regulating conflict through compromise which can eventually make the 'co-operating two sides' position viable.

back as Britain which is still paying the penalty of being pioneer industrializer. Most other countries share something of the late-development syndrome shown most obviously by Japan. Thus factory union locals and factory/company agreements have long since been standard practice in the United States. In many other respects, too, America is further along the road. In an interesting 1958 article, Arthur Ross asked 'Do we have a new industrial feudalism?'[71] His answer was 'no', by which he meant that the undoubted decline in turnover was not exclusively due to corporation welfare, the effect of seniority privileges, pension rights, etc. When he comes to analyse trends in voluntary quit-rates over this century, however, he refers to many of the features discussed here as part of a move in 'the Japanese direction'. He attributes a big decline in turnover in the 1920s, to the introduction of professional personnel management: the effect of managers learning with 'the shock of original discovery . . . that workers were human beings' and trying as a result to decasualize and systematize the whole employment relationship. He finds part of the decline to be due to the spread of tolerated unionism, providing new ways of expressing discontent besides walking off the job, and it is inferable from his argument that part is also due to the increasing proportion of large firms, since 'large firms tend to have low turnover rates, probably because of abundant opportunities for promotion and transfer'. The growing importance of internal promotion is a key element in the change. An excellent recent study[72] argues that America hardly has a traditional-type labour market any more: most workers are involved in an 'internal labour market' – internal to a specific enterprise which has a limited number of (lower level) entry ports for workers and fills its vacancies at other levels internally. In the terms of this book they are well on the way to an 'organization-oriented employment system' – a change which the authors ascribe to the increasing enterprise-specificity of skills, the increasing resort to on-the-job training, and the force of custom. Another straw in the American wind is the grant of seniority increments (as distinct from the career progression through a hierarchy of jobs just referred to). A recent study found that 45% of wage contracts in manufacturing provided not for a single rate but for rate ranges for each job, progression up the scale being based on length of service, merit or a combination of both.'[73]

[71] *American Economic Review*, vol 48, Dec. 1958, pp. 903–19.

[72] P. B. Doeringer and M. J. Piore, *Internal Labor Markets and Manpower Analysis*, 1971.

[73] Bureau of National Affairs, 'Basic Patterns in Union Contracts', February 1971, quoted in Income Data Services Ltd, *Incomes Data Study No. 11, Service Pay*, p. 6.

Similarly in Europe the West German rationalization of union structures by industry and the co-determination arrangements are well known. In France, the events of May 1968 and General de Gaulle's espousal of the participation slogan in his subsequent election campaign have brought many innovations (either by legislation or by agreement between the employers' association and the major unions) which have consolidated and universalized practices gradually developed in 'advanced' enterprises over previous decades. 'Mensualization' will now give all workers the security, sickness and pension benefits formerly reserved for white-collar workers. Seniority premia can add up to 15% to wages. Profit-sharing is now required by law. So is the joint administration of training schemes by committees of management and workers. Meanwhile the pattern of bargaining has been changing to give greater prominence to enterprise agreements negotiated by enterprise committees, rather than to industry-wide agreements – a recognition that industrial bargaining for industry-wide terms of employment, 'a system well adapted to an economy where the work-force moves from job to job according to the fluctuations of the market, is much less well adapted to an economy of large enterprises which plan for the medium and long term and in which the worker's aim is to improve his place within the organization.'[74] One of the major trade union federations, the CEDT, has decided to ride with, not against, this particular current, concentrates on strengthening the enterprise bargaining structure and has, since 1970, espoused the 'democratic corporatist' ideal of worker self-management.'[75]

A Dutch example reported in the British press shows an even closer approach to the Japanese model. In a general reform of the employment system at the Hoogovens steel works, all distinctions between hourly-rated and salaried workers were removed. Time clocks were abolished; all 21,000 employees were put on monthly salaries with uniform principles for pension and holiday rights; salaries were based on job evaluation, length of service, and for some workers group performance bonuses; and all formal barriers to promotion and transfer were removed.[76]

WHAT IS NOT LIKELY TO HAPPEN
Finally, a qualification. The trends discussed here as 'moves in the

[74] J. D. Reynaud, S. and J. Dass, P. Maclouf, 'Les évenements de mai et juin 1968 et le systeme francais de relations professionales', *Sociologie du Travail*, 13, i, Jan.–March 1971, p. 93.

[75] Ibid, part 2; 13, ii, April–June 1971, p. 204.

[76] *The Financial Times*, 23 December 1970, and Income Data Services Ltd, op. cit., p. 7.

Japanese direction' are only trends towards certain salient features of the Japanese system of welfare corporatism – factory and company based trade union and bargaining structures, enterprise welfare and security, greater stability of employment and integration of manual workers as 'full members' of the enterprise, greater bureaucratization and a co-operative or corporate ideology. It is not suggested that *all* the features of the Japanese system are likely to appear in Britain. Specifically:

1. Even if the factory or company-based bargaining system becomes the dominant form in the large corporation, it is unlikely, given that Britain has once had an industry-wide bargaining system, that the smaller enterprises will drop out of the collective bargaining structure and become largely un-unionized as in Japan. In, for example, the electrical contracting industry in which firms employing less than a hundred workers number two and a half thousand, the existing system of industry-wide bargaining may well persist.[77]

2. Secondly, there is no reason for expecting there to be reproduced in Britain those features of the Japanese employment system which are most clearly derived from traditional Japanese cultural patterns – the proliferation of status hierarchies, the easy acceptance of deference to organizational superiors, including the acceptance of assessment for merit pay; or the 'devotion' to work which subordinates private life and the claims of the family to the claims of the organization. The resistance to 'corporatism' of this kind in Britain is strong – see the remarks of Allan Flanders quoted earlier. These, in any case, are characteristics which Japanese enterprises are likely to shed with greater affluence and deeper rooting of egalitarian ideals, but without any necessary consequent changes in the main outline of 'the system'. (Some have changed already: unions have eliminated merit assessment in the posts and telegraphs corporation, for example.)

3. Thirdly, the trends towards welfare corporatism in the early industrializing countries have run parallel to a trend towards welfare *statism* and increasing central political management of the economy. There is no reason to expect the latter trend to be reversed; consequently the forms of welfare corporatism evolved are likely to be somewhat different from the Japanese pattern where welfare corporatism developed, as it were, ahead of state forms of welfare collectivism, and corporations are more autonomous units. Thus, there is no reason to believe that enterprise welfare will ever assume quite the

[77] See the evidence of Allan Flanders to the Donovan Commission *Evidence* 1962, p. 2781, para. 9919 and the Commission's *Report*, para. 167.

same importance as compared with state welfare in England as in Japan. Similarly, one would expect a further evolution of the mechanisms which have been developed most fully in Scandinavian countries for the welfare, pay and status of individual workers to be much affected by central decisions in which organizations of trade unions and employers at the *national* level take part. This may, however, be a case of convergence from both sides. State welfare is of increasing consequence as a supplement to enterprise welfare in Japan, too, and there is already much talk in Japan of the need for an incomes policy in the formation of which unions and employers would be represented through national organizations.

PART THREE

The Past and the Future

Chapter 14

The Origins of the Japanese Employment System

There was a time when the differences between the market-oriented British employment system and the organization-oriented Japanese system would have been happily ascribed to 'the unique genius of the respective races' and one would have left it at that. Nowadays, given the prevalence of theories about the 'structural requisites' of industrialism, one is urged to probe further. How *is* one to explain these differences?

The most favoured explanations have been of two kinds. The first is that Japan is backward in her progress to modernity (seen as a unilineal scale of development) but she will catch up – indeed, that she *is* catching up as the increase in labour mobility shows. This is not very convincing. Chapter 12 has already assessed the likelihood of a change to a more market-oriented system in Japan and suggested that the balance of probability is against it going far. Chapter 11 made the point that Japan's welfare corporatism is a far cry from the paternalism of early British industrialization: 'arrested development' is no explanation for it.

The second kind of explanation appeals to cultural differences. The contrast between the two systems springs from differences in the continuing cultural predispositions of the two peoples which have remained relatively constant since pre-industrial times. The stirring and spicing and baking process of industrialization may have been the same in both cases, but if you start off with a different cultural dough you end up with a different social cake.

Several times we have had occasion to refer to such differences – chiefly the differences in the individualist/groupishness dimension, in attitudes to age in particular and to authority in general, in the attitude to work. These cultural tendencies may seem to explain why the Japanese should feel reasonably comfortable in the institutions they have, and the British in theirs. But that does not explain *how* either people got their institutions. Did they (a) *create* them *de novo* to conform to their cultural predispositions? Or (b) did they (or at least the Japanese, for the British hardly had that option) choose their institutions off the peg, as it were, looking around the world at the various models and choosing the one that conformed to their cultural purposes, or, perhaps, eclectically synthesizing one of their own – much as they chose a British navy and a Prussian army organization? Or (c) were these cultural predispositions already, in the pre-industrial period, embodied in embryo institutions which have gradually evolved into the modern system with little conscious choice – so that there is not just the continuity of cultural congruence, but direct *institutional* continuity between pre-industrial and industrial Japan?

In Japan's case, the answer, as we shall see, is a bit of all three. Before offering the evidence, let us note in passing that there is a third, less common, kind of explanation which can be given for the differences between Britain and Japan. That is the explanation in terms of a 'late development effect', already hinted at in Chapter 13 with its suggestion of a revised line of evolutionary development along which Japan may be said to be ahead of Britain. That third set of factors will be considered in the next chapter. In this chapter, dealing with Japan's industrializing century, we shall be concerned to tease out the answer to the questions just raised about the second, the cultural, set of factors: how far is there direct institutional continuity in employment institutions from the Tokugawa period to the present day; how far was there conscious invention or conscious borrowing of new institutions?

TOKUGAWA PATTERNS[1]

Only a tiny proportion of the population of Japan in 1860 (perhaps as small as 5%) was engaged in regular wage employment of any kind. (If one excludes, that is, the Samurai whose heritable rice stipends were ambiguously seen either as an unconditional feudal right or as a reward for current service.) Agriculture was, as it has largely remained today, entirely a peasant family-farm agriculture. There was a certain amount of casual daily hire at peak periods, though within the framework, often, of on-going patron-client relations which blurred with gift-giving, feasting and voluntary 'service', the contractual nature of employment. In some areas the richer families had living-in servants, both domestic servants and farmhands. These were usually taken in late childhood and stayed until marriage or beyond. They were rewarded with their keep, with 'second-class membership'

---

[1] The following three pages draw heavily on an unpublished paper by R. M. V. Collick.

status in the family, with an annual rice payment to their parents, and with the eventual prospect of a small dowry.

Very similar but more clearly elaborated employment relations were found in what was conventionally described as the 'townsman's class' where the bulk of the employees were to be found. This embraced a large spectrum from the rich merchant houses engaged in multifarious banking and wholesale commodity trade, through the specialist dealers organizing production on a putting-out basis, and the bespoke tradesmen who served the wealthy as armourers or interior decorators, to the small artisan families who made the umbrellas and lanterns and clothing and writing brushes – the commodities which were sold ready made rather than commissioned. These, again, were family enterprises. Any one of them might expand the family labour force by taking in outsiders as second-class family members in much the same way as rich peasants did. The contract would be long term; 'wage' payments made twice-yearly (Michaelmas and Lady Day, as it were); and the employer would feed and clothe and accept some paternal responsibility, looking after the sick, arranging marriage, and so on.

This type of employment – as a means of expanding a basically family enterprise – was most elaborately formalized in the great merchant houses[2] where a regular career progression was available. Errand boy/apprentices would be recruited at the age of ten or eleven or even earlier. Their training was specific to the business of the house (apart from such general skills as writing and the use of the abacus for which the employer might send them to a teacher). Gradually they moved through a clear hierarchy based strictly on seniority rather than performance. Each promotion was marked by a minor *rite de passage*, by the adoption of a new hair style or type of clothing, by express permission to smoke or visit brothels, by an increase in pocket money, or a decrease in the proportion of notional wages which the paternal employer compulsorily saved. Beyond the top position of manager lay the further possibility, for the most able or most favoured, of the chance to set up a 'branch family', taking the main family's name, and receiving a small slice of its business.

Employment relations were somewhat different among the most skilled artisans, though the degree of difference depended on the type of trade. Those in settled family-based lines of production – lacquer-workers, armourers, makers of fine papers – had systems of apprenticeship, continuing service and branching very similar to

---

[2] A colourful account of these employment practices can be found in: Miyamoto Mataji, *Kinse shōgyō keiei no kenkyū*, 1948 part 2, ch. 1.

those of merchant families, though there was probably a good deal more movement between employers in practice than in the case of merchant houses, since the skilled artisan had a more definite transferable skill to sell. This was much more definitely the case in the geographically more mobile construction trades.[3] The apprentice who completed his learning term and his further term of 'thank you' service might well, as a journeyman, leave his original master and work for several other masters before (if ever) he became a master himself. There was, therefore, something much more like a labour market in these trades; wages varied according to skill rather than being conventionally determined on seniority principles.

These settled, long-term, family-extension type of relationships were the predominant, but not the only, form of employment in traditional Japan. Some of the larger merchant houses increasingly resorted to servants/workers hired on annual or six month contracts to do the more menial fetching and carrying and cleaning jobs. They might be hired at any age, and although they might still live in, would have none of the prospects of advancement of the regular employees hired as apprentices. Many such family enterprises also supplemented their labour force occasionally – or even regularly – with casual labour hired from day to day. The big towns had regular licensed contractors who supplied such labour. Some of the rural silk-reeling concerns offered seasonal work to girls on a similar daily basis, and the early weaving establishments probably paid by the piece, as was understandable in enterprises which grew from a cottage putting-out system. Equally uninvolved in any guaranteed secure relationship were the labourers at the docks and on the trunk roads, at major construction sites, in the forests and in the mines. A depressed underclass, unmarried and hardly able to aspire to married respectability, they sought protection in what anthropologists call 'fictive kin groups'. Paternalistic bosses, with the requisite age experience and toughness, offered protection and the opportunity for jobs to their client 'children' – in exchange for loyal service and unquestioning acceptance of the fact that their *oyabun* 'father' took a share of the proceeds of their labour.

THE MODERN PERIOD[4]

All of these patterns of employment were continued in one form or another in the modern period. But as Japan became transformed by

---

[3] Endō Motoo, *Shokunin no rekishi*, 1956, pp. 86–106.

[4] The most useful studies of these developments, on which this account is largely based, are: Hazama Hiroshi, *Nihon rōmu kanrishi kenkyū*, 1964; Hyōdō Tsutomu, *Nihon ni okeru rōshi-kankei no tenkai*, 1971; Sumiya Mikio, *Nihon chindrōdōshi-ron*, 1955; Koji Taira, *Economic Development and the Labour Market in Japan*, 1970.

the importation of foreign machine technology and foreign institutions in the period after 1870, new types of employment relationships were inevitably thrown up. Sheer size of organization made existing models inappropriate. For the purposes of potting history it is most convenient to separate four spheres of employment: firstly, mining, dockwork, construction and other enterprises which used large numbers of men in simple unskilled, often dangerous and brutalizing occupations, a large proportion of them men who had a low probability of ever marrying; secondly, the textile trades, ceramics and other light industries, which relied predominantly on the labour of young unmarried girls; thirdly, the engineering and shipbuilding trades and large-scale transport which employed mostly men, a relatively high proportion of the skilled, and most of them who were of the appropriate ages, heads of families; and fourthly the commercial and financial institutions and the staff employees of firms in the other sectors just mentioned.

The first, the 'rough' unskilled bachelor industries soon formalized within a larger capitalist framework the labour system based on the 'fictive kin' relationships just described. The 'fathers' (*oyabun, oyakata*), the bosses of the *hamba* or *naya* doss-houses which gave the system its name provided the shelter, the food (and drink), and the opportunity to work that their underlings needed, the doss-house group provided the camaraderie and the emotional support and physical protection which compensated for the lack of a settled family life. The boss organized the work, in effect as sub-contractor to the company, keeping what he considered a fair share of the proceeds, and deciding himself how to share the rest among his subordinates. 'Elder brothers' in the doss-house might be entitled to a little more than 'younger brothers', other things being equal, but by and large shares were supposed to depend on the amount of work done. The ethic of 'paternal' care and 'filial' loyalty was often, however, a thin veneer for a ruthless form of exploitation in which the mine-owners and the bosses acted in collusion. The workers were not tied down by bonds of sentiment or the prospect of advancement, but by a system of permanent indebtedness backed up by physical coercion which geographical isolation made the more effective – as the Tokyo intellectual world was shocked to discover in 1888 when a reporter smuggled himself into the fortress-like mining island of Takashima and subsequently 'escaped' to write a series of sensational articles about his experiences.

ENGINEERING AND SHIPBUILDING

The engineering industries need looking at more closely since it is there that one can see some of the various elements of modern welfare corporatism being pieced together. The pace-setters were the government arsenals and shipyards. These were the first large enterprises – the Yokosuka yard had 600 workers already in 1868 and had nearly tripled in size by 1881. In 1899 the military and naval establishments still employed 54% of the forty-six thousand workers in the larger engineering establishments (over ten workers) and after the expansion of the Russo-Japanese war they had 63% of a labour force more than three times that size.[5] The state sector was further enlarged in that decade by the addition of a nationalized railway system and the state steel works of Yawata.

A good deal of documentation concerning the Yokosuka yard still survives – at least concerning the formal system, if not its actual operation.[6] It had been started by the Tokugawa government with considerable French assistance, and continued by the new Imperial government. Its management system, like that of other enterprises started by feudal governments in the 1860s, had to be created *de novo*, for the traditional employment patterns provided no obvious model for enterprises created by a bureaucracy rather than by a family. The system changed gradually in response to (a) the change in the controlling bureaucracy from a hereditary status base to new more rationalized and meritocratic forms, (b) the development of Japanese technical competence and the departure of foreigners, (c) increase in size, and (d) the accumulation of experience and of experimentation with organizational devices. Several features of the Yokusuka system as it had developed by 1880 are worth noting in the light of later developments.

1. The first is the minute detail in which every facet of personnel administration was regulated. Job specifications and careful delimitations of authority, procedures for recruitment, promotion, and leave (what form and whose signature, counter-signed by whom) are laid down with a precision modified only by the frequent phrase: 'However, in exceptional circumstances, exceptions may be made.' In the early years, to be sure, production management was entirely the work of the team of forty-five French engineers and craftsmen who arrived in 1866. The twenty-odd Samurai managers listed in the 1869 establishment were solely concerned with personnel matters. (By 1873, however, there were thirty-eight Japanese technicians: by 1876 the foreign staff was reduced to twenty-five and rapidly tailed off thereafter.) There was, therefore, plenty of scope for inventing

5 Hazama, op. cit., p. 436.
6 The following details concerning the Yokosuka shipyard and arsenal are all taken from the documents quoted in Hazama, op. cit., pp. 399–435.

regulations and procedures to keep themselves occupied (and, in a state organization, no profit motive, inducing cost-consciousness, to act as a deterrent). But the sophistication and detail of the regulations and their style – their mixture of rational-legal precision (if x, then y shall be done) with didactic exhortation – clearly betray their origins in the traditions of the feudal bureaucracies which had evolved to a surprising degree of formal elaboration in the preceding two and a half centuries. The regulations of the Yokosuka shipyard provide a link in the chain of direct institutional continuity from such organizations as the fief-governed schools of the Tokugawa period to the elaborate rule books of modern Japanese enterprises.

2. Status distinctions were sharp, reflecting the social distance between the Samurai warriors and common people which still until the 1870s, entailed substantial legal as well as social privilege. In a semi-military society the authority of management was strong. 'Workers who, having registered in the morning, slip out of the factory and take advantage of the crush at the gates at lunchtime to slip back in and sign off, shall, after careful investigation, be made to stand tied to a stake for three hours in the afternoon beside a board on which is written the offender's name, shop and offence. In addition they shall lose a day or more's wages.' (1873). As the society changed, however, and the automatic prestige of Samurai status diminished, and as recruitment to managerial ranks came to depend on educational qualifications so that managerial status and Samurai ancestry ceased always to coincide, styles of authority were somewhat modified.

3. One important modification was the creation in 1882 of a work-gang system. (It came, not surprisingly, at a time when Japanese managers were starting, not just to enforce attendance, but to replace the French in supervising the work process itself.) From five to fifteen workers were grouped in relatively permanent work-groups under a foreman leader who was 'to be himself a model of correct behaviour, to guide and exhort the members of his group in accordance with the orders of his superior, to make sure that they obey the regulations, to admonish them when they are in error, and to unite them in earnest industrial endeavours'. The memorandum sent to the Navy Ministry requesting permission to institute the system (accompanied by a careful drawing of the cap with which the new foremen were to be issued) explains that direct control of a large and growing workforce by the technicians had become impossible and that the senior workers who were in theory supposed to guide the others did not do so because their responsibilities were not clear.

How much this system owed to knowledge of foreign practices is not clear. The cap was certainly an import, but the system came in 1882 after most of the French had left. What is clear is its roots in Japanese culture – in the moralism of the passage quoted, and in another of the twenty-one articles of the work-group rules which stated: 'any shirking, misconduct or breaking of the regulations by any member of the group shall be considered the responsibility not only of the individual concerned, but of the group as a whole'. Here was a creative application to industry of an old method of political control long familiar in China and Japan and institutionalized in seventeenth-century Japan as the *gonin-gumi* system – the 'five household' (more often ten or more in practice) collective responsibility system. The very title given to the foremen (*gochō*) reveals how explicitly the model was adopted. Here, then, is a link between the institutions of the Tokugawa period and the 'groupishness' characteristic of workshop organization today. Note, though, that it is not simply, like the continuity of bureaucratic styles, a matter of inertia, of the unconscious persistence of habits of mind. It rested on that, too, but required also a conscious act of institution building, a reinterpretation of those values and habits of mind in organizations adapted to the new setting.

4. The assumption that work comes first, that a man's work role dominates his other roles, that a man's primary mode of self-definition was in terms of his membership in the firm (see p. 209 for the modern manifestation of this syndrome) may be found in another article of the work-group rules. 'The foremen should take careful note of the members of his group, *not only*, *of course*, *when at work*, *but also at other times* and according to what he hears and sees should report accurately to his superiors, either favourably or unfavourably.' (My italics.)

5. In a Japan with no traditions of the kind of metalworking skills the dockyards required, new workers had to be trained. (Ships' carpenters, caulkers and sailmakers had talents close enough to those required for the new techniques to be adaptable.) From its beginnings in 1866 the yard had built its own school which had a course for full-time engineer/technician apprentices, another course for craft apprentices who spent half-day in the school and half-day in the yard, and in the early years a mixture of general education and training in industrial drawing etc. for workers who were being groomed for foremanship.

6. Having trained workers the problem was to keep them. As private jobbing engineers started up in the last quarter of the century

competition for skilled workers increased. Private firms, unhampered by bureaucratic regulations and fixed budgets could often offer attractive wages to workers whose skills were in scarce supply. The documents clearly reveal the continuing concern of the Yokosuka management with this problem. Three institutional devices were introduced to deal with it.

a. From the first, clear status distinctions were introduced between 'regular workers' who were guaranteed some permanency of employment, and other workers who were taken on for periods when there was work for them to do, or on a casual daily basis. The 1869 establishment has exactly the same three-fold distinction as the 1969 Hitachi establishment. There were regular workers, temporary workers on production work who could be promoted to regular status, and mere fetchers and carriers and sweepers. The last group was composed in 1869 of 35 paupers and 17 convicts.

b. In 1873 most of the existing regular workers – perhaps about one in seven or one in eight of the daily muster – were given a new status as monthly salaried workers. Their monthly pay continued during sickness, though they received overtime premia when they worked more than ten hours a day. The memorandum recommending this change to the Ministry explicitly spoke of it as the best means, within a limited budget, of countering the higher wages offered by other employers. Part of the wages of these 'staff workers' was compulsorily saved against their retirement.

c. For other workers a long-term contract system was introduced. Workers 'signed on' for a period which varied according to age, ranging from ten years for those aged 15 to 19, to one year for those approaching 40. At the end of the contract they were entitled to a bonus of fifteen days' pay for each year of service. The dockyards could also offer the additional inducement of exemption from compulsory military service.

At least two elements of institutional continuity are to be found in these measures. The compulsory saving system was characteristic of Tokugawa merchant houses. Secondly, the original title of the regular workers at Yokosuka was *kakae shokunin* – 'retained craftsman', a term which reflects a standard Tokugawa practice. Feudal lords who had a good armourer whom they did not wish to lose to another fief would pay him a retainer in the form of an annual rice stipend. (Until the monthly salary system was started in 1873, in fact, senior workmen still received a monthly rice stipend as well as their cash wage.) These elements of continuity are not unimportant, but for the most part these measures to 'stabilize' the workforce represented a new

383

response to a new problem, newly created by the development of an embryo free labour market.

7. Recruitment procedures became formalized at an early stage. Already in 1872 there were regular 'intakes' of new workers three times a year, though this was later modified to once a month. By the late 1880s selection procedures were formalized here just as (under the joint influence of Europe and ancient China) they had been in other spheres of the government bureaucracy. Would-be recruits with no work experience were given a formal test of reading, composition and arithmetic. The yard clearly saw no point in wasting training on workers who were not intelligent enough, or educationally well enough prepared, to take advantage of the training.

8. Finally, the wage system of the Yokosuka yard is worthy of note. The early regulations gave discretion to supervisors to fix individual wages within certain ranges, but the scales were soon formalized. Only in the very first wage scale of 1872 is there any suggestion of a differential price for different *kinds* of skills. Then there was a scale for shipwrights divided into six grades ranging from 28 to 38 sen a day, and another scale for other kinds of craftsmen with only three grades ranging from 28 to 34 sen. These craft distinctions almost immediately disappeared, however, and at the same time the grade divisions became finer, the scales longer and steeper. By 1883 there was a 17-step scale – one grade of probationary worker, three grades of apprentices (13 to 20 sen a day), eight grades of craftsmen (25 to 60 sen a day) and five grades of master craftsmen (rising to 120 sen a day). Promotion from grade to grade depended on twice-yearly merit assessments – 'how far a man has advanced in skill and how diligently he works'.

The reference to diligence suggests that seniority played a big part in determining promotions, that this was already an organization-oriented rather than a market-oriented wage system. Although there appear to be no memoranda to prove the point, the scales seem designed to provide incentives to stay with the firm, rather than to give managers wide latitude in bargaining to attract skilled workers. For a single enterprise to operate such a system, however, was not enough. It was not until such practices became general, several decades later, that the 'Japanese system' settled into its present form.

FURTHER EVOLUTION
Government arsenals and shipyards of the 1880s clearly were in many respects prototypes of the modern Japanese system: bureaucratic proliferation of regulations, groupishness, the moralism of the total

commitment, the permanent/temporary worker division, in-firm training, long service incentives, careful recruitment selection, and organization-oriented rather than market-oriented incremental wage scales are all there. Some of these elements can be traced to unconsciously carried-over habits of behaviour, some to conscious adaptation to a new setting of institutions of the feudal period, some (like the work-group system) to conscious adaptations in a new industrial setting of institutional forms found *outside* of traditional employment patterns, some to institutional innovation in response to the entirely new situational demands of the economic and social framework in which these enterprises operated.

'The system' was far from complete, however. The Yokosuka enterprise was a micro-polity; it was not yet a macro-family. To produce the 'enterprise family system' of pre-war Japan some new institutional features were needed, and above all a new ideology. It also has to be explained how and why the employment practices of state enterprises should have spread.

The main motive forces for these developments had three main origins. First, employers continued to be preoccupied with the problem of reducing turnover and retaining their skilled workers. A second factor was the growth of general social concern with working conditions in mines and textile factories which were thought to be inhuman by the humanitarians, degrading and immoral by traditional Confucianists, and dangerously productive of social tensions by the enlightened technocratic bureaucracy. Thirdly this alarm was brought home eventually to the industrialists themselves as labour unrest began to spread and the first strikes and unions were organized.

PRIVATE SECTOR ENGINEERING
It was some time before really large-scale private engineering firms appeared. It was not until the Russo-Japanese war of 1904–5 that the ancestor of the modern Tōshiba, started as a small jobbing workshop in 1869, first employed more than a thousand workers. The Mitsubishi shipyard in Nagasaki grew more rapidly. It was already a large government concern when Mitsubishi leased it in 1882. By the time it acquired full ownership rights three years later, nearly 1500 workers were employed.

In their early stages the private firms had little of the formal bureaucratic organization of the government concerns. Their work organization lay somewhere between that of the arsenals and that of the mines. The key figures were the senior skilled workers, the *oyakata* bosses on whom employers largely relied to train and control the work force. Sometimes, in the early period, the *oyakata* took personal apprentices, boarded and fed them, collected such wages as were due to them – and gave them a share. These practices derived directly from the traditions of the Tokugawa artisan. In some establishments master craftsmen personally controlled a team not only of apprentices proper, but also of older workers, and bid against other master craftsmen for jobs, sharing the proceeds at their own discretion among their team. Some factories, in fact, were little more than a congeries of little workshops, each owning its own tools.

Such systems became rarer, however, by the end of the century. In the larger yards and factories all workers were directly employed; the *oyakata*, given formal authority in the system as foremen or supervisors often had the power to hire and fire, and a decisive say in the fixing of individual wages; they had charge of training apprentices, and in off-duty relationships something of the old exchange of service and protection might prevail – the juniors running errands for the *oyakata* and relying on him to bail them out or talk them out when they got into trouble with the police, to fix things with parents when they got into trouble with a girl. But the *oyakata*'s authority was increasingly circumscribed as the direct relationship between the worker and the firm was strengthened – through tighter managerial control of personnel matters, through more formal bureaucratic regulation of wage matters, and through increasing control of the firm over training.

One factor which facilitated these developments was the growth in technical secondary and higher education, increasing the supply of managers capable of exercising closer control over the work process. (The Mitsubishi shipyard increased its managerial staff by nearly 50% between 1897 and 1900 with little increase in the manual work force.[7]) Another factor was increase in size. As more and more firms – the Shibaura engineering works, the railway works at Omiya and so on – approached the size of the Yokosuka shipyard or the Tokyo arsenal, so they came to take on some of the characteristics of those government enterprises. The Mitsubishi shipyards at Nagasaki – for a long time easily the biggest private concern and the direct heir of a government organization – was always in the vanguard in the process of formal rationalization of organization and procedures.

There were two chief motives for cutting the *oyakata* down to size. The first was because they clearly abused their power and this affected morale and the quality of work. In regulations recorded for Shibaura in 1899 and the railway workshops in 1900, the system of competitive ganger-subcontracting was revised: they were no longer allowed to

[7] Hyōdō op. cit. p. 111. Unless otherwise stated this account of developments in private engineering is derived from Hyōdō, pp. 55–270.

distribute rewards at their discretion. Either the original tender had to specify the shares of each member of the workgroup, or they were left to be determined unilaterally by managers. (The latter was the case at Yokosuka where the competitive subcontracting system was *introduced* from private industry in 1901.) The clean-up of the system at Shibaura was only accomplished by dint of sacking some well-entrenched *oyakata* bosses – what the firm's history refers to as a 'routing of the feudal barons'.

A second major concern was the increasingly acute shortage of skilled labour as the growth of industry accelerated during and after the Sino-Japanese war of 1894–5. The total engineering workforce (in registered factories employing ten or more workers) grew slowly to only 13,000 in 1890. In the next five years it more than doubled; in the next five years it nearly doubled again (despite a recession in 1898–9), and between 1900 and the ending of the Russo-Japanese war in 1905 it increased nearly two and a half times to 150,000. There was no real shortage of recruits into industry. The children of the urban working class probably provided most of them: surrounding rural areas offered many more. The problem was to train them, and having trained them, to keep them.

The formal classroom-type training started at the Yokosuka shipyard in the very early period had mostly been for the *new* trades – iron-working, founding, turning, boilermaking. The ships' carpenters, sailmakers, caulkers came from the older wooden shipyards. Their skills were reproduced by the personal apprenticeship methods traditional to those crafts. As a first generation of skilled craftsmen in the new trades matured, these same traditional methods of personal apprenticeship began to function for them too. In Yokosuka, the emphasis on the formal schools increasingly shifted to training not craftsmen but technicians, so that even in the government yards it was increasingly left to the *oyakata* to take disciples for craft training as a means of building up their own, personally loyal, work-groups.

But this proved increasingly inadequate. The *oyakata* were not necessarily good teachers, nor much concerned with their apprentices' training. Most of the big firms in the late 1880s and 1890s introduced regulations for the direct employment of apprentices at wages supplied by the firm, not by the *oyakata*. Frequently the rules involved bonding arrangements to work for the firm for three or more years after completing the apprenticeship (the traditional 'thank-you service') and there were bonuses and compulsory savings systems to reinforce the spirit of contractual fidelity.

It was still largely an informal training – standing by the *oyakata* – but the managers supervised it and some formal elements were built in. Mitsubishi started its own school in 1890, though this too, like the Yokosuka one, soon gave prime emphasis to the training of technicians.

By this time, the *nation*'s need for industrial training was widely discussed in the Press and in the speeches of politicians and educators. A number of public apprentice schools were started. By 1900 they had a total of some 1,700 pupils, with an equal number in industrial supplementary schools offering evening classes. Engineering firms could send their young workers to these schools in the evenings or on part-time day release. These schools did not solve the craftsmen problem, however. Most of their graduates proceeded not to the shop floor but to further higher level courses to become technicians.

Least of all did these schools solve the training problems of the small firms. They were apt to solve them at the expense of the large firms. According to one of the fragmentary pieces of evidence, the Mitsubishi school produced 185 trained men between 1904 and 1910. Only 78 were still working for the firm in 1912. It is not surprising that concern about turnover was at its most acute in the large firms.

It was the largest of the large firms – Mitsubishi – which in 1897 took the lead in another innovation designed to help stabilize the workforce – the establishment of a formal welfare fund. Mitsubishi's scheme provided sick pay and retirement benefits with employer and employee sharing equally the contribution cost. In one sense this was a natural concomitant of the attempt to reduce the power of the *oyakata* for it was the *oyakata* who had traditionally 'looked after' his men, and the profits of his exploitative power over them had been the means by which he could do so. An alternative type of accommodation to the diminished social security role of the *oyakata* was the formation of a *workers'* mutual aid friendly society. The first one in Japan to be organized on a large scale on Western lines was the Metalworkers' Union formed in 1897, the same year as Mitsubishi's scheme. However, as one of its organizers lamented, 'it foundered on beri-beri'. Its scale of contributions and sick payments had not taken full account of the incidence of that deficiency disease. By contrast employer-sponsored schemes like those of Mitsubishi were not prone to collapse for the lack of 500 yen in the bank.

All the evidence seems to indicate, however, that at the turn of the century – despite the bonding systems, despite the contract/bonus system, despite the prospects of promotion up skill/seniority scales, despite welfare security schemes – both in the private and the public sector of the engineering industry turnover rates were high – with the separation rate rarely running at less than 50% a year and frequently over 100%. Contemporary descriptions suggest that there were three types of workers. First there were the 'loyalists' who stayed with their firm and had hopes of promotion to the rank of foreman or better. Surveys done around the turn of the century found in the older established firms a core of 15–20% of workers who already had more than five years of service. Secondly, there were the ambitious experience-earners – men who moved around to gain experience with the ultimate purpose of setting up on their own. The old Tokoguwa tradition of artisan independence still pervaded this factory world and the vigorous growth of small sub-contracting firms – set up, often, in a backyard with a second-hand lathe – and the important role they played in Japan's development are testimony to the strength of that ambition and the relative frequency of its fulfilment. Thirdly, there were the 'travellers', large numbers of skilled workers who inherited the footloose traditions of the construction industry artisans of the Tokoguwa period. Often with an unsettled family life (bachelors made up 41% of the Nagasaki shipyard workers – all ages – in 1901), they were men who depended on nothing but the skill they had to sell in the market. They were confident, proud, quick to anger and quick to abandon one employer for another who, with rush orders on hand, was prepared to offer a few sen a day extra in wages. The manager of the Nagasaki yard complained in 1899 he was 'acting as a labour bank'. When business was good in the smaller firms the 'travellers' all took off for the higher wages. When business got slacker, back they came to the steady work and the bureaucratic wage-scales of the shipyard.

It was the more skilled and responsible of these 'travellers' who formed the core of the Metalworkers Union when it was founded in 1897. They were the men who had the wide personal connections across the industry through which the union message could run. They were the men who had a prime interest in the independent social security scheme, the job vacancy information service, and the travel-loan service (to workers taking up new jobs in distant parts) which were some of the union's main features. The leading lights of the union, said an intellectual who was one of its organizing spirits, were mostly 'travellers, men of some experience, men with a good deal of skill and personal confidence in it, men who believed that the sun shone wherever you happened to be'. They were not, said he, referring with scorn to the first, 'loyalist' category of workers: 'men who stick for ever to the same old job, bowing and scraping to the foreman and superintendent, scuttling around with their little presentation boxes of cakes hoping to get a rise in salary'.

It was to be some years before the bigger employers found the means of making the loyalist 'bower and scraper' the typical member

389

of the workforce. At the turn of the century, as the number of enterprises – the number of alternative employers – in a few concentrated areas grew, Japan was developing a standard European-type market for engineering skills. When the new union in 1897 declared its intention of being a craft union, it was partly transferring, as a leading article in its journal said, 'the experience of Europe and America' which has proved among other things that 'organized labour can control its entry to and departure from the market . . . when times are slack a powerful union can maintain wages while aiding those who lose their jobs. . . .' But the Japanese situation was sufficiently like that of Europe and America for Western experience to *seem* to be transferable, for the reference to 'the market' to seem plausible – even though the union never actually managed to bargain for wage rates before its collapse in 1900.

In fact, wage systems did diverge considerably from the principle of a 'going rate' for a particular skill. Most firms followed the Yokosuka government yard in having broad ranging scales, though some had a number of slightly different scales for different trades. How steep the scale progression *normally* was, is uncertain. It seems that where scales nominally ran from 100 (at the end of an apprenticeship) to 300–400, only foremen and vice-foremen occupied the higher reaches, and an ordinary worker, if not promoted, was unlikely to go beyond 200 – though this still represented a considerable premium for experience.

These wage-scales by no means prevented mobility. A man could be slotted into the scale at a point befitting his age and experience. Nevertheless, the fact that men were (*vide* the Yokosuka promotion rules quoted earlier) promoted for diligent co-operativeness and regular attendance as well as skill, must have meant (a) that many reached a wage level by seniority which their skill would not buy elsewhere, and (b) that some younger workers who valued security were prepared to start lower down the ladder in the hope of reaching such a position. The deepening and conventionalizing of these trends was a major factor in consolidating the 'Japanese system'.

OTHER SECTORS

Already in these changes in the private engineering sector one can see foreshadowed many elements of 'the Japanese system', most of them following the innovations of the Yokosuka shipyard in the early decades. Certain other crucial elements had to be added, however, before the system settled into its final pre-war mould – notably the ideological element. Some of these other elements had their origins elsewhere – in the girl-employing textile trades, in the unskilled/semi-skilled male mining industry, and among the white collar staff of financial and commercial houses and of the large engineering firms themselves.

To take the last first: it seems that there were two main influences. The old 'house traditions' of some of the older concerns – like Mitsui and Sumitomo – which had their roots deep in the Tokoguwa period provided the principle of 'lifelong employment' beginning with a youthful apprenticeship and ending as a trusted manager or founder of a new 'branch house'. The second influence – the bureaucratic structure of government and of the early state concerns – provided a model of formal structure in which the principle could be reinterpreted – most naturally, for instance, for Mitsubishi whose founder had himself begun as the manager of a trading enterprise established by the Tosa fief bureaucracy. In this sphere, too, the turn of the century marked a departure of importance. Until the 1890s the salaries and prospects of employees in private industry had been inferior to those in government. Cash incomes apart, the man of business was awarded no great social honour. Fighting and governing were the only noble occupations according to Samurai tradition. Consequently, the ambitions of any bright educated youth were always directed to the civil service. By the 1890s, however, the institutions of higher education were beginning to turn out more graduates than government could absorb. This coincided with the arrival in Mitsui of a determined manager bent on reform. He greatly increased salaries. Mitsui, and in turn the other big Zaibatsu firms, became attractive prospects to university graduates and (since the available graduates were new graduates) the entry-at-the-bottom, lifetime career structure soon became established. The other big change of the first decade of the century was the development of profit-sharing bonus schemes as a means of enhancing the loyalty and commitment of staff employees. At first confined to directors they were later (in Mitsui after a protest movement led by a man who later became a Minister of Finance) extended in most firms to all staff employees.[8]

The second of the other sectors – mining and similar trades – was chiefly of importance because the mines epitomized for the general newspaper-reading public the brutish evils of industrialization. The revelations about the degrading conditions in the Takashima mines and the exploitative doss-house system of indirect labour led to the enactment of the Mining Regulations of 1890 and stimulated the demand for a more general factory act on the model of European laws. The mining industry was not the source of institutional innovations. It did, however, provide an important stimulus to the ideo-

[8] Taira, op. cit., pp. 117–18.

logical debate – as, later, did the publication in 1899 of a series of powerful newspaper articles on conditions in the factories and industrial slums, followed by a coldly factual, but for that reason all the more impressive, survey published by the Ministry of Agriculture and Commerce in 1903.

A fascinating glimpse of the state of opinion about industrial relations is given by the debates of a special committee of officials and industrialists which met in 1896 and 1898 to consider proposals for factory legislation drafted by Ministry officials.[9] The industrialists, not unnaturally, were opposed to the bill. All was well, argued some, there was no need to resort to these desperate European expedients because of the very special character of Japanese traditions – 'a warm spirit of family harmony' prevailed in the factories 'where old helped the young, and youth aids age, where joys and sorrows are mutually shared'. A law which coldly specified rights and duties would destroy the fine basis of morality and trust on which good relations depended. The proponents of the bill were prepared to make polite concessions to such views. One argument was that paternal benevolence might now be general among employers and things would be all right as long as industry remained in the hands of the 'present generation of warm-blooded men brought up in the traditional Japanese education'. But, 'we are now importing western education, and if one looks at the customs of Europe, as the notion of mere capitalists, of the power of capital, gathers strength and the single-minded concentration on profits, then we shall lose the traditions we were brought up in and eventually we must face it that there will be a tendency for the blood to run colder in people's veins,[10]

Others went further. There may be something of a family atmosphere in the smaller workshops, but can one talk of a family relationship between employer and employee when they don't even know each other by sight?[11] The first wave of strikes in 1897 should surely shatter these illusions. How to adapt traditional principles to *large* enterprise was something that had to be invented or *learned* and backward Japanese industrialists could well take a leaf out of European books. A senior official commended to his compatriots the model of his friend, a British industrialist who owned a factory just

[9] These debates have been reprinted. Nōshōkō Kōtō Kaigi, *Giji sokkiroku* (and Daisankai, ditto), reprinted in Obama Ritoku (ed.), *Meiji bunka shiryō sōsho*, 1961. Brief accounts may be found in Byron K. Marshall, *Capitalism and Nationalism in Pre-war Japan*, 1967 and R. P. Dore. 'The Modernizer as a Special Case: Japanese Factory Legislation 1882–1911', in *Comparative Studies in Society and History*, vol. 11, no. 4, October 1969.
[10] Masuda Takashi, the 1896 meeting, p. 56.

392

outside Manchester. The small town was, in fact, built around the factory. The owner was the grandson of the founder and many of the workers were third generation workers. The owner contributes largely to the upkeep of a hospital, a local school and a church where every Sunday 'he goes to worship with his workers since all are equal in Christ'. He opens his grounds to them for an annual fete when the gardens are at their prettiest, and the way in which he returns his people's affection in a near-feudal relationship is clearly evident in the way the workers touch their caps to him and in the kindly words he addresses to their children when he meets them in the street.[12]

Some were prepared to use the law to develop these new models of large-scale paternalism. As a concession to industrialists who stood to lose from the bill's regulation of hours of work and safety conditions, the draft included provisions for a worker registration system which would prevent employers from poaching each others' employees. As a cheap means of dealing with the labour-shortage problem and the difficulty of keeping skilled workers (i.e. without raising wages) this had an obvious appeal to employers except to those who were paying high wages and doing rather well in the competition, or those who had a sophisticated ideological commitment to free-market *laissez-faire* capitalism. One man on the frontier between business and government, a director of the Industrial Bank, explained how these measures might help to build the new pattern of industrial relations. 'The object is to try as far as possible to maintain, or as far as possible to establish even in the big factories the family-like relationships which we have at present in Japan, so that we can prevent the kind of antagonism between capitalists and workers which results in such things as strikes.' He adds, interestingly, that there is a better chance of establishing such socially responsible patterns of management in Japan than elsewhere because there was, in the typical Japanese company, a greater divorce between ownership and control than was to be found in the one-man enterprises of the West. 'Consequently they have a tendency to seek not simply the profits of the shareholders, but also to be able to seek the profit of the company as a whole.'[13]

It was pre-eminently firms in the textile sector with its predominantly female labour force that made the earliest experiments in building up 'family-like relationships' on a corporate scale. If the engineering establishments like Yokosuka provided many of the bureaucratic

[11] From the 1898 meeting, p. 194.
[12] Kaneko Kentarō, 1896 meeting, p. 53.
[13] Shimura Gentarō, 1898 meeting, p. 106.

work-organization ingredients of the Japanese system, the textile factories provided the extra-factory welfare elements, the uplift, and the ideology. This is not, perhaps, surprising. Adolescent girls are more likely to stimulate paternal proclivities in tough employers than adult male engineering workers.

It was some time, however, before the profit motive sought the support of such magnanimous instincts. While there were doubtless always a number of personally paternalistic small employers in the silk-reeling and cotton-spinning establishments, larger firms had often adopted quite different methods. The problem they faced in common, after the rapid expansion of the industry by 1890, was a shortage of labour. There was not an endless supply of 13-year-old farmgirls willing to be persuaded, by cash advances to their parents, to give five years of their life to a textile factory with about equal chances of ending with a small dowry or a mortal dose of tuberculosis. Recruiting costs rose, despite non-poaching demarcation agreements between employers who divided the villages of their hinterland between them. Higher recruiting costs were compensated for by longer hours of work.

'The consequences of the steps taken by the employers were, however, that in addition to ill health and accidents induced by long hours of intensified labour under poor working conditions, the workers' efficiency was reduced because of absenteeism, sabotage, strikes and, in many cases, desertions. With deterioration of employee morale, the employers turned more and more to coercive measures to increase production. The measures entailed greater expenses for supervision and policing, which offset low wages and cheap facilities. At the same time recruitment expenses increased in the countryside, for the misery of factory life, which became known through rumours, agitation or from the workers who returned home sick and disabled, raised the psychological cost of transfer from farm to factory. Thus actions taken in the hope of reducing labour costs in the short run proved self-defeating in the long run.'[14]

'We textile manufacturers are much misunderstood', said Mutō Sanji, president of one of Japan's largest spinning firms (a Mitsui enterprise), in February 1902.

'We are constantly under attack. Recently we have seen the appearance of a group of people calling themselves Socialists who claim that we are cruelly treating the operatives in our factory. . . . The government authorities are talking of the need for a factory act

[14] Taira, op. cit., pp. 108–9.

that will regulate hours and seek to interfere in all sorts of ways on the grounds of hygiene or educational need. . . .'[15]

Three months later the same Mutō instituted the first of, according to one historian's count, thirty-nine separate welfare measures designed to create the firm-as-extended-family system of the Kanegafuchi spinning company. Already it had something of a reputation as a progressive firm. Breaking into the Kobe area with a new factory in 1896 it had been forced to attract labour by paying wages above the rate agreed by the local manufacturers association, and had refused to join the association when pressed. The firm was already spending the princely sum of 50 yen a year on morally improving lectures and lantern shows for its girls, and had a room in the dormitories for sewing classes, and also something of a sick bay. But the new measures instituted in the years 1902–7 were part of a new, deliberately innovative and single-minded strategy – to get higher profits (and, doubtless, to head off the clamant socialists and government officials) not by making the workers fear and respect the firm, or by appeal only to their material instincts, but by implanting in them a spirit of affection and gratitude to the firm and its president.

Not all the institutional devices were by any means *original* inventions. Mutō claims to have found the inspiration for many of his plans in Krupp and the National Cash Register Corporation.

They included a crèche for working mothers, a workshop environment improvement fund with a claim to a percentage share of profits, much improved bathing and recreational facilities in the dormitories, an improved company housing scheme for married employees, subsidized consumer co-operatives for those living in company houses, a suggestions scheme, a complaint box grievance procedure (*not* for anonymous complaints, however), a company news sheet (distributed also to the home villages from which the girls were recruited), a separate girls' magazine for the younger operatives, a kindergarten to absorb the noisy children of night workers who needed to sleep in the daytime, well endowed schools for girl operatives (teaching regular school subjects to the younger ones and the womanly arts to the older), an apprentice training school for male maintenance workers, and a sick pay, pension and welfare fund (modelled on Krupp's) covering, for example, funeral expenses for members of the workers' family, paid for by equal contributions from the worker and the firm.

Slowly these innovations spread – from the textile firms to other

[15] Hazama, op. cit., p. 310. This account of the Kanegafuchi reforms is taken from Hazama, pp. 311–17.

branches of industry including engineering.[16] So, too, did the ideology. Those who had spoken earlier of the roots of Japanese industrial relations in Japan's noble ethical traditions had never been clear which of the five 'basic human relationships' of neo-Confucianism formed the relevant paradigm – the father-son relation or the master-servant relation. As the ideology began to crystallize in the first decade of this century, however, there was no longer any doubt that the family relationship offered the most 'bite'. Again a government concern played an important vanguard role; after railways were nationalized in 1906 the new corporation soon developed the clan-like characteristics for which it is still famous. The Minister of Communications (1908–11) largely responsible for these policies explained in a speech:

> '. . . all railroad workers should help and encourage one another as though they were members of one family. A family should follow the orders of the family head and, in doing what he expects of them, always act for the honour and benefit of the family. I attempt to foster among my 90,000 employees the idea of self-sacrificing devotion to their work. I also preach the principle of loving trust. . . .'[17]

THE FINISHING TOUCHES

The shape of employment systems to come was already becoming clear in the first decade of this century. It remains to list briefly some of the main factors which led from these beginnings to the final crystallization of pre-war corporate paternalism in the decade around 1920, and thence to the welfare corporatism of the present day.

1. The most important was the great acceleration in the pace of Japanese industrialization during the First World War, the accompanying shortage of workers, the growth of worker organization, inflation and the increasing resort to strikes. These greatly increased the attractiveness of measures designed to stabilize and to evoke loyalty in the workforce.

2. The strikes, followed in 1918 by the Rice Riots and increasing tenancy unrest, prompted a series of measures by the government and the related official, educational and industrial wings of the new Japanese establishment, to counter the appearance of dangerous divisions in society. Their aim was partly to repress (preferably by didactic, but when necessary by coercive methods) partly judiciously

---

[16] Hazama, op. cit., p. 525.
[17] Gotō Shōijrō, quoted in B. K. Marshall, op. cit., p. 72.

to *accommodate* the claims of the ordinary Japanese citizen to have more control over his fate. Like the eventual grant of universal manhood suffrage in 1925, the Conciliation Society played a large role in devising such modes of accommodation. It was founded in 1919, at about the same time as Britain's Industrial Welfare Society and with similar aims – though with much greater impact. Staffed by intelligent officials, whose reports often excoriated ruthless and unreasonable employers and landlords as much as turbulent and ungrateful workers and tenants, its industrial policy was largely concerned not only with promoting the new, firm-as-family ideology and all the welfare measures and systems which supported it, but also to the development of workers' councils and consultative committees as a means of co-opting the union movement within the structure, finding means of channelling grievances and enhancing commitment. Sham though many of these councils were, they were by no means all without substantive significance. They did represent a genuine step towards constitutional, and away from arbitrary management.[18]

3. The threat posed to employers by the growth in the union movement generally in the middle and late twenties helped in another way to reinforce the system. Wage patterns and the labour market situation were already such that, except in a very small number of trades like printing, the enterprise unit rather than craft groups proved the natural basis of organization, thus, in a sense, reinforcing enterprise consciousness.

4. One further means of 'binding' workers to the firm, of strengthening their identification with it, was to extend to them the sort of twice-yearly bonus provisions – related to the profits of the firm – hitherto reserved for staff workers. (Many of the other welfare and security measures, too, of course, could be seen as extensions downwards of patterns which developed in the staff grades of the big firms.)

5. Secular trends affected the character and ideology of both managers and workers. As for workers, a union organizer in the 1890s (see p. 387) had pointed to the difference between the sycophantic climber who stayed with the firm and the mobile skilled confident craftsman. More universally prolonged primary education, with its inculcation of foresight and prudence, the gradual penetration, as living levels slowly rose, of the bourgeois values of security and the desire for a settled family life, reduced the proportion in the

---

[18] See G. O. Totten, 'Collective Bargaining and Works Councils as Innovations in Industrial Relations in Japan During the 1920s', in R. P. Dore (ed.), *Aspects of Social Change in Modern Japan*, 1967, and Hyōdō, op. cit., pp. 367–403.

workforce of the tough self-confident 'travellers' apt to boast like the old Edo artisan, that they 'never carried money over from one day to the next'. The key period, of dramatic falls in separation rates, was the first half of the 1920s. In the Kobe shipyards, for instance, the separation rate fell from nearly 60% p.a. in 1919 to less than 10% in 1926.[19]

Among managers, too, the proportion of graduate employee managers increased and the proportion of entrepreneur managers decreased. The new breed was a smoother, less aggressive type, of a calculating and manipulative rather than tough coercive bent – the sort of managers, in fact, like Mutō of Kanegafuchi or Minomura of Mitsui, who had been responsible for the original innovations which created the Japanese system.[20] It was not just that a new breed of men were in control – they were also in a structurally different situation as the big *zaibatsu* conglomerates owned an increasing share of manufacturing industry. They were career managers in an industrial bureaucracy – and a bureaucracy, at that, which was becoming, by its own processes of internal elaboration, steadily more bureaucratic.[21]

6. Another essential element in the development of 'the system' was the emergence of considerable wage differentials between large and small firms. The available statistics seem to show that in the first decade of the century the average small firm paid wages not so much smaller than the average large firm. Figures for 1909 suggest that employees in firms with four to nine workers received about 88% of the average wage of workers in firms with over a thousand employees. This is the sort of differential found in Western industrial countries today. By 1914 the differentials had slightly widened as the large firms put up their shutters against the market; by the 1930s decisively so. Differentials then reached the ratios maintained in the 1950s. Union activity in large firms may have been one contributing factor; the depression was another. In the labour-market-oriented small firms wages fell, while institutional rigidities kept them higher in the large enterprises. In those firms the answer to the depression was dismissal – though by this time chiefly of temporary workers. See below.[22]

7. The last point indicates another feature which became generally institutionalized in this period – the temporary/permanent worker division. It had (p. 381) already appeared in a rudimentary form in

[19] Hyōdō, op. cit., p. 405.
[20] Taira, op. cit., p. 101.
[21] Hazama, op. cit., p. 488.
[22] Taira, op. cit., pp. 175–7; Hyōdō, op. cit., pp. 473–6.

Yokosuka in the 1870s. It was an inevitable consequence of the development of an organization-oriented employment system, offering workers long-term career prospects, pensions and welfare measures designed to provide long-term work incentives, in an economy very much subject to short-term business fluctuations. Temporary workers, not admitted to the enterprise family, enjoying none of the privileges of the permanent workforce and dismissible whenever times were bad, offered the necessary flexibility.[23]

8. The final crucial element in the structure was the practice of hiring new recruits exclusively, or almost exclusively, from young school leavers. Where incremental scales are conventionally age-related – as they inevitably came to be – there is an obvious rationality in preferring a young recruit who can be put at the bottom of the scale to an older one who has to be fitted higher up, if both are equally without relevant training. It was a long time, however, before employers came to prefer to recruit a 15-year-old and train him rather than to recruit an already-skilled man from the market. That happened only when: (a) other large employers became more successful in holding on to workers who were already trained so that there were fewer seeking jobs in the market; (b) technology becoming diverse and complex employers needed more specific skills; (c) the ideology developed its own independent momentum and reinforced the value placed on loyalty and long service and being 'born into' the firm at a normal early age; (d) more directly, the need to preach loyalty to counter left-wing ideas placed a premium on catching workers young enough for 'spiritual education' to 'take'; (e) the cultural unity of the country, and the standards of literacy and epistolary skill, reached the point at which recruitment of the very young from rural areas to urban factories became easy; and (f) the period of schooling lengthened so that it became reasonable to move straight from school to factory and the schools became obvious recruiting grounds.

The 1920s were the crucial period in this respect too. Annual April recruitment of new school-leavers (those who had had their six years of compulsory plus two years of non-compulsory upper-primary education) started at the Kure shipyards in 1919 and at Mitsubishi's Nagasaki yards a year later.[24] Other firms soon followed suit. This was also the crucial period for another related development – a big expansion of enterprise training schools. One after the other leading firms started schools in the decade after 1918, abandoning any further

---

[23] Hyōdō, op. cit., pp. 428–30; Hazama, op. cit., pp. 495–9.
[24] Hyōdō, op. cit., p. 421.

reliance on farming out their apprentices – for less adequate and specialized training – to public night-schools.[25]

Thus was the pre-war pattern of corporate paternalism established. It was in some respects reinforced, in others transmuted – sufficiently so for 'welfare corporatism' now to be a more appropriate name – in the late forties. Many of these changes have been mentioned earlier in this book.

1. First, the drastic decline in production levels and in real wages in the aftermath of the war wrenched the wage system even further away from market principles than it had been. The new unions and management were prepared to agree that the only fair way to distribute starvation wages was in rough relation to the number of people in danger of starving. Hence large portions of the wage bill reserved for family allowances; hence a reinforcement of seniority scales because they roughly related wages to a rising scale of family responsibilities.

2. Given the strength of enterprise consciousness and the absence of a market-based wage system, it was inevitable that when powerful unions developed they should have been *enterprise* unions. They played a powerful role in entrenching the system (a) by being able to demand and fight for security of employment, and (b) by their very existence reinforcing enterprise consciousness.

3. And also by effecting a change in the system which made it viable in a country now officially based on a democratic ideology rather than an authoritarian one – i.e. by greatly reducing the status distinctions and the differences in security and material privilege between manual and staff workers, by taking a share in the administration of welfare schemes, by bargaining hard over wages, and generally by giving the system a big push in the direction in which the Conciliation Society had been nudging it in the 1920s – towards constitutional management. Post-war management ideology dropped the firm-as-family motif, and while still stressing group identity dwelt more on collateral solidarity than on vertical ties of loyalty.

4. The powerful bargaining strength of unions in the large efficient firms made it possible for them to push wages up against the limit of 'capacity to pay' and thus maintained wide differentials in *average* wages between them and the small less efficient firms with no unions or only weak ones. This had the further effect of enhancing the

[25] Ibid., p. 407.

attractiveness of the large firms and the willingness of young school leavers to enter them for very low starting wages – which in turn reinforced the steepening of the age/wage progression.

We can now give an answer to the questions with which we began this chapter.

Some, but on the whole, very few, of the features of 'the Japanese system' are the result of direct continuity from the feudal period – of institutional inertia, the continuance from unconscious habit of certain patterns of behaviour. Formal practices like the year-end and mid-summer bonuses come into this category, so do the patronage relations between master-craftman and journeyman, transmuted into the 'diffuse' relationship of foreman and worker in the modern factory.

Some elements, like the permanent/temporary worker division or incremental wage scales (and perhaps even the bonuses put in the last category) are the result of conscious adaptation of earlier *employment* patterns.

Some features, like the collective responsibility of work-groups, or like many of the patterns of bureaucratic organization, are conscious adaptations to industry of institutional forms developed in the feudal period *outside* of industry – primarily in the Samurai bureaucracies of the fiefs and of the central government.

Some features are consciously borrowed from abroad – like the National Cash Register's news-sheet and the Krupps-style welfare fund.

Some features, like many of the innovations in wage systems, seem to be wholly indigenous inventions.

If, then, institutional inertia is only a small part of the explanation for the system compared with the cumulation of many innovative acts of conscious choice, the next question to ask is why did Japanese industrialists make certain kinds of choices.

A possible answer: because of their ideology, because of the Confucian world view inherited from the Tokokugawa period, modified only by its adaptation to the exigencies of a modernizing 'new state'. It is not a bad answer. Ideology was relevant in at least three ways.

First, the modified Confucian world-view which prevailed in late nineteenth-century Japan assumed original virtue rather than original sin. Confucianists in positions of authority – whether in Tokugawa Samurai bureaucracies, in Japanese nineteenth-century railway workshops, or in modern Peking party offices – have been rather less predisposed than their Western counterparts to see their subordinates as donkeys responsive to sticks and carrots, and more disposed to see them as human beings responsive to moral appeals. Japanese industrialists' view of man (like Robert Owen's, for that matter) made them believe in the *efficiency* of benevolence in evoking loyalty, and of trust in evoking responsibility. This clearly, for any given set of objectives, predisposed them to certain choices of means rather than others.

Secondly, it helped *shape* some of those objectives. Among the things that private industrialists and managers of government corporations wanted was to appear in the eyes of their fellow countrymen as good moral citizens – particuarly when businessmen were having a hard time raising their social status relative to that of civil and military servants of the state.[26] Given the ideology of the time, the image to which they had to conform was that of the benevolent paternalist, the *leader* of a large workforce in the campaign to make the country strong, not the exploiter of others for purely selfish purposes. Mere ostentatious wealth, with a reputation for the forcefulness and intelligence which had earned it, were not enough to secure the highest reputations in Japanese society.

Thirdly, the ideology affected the relative weights that industrialists and managers gave to *different* objectives. They were concerned with their public reputation, but they were also concerned with profits, with expansion of the enterprise, or with (in the case of managers of the state concerns) efficient organization as an end in itself. The fact that their ideology was one which emphasized honour and respect compared with other satisfactions, perhaps led them to put greater weight on the first of these concerns than do industrialists in most other societies.

But that is not to deny the very great importance of their concern with profits, with expansion, and with efficiency. It is a safe bet that they would have been most particularly well disposed towards innovations which not only enhanced their public image, but *also* contributed to greater efficiency, greater profits, faster expansion.

It seems, to judge from the record of GNP growth, that the system which was created *did* so contribute to efficiency, profits and growth. Their innovations were 'rational'. But why should 'rationality' have pointed to one kind of managerial policy in capitalist Japan, but to quite different kinds of policies in capitalist Britain? Was it because the *objects* on the receiving end of managerial policy – the workers, their values and attitudes – were different as between the two countries?

[26] See B. R. Marshall, op. cit., *passim*.

Partly, perhaps (see the first point made above about ideology) but that is far from the whole story. One needs to rephrase the question. Why should 'rationality' have pointed to one kind of managerial policy in capitalist Japan *in 1900–20 when the 'Japanese system' was becoming institutionalized*, and to quite different kinds of policies in capitalist Britain *in the mid-nineteenth century when British employment institutions and industrial relations were becoming institutionalized*?

Because between, say, 1850 and 1920 the world had changed in significant ways; because the objective structure of opportunities and constraints, and hence the means by which profits and growth can be maximized, can never be the same for the late developer as they were for the early developer.

It is to the possibility of formulating a typical 'late development pattern' of industrial relations that the next and final chapter is devoted.

Chapter 15

Late Development

'The basic principle of the nineteenth-century British private enterprise economy was to buy in the cheapest market and to sell in the dearest. For the employer to buy labour in the cheapest market implied buying it at the lowest rate per unit of output; i.e. to buy the cheapest labour at the highest productivity. Conversely, for the worker to sell his labour in the dearest market meant logically to sell it at the highest minimum price for the minimum unit of output.[1]

To be sure, as Hobsbawm goes on to point out, this principle underlying all contemporary theorizing about the industrial situation was not completely assimilated by workers and employers 'as the rule of the game' until towards the end of the century, in the final stages of the Great Depression. Earlier it had been modified in practice by custom and convention – by notions of 'a fair day's work for a fair day's wage', of the need to provide a subsistence minimum, of a 'proper' skilled/unskilled differential, of paternalistic obligation, and of the duty of faithful service. But already by the middle of the century the 'new model' of unionism had developed all kinds of devices which assumed the dominance of market principles and were designed to improve the bargaining power of workers acting collectively in the market – restrictions on entry into the trade, unemployment benefits, emigration benefits, allowances which rationalized older tramping systems and helped workers to move from labour-surplus areas to labour-scarce areas, and so on. And by mid-century, the experience of market fluctuations was sufficiently ingrained for both employers and workmen often to prefer a shorter hiring period to a

[1] E. J. Hobsbawm, 'Custom, Wages and Work-load', in A. Briggs and J. Saville, *Essays in Labour History*, 1960, p. 113. Also in E. J. H., *Labouring Men*, 1964.

long one, so as to keep open their options for driving a better bargain if the market situation should change.[2]

Was there, then, no British employer who saw himself faced with the same problems as the innovating Japanese employers described in the last chapter, and none who sought to solve them by similar devices, similarly deviating from strict market principles? Far from it. At certain periods there were loud complaints of shortage of skilled workers; there were constant denunciations of the instability and unreliability of the work force. A number of individual 'progressive employers' reacted to such problems by experimenting with institutional devices very similar to those which became standard in Japan. But there were never *enough* of them to make any impact on the system as a whole – until, as Chapter 13 has suggested, the last decade.

The early tentative moves in this direction were of several kinds. There were, to begin with, 'traditional paternalists' in the terms of Chapter 10 – employers who 'looked after' their workers, meeting family crises with (discretionary) private charity, building schools for their children, and hospitals and churches for the (usually small, one-factory-town) communities in which they lived. Such was the enterprise of the Quaker Bright family in Rochdale,[3] which may well have been the one with the touchingly 'near-feudal' relation between master and man held up as a model for Japanese employers in the 1898 debates in Tokyo (see p. 391). Such, too, across the Atlantic, were the cotton mills of New England which in many respects treated their girls in much the same way as Japanese employers were to do later in the century.

And already, before the end of the eighteenth century, there was a beginning of non-discretionary rule-bound enterprise welfare. Boulton and Watt, for example, the makers of steam engines, as well as pioneering apprentice schemes, taking their workers on outings and 'looking after' senior and experienced workers with special wage increments, also set up a contributory sickness insurance fund for their workers[4] – a move towards welfare 'as of right' rather than from benevolence. Robert Owen's paternalism, though if anything more authoritarian than Boulton's, since he saw himself as having a stern moral duty to direct his workers into virtuous paths, was also very

---

[2] Ibid., p. 121. Recall, also, the modern reluctance to put verbal agreements in writing. One imagines, though, that as, with experience, people began to recognize the pattern of the trade cycle there ought to have emerged a preference for long-term contracts by workers at the peaks and by employers at the troughs of the cycles.

[3] R. Bendix, *Work and Authority in Industry*, Harper Torchbook edn., 1963, p. 49.

[4] Eric Roll, *An Experiment in Industrial Organisation*, 1930, reprinted 1968.

much rule-prescribed as well as discretionary; his famous system of aggregating and rewarding good conduct marks was an example.

Owen's emphasis on rewards was one of his outstanding deviationist features. The part of tradition that most employers retained and codified was the stern paternalism of swingeing disciplinary regulations, the point of which for some employers was that they offered a means of reducing wages. Rewards tended to become assimilated into a contractual system of incentive payments little different from piecework. But other enterprises did retain systems of rewards and bonuses which were intended to have symbolic as well as material importance, and to bind men to the company 'by as many ties as possible' – the railways for instance.[5] Other means of stabilization were developed by employers who were concerned about the loss of skilled workers poached by other firms – especially in the early period of industrialization.[6] These remedies included long-term contracts,[7] mutual non-poaching agreements between companies and even, in 1840, a suggestion for legislation to establish a registry of servants somewhat similar to that proposed in the early drafts of the Japanese Factory Law.[8] The railways, which required skilled and responsible workmen and were not so bound by the fixed-price-for-equal-skills traditions of older trades, developed *de facto* seniority systems of promotion[9] and even of wage increments within grades. They frequently housed their workers too, as, of course, did many other employers.[10] At the end of the century some of the gas companies, jolted out of their complacency by a wave of labour troubles, tried to outbid the unions with co-partnership schemes.[11]

But most of these embryonic trends were aborted. Boulton and Watt's successors swept away the insurance scheme as part of their moves to rationalize the business – moves which included the development of piecework systems for steam-engine building as a means both of labour control and of unit cost accounting. Robert Owen, though about the only 'progressive' employer who bothered to write about his methods and actually *advocate* them as part of a consistent philosophy, had few imitators and, indeed, many implacable enemies. Ideas for a registry of servants made no headway; it was,

[5] P. W. Kingsford, *Victorian Railwaymen*, 1970, p. 28.
[6] S. Pollard, *The Genesis of Modern Management*, 1965, pp. 169 ff.
[7] Ibid., p. 191.
[8] Kingsford, op. cit., p. 11.
[9] Ibid., p. 145.
[10] Pollard, op. cit., p. 200.
[11] E. J. Hobsbawm, 'British Gas Workers 1873–1914', in *Labouring Men*, 1964, p. 171.

indeed, given the prevailing market philosophy, hard among manufacturers to stir up any genuine indignation against 'poaching' unless
it actually clearly involved the capture of technical secrets.[12] The
seniority system on the railways was entrenched in large measure as a
result of union pressure, not as a result of management policy.
Employers were reluctant to admit mere length of service as a justification for promotion or an increase in wages and sought to insist
that they could be justified only by a real change in the nature or
quality of services rendered – otherwise, said one management in
1868, pay 'will cease to be measured by the natural relations of supply
and demand, and will be raised from time to time upon conventional
feelings to a standard more than the market value of the services
rendered'.[13] So few were the employers who saw their housing scheme
or their works farm and dairy, or their factory provision shop as a
means of improving their workers' health and comfort, or as a means
of earning gratitude for their benevolence; so many saw it as yet
another market relation with their workers in which they could ex-
ploit their superior bargaining power for all it was worth and, in
Alfred Marshall's words, get 'back by underhand ways part of the
wages which they nominally paid away',[14] that the employer's
tommy shop and the tied cottage became for trade unions something
to be entirely abolished, not something to be improved. Co-partnership persisted in some gas companies until nationalization, but made
little difference to their employment patterns in other respects.

In Japan a sufficient number of firms in a sufficiently dominant
position deviated far enough from market principles of employment
to form a 'critical mass' capable of changing the character of the
system as a whole. In Britain, on the other hand, the deviants were
few and of feeble influence: the market principle won. Let us list
some of the factors which explain that difference. The relevant time-
periods considered are roughly Japan from 1880 to 1930 and Britain
in the first three-quarters of the nineteenth century.[15]

---

[12] Pollard, op. cit., p. 169.
[13] Kingsford, op. cit., p. 145.
[14] G. W. Hilton, *The Truck System*, 1960.
[15] No strictly comparable phasing is possible, of course, since Japan did *not*
repeat Britain's history. Some of the obvious growth indicators of levels of
industrialization do not move together. Britain, for example, had less than 40%
of employed males in agriculture well before the end of the eighteenth century.
In Japan that point was reached in the 1930s, by which time Japan had nearly
10% of employed males in the metal trades, a point which Britain did not reach
until after 1850. Textile workers made up 24% of the total labour force in Britain
according to the 1856 census. They never reached 10% in Japan.

407

RELEVANT DIFFERENCES

1. In contrast to the Confucian ideology discussed in the last chapter, the ideology of market individualism was already deeply entrenched in Britain *before* industrialization began. It was the Communist Manifesto, echoing the words of Carlyle a decade earlier, which made famous the phrase 'cash nexus' to describe the only thing that remained to bind employer and employee, but already, half a century before that, Adam Smith was speaking most naturally of labour as a commodity like any other commodity, differing only in that the long-term effect of its price on supply was *more* long-term than for most other commodities since it operated through the Malthusian checks on the one hand, and earlier marriage and healthier breeding on the other. Legislative attempts to keep the employment relation market-pure and unencumbered by the paternalistic trickery of payment in kind were already three and a half centuries old before the industrial revolution began. The earliest statutory prohibitions of truck payments go back to 1411.[16]

The difference in prevailing ideologies between the two countries correlates clearly with differences in pre-industrial economic organization. Agriculture and handicrafts remained in Japan a family affair to which the Confucian ideology was well adapted: British agriculture was already largely organized on a capitalist basis with a thriving market in free wage labour well before industrialization began. It is not surprising that the market principle became deeply entrenched, not only in the theories of Scottish economists, but also in the everyday expectations and assumptions of those who bought and sold labour.

2. A more specific aspect of the last point is the very wide spread of the putting-out system in British industry before and in the early days of the industrial revolution. The piecework pattern of payment survived its transformation into a factory system and this doubtless helps explain the prevalence of this form of wage payment – so much the purest expression of the market principle that Marx saw it as the system best suited to capitalism.[17] Putting-out manufacturing was not so highly developed in nineteenth-century Japan. Above all there is no gradual transition to factory production. The new factories brought in new technology and new organization, very often in quite different locations from the cottage industry areas.

3. A *laissez-faire* market economy is an individualistic economy.

[16] G. W. Hilton, *The Truck System*, p. 64.
[17] E. J. Hobsbawm, 'Custom, Wages and Work-load', p. 131.

Once the bonds of fief, of manor, of guild and corporation are loosened, the political and the economic community are separated. Economically the individual is atomistically alone in the national market. 'The free man', said the Revd. Joseph Townsend, in the famous pamphlet in which he spoke of hunger as the necessary, peaceable and silent stimulus to useful labour, 'should be left to his own judgement and discretion'.[18] If he cannot survive it is to the politically defined community that he turns, not to the enterprise, for the new enterprise is not a politico-economic unit as the old guild was; it is an economic enterprise *tout court*. The survival of an interventionist philosophy in the political sphere (for the victory of *laissez faire* thinking was never complete in England)[19] in fact facilitated the adoption of impersonal market individualism in the economic sphere proper. The Speenhamland system forcefully illustrated both the new assumption that securing a subsistence minimum was not the business of the employer but of the local political community, and also the fact that the political community was prepared to accept these responsibilities. Soon after, foreshadowing Britain's slow transition from benevolently paternalist interventionism to a more egalitarian collectivism, workers began increasingly to re-create new communities, in friendly societies and trade unions, based on similarity of interest in the market rather than on association in the place of work. By the 1830s Britain already had, in the Corn Law League and the Chartists, formal political organizations self-consciously representative of different social classes.[20]

Hence, unlike the much more 'cellular' society of Japan at the turn of the century where charity and paternalistic duty were expected to begin at home among one's own employees and subordinates, in Britain discussion of the duty of the higher classes to the lower had already shifted onto the plane of national politics centring around Poor Laws and Factory Acts, hospitals, and later, state pension schemes. Not local, but national collectivist solutions were sought to the problem of insecurity and misery. The Owenite impulse was carried forward to the search not for new management styles but to legislative solutions; the thought that welfare and security were the state's job absolved employers from action and left their consciences clean.

[18] *A Dissertation on the Poor Laws by a Well-wisher of Mankind*, 1786, quoted in Bendix, op. cit., p. 74.

[19] For helping to sort out my ideas on this score I am indebted to Barry Supple and to his 'Legislation and Virtue: an Essay on Working-class Self-help and the State in the Early Nineteenth-Century.' (mimeo.)

[20] A. Briggs, 'The Language of "Class" in Early Nineteenth-Century England', in A. Briggs and J. Saville, op. cit., pp. 66–9.

4. The battles fought at this political level over the development of social legislation not only changed Britain, they also, when conjoined with other similar battles fought in Europe and America, changed the world. The fact that Japan started industrialization 'late' is all important. Ideologies are not confined within frontiers. There are such things as world 'norms' concerning the range of employment relations which are feasible and desirable. Nowadays these norms are codified in conventions and resolutions of the International Labour Organization. In the nineteenth century they were much more diffusely defined, but still real, as the slow progress of the abolition of slavery demonstrated. These norms were very different in the first decade of this century when Japan's industrial institutions were taking shape from what they had been in Britain's industrial infancy a century earlier.

Over-schematizing one might summarize as follows. Free market principles of employment have a natural appeal to employers in a world where unions do not exist or are prohibited by law. They become less attractive to employers when trade unions win their right to exist and so severely limit the employer's bargaining superiority. But by the time this happened in Britain, by the time employers began to have material incentives for seeking alternatives, the existing market principles were so firmly entrenched – and so reinforced by the pattern of trade unionism itself – that change was difficult. Employers had, in any case, lost their power unilaterally to change institutions without the co-operation of the unions.

Japanese employers, on the other hand, could see the writing more clearly on the wall. The inevitability of strikes and class conflict is occasionally predicted – though not always accepted – in the debates over factory legislation in the last decade of the nineteenth century. A decade and a half later there was little doubt as to what was in store. By 1922, when employment relations were still in a fluid state, international respectability required Japan to give trade unions an accepted place in the political firmament by allowing them to choose a representative to attend the Conference of the ILO. Japanese employers, therefore, knew that they had to live with unions at an early stage; they were able to adjust to that future prospect by institutional innovations *before* the unions became so strong that their options were foreclosed – while they still had a large measure of control over the situation.

5. Universal primary schooling was a late development in the history of British industrialization. Japan, by contrast, had probably 90% of its boys attending standardized and reasonably efficient

primary schools at the beginning of this century, at a time when there were still fewer than eighty factories employing more than five hundred workers. Preferential employment of young school leavers was an option open to early Japanese industrialists more clearly than to their earlier English counterparts. It is not surprising that they should have taken it. All questions of literacy and numeracy apart, the schools had disciplined the new generation to habits of time-keeping and steady application which their parents often lacked. The schools provided convenient recruiting grounds where teachers' reports, school records and later the firm's own dexterity and intelligence tests could *select* recruits and make sure that the big firms like Mitsubishi which pioneered school-leaver recruitment could cream off each age group. 'Creaming-off' was possible because although there was a shortage of skilled workers and of girl school-leavers willing to enter textile factories, there was never a shortage of boy school-leavers, and the big firms from an early stage offered better employment prospects and so could attract the cream.

6. The differential development of industry and education is part of the late-development effect. Late-developing societies generally find it easier to build a modern educational system than to build a modern manufacturing industry. One might also consider it as typical of the late-development syndrome that Japan developed a modern industry *without* the slow penetration of capitalist wage relationships in agriculture which preceded Britain's industrial revolution. Japan's agriculture has remained a structure of *family* holdings employing little wage labour. Add to the picture: (a) primogeniture inheritance, (b) the fact that, with the average size of holding down to two acres, the available land was already filled up, and (c) the fact that improved public health and nutrition enhanced the survival chances of children. More families had surviving, non-inheriting younger sons. The opportunities for younger sons to be adopted into existing land-holding families which lacked heirs also diminished. Younger sons, therefore, were increasingly marked out from childhood as destined to leave the village. They came on the market at the end of their schooling conditioned to look not for a few years' work with the hope of returning to the village, but for a career – and ready to accept low wages for the guarantee of good prospects. The fact that the culture of the Japanese peasant family in which they grew up was already a quite economically rational one, calculating to *long* time horizons, reinforced these preferences.

7. Another likely reason why Japanese employers were more prone than their earlier British counterparts to be attracted to the idea of

411

recruiting youngsters is because they were more likely to have to do their own training anyway. Late developing Japan imported the latest nineteenth century and twentieth century techniques into a society where traditional artisan skills resembled those of sixteenth or seventeenth century Europe. Japan had to make a technological leap – whereas Britain made a shuffling technological advance. The smooth progression from the artisan skills of eighteenth-century Britain to the factory engineering skills of the next century is reflected in the continuity of apprenticeship systems and modes of skill certification throughout the transition from guilds to unions. New inventions came gradually and in penny packages; the workmen acquired the new skills they involved as a topping up of their existing skills, and passed them on to their successors. In Japan there was little such continuity. In the shipyards, the traditional-style caulkers could be upgraded to handle the new imported techniques, but iron-using shipwrights had to be trained from scratch – and only the employer could do it.

This is, to be sure, a difference of degree. Some British advances were *big* advances. When Boulton and Watt started making their steam-engines in Birmingham they sent agents and letters to Liverpool and Manchester and Cornwall to recruit watchmakers and tool-makers and turners and moulders.[21] They *naturally* turned to the market to fill their needs, but found that it was difficult to upgrade the workers they recruited to cope with the finer tolerances they required. They finally developed their own seven-year apprenticeships to fill the gaps. But such situations were exceptional in Britain: very common in the more discontinuous, compressed technological development of Japan.

8. Another difference explains why – quite apart from the problems of initial introduction of new techniques – worker-to-worker transmission of techniques through informal apprenticeship systems was less adequate in Japan than in Britain to satisfy the demands of industry: Japanese industry expanded faster than Britain's.[22]

[21] See Pollard, op. cit., p. 170.

[22] If one takes overall estimates of growth rates in manufacturing, mining and building as an index, the most easily available comparisons are between compound annual growth rates for (overlapping) 30-year periods in England and for consecutive five-year periods in Japan. The British figures range between 2·7 and 4·7 for 1801–1901 (crude average: 3·3); the Japanese figures range between 2·9 and 8·6 (crude average: 6·3). In terms of employment, the growth in the number of factory workers (in registered establishments with more than ten workers) was at an average compound rate of 4·9% in Japan between 1886 and 1920. In Britain, between 1835 and 1874 factory employment in the cotton and woollen industries increased at a rate of 3·4% per annum. Okawa Kazushi *et al.*, *Nihon keizai no*

9. Just as important, perhaps, is the fact that Japanese industry grew more steadily.[23] The cycles of boom and slump were not so lengthy; the troughs not so deep, their effect in tempering optimism about the prospects of long-term growth not so devastating. Japan, like all follower countries, knew better where she was going. The present of the more advanced countries offered an image of her future.

Let us twist some of these strands together. The Japanese employer had reasons for recruiting young school-leavers and training them that the British manufacturer hadn't – their easy availability, their cheapness, their disciplined willingness to learn, and the fact that, because of the technological leap and the faster rate of growth, the market could not provide for his needs so that he would have to do his own training anyway. His experience of steadier growth made him more optimistic about the future: he could calculate that if he invested in training and devised schemes to keep his workers in order to recoup his investment, market conditions would be likely to *allow* him to keep them fully occupied. Seniority scales and other long-term incentives followed naturally – and were that much easier to afford since the young workers, competing for entry into the firms which offered good prospects, were hirable at such low initial wages.

10. There is another possible factor in the willingness to pay seniority premiums and to spend money on welfare facilities, etc. The Japanese engineering industry started late, with more advanced capital-intensive technology than the early British industry, using expensive imported machines. It is probable – though there are no decisive figures to prove it – that labour costs represented a smaller proportion of total costs for the average Japanese manufacturer than for the average British manufacturer at a comparable stage of development – despite some evidence that machines were lavishly

seichōritsu, 1955, pp. 21 and 83–5; B. R. Mitchell and P. Deane, *Abstract of British Historical Statistics*, reprinted 1971, pp. 188, 199; P. Deane and W. A. Cole, *British Economic Growth, 1688–1959*, 1962, p. 170.

[23] In only 12 of the 35 years 1886 to 1920 did the number of registered factory workers in Japan decline over the previous year; the declines were small and only once, when a fall of some 18% was spread over the period 1890–3 did they continue for more than one year (Okawa, op. cit., p. 83–5). Comparable British indexes are hard to find, but to take one easily to hand: in 19 of the 35 years from 1855 to 1889 the recorded production of iron ore fell below the previous year's total. This included three periods when the decline continued for three successive years, and the 5-year decline of the Great Depression – a fall of 27% from 1882 to 1887 (Mitchell and Deane, op. cit., p. 129). For other indicators of the amplitude of the British trade cycle – including the estimate of a 50% fall from peak to trough in the depression of the early 1840s, see W. W. Rostow, *The British Economy of the Nineteenth century*, 1948, p. 44.

over-manned.[24] A 5% increase in labour costs would therefore have less serious implications for the health of the business.

11. A further aspect of cost structure: leaving plant idle is more serious the higher the ratio of the loss incurred by leaving capital unutilized to the saving from not paying the wages of the worker who would otherwise have worked it. Hence absenteeism and high turnover were more seriously costly to the heavily capitalized Japanese employer who bought his machines from high-wage foreign countries and employed cheaper local labour. Hence a stronger incentive for him to find ways of 'stabilizing' even semi-skilled machine-minding workers.

12. The late starter begins with advanced production technology. He is also likely to start with advanced organizational technology. Another important difference – remarked on by Japanese contemporaries as a reason why Japan could develop more orderly employment practices (see p. 391) – was that whereas the owner-managed firm predominated in the British economy until an advanced stage, Japan was dominated by corporate organizations from the very beginning – and as the last chapter showed it was they which were responsible for the crucial innovations in the employment field. Some of these corporate organizations were state organizations where concern for profits was minimal: others were parts of the large Zaibatsu empires which increasingly dominated the private sector. The relevant features of these corporate organizations, as compared with owner-managed firms, were:

a. Their greater security of prospects, obvious in government enterprises, and in the Zaibatsu firms a consequence of their oligopolistic position in internal markets, the size of their financial resources, and their political influence. This security conduced to more long-term calculations of the costs and benefits of employment policies.

b. Their greater size – a necessary precondition for successfully operating a career structure for manual workers.

c. Their bureaucratic management structure – in the private firms no less than in the government enterprises partly because the former were modelled on the latter. The fact that the recruitment and promotion patterns which provided the career structure for managers were highly elaborated and entrenched at an early stage (unlike the nineteenth-century British pattern of market recruitment or family

[24] David Landes, 'Japan and Europe' in W. W. Lockwood (ed.), *The State and Economic Enterprise in Japan*, 1965, p. 117.

414

recruitment of managers) made it easier to extend those patterns to manual workers.

13. The dualism which developed in Japan's sponsored industrialization between the large bureaucratic capital-intensive firms which benefited from state sponsorship and the small private firms which did not, reflected a difference in capacity to pay which – as soon as trade union organization started – made enterprise unions, which could push each employer to the limit of his capacity to pay, a natural form of organization. Since the development of lifetime employment patterns preceded the development of effective trade unions, the enterprise form was the natural one anyway. The electrician in one firm who does not expect to be in the labour market again, has no great interest in the wages paid to electricians in other firms. A nineteenth-century Birmingham moulder who never knew when he would be stood off and looking to another small foundry for employment had every interest in the local market.

Another difference relevant to the pattern of trade unionism: British unions were created and achieved definite organizational shape at a time when they were anathema to employers; they therefore *had* to meet off the factory premises – often with secret society rituals. In the post-war period, when the Japanese union took shape, no employer dared question the unions' right to exist. They could organize openly on the premises. This also helped to make them workshop-based.

And, as has been pointed out several times before, the enterprise-based union serves very much to reinforce the whole employment system.

LATE AND LATER DEVELOPMENT

All these differences between Britain and Japan in particular can be generalized as differences between early developers and late developers in general – as part of a general late capitalist development syndrome. In fact, the later development takes place the more pronounced these late-starter characteristics are likely to be, the more marked the late development effect in industrial relations. The later industrialization begins:

– the less likely (see Gerschenkron on the psychology of backwardness[25]) that it will be dominated by a *laissez-faire* philosophy, the more likely that the state will play a predominant role,
– the less chance of any repetition of the slow evolution of putting-

[25] A. Gerschenkron, *Economic Backwardness in Historical Perspective*, Praeger paperback, 1965. The essay of that title.

out systems into factory systems or of a slow transformation of peasant into capitalist agriculture preceding industrialization,

– the more likely the development of school systems is to precede the development of a substantial manufacturing sector,

– the bigger the technological leap from traditional skills to those required by the new technology imported from the advanced countries,

– the bigger the organizational leap; the more likely industry is to *begin* with rationalized bureaucratic forms of organization including specialist personnel managers operating objective recruitment and promotion schemes – the more so if, as is likely, the state plays a direct role in the industrialization process through state corporations or partnership schemes,

– the more the norms diffused to the late starter from the industrialized countries are likely to stress the rights of trade unions and workers and the need to treat workers as human beings not as mere sellers of a commodity called labour. Corporations in the contemporary late-starter countries, sending their personnel officers to business schools in Europe and America, *begin* industrialization under the influence of human relations theories and Y-theories, and theories about the virtues of consultation with workshop representatives,

– the more secure the big firms (because the state cannot afford to let them collapse) and the more plan-oriented the management (partly as a result of the absorption of advanced-country business techniques) and the longer the time horizon for the cost-benefit calculation of personnel policies,

– the sharper the dualism between the big firm sector characterized above and the small firm sector, the more privileged the big sector workers, the more their unions are concerned with job security, and the more likely plant or enterprise-based organization.

It is not hard to find evidence for some of these propositions in the contemporary developing world. Whatever the structure of national trade unions, the effective units of labour organization are commonly plant or enterprise units. Except where governments intervene to control wage settlements, industrial bargaining is rare; plant or enterprise bargaining is the norm. Wage differentials between the big corporate firms and the more traditional sector are considerable. Seniority incremental scales are common.[26] Job security is not only a

[26] As a Nigerian government report put it, a few years after independence, 'persons in the wage-earning class, in the same way as persons in the salary earning class, are entitled to certain prospects in respect of their employment . . . a remuneration . . . sufficient to maintain an ever-increasing family. . . . A person

preoccupation of the unions; it is often heavily reinforced by the law. A distinction between 'permanent workers' and 'temporary workers' is very generally recognized in developing countries. Many firms provide extensive welfare facilities for their employees – including expatriate firms which provide less generous facilities in their home countries. Many run expensive training schemes.

Equally, one might find confirmation in the history of European industrialization. Germany, a later starter than Britain, has always had more organization-oriented, less market-oriented forms of employment than Britain. The post-war reconstruction built on and amplified these characteristics rather than simply creating them.[27] Even the United States, for all that its later industrialization was in most other respects, particularly the role of the state, quite dissimilar to that of Germany, did at least develop a pattern of trade union organization firmly based on the plant and enterprise rather than on the local market. In fact, there is a good case for saying that it is Britain rather than Japan which stands out as exceptional (and after all only one country *can* be the first to industrialize) in having such a thorough-going market-oriented pattern of employment.

THE PATTERN OF CAUSATION

In this chapter we have been concerned not with those features of the Japanese and British systems which seem clearly to owe a lot to the inertia of behaviour – different kinds of authority relations and different patterns of work group formation, for example – but with certain kinds of formal institutional innovations which were generally adopted in Japan and not generally adopted in England – and with the reasons for the difference. Attitudes and values, it was suggested at the end of the last chapter, clearly had something to do with it. First, the attitudes and values of workers in Japan probably made the innovations more likely to have their desired effect than they would have been if British workers were involved. Second, the attitudes and values and explicit ethic of Japanese employers was more congenial to those innovations; the institutions concerned seemed more in keeping with their basic sense of propriety than they would have done to their British counterparts.

who is engaged as a labourer should be given . . . a long scale with efficiency bars . . . to act as an inducement to greater effort, productivity and the inculcation of a sense of duty; more so as the Nigerian labour pool is increasingly going to be made up of school-leavers rather than illiterates as at present.' Government of Nigeria, *Commission on the Review of Wages, Salaries and Conditions of Service of the Junior Employees of the Government of the Federation and in Private Establishments*, The Morgan Commission, 1964, p. 8.

[27] R. Dahrendorf, *Society and Democracy in Germany*, 1968, chs. 11 and 12.

The present suggestion is that other factors also counted. These innovations were more likely to have *profitable* results for Japanese manufacturers at the turn of the century than for British manufacturers earlier for reasons quite beside the specifically national cultural predispositions of the workforce. These are reasons which have to do: (a) with the different structure of economic opportunities and constraints which the late-development situation presents, and (b) with differences in values – in the way people perceive and define their advantages – which derive not from differences in national character but from situational differences (e.g. being a graduate employee manager rather than a classical entrepreneur, or being a primary school graduate rather than an illiterate migrant from rural areas); these situational differences being *also* a consequence of the difference between early and late industrialization.

It is hard to say how *much* causal weight to attach to the different factors. A seniority wage system was both consonant with Japanese conceptions of age hierarchy, and also a rational means for employers to get the most out of their workers at least cost. Supposing there had not been such a neat coincidence? What about features that were culturally and ideologically congenial but not advantageous – or the other way around? Which consideration would have won?

Marxists and neo-classical economists ought in principle to agree that of course material interests would have won. In practice, the majority of economists on whom I have tried these ideas appear very reluctant to give up their assumption that the British market-oriented system is somehow 'normal' and the Japanese a curious deviation to be ascribed wholly to very special 'cultural factors'. Probably this is because the notion of a specific late-development effect casts doubt on the validity of all universal models either of economic growth or of rational labour market behaviour; it is just more comfortable to take it as self-evident that the Japanese are peculiar.

The matter is, however, open to empirical test – by examining in detail the employment systems of other developing societies in Africa and Asia and Latin-America which share (in even higher measure) the 'late development effect' with Japan, but have quite different cultural proclivites. This would show which are those elements of the Japanese-type organization-oriented system which offer such overwhelming advantages in the late developing situation that they are likely to be adopted whatever the ethical and ideological propensities of the society concerned, and which, by contrast, do not occur in other late-developers and can therefore be assumed to have required the extra push of cultural congeniality to cause the Japanese to adopt them.

But that is matter for another book.

CONVERGENCE

A final word to relate the discussion of the last two chapters to the conclusions of Chapter 13. Two main features – increasing organizational and technological complexity and the increasingly strong assumption of status-equality were credited in that chapter with shifting the British system 'in a Japanese direction'. They are, of course, features very closely linked to elements of the late development effect discussed above. And the last question asked – which of the features of the organization-oriented pattern of employment are so overwhelmingly 'rational' that they would 'take' in any late-starter situation and which not – is cognate with the question: how imperatively do the needs for handling complex technology and organization and for meeting demands for status equality impose identical institutional solutions on all advanced industrial economies, and how far do these 'prerequisites' shape the character of industrial societies.

Reflection on the histories of Britain and Japan helps to clarify the continuing sources of diversity. One, clearly, lies in the different pre-industrial histories of different countries. Even within the European cultural tradition and within the same capitalist bloc differences in the pre-industrial society remain clearly marked in the modern social structure – as between, say, Britain and Germany. These differences become more pronounced when one compares Japan – the only advanced industrial country whose traditional culture owed almost nothing to Mediterranean origins – with all the others which share the Judaeo-Graeco-Roman traditions.

Secondly, diversity springs from the exigencies of other overriding imperatives; the incidents of war and revolution, the ideological convictions of particular elite groups, the country's strategic role, its racial composition and the tension it generates, the size and resources of the country, its population density and all the other factors which affect the strength and direction of state control over the economy and the society.

The third source of diversity is the one which these last two chapters have highlighted. The way a country comes to industrialization can have a lasting effect on the kind of industrial society it becomes. It will be a long time before Britain loses the marks of the pioneer, the scars and stiffnesses that come from the searing experience of having made the first, most long-drawn-out industrial revolution. The slowness of the process gave time for the classes gradually to draw apart and over generations to develop their own quite separate cultures before the elite awoke to a realization of what was happening to the cohesion of their society and began grudgingly to accept a new collectivism. That is a legacy underlying many features of Modern Britain, like the antique inflexibility of her trade union institutions. It is a legacy which will be with us for some time to come, and which will continue to differentiate Britain from a society like Japan which jumped from a feudal form of corporatism to a modern form of enterprise corporatism without ever experiencing either the sturdy independence or the callous indifference to one's neighbour of a thorough-going *laissez-faire* market economy.

Appendix: The Interview Survey

For reasons explained in the foreword it was not possible to conduct the interview survey at the factories originally studied in Britain. The Glasgow boilermaker firm of Babcock & Wilcox and the Chelmsford factory of Marconi were substituted. In each British factory a random sample of weekly-paid workers (British-born in so far as origin could be identified) was drawn from employee records; in Japan from the corresponding manual worker grades. Reserve lists were prepared to substitute for non-contacts or refusals, but in Britain their use was subject to the constraint that the substitute had to belong to the same category – skilled, semi-skilled, labourer or apprentice – as the original sampled individual so that the balance of skill levels in the final sample continued to reflect that in the factory as a whole. (Skilled workers represented 41% in Babcock, 35% in Marconi and 31% in Appleby Frodingham according to the firms' classification, 55%, 52% and 37% respectively according to the respondents' own classification.) Similar control over adjustments was possible at the Hitachi factories using the upper, middle and lower bands of the skill-grading system, but not at the Yawata steel factory. Interviews were conducted between August and December 1969 at home in the evenings or at weekends, though at Hitachi some long-distance commuters were interviewed in a room at the trade union headquarters and at Yawata in a rented community hall near the works. Interviewers were N.O.P. staff interviewers in Britain; Professor Hazama and students under his direction in Japan. Each interview lasted between 40 and 100 minutes. Copies of the interview schedule may be obtained (at the cost of Xeroxing) from the author. Details of sample size and response rate are as follows. Non-contacts, which seem (though the records are not complete) to have been a higher proportion of failures at the other British firms than at Babcock's, were frequently due to the failure of employee records to record changes of address.

	Original sample	Refusals	Non-contacts	Sub-stitutes	Com-pleted	Usable
Engineering firms						
Babcock & Wilcox	150	29	17	43	147	147
Marconi	150	50		35	135	135
Furusato	150	34		30	146	146
Taga	150	39		30	141	141
Steel firms						
Appleby Frodingham	300	105		119	314	274
Yawata	300	72		60	288	288

421

Index

Abegglen, James 31
ability 70
absenteeism 26, 96, 188, 238, 243, 414
accountants 37, 43
AEF (Amalgamated Engineering Federation) 125, 131, 133, 155, 344, 346
affectivity 270, 274
affluence 21
Africa 12, 418
age 41
 of work force 31
 at first birth 34
 and authority 254
 see also seniority
aggressiveness 187
agriculture 246, 376, 411
A-level 46
alienation 87, 229, 277
All-Japan Seamen's Union 324
ambition 213
American Occupation Administration 115–19, 328
Appleby Frodingham 14
apprentices 72–3, 109, 322, 386
apprenticeship 55–9, 378, 386–9, 412
architecture 21
aristocracy 254
armaments 167
army 275, 338, 358
artisan 386
ASTMS (Assoc. of Supervisory Technical and Managerial Staffs) 129, 135, 363
ascription/achievement 270–2
assembly lines 26, 61, 92, 131, 245

AUEW (Amalgamated Union of Engineering Workers) see AEF
authority/authoritarianism 186, 188, 217, 219, 222–61, 358, 363, 381, 400
Azumi, K. 49, 294

Babcock & Wilcox 14, 160, 196
badge 24, 214, 257
bank capital 330–1
bargaining 108
Becker, G. 72
Bendix, R. 307, 405
benevolence 402
Bentley, F. R. 347
Berg, I. 47
Bescoby, J. 342, 353
Bolle de Bal, Marcel 349
bonding 387
bookishness 71
bonuses see wages
Bouglé, C. C. A. 10
Boulton, S. 405–6, 412
Bradford factory, general character 21–9
Bridlington agreement 344
Briggs A. 404, 409
Bright, J. 405
British Civil Service 68–9
British Institution of Mechanical Engineers 53
British Legion 275
British Leyland 338, 348, 353
British Steel Corporation 14
Broadbridge, S. 302–3
Brown, W. 348
Bugler, Jeremy 345

Myers, F. 354
my-home-ism 212, 221

Nakane, Chie 250
National Board for Prices and Incomes
82, 347, 349–50, 351, 354, 355,
356, 359
National Cash Register Corporation
395
national character 13, 212, 218, 237,
248, 296–8, 375, 419
National Coal Board 360
national income 330–1
National Movie and Theatre Workers'
Union 324
nationalism 22–3, 51, 275
naya system 379
Nelson, Lord 23, 127
New Year gifts 235
Nigeria 417
night-school 56
night work 97
Nippon Steel Corp. 14
Nissan Automobiles 328
Northcote-Trevelyan Report 229–30
Norwegians 218

Obama, Ritoku 392
Odaira, N. 23, 51
Odaka, K. 290
OECD 294
Oji Paper Works 328
Okawa, K. 412
Okōchi, Kazuo 195
Okurashō 267
O-level 54
organization charts 224
organizational complexity 339, 367
organizational size 414
organizational structures 138, 416
original sin 234, 277
Osborn, John H. 363
Outward Bound 58, 208
overtime 74–5, 79, 96, 116, 168, 174–5,
181, 185, 190, 210, 247, 359
Owen, R. 402, 405, 406
ownership and control 393, 414
Oxbridge 290
oyabun, oyakata 378–9, 386–9

Parker, S. R. 158–9, 341

Parsons, T. 269.
part timers 33, 39
particularism/universalism 61, 65, 212,
230, 270, 273–4
paternalism 265, 269–75, 301, 303,
375, 377, 392, 405–6
patriotism *see* nationalism
payment by results *see* wages, piecework
pensions 97, 202, 205, 207, 219, 255,
322, 368, 399
performance 226, 230, 271, 314, 377
permanent employment 31–41, 70,
74, 186, 214, 222, 311, 320, 336,
391, 399
person-related payments 99
personal connections 61
personality, consistency in 280
personnel managers 145, 159, 165,
172, 214, 357, 380
personnel policies 134
Phillips, D. 276
physical jerks 24, 175
physically handicapped 70
PIB *see* National Board for Prices
and Incomes
piecework *see* wages
Pilkingtons 343, 345–7
Piore, M. J. 368
planning 357
plant negotiation 174
police 338
political parties 288–9
politics 10, 193, 280, 284–92, 334, 397
Pollard, S. 406–7, 412
pool-leader 59
poor laws 409
positivism 51
'posting' 33, 40, 210, 247, 250, 278,
308
post-war reconstruction 23
Prefectural Labour Federation 122
prestige and authority 259
prestige of business 391
Pressed Steel Fisher 348
Prices and Incomes Policy 148, 200,
340
pride in skill 114, 127, 185, 246, 262,
277, 389
primogeniture 411
privacy 207, 212
privatization 292

private enterprise 90
prizes *see* rewards
production orientation 21
productivity 148, 151, 185, 200, 302
productivity bargaining 145, *see also* industrial relations, plant level negotiations
productivity consciousness 117
professional associations 71
profits 37, 151, 266, 402, 418
progressive employers 405
promotion 41, 67–70, 78, 99–103, 112, 147, 156, 159, 191, 224, 226, 230, 250, 350, 355, 384
public *v.* private 211–12
putting-out system 408, 416
Pym, D. 347

quality control 54, 88
questionnaire survey *see* survey
quotas 168

radical students 213
railways 343, 354, 396, 401, 406–7
Raleigh 348
ranks – and functions 67
rate fixing 79–94, 142, 147, 151, 170
rationality 402–3, 418
recession 38
records 67
recruitment 31, 33, 39, 69, 71–2, 97, 169, 212, 270, 305–8, 321, 384, 394, 399, 411
  craftsmen 54, 60–1
  mid-career 308
  of managers 41–9
  technicians 54, 60–1
  tests 49, 57, 64
redundancy 35–41, 118, 132, 147–8, 156, 161, 336, 353
Redundancy Payments Act 37, 40, 147, 200, 353–4
research methods 13, appx.
responsibility 402
retirement 129, 202, 216, 219, 272
retirement pensions 201
rewards 58, 66, 195, 242, 406
Rice Riots 396
rights–consciousness 189–191, 195, 241
ringi system 227–8
Robens, A. 365

Roberts, B. C. 344, 346
Robinson, Derek 350
Rochdale 405
Rōdōshō 310–14, 319, 327, 330
roles 213, 382
Roll, E. 405
Rolls Royce 348
Ross, Arthur 368
Rostow W. W. 413
Royal Commission on Trade Unions and Employers' Associations 136, 141–2, 158, 340, 348, 352, 360, 363, 366
rules – works rules 187, 244, 261, 357, 379

safety 23–4, 199, 189, 244
salaries *see* wages and salaries
samurai 211, 376, 380
sandwich courses 45–6
Saville, J. 404
savings and loan schemes 203
Scamp, Jack 134
Scanlon Plan 113
schools 61, 65
scientism 106, 318
Scott Bader 366
seamen 324, 327
secrecy 150–1, 164
secretaries 32
security 68, 215, 226, 352–3, 359, 388, 390, 397, 400, 416
self-criticism 63
self-management 365
seniority 24, 41, 95, 99, 105, 107, 133, 147–8, 156, 179, 191, 226, 230, 276, 301, 308, 351, 352–5, 368, 375, 377, 406–7, 413, 418, *see also* wages and seniority
separation rate 34, 100, 311
sex roles 252–3
Shanks, Michael 356
shareholders 222–3, 265–6, 330–1, 358, 363, 393
Shell 338
Sheth, N. R., 273
Shimura, G. 393
Shinsanbetsu 125
Shinto 23
shipbuilding 379
shipyards 35
shop-floor bargaining 79–82, 108

shop stewards 67, 80, 84, 88, 92, 131–
135, 146–7, 150, 156–60, 182–6,
206, 341, 357, 359, 361
chief s.s. 43, 132, 142, 149, 159,
207
committees 126, 132, 155, 324
facilities for 142
see also unions, industrial relations
sick payments 36, 77, 96–7, 136, 187,
201, 203, 205–7, 215, 219, 255,
272, 388
signature seals 227–8
'sincerity' 51
Sino-Soviet conflict 288
skill certification 54, 58, 62, 72, 105,
128, 147
skill classifications 77, 111, 345
skill obsolescence 38
skill Olympics 63
Slaughter, C. 282
slogans 23, 209–210, 239
Smith, A. 406
smoking 245
social democratic revolution
in industry 115–19, 140, 219
social evolution 10, 375
social gatherings 52, 58, 137, 189,
194, 205, 207, 209, 214, 220, 235,
274
socialization 50
Society for Service to the Nation
through Industry 116
Sōhyō (Japan General Council of
Labour Unions) 125, 285–6, 315,
327–9, 332, 334–5
solidarity 139, 206, 291
songs, factory 52; union 164
specially titled workers 100, 102, 258
Speenhamland 409
sports facilities 204–5
sportsmen 65
spring offensive 138, 176–8, 198, 325,
334, 347
staff 119
Stalker, G. M. 225
state control over industry 286
status 170
status differences 25, 43, 95–6, 119,
170, 173, 219, 255–8, 262, 284,
325, 346, 352, 362, 381, 383
status system 222, 251
Stinchcombe, A. L. 138

strikes *see* industrial relations, strikes
student apprentices 45–6
study groups 53, 66
sub-contracting 29, 39–40, 167–8, 194,
202, 247, 302–3, 336, 379
submissiveness 247–9, 262, 375
suggestions schemes 240–1
Sumitomo 391
Sumiya, M. 378
supertax 269
supervision *see* foreman
Supple, B. 409
survey 13, 34–5, 67–8, 127, 158–62,
186, 191–2, 195, 196, 206, 214–18,
231–2, 248, 254, 269, 291, 316,
318, 319
method 14, 421

Taga factory, general character 21–9
Taira, K. 302, 308, 378, 398
Taiwan 167
Takashima 391
take-overs 37
Tannenbaum, Frank 365
technical colleges 45–6
technicians 54, 100, 107, 309
technological change 38, 66, 184, 186,
309, 320, 335, 412
technological determinism 10
technologists 55
technology 412, 416
temporary worker 32–3, 38, 70, 308,
309, 322, 325, 383, 398, 417
tertiary employment 310
textiles 394–6, 405
Thomas, C. K. 338
Thomas, Michael 360
time clocks 81, 84, 96, 356, 369
titles 258
toilets 256
Tokugawa period 376
Tokyo arsenal 386
Tokyo Imperial University 289
Tokyo University of Technology 47
tool ownership 231
tool-room 94
Tōshiba 385–7
Totten, G. O. 324, 397
Townsend Revd. J. 409
trade unions *see* unions
trade cycle 404, 413
trade restrictions, American 167